The Guardian Guide to Parliament

The Guardian Guide to Parliament

guardian.co.uk/politics

Edited by Julian Glover

Associate editors:
Jennifer Smookler and Ian Valvona

ATLANTIC BOOKS

LONDON

First published in 2001 by Guardian Books,
an imprint of Grove Atlantic Ltd

Copyright © Guardian Newspapers Ltd 2001

Additional research by the *Guardian*'s Research and Information Department
Copy-edited by Richard Moriarty

10 9 8 7 6 5 4 3 2 1

A CIP catalogue record for this book is available from the British Library.

1 903809 11 8

Printed in Great Britain by CPD, Ebbw Vale, Wales
Designed and typeset by Penny and Tony Mills

Grove Atlantic Ltd
29 Adam & Eve Mews
London W8 6UG

Contents

Introduction

Michael White

On a bad day in parliament you do not have to sit in the steeply raked press gallery above the House of Commons to smell the rot. Peter Mandelson once suggested that representative democracy is gradually giving way to direct democracy – the mouse and the focus group, instead of the ballot box and the hustings. It certainly feels that way on an average Monday or Thursday.

Built with high-minded austerity after its destruction by a German bomb in May 1941, the chamber of the Commons stands apart from the camp Gothic excesses that make up the remainder of Pugin and Barry's Thamesside masterpiece. Moving very slowly with the times, it was relit for television in 1989.

The presence of television cameras may not have destroyed the parliamentary illusion single-handedly, but it has certainly helped. Busy MPs, reeling under ever-larger torrents of constituency demands, can keep an eye on the chamber through the TV monitor in their offices, which leaves them free to get on with what many think of as their "real" work.

Ditto the political correspondents. Ditto conscientious voters with access to the parliament channel. All can watch from afar and, in doing so, see for themselves the impotent nakedness of an ill-attended chamber – all that empty green leather, so unsuitable for television – where inexperienced ministers fob off deferential backbenchers about statements they may already have made on BBC Radio 4's *Today* programme.

And yet, in November 1990, the same television cameras allowed the same voters to watch the improbable oratory of Sir Geoffrey Howe – Mogadon Man himself – destroy the most powerful premiership since Churchill's. It magnified the speech's impact, and sealed Margaret Thatcher's doom.

What is more, if parliament is in decline, it always has been, at least since the modern Palace of Westminster opened for business more than 150 years ago. As Fleet Street's senior political columnist, Alan Watkins, writes from time to time, the old lady is always being killed off by MPs and pundits. Then, just as she is being wheeled into the mortuary, she sits up in bed and asks for a cup of tea.

In two tours of duty at Westminster, spread across 25 years, I have seen the old place's fortunes fall and rise and then fall again to its present low public standing: as a legislative rubber stamp for Tony Blair's well-meant, but sometimes foolish, administration.

Since the June 7, 2001 election, there have been signs that the backbenches are poised to reassert themselves more forcefully. In July 2001, a cross-party rebellion over the sacking of two select committee chairmen garnered enough support from the Labour backbenches to defeat Tony Blair's government for the first time in the Commons.

And as Paul Flynn writes on page 333, senior MPs, many of them ex-ministers, have formed a Parliament First group. Was it all just a brief rush of post-election blood to the head, prompted by tiredness and the heat of July 2001?

Hopefully not, and in the cycle of things it is about time. In 1997 New Labour MPs were loyal and grateful to Blairism; old Labour lags had spent 18 years repenting the pleasures of self-indulgent indiscipline – and been free to watch the Tories catching the disease. The effects of the political penicillin were bound to wear off.

When I first arrived in the press gallery in 1976, I found a Labour government, newly led by Jim Callaghan, facing the worst social and political crisis since the Second World War.

The Labour minority years were hell for Mr Callaghan, but exciting for MPs and the press. They felt important, the Commons bars were full every night, ministers were solicitous; even the Liberals enjoyed a self-important Lib–Lab pact with Labour, while the SNP (all 11 of them) were both wooed and feared.

Every vote counted and when, three weeks into my new career, Labour fiddled a vote on the nationalisation of the shipbuilding and aircraft industries (how quaint the phrase now sounds!), a young thruster called Michael Heseltine picked up the mace, the symbol of parliament's authority, and waved it menacingly at the Labour benches where "The Red Flag" was being sung.

Yes, 'The Red Flag", not "Things Can Only Get Better". Parliament mattered, and Margaret Thatcher's rampant Tory opposition was trying to harry Callaghan's regime into an early grave. When in danger of losing a vote, Jim's wily whips sent their troops home and lost 300–0, giving Mrs T a meaningless win.

It was called "rug pulling" and it worked until the fateful motion of confidence – lost by one vote on March 28, 1979 – that triggered the first fall of a government on a direct vote of the Commons since 1841.

That night Neil Kinnock led the singing of That Song again. Thatcherism arrived soon after.

It was Thatcherism that first broke the spirit of the Commons. Initially the trench warfare was magnificent, both across the chamber and within the ranks of the main parties. Thatcher and her shock troops – Howe, Lawson, Ridley, Tebbit – faced opposition from one-nation Tory wets – in cabinet, the Jim Priors and Ian Gilmours and, outside it, the glowering Ted Heath. The fight was ideological too.

The battle was also aided by a shadow cabinet stuffed with an array of not only talented, but battle-hardened ex-ministers, whose experience stretched back to 1945. Lieutenant Callaghan RN, Major Healey, beachmaster at the Anzio landings in Italy, Captain Roy Jenkins of Bletchley Park (Enigma) fame, Flight Lieutenant Benn and their like were still active. So was Brigadier Enoch Powell. That too was a shrinking pool of experience.

Gradually Mrs Thatcher's successes and her majorities cowed the Commons. Though the Tory poll-tax revolt of 1989 showed she never crushed dissent entirely, the decisive opposition came on the streets and in the ballot boxes.

Neil Kinnock, by now in double-breasted suits, led the long march back to the electable centre ground. Professional politicians in their early 30s, better educated but less experienced in life, accentuated the change. So did unelected spin doctors. The "poodle parliament" jibe, a century old, was revived.

That the Commons could still inflict damage on governments was amply demonstrated by the ever-faster Eurosceptic destruction of John Major and his 21-strong majority after 1992. And Mrs Thatcher's creation of a proper select committee system in 1979 (an oversight for which her first leader of the Commons, Norman St John Stevas deserves credit) had handed MPs another lever to use against the executive.

But the exuberant parliamentary mood of the 70s, 80s and early 90s soon faded. Ideological politics was replaced by a more managerial kind, by the growing power of Brussels to restrict sovereign legislation and (in the courts) by judicial review.

Devolution was another blow to Westminster, albeit nobly self-inflicted. The exponential growth of 24-hour multi-option media, committed to infotainment rather than civic space, also gave an increasingly apolitical and undeferential electorate other things to do with their spare time than worry about the chairmanship of the 1922 committee.

Yet the rise of single-issue pressure groups – some aggressively militant on the terrorist model – of email and telephone canvassing, of pollsters, focus groups and other manifestations of the direct democracy question have not delivered what their proponents predicted.

Neither e-politics nor riots in Seattle and Genoa – Bradford and Burnley too – can claim to have got it right.

In this fast-changing situation, where the old levers no longer seem to work properly, MPs are struggling to evolve a new role, as campaigners and facilitators, as well as holder-to-account of the mighty, their ancient function.

It must be a role that goes beyond giving a soundbite to *The Six O'Clock News* on College Green and it is far from clear how it will develop. But it is also too soon to wheel the old lady into the mortuary fridge just yet.

Michael White is the political editor of the *Guardian*.

The House of Commons

The New MPs

Andrew Roth

Deciding which new MPs will thrive as parliamentarians is a mug's game. It is almost impossible to anticipate which qualities will carry over successfully into the Commons from previous careers. If there were a sure formula for anticipating applause-winning Commons successes on the basis of storming Tory redoubts, then Liberal Democrat Sue Doughty's unexpected capture of Guildford – a victory almost as spectacular as the Liberal party's famous 1964 byelection win at Orpington – would enable her, as Guildford Girl, to emulate the enviable record of Orpington Man, Eric Lubbock.

The difficulty lies in transmuting outside talents into the peculiar mixture required to thrive as an MP. Alan Reid, who has come in for the Lib Dems in Argyll and Bute, ranks higher than his colleague Dr Evan Harris as a chess player (Mr Reid once played grand master Nigel Short) but it cannot be assumed he will be more astute at moves on the parliamentary chessboard than the 1997 vintage MP for Oxford West and Abingdon, who has been returned with an enhanced majority.

Of the 1997 intake, nobody could have anticipated the much greater parliamentary success of John Bercow over his fellow right-wing Tory, Dr Julian Lewis. Better educated, Dr Lewis has a fearsome reputation as a more-than-academic Cold War polemicist. But Mr Bercow unveiled a talent for parliamentary tactics and timing, plus a phenomenal memory which brought him to the front bench, where he underpinned and often outshone Ann Widdecombe.

I burned my fingers picking winners decades ago, when it seemed simpler, certainly on the Labour side. In the old days, some constituency activists chose their candidates by talent-spotting crusading speeches at Annual Conference. Like the activists of Oldbury and Halesowen, I thought that John Horner, the general secretary of the Fire Brigades union, and a powerful conference orator, might emerge as "another Aneurin Bevan". Alas, all he became was a good constituency MP.

As Transport and General Workers' Union leader, Frank Cousins showed that the formidable qualities needed to reach the top of a union do not necessarily translate into parliamentary skills, particularly in middle age. Cousins, like his predecessor, Ernest Bevin, never managed to master the indirect language spoken in the Commons. But with Bevin it did not seem to matter.

Labour talent-spotting became more difficult with the introduction of "one member, one vote" to select candidates, except when Number Ten or Millbank bends the rules or twist the arms of retirement-age sitting Labour MPs to parachute in Blairite favourites.

A handful of over-publicised parachutists apart, the ordinary candidate is selected by the votes of some 350 party members, who tend to pick known and trusted local worthies such as council leaders.

In Ashton-under-Lyne, Robert (now Lord) Sheldon informed his party early enough of his imminent retirement, to avoid last-minute parachutists. The party duly chose, by a margin of three votes, the 52-year-old councillor, David Heyes, recently manager of the local Citizens' Advice Bureau, an Open University graduate and a longtime trade union activist. With the loyalism inbred in local councils and unions, such low profile new MPs tend to be fairly docile.

Despite this, I would still place small bets on a handful of New Labour MPs who have used local roots or union links to work the system.

Something can be expected from two local boys who made good: Paul Farrelly (Newcastle-under-Lyme), until recently the city editor of the *Observer*, and Andy Burnham (Leigh), a former adviser to the culture secretary, Chris Smith. Both have been politically energised by events in the recent past. Farrelly, the son of an Irish immigrant who came to Newcastle-under-Lyme to lay pipes for British Gas, went from Oxford to a fatcat city job. He was blasted out of this by the privatisation of British Gas, which, under its new profit-hungry management, brutally sacked his foreman father when it contracted out its pipelaying.

Farrelly became a journalist, became active politically in his home town, and was duly anointed heir to the Golding dynasty there.

The defeat of the 1984–85 miners' strike politicised Andy Burnham, who was brought up in the Lancashire coalfield. In its wake he joined the Labour party locally. After Cambridge he worked in politics in London. When Lawrence Cunliffe retired from Leigh, encompassing the Lancashire coalfield, Andy became his successor by telling local selectors that it had been his advice that had secured special recreation facilities for the devastated former coalfields and free television licences for over-75s.

I would also put a small wager on the impact of Kevan Jones, Giles Radice's very different successor at Durham North, a GMB union seat. He did not give up his post as the GMB's top political man in the north to become a Commons cipher. My guess is that he will add parliamentary muscle to his union's resistance to Tony Blair's enthusiasm for creeping privatisation.

One of Wales's most attractive newcomers is Rhodri Morgan's admiring replacement at Cardiff West, the half-Irish, half-Welsh Kevin Brennan, who has scored points already with a brilliant maiden speech.

Among the over-publicised few Labour parachutists, the future of Shaun Woodward (St Helens South) looks doubtful because his perceived arrogance makes him the most disliked newcomer, even among those who are not influenced by the *Daily Mail*'s stunt of foisting stage butlers onto him. Tony Blair's efforts to find him a seat were only understandable as a signal to defection-prone Tory MPs, saying, "If you come over, we'll take care of you."

David Miliband is a sharp contrast. He inherited the fine brain of his late father, the LSE lecturer, Ralph Miliband, but reacted – as did friends like me – against Ralph's move to the left.

Miliband came out of Blair's inner sanctum, where he wrote the election manifesto. He was welcomed by his predecessor at South Shields, David (now Lord) Clark, and the local party, who like big hitters. In his first week as an MP he was rewarded with a place on a Brussels committee thought to have been reserved for Peter Mandelson.

Among the Tory newcomers, all bets came off when Kenneth Clarke plumped his candidacy into the leadership candidates' crowded pool. Among those who decided to gamble on Ken is Henley's new MP, the serio-comic editor of the *Spectator*, Boris Johnson, previously a sharp critic of Brussels. The gamble did not pay off: Boris may find he has plenty of time for the *Spectator*.

Among the most relieved by Iain Duncan Smith's win was Andrew Rosindell, the ultra right-wing Europhobe who won back his home town, Romford, from a weak Labour incumbent. This win was widely predicted by fellow zealot-graduates of the Federation of Conservative Students.

Almost certain to thrive is George Osborne, who retook the normally safe Tory Tatton from off-white-suited Martin Bell, who had erased the stain of Neil Hamilton's occupancy. As William Hague's able former speechwriter, this well-to-do new MP has faced the torment of deciding on which new Tory leadership bandwagon to leap.

I would also place a small wager on the ability to advance of Adrian Flook, who retook Taunton from the anti-hunting Lib Dem, Jackie Ballard. Where Jackie turned doubters into opponents, Flook, a quiet critic of hunting, did not antagonise electors, listening sympathetically to those pushed his way. His manner of victory did not resemble his name.

Andrew Roth is the publisher of *Parliamentary Profiles*.

Maiden Speeches

Matthew Tempest

It is a fact of some pathos that most MPs make their maiden speeches before an audience smaller than any that they had on the stump campaigning.

Detached, apathetic, and partisan as most election events are these days, it still must have come as a disappointment to many of the 99 new MPs elected in 2001 to find that so many of their 658 colleagues could find more pressing engagements than listening to new MPs make their first speeches.

This is a shame, as most maidens, prescribed as they are, reveal a lot about incoming members, their constituencies, and their humour.

The unwritten rules of a successful maiden dictate that one should first praise one's predecessor (succinctly if from another party, sycophantically if from your own) and then compose a paean to the beauty of the constituency before offering a foretaste of the one particular hobbyhorse of an issue you will flog to death during the next five years.

As the new Liberal Democrat member for Orkney and Shetland, Alistair Carmichael, admitted in his maiden speech after the 2001 election, "It is traditional in this House to pay tribute to one's predecessor. It occurs to me, having observed the debate on the Queen's speech over the past few days, that this is perhaps a tradition which it is open to some honourable members to observe through gritted teeth and with their fingers crossed behind their back."

The new Ron Davies, Wayne David of Caerphilly, was curt in his tribute to the man who had been keeping his seat warm: "My immediate predecessor was Ron Davies, a former secretary of state for Wales. He made a huge contribution to the achievement of Welsh devolution." The End.

Take this example of a gleaming double-edged sword from Patrick Mercer, the new Tory boy in Newark, on his Labour predecessor, who was acquitted on appeal of falsely declaring election expenses: "Mrs Fiona Jones was my immediate predecessor in Newark and her achievements probably speak for themselves. I believe that she is now having more time to spend with her family."

David Cameron, who inherited the safe Tory seat of Witney from the turncoat Shaun Woodward, was no less cutting: "I know that it is traditional to pay tribute to one's immediate predecessor and I have no hesitation in saying that I agreed with almost everything that he said in the first half of the previous parliament, when he was a trenchant critic of the government.

"He remains a constituent and a not insignificant local employer – not least in the area of domestic service. We are, in fact, quite close neighbours. On a clear day, from the hill behind my cottage, I can almost see some of the glittering spires of his great house."

Some MPs truly are a hard act to follow, as this extract from Strangford MP

Iris Robinson's maiden speech reveals: "John Taylor has been a district councillor, a member of the Stormont parliament, the Northern Ireland forum, the Northern Ireland constitutional convention, three assemblies, this House, the European parliament, the Council of Europe, and now the other place." Beat that if you can.

The Order of the Brown Nose 2001 goes to young Jonathan Djanogly, stepping into John Major's shoes in Huntingdon. "John Major is a perfect gentleman – a man of immense charm and warmth, who is kind and dedicated to public service. As prime minister, he proved himself a true statesman: on the one hand, showing courage and determination in his conduct of the Iraqi conflict and, on the other, displaying his qualities as a peacemaker in his relentless pursuit of a lasting settlement in Northern Ireland."

But for some assiduous new boys, a maiden is not quite what it seems. Take Leigh's Andy Burnham: "For someone making his maiden speech, I am in the unusual position of already having made history in the House. On October 26, 1996, *The Times* reported: 'The mobile phone has finally breached the last bastion of low-tech tranquillity: the House of Commons.'

"Today I own up as the naive researcher who made that historic call. I can only hope that my future contributions to the House will be less irritating than that one."

Giving a guided tour of one's constituency is always a good opening gambit as well.

Insularity of the island-race mentality had got to the Isle of Wight's Andrew Turner, who trumpeted his constituency's Garlic Festival: "There one can sample not only garlic bread and garlic mushrooms, but garlic beer, garlic honey and garlic ice cream."

Other constituencies don't necessarily pack the same punch. Ian Lucas told of the charms of Wrexham: "My first constituency engagement after my election was a community litter pick, which was enjoyable."

And full marks for honesty to Adrian Flook, the new Tory in Taunton, who enlightened MPs with the news that "for those who do not know, it rains quite a lot there."

Dai Havard, Merthyr Tydfil and Rhymney's new MP, decided to make sure the Hansard reporters in the press gallery upstairs were still awake with this snippet: "Diolch yn fawr i chi a diolch yn fawr iawn, Madam deputy speaker. I hope to catch your eye again."

Caernarfon's chosen son, Hywel Williams, commented mournfully: "My constituency is an area of astonishing natural beauty, but, as the saying goes, 'You can't eat the scenery.'"

More traumatic were the hurdles facing Parmjit Dhanda, who took over in Gloucester from Labour's Tess Kingham.

"After my selection, but before it realised what a splendid fellow I am, my newfound friend, the *Citizen* [a local newspaper], wrote: 'Labour can kiss goodbye to this seat. They might as well hand it over to the Conservatives now. The Labour party in Gloucester has made the same mistake as the Tories in Cheltenham when they chose a black barrister as candidate and handed the seat to the Liberal Democrats. Mr Dhanda could withdraw to allow another candidate to be adopted.'"

[Hon. members: Shame.]

"I am not making this up, honestly. The *Citizen* said: 'Things were so much easier' – this may appeal more to older Labour members than to me – 'when candidates were picked by a handful of party elders in a smoke-filled room rather than the whole party membership.' Most painfully of all, not for me but for the residents of Gloucester, the *Citizen* was 'sad to say, many of the voters of Gloucestershire have yet to reach the advanced state of consciousness to accept a foreigner as their local MP'.

"The people of Gloucester proved that they are better than that, and I stand here as the very proud member of parliament for Gloucester."

Touché.

Matthew Tempest is a correspondent for *Guardian Unlimited Politics.*

MP Profiles

The following pages contain a short description of the interests, parliamentary activities and backgrounds of each of the 659 MPs in the House of Commons.

The top line gives the MP's name and the title they choose to use in parliament. This is followed by details of their seat, any previous seats held and the 2001 election result.

Where available, the description includes a quote from Andrew Roth, a political biographer and researcher who has been following parliament for the past 50 years. The quotes come from his series *Parliamentary Profiles*.

For MPs first elected in 2001, the description includes a quote from the MP's maiden speech, from the candidate during the campaign, or from a commentator.

The recent parliamentary activity description includes notable ministerial and shadow positions since 1997 and significant positions before then, current and some previous committee memberships, and campaigning and party activity. For a breakdown of abbreviations see the table on the next page.

The description is not a full history of all posts held by an MP: for this, see www.guardian.co.uk/politics/aristotle.

The background description mentions significant former positions held by the MP. It is not a full description of their career.

Where possible, the page also includes the MP's date and place of birth, together with short details on their education and their constituency.

Department Abbreviations

Cabinet Office	CO
Department of Culture, Media and Sport	DCMS
Department of Education and Skills (from 2001)	DFES
Department of Education and Employment (to 2001)	DFEE
Department of Environment, Food and Rural Affairs (from 2001)	DEFR
Department of Health	DoH
Department of International Development	DFID
Department of Trade and Industry	DTI
Department of Transport, Environment and Local Government (to 2001)	DETR
Department of Transport, Local Government and the Regions (from 2001)	DTLGR
Department of Work and Pensions (from 2001)	DWP
Foreign Office	FCO
Home Office	HO
Lord Chancellor's Department	LCD
Ministry of Defence	MoD
Ministry of Agriculture, Fisheries and Food (to 2001)	MAFF
Northern Ireland	NI
Northern Ireland Assembly	NIA
Northern Ireland Executive	NIE
Northern Ireland Office	NIO
Scotland Office	SO
Wales Office	WO

A

Abbott, Diane
Labour MP for Hackney North and Stoke Newington since 1987

Majority: 13,651 (46%)
Turnout: 49%

	Votes	Share %	Change %
Diane Abbott, Labour	18,081	61	−4.2
Mrs Pauline Dye, Conservative	4,430	15	−1.9
Meral Ece, Liberal Democrat	4,170	14.1	3.9
Chit Yong, Green party	2,184	7.4	n/a
Sukant Chandon, Socialist Labour party	756	2.6	n/a

Andrew Roth says: "highly intelligent, sarcastic, pugnacious extrovert"

Parliamentary career: public administration committee (2000–2001); Treasury committee (1997–2001); foreign affairs committee (1997–2000); Labour party NEC (1994–97); first black woman MP
Background: press officer, Lambeth Council and GLC; TV journalist; HO trainee civil servant
Born: September 27 1953 in Paddington, London
Education: Harrow County Girls' Grammar School
Higher education: Cambridge, Newnham
Constituency: one of the most deprived areas in London; significant ethnic-minority population

Adams, Gerry
Sinn Fein MP for Belfast West since 1997; Belfast West (1983–92)

Majority: 19,342 (47.2%)
Turnout: 68.7%

	Votes	Share %	Change %
Gerry Adams, Sinn Fein	27,096	66.1	10.2
Alex Attwood, Social Democratic and Labour party	7,754	18.9	−19.8
Eric Smyth, Democratic Unionist party	2,641	6.4	n/a
Chris McGimpsey, Ulster Unionist party	2,541	6.2	2.8
John Lowry, Workers' party	736	1.8	0.2
David Kerr, Third Way	116	0.3	n/a
Rainbow George Weiss, Ind Vote	98	0.2	n/a

Andrew Roth says: "complicated and elusive ... cold blooded, articulate and intelligent"

Parliamentary career: has not taken his seat in parliament
Background: founding member of civil rights movement in Northern Ireland; president of Sinn Fein (1983–); author of books on Northern Ireland; barman
Born: October 6 1948 in Belfast
Education: St Mary's Christian Brothers' School, Belfast
Constituency: very nationalist inner-Belfast stronghold around the Falls Road

Adams, Irene
Labour MP for Paisley North since 1990

Majority: 9,321 (34.4%)
Turnout: 56.6%

	Votes	Share %	Change %
Irene Adams, Labour	15,058	55.5	−4
George Adam, Scottish National party	5,737	21.1	−0.8
Jane Hook, Liberal Democrat	2,709	10	3.1
Craig Stevenson, Conservative	2,404	8.9	−0.7
Jim Halfpenny, Scottish Socialist party	982	3.6	n/a
R Graham, ProLife Alliance	263	1	−0.6

Andrew Roth says: "tough minded and tough talking"

Recent parliamentary career: Scottish affairs committee (1997–2001)
Background: councillor at 24; youngest JP in Scottish history; secretary to late husband, Allan Adams MP (1986–90)
Born: December 27 1947 in Paisley
Education: Stanley Green High School, Paisley
Constituency: Scotland's fifth largest town, by River Clyde, includes Glasgow Airport and Renfrew

Ainger, Nick
Labour MP for Carmarthen West and South Pembrokeshire since 1997; Pembroke (1992–97)

Majority: 4,538 (12.3%)
Turnout: 65.3%

	Votes	Share %	Change %
Nick Ainger, Labour	15,349	41.6	–7.5
Colin Schrader Schrader, Conservative	10,811	29.3	2.7
Llyr Hughes Griffiths, Plaid Cymru	6,893	18.7	6
William Jeremy, Liberal Democrat	3,248	8.8	0.6
Ian Phillips, UK Independence party	537	1.5	n/a
Nick Turner, Customer	78	0.2	n/a

Andrew Roth says: "highly active and well regarded local job and environment defender"

Recent parliamentary career: government whip (2001–); PPS to secretaries of state for Wales (1997–2001); administration committee (2001–)
Background: marine rigger (1977–92); supports Amnesty, Friends of the Earth, League Against Cruel Sports, RSPB, Greenpeace
Born: October 24 1949 in Sheffield
Education: Netherthorpe Grammar School, Staveley
Constituency: mixed West Wales seat, part urban Carmarthen, part rural Pembrokeshire; former home of Dylan Thomas

Ainsworth, Bob
Labour MP for Coventry North East since 1992

Majority: 15,751 (42.2%)
Turnout: 50.4%

	Votes	Share %	Change %
Bob Ainsworth, Labour	22,739	61	–5.2
Gordon Bell, Conservative	6,988	18.8	–0.5
Napier Penlington, Liberal Democrat	4,163	11.2	3.2
Dave Nellist, Socialist Alliance	2,638	7.1	n/a
Edward Sheppard, British National party	737	2	n/a

Andrew Roth says: "Coventry-centred mainstream trade unionist still indignant about injustice to the underprivileged"

Recent parliamentary career: junior minister, HO (2001–); junior minister, DETR (2001); government whip (1997–2001)
Background: sheet metal worker, Jaguar Motors (1971–91); shop steward for TGWU (then MSF); deputy leader of Coventry Council
Born: June 19 1952 in Coventry
Education: Foxford Comprehensive School, Coventry
Constituency: industrial Coventry seat with much council housing

Ainsworth, Peter
Conservative MP for East Surrey since 1992

Majority: 13,203 (28.0%)
Turnout: 62.7%

	Votes	Share %	Change %
Peter Ainsworth, Conservative	24,706	52.5	2.4
Jeremy Pursehouse, Liberal Democrat	11,503	24.5	2
Joanne Tanner, Labour	8,994	19.1	−2.1
Anthony Stone, UK Independence party	1,846	3.9	n/a

Andrew Roth says: "pragmatic and functional politician with little interest in ideologies"

Recent parliamentary career: shadow secretary of state, DEFRA (2001–); shadow secretary of state, DCMS (1998–2001); deputy chief whip (1997–98)
Background: investment analyst; company director; research assistant to MEP (1979–81)
Born: November 16 1956 in Hampshire
Education: Ludgrove School, Wokingham; Bradfield College, Berkshire
Higher education: Oxford, Lincoln
Constituency: wooded, hilly commuter villages south of London by Kent border

Alexander, Douglas
Labour MP for Paisley South since 1997

Majority: 11,910 (39.0%)
Turnout: 57.2%

	Votes	Share %	Change %
Douglas Alexander, Labour	17,830	58.4	14.3
Brian Lawson, Scottish National party	5,920	19.4	−13.1
Brian O'Malley, Liberal Democrat	3,178	10.4	−0.6
Andrew Cossar, Conservative	2,301	7.5	0.5
Frances Curran, Scottish Socialist party	835	2.7	n/a
Patricia Graham, ProLife Alliance	346	1.1	−1.4
Terence O'Donnell, Independent	126	0.4	n/a

Andrew Roth says: "Buchan-inspired, Brown-encouraged Scots New Labour enthusiast"

Recent parliamentary career: minister of state, DTI (2001–)
Background: solicitor; Labour's 2001 election coordinator; parliamentary officer and speech writer for Gordon Brown
Born: October 26 1967 in Glasgow
Education: Park Mains High School; Lester B Pearson College, Vancouver
Higher education: Edinburgh University; University of Pennsylvania
Constituency: includes most of Paisley town centre, west of Glasgow

Allan, Richard
Liberal Democrat MP for Sheffield Hallam since 1997

Majority: 9,347 (24.4%)
Turnout: 63.4%

	Votes	Share %	Change %
Richard Allan, Liberal Democrat	21,203	55.4	4.1
John Harthman, Conservative	11,856	31	−2.1
Gillian Furniss, Labour	4,758	12.4	−1.1
Leslie Arnott, UK Independence party	429	1.1	n/a

Andrew Roth says: "bright, busy and hardworking"

Recent parliamentary career: Lib Dem spokesperson, information technology (2001–); chair, information committee (1998–2001)

Background: developed information systems for the NHS; field archaeologist; Avon councillor
Born: February 11 1966 in Sheffield
Education: Oundle School
Higher education: Bristol Polytechnic; Cambridge, Pembroke
Constituency: grand, hilly, suburban Sheffield seat beneath Peak District hills

Allen, Graham
Labour MP for Nottingham North since 1987

Majority: 12,240 (40.8%)
Turnout: 46.7%

	Votes	Share %	Change %
Graham Allen, Labour	19,392	64.6	−1.1
Martin Wright, Conservative	7,152	23.8	3.5
Rob Lee, Liberal Democrat	3,177	10.6	2.6
Andrew Botham, Socialist Labour party	321	1.1	n/a

Andrew Roth says: "a forceful agitator for pluralism, modernisation of parliamentary democracy and US-style separation of powers"

Recent parliamentary career: government whip (1997–2001)
Background: GLC senior officer; trade union officer (GMB); researcher for Labour party; author; talented cricketer
Born: January 11 1953 in Nottingham
Education: Forest Fields Grammar School
Higher education: Leeds University; London Guildhall
Constituency: council estates and manual workers on northern edge of Nottingham

Amess, David
Conservative MP for Southend West since 1997; Basildon (1983–97)

Majority: 7,941 (21.2%)
Turnout: 58.3%

	Votes	Share %	Change %
David Amess, Conservative	17,313	46.3	7.5
Paul Fisher, Labour	9,372	25.1	2.3
Richard de Ste Croix, Liberal Democrat	9,319	24.9	−8.2
Brian Lee, UK Independence party	1,371	3.7	n/a

Andrew Roth says: "cheerleader for Essex Tory proles and originator of the 'I love Basildon' campaign"

Recent parliamentary career: health committee (1998–)
Background: company director; partner in employment consultancy; underwriter; junior school teacher for a year
Born: March 26 1952 in Plaistow
Education: St Antony's Junior School; St Bonaventure's Grammar School
Higher education: Bournemouth College of Technology
Constituency: smart, western part of Essex seaside town; includes Leigh-on-Sea and Westcliffe-on-Sea

Ancram, Rt Hon Michael
Conservative MP for Devizes since 1992; Edinburgh South (1979–87); Berwickshire and East Lothian (1974)

Majority: 11,896 (22.4%)
Turnout: 63.7%

	Votes	Share %	Change %
Michael Ancram, Conservative	25,159	47.3	4.5
Aubrey Ross, Labour	13,263	24.9	0.7
Helen Frances, Liberal Democrat	11,756	22.1	−4.4
Alan Wood, UK Independence party	1,521	2.9	n/a
Ludovic Kennedy, Independent	1,078	2	n/a
Ms Vanessa Potter, Official Monster Raving Loony party	n/a		

Andrew Roth says: "witty, urbane English-accented Scots aristocrat"

Recent parliamentary career: deputy leader and shadow foreign secretary (2001–); challenged for the party leadership (2001); chairman, Conservative party (1998–2001); opposition spokesperson, constitutional affairs (1997–98)
Background: son and heir to the 12th Marquess of Lothian; advocate; commercial farmer in family agricultural firm; public relations consultant
Born: July 7 1945 in London
Education: Ampleforth
Higher education: Edinburgh University; Oxford, Christ Church
Constituency: traditional Wiltshire farming seat, downland and small towns

Anderson, Rt Hon Donald
Labour MP for Swansea East since 1974; Monmouth (1966–70)

Majority: 16,148 (53.7%)
Turnout: 52.5%

	Votes	Share %	Change %
Donald Anderson, Labour	19,612	65.2	−10.2
John Ball, Plaid Cymru	3,464	11.5	8.1
Robert Speht, Liberal Democrat	3,064	10.2	1.3
Paul Morris, Conservative	3,026	10.1	0.8
Tony Young, Green party	463	1.5	n/a
Tim Jenkins, UK Independence party	443	1.5	n/a

Andrew Roth says: "anti-racist, pro-EU moderate idealist"

Recent parliamentary career: chair, foreign affairs committee (1997–); restored to position after parliamentary revolt (2001)
Background: Swansea-born barrister; consultant, and lecturer in US and comparative government; diplomat and adviser on Europe
Born: June 17 1939 in Swansea
Education: Swansea Grammar School
Higher education: University College, Swansea; Inner Temple
Constituency: docks and factories to east and north of Wales's second city

Anderson, Janet
Labour MP for Rossendale and Darwen since 1992

Majority: 5,223 (12.7%)
Turnout: 58.9%

	Votes	Share %	Change %
Janet Anderson, Labour	20,251	49	−4.6
George Lee, Conservative	15,028	36.3	4
Brian Dunning, Liberal Democrat	6,079	14.7	4.1

Andrew Roth says: "feminist loyalist apparatchik, music-lover and former Sunday trading lobbyist"

Recent parliamentary career: catering committee (2001–); junior minister, DCMS (1998–2001); government whip (1997–98)
Background: journalist on the Scotsman and Sunday Times; researcher for Barbara Castle, Jack Straw, and Margaret Beckett; multilingual
Born: December 6 1949 in Newcastle upon Tyne

Education: Kingsfield Comprehensive School
Higher education: University of Nantes, France; Central London Polytechnic
Constituency: small towns, valleys, and moors in east Lancashire

Arbuthnot, Rt Hon James
Conservative MP for North East Hampshire since 1997; Wanstead and Woodford (1987–97)

Majority: 13,257 (30.2%)
Turnout: 61.6%

	Votes	Share %	Change %
James Arbuthnot, Conservative	23,379	53.2	2.3
Mike Plummer, Liberal Democrat	10,122	23	0.3
Barry Jones, Labour	8,744	19.9	3.9
Graham Mellstrom, UK Independence party	1,702	3.9	n/a

Andrew Roth says: "bright right-wing chancery barrister from a good parliamentary stable"

Recent parliamentary career: intelligence and security committee (2001–); opposition chief whip (1997–2001)
Background: son of a Tory MP and political canvasser from the age of five; barrister; Lloyds underwriter
Born: August 4 1952 in Deal, Kent
Education: Eton College
Higher education: Cambridge, Trinity
Constituency: fast-growing Home Counties suburbs and villages, near M3

Armstrong, Rt Hon Hilary
Labour MP for Durham North West since 1987

Majority: 16,333 (41.6%)
Turnout: 58.5%

	Votes	Share %	Change %
Hilary Armstrong, Labour	24,526	62.5	–6.3
William Clouston, Conservative	8,193	20.9	5.6
Alan Ord, Liberal Democrat	5,846	14.9	4.1
Joan Hartnell, Socialist Labour party	661	1.7	n/a

Andrew Roth says: "a worthily competent regionalist and deeply-committed reforming missionary for her area"

Recent parliamentary career: chief whip (2001–); minister of state, DETR (1997–2001)
Background: social and community worker; lecturer in community and youth work; researcher for her Labour MP father; Durham councillor
Born: November 30 1945 in Sunderland
Education: Monkwearmouth Grammar School
Higher education: West Ham Technical College; Birmingham University
Constituency: hilly, ex-industrial, ex-mining, isolated small towns

Atherton, Candy
Labour MP for Falmouth and Camborne since 1997

Majority: 4,527 (9.7%)
Turnout: 64.3%

	Votes	Share %	Change %
Candy Atherton, Labour	18,532	39.6	5.8
Nick Serpell, Conservative	14,005	29.9	1.1
Julian Brazil, Liberal Democrat	11,453	24.5	–0.7
John Browne, UK Independence party	1,328	2.8	n/a
Hilda Wasley, Mebyon Kernow	853	1.8	1.4
Paul Holmes, Liberal	649	1.4	0.4

Andrew Roth says: "a stimulating hybrid of Peter Mandelson and Dawn French"

Recent parliamentary career: introduced private member's bill to bring in an age equality commission (2001); education and employment committee (1997–2001); employment subcommittee (1997–2001);
Background: freelance journalist; probation officer; MP's researcher; Islington councillor and mayor; mother was mayor of Falmouth
Born: September 21 1955 in Surrey
Education: Sutton High School; Midhurst Grammar School
Higher education: North London Polytechnic
Constituency: once centre of tin mining industry, now Cornish port and holiday resort

Atkins, Charlotte
Labour MP for Staffordshire Moorlands since 1997

Majority: 5,838 (13.7%)
Turnout: 63.9%

	Votes	Share %	Change %
Charlotte Atkins, Labour	20,904	49	–3.2
Marcus Hayes, Conservative	15,066	35.3	2.8
John Redfern, Liberal Democrat	5,928	13.9	1.8
Paul Gilbert, UK Independence party	760	1.8	n/a

Andrew Roth says: "loyal, computerphile enthusiast for raising educational standards"

Recent parliamentary career: PPS to Baroness Symons (2001–); committee of selection (1997–2001); education and employment committee (1997–2001); education subcommittee (1997–2001)
Background: Unison parliamentary officer; NUJ press officer; Wandsworth councillor
Born: September 24 1950 in Chelmsford
Education: Colchester County High School
Higher education: London School of Economics; School of US Studies, London
Constituency: borders Cheshire and Peak District, hill farming, dairies and textiles

Atkinson, David
Conservative MP for Bournemouth East since 1977

Majority: 3,434 (9.6%)
Turnout: 59.2%

	Votes	Share %	Change %
David Atkinson, Conservative	15,501	43.3	1.9
Andrew Garratt, Liberal Democrat	12,067	33.7	2.3
Paul Nicholson, Labour	7,107	19.9	–1.2
George Chamberlaine, UK Independence party	1,124	3.1	n/a

Andrew Roth says: "the James Bond of the Christian right"

Recent parliamentary career: opposition whip (2001–); UK representative on the Council of Europe (1987–2001); member of several other European committees
Background: company director; marketing executive; interest in alternative therapies, mental health, IT; Southend councillor
Born: March 24 1940 in Westcliff-on-Sea
Education: Alleyn Court School; St George's School, Weybridge
Higher education: Chelsea College of Automobile and Aeronautical Engineering; Southend College of Technology
Constituency: retirement and tourist resort, south coast seaside, east Bournemouth and Poole

Atkinson, Peter
Conservative MP for Hexham since 1992

Majority: 2,529 (6.0%)
Turnout: 70.9%

	Votes	Share %	Change %
Peter Atkinson, Conservative	18,917	44.6	5.8
Paul Brannen, Labour	16,388	38.6	0.3
Philip Lathan, Liberal Democrat	6,380	15	–2.4
Alan Patterson, UK Independenceparty	728	1.7	n/a

Andrew Roth says: "the unbridled voice of the constituency's big farmers, the Countryside Alliance and newspaper moguls"

Recent parliamentary career: opposition whip (1999–); Scottish affairs committee (1997–); court of referees committee (1997–); PPS to Lord Parkinson (1997–99)
Background: locally-born journalist turned public affairs consultant; Wandsworth councillor
Born: January 19 1943 in Corbridge, Northumberland
Education: Cheltenham College
Constituency: huge, rural, agricultural seat, stretches south of River Tyne to Scottish border, includes part of Hadrian's Wall

Austin, John
Labour MP for Erith and Thamesmead since 1997; Woolwich (1992–97)

Majority: 11,167 (33.5%)
Turnout: 50.3%

	Votes	Share %	Change %
John Austin, Labour	19,769	59.3	–2.8
Mark Brooks, Conservative	8,602	25.8	5.6
James Kempton, Liberal Democrat	3,800	11.4	–0.6
Hardev Dhillon, Socialist Labourparty	1,180	3.5	n/a

Andrew Roth says: "as fierce a campaigner against local short-changing on employment, NHS and fire services as he is against Turkish or Serbian aggression"

Recent parliamentary career: unopposed bills panel (1998–); health committee (1997–)
Background: community relations officer (1972–92); medical laboratory technician; Greenwich councillor and mayor who introduced London marathon
Born: August 21 1944 in Blaby, Leicestershire
Education: Glyn County Grammar School, Epsom
Higher education: Bristol University; Goldsmiths' College, New Cross
Constituency: new south London riverside town, problems with housing, crime, and racial tension

B

Bacon, Richard
Conservative MP for South Norfolk since 2001

Majority: 6,893 (12.3%)
Turnout: 67.6%

	Votes	Share %	Change %
Richard Bacon, Conservative	23,589	42.2	2
Anne Lee, Liberal Democrat	16,696	29.9	1.6
Mark Wells, Labour	13,719	24.5	1.6
Stephanie Ross, Green party	1,069	1.9	1.1
Joseph Neal, UK Independence party	856	1.5	n/a

David Hencke, the *Guardian*: "Richard Bacon has called for the abolition of the European parliament and commission"

Recent parliamentary career: entered parliament 2001; public accounts committee (2001–)
Background: public relations consultant; managing director; Barclay's investment banker; financial journalist
Born: September 3 1962
Education: King's School, Worcester
Higher education: London School of Economics
Constituency: rural, middle class, some commuters, small towns and many villages

Bailey, Adrian
Labour MP for West Bromwich West since 2000

Majority: 11,355 (35.7%)
Turnout: 47.7%

	Votes	Share %	Change %
Adrian Bailey, Labour	19,352	60.8	9.8
Karen Bissell, Conservative	7,997	25.1	–8.8
Sadie Smith, Liberal Democrat	2,168	6.8	–2.7
John Salvage, British National party	1,428	4.5	0.3
Kevin Walker, UK Independence party	499	1.6	0.3
Baghwant Singh, Socialist Labour party	396	1.2	n/a
Baghwant Singh, Socialist Labour	n/a		

Maiden speech: "[I have] worked for the cooperative movement and am committed to the principles of cooperation and mutuality"

Recent parliamentary career: Northern Ireland affairs committee (2001–); entered parliament 2000 byelection
Background: political organiser, Co-operative party; librarian for 11 years; deputy leader of Sandwell Council
Born: December 11 1945
Education: Cheltenham Grammar School
Higher education: Exeter University; Loughborough College of Librarianship
Constituency: at the heart of the Black Country, old industrial communities, manual workers, mainly urban

Baird, Vera
Labour MP for Redcar since 2001

Majority: 13,443 (35.2%)
Turnout: 57.7%

	Votes	Share %	Change %
Vera Baird, Labour	23,026	60.3	–7
Chris Main, Conservative	9,583	25.1	2
Stan Wilson, Liberal Democrat	4,817	12.6	3
John Taylor, Socialist Labour Party	772	2	n/a

Maiden speech: "as a criminal lawyer, I am interested in issues of crime control, access to justice, the courts and criminal sentencing"

Recent parliamentary career: entered parliament 2001; joint committee on human rights (2001–)
Background: one of the UK's top criminal lawyers; deputy head of Michael Mansfield QC's law chambers in London; visiting Oxford fellow (1999)
Born: February 13 1951 in Oldham
Education: Chadderton Grammar School for Girls, Oldham
Higher education: London University; Open University
Constituency: chemical industry and steelworks; purpose-built towns on the Cleveland coastline

Baker, Norman
Liberal Democrat MP for Lewes since 1997

Majority: 9,710 (21.3%)
Turnout: 68.5%

	Votes	Share %	Change %
Norman Baker, Liberal Democrat	25,588	56.3	13.1
Simon Sinnatt, Conservative	15,878	35	−5.6
Paul Richards, Labour	3,317	7.3	−3.3
John Harvey, UK Independence party	650	1.4	n/a

Andrew Roth says: "hit the parliamentary scene running, spraying questions in all directions"

Recent parliamentary career: asked the written question that led to the resignation of Peter Mandelson MP (2001); Lib Dem spokesperson, HO (2001–); joint committee on human rights (2001–); broadcasting committee (2000–2001); Lib Dem spokesperson, environment and Millennium Dome (1997–99)
Background: teacher of English as a foreign language; MP's researcher; environmental campaigner; regional director, Our Price Records; Lewes councillor
Born: July 26 1957 in Aberdeen
Education: Royal Liberty School, Romford
Higher education: Royal Holloway College, London; Bedford New College
Constituency: old fashioned small town east of Brighton, contains Glyndebourne

Baldry, Tony
Conservative MP for Banbury since 1983

Majority: 5,219 (10.2%)
Turnout: 61.8%

	Votes	Share %	Change %
Tony Baldry, Conservative	23,271	45.2	2.3
Leslie Sibley, Labour	18,052	35	0.2
Tony Worgan, Liberal Democrat	8,216	16	−0.7
Bev Cotton, Green party	1,281	2.5	1.6
Stephen Harris, UK Independence party	695	1.4	n/a

Andrew Roth says: "a split personality: sometimes a pompously middle class climber, sometimes an engagingly pragmatic wet"

Recent parliamentary career: standards and privileges committee (2001–); trade and industry committee (1997–2001); minister of state, MAFF (1995–97)
Background: barrister; publisher; Territorial Army officer and honorary colonel
Born: July 10 1950 in Middlesex
Education: Leighton Park School, Reading
Higher education: Sussex University
Constituency: rural north Oxfordshire town with fast-growing economy thanks to M40

Banks, Tony
Labour MP for West Ham since 1997; Newham North West (1983–97)

Majority: 15,645 (53.5%)
Turnout: 48.9%

	Votes	Share %	Change %
Tony Banks, Labour	20,449	69.9	−3
Syed Kamall, Conservative	4,804	16.4	1.4
Paul Fox, Liberal Democrat	2,166	7.4	0
Ms Jackie Chandler Oatts, Green party	1,197	4.1	n/a
Gerard Batten, UK Independence party	657	2.2	n/a

Andrew Roth says: "quick witted, verbally incontinent, hard-left former rebel"

Recent parliamentary career: accommodation and works committee (2000–); procedure committee (1999–2001); junior minister, DCMS (1997–99); ran failed British bid for 2006 World Cup
Background: head of research, AUEW trade union; supports animal welfare and football
Born: April 8 1943 in Belfast
Education: Archbishop's Tenison Grammar School
Higher education: London School of Economics; York University
Constituency: innercity, large Afro-Caribbean and Asian population

Barker, Gregory
Conservative MP for Bexhill and Battle since 2001

Majority: 10,503 (23.4%)
Turnout: 64.9%

	Votes	Share %	Change %
Gregory Barker, Conservative	21,555	48.1	0.0
Stephen Hardy, Liberal Democrat	11,052	24.7	–0.8
Anne Moore-Williams, Labour	8,702	19.4	1.3
Nigel Farage, UK Independence party	3,474	7.8	n/a

Maiden speech: "few people realise that Bexhill was the birthplace of British motor racing and next year we look forward to celebrating the 100th anniversary of the first motor race along the seafront"

Recent parliamentary career: entered parliament 2001
Background: corporate finance adviser; worked for Russian oil industry; director of recruitment agency; Territorial Army soldier
Born: March 8 1966 in Sussex
Education: Steyning Grammar School; Lancing College, West Sussex
Higher education: Royal Holloway College, London
Constituency: coastal strip between Hastings and Eastbourne plus Sussex wooded countryside

Barnes, Harry
Labour MP for North East Derbyshire since 1987

Majority: 12,258 (29.1%)
Turnout: 58.9%

	Votes	Share %	Change %
Harry Barnes, Labour	23,437	55.6	–4.9
James Hollingsworth, Conservative	11,179	26.5	1.3
Mark Higginbottom, Liberal Democrat	7,508	17.8	3.5

Andrew Roth says: "hyperactive, Campaign Group nuclear pacifist ... a mixed-doctrine member of Labour's core awkward squad""

Recent parliamentary career: Northern Ireland affairs committee (1997–); backed help for exiles driven fron Northern Ireland by the IRA; campaigned for the Labour party to organise in Northern Ireland; registered 75 rebel votes (1992–96)

Background: lecturer in government, politics and industrial relations, Sheffield University; railway clerk
Born: July 22 1936 in Easington, County Durham
Education: Easington Colliery Secondary Modern School; Ryhope Grammar School
Higher education: Hull University; Oxford, Ruskin
Constituency: kidney-shaped former mining constituency at northern end of Derbyshire

Baron, John
Conservative MP for Billericay since 2001

Majority: 5,013 (11.0%)
Turnout: 58.1%

	Votes	Share %	Change %
John Baron, Conservative	21,608	47.4	7.6
Amanda Campbell, Labour	16,595	36.4	−0.9
Frank Bellard, Liberal Democrat	6,323	13.9	−1.9
Nick Yeomans, UK Independence party	1,072	2.4	n/a

Maiden speech: "Billericay has historical connections with the pilgrim fathers…those men and women escaping the heavy hand of government"

Recent parliamentary career: entered parliament 2001
Background: company chairman; captain, Royal Regiment of Fusiliers
Born: June 21 1959
Education: Queen's College, Taunton
Higher education: Cambridge, Jesus College; Royal Military Academy, Sandhurst
Constituency: Basildon without Basildon New Town; commuter belt, owner-occupier Tory territory, once held by Teresa Gorman

Barrett, John
Liberal Democrat MP for Edinburgh West since 2001

Majority: 7,589 (19.3%)
Turnout: 63.8%

	Votes	Share %	Change %
John Barrett, Liberal Democrat	16,719	42.4	−0.8
Elspeth Alexandra, Labour	9,130	23.1	4.3
Iain Whyte, Conservative	8,894	22.5	−5.5
Alyn Smith, Scottish National party	4,047	10.3	1.5
Bill Scott, Scottish Socialist party	688	1.7	n/a

Maiden speech: "While we are here and grappling with the problems of the western world, I hope that we never forget those in the third world who are desperate to fill their empty bellies while burdened with debt to the richest nations on the planet"

Recent parliamentary career: entered parliament 2001
Background: company director; involved in Edinburgh Film Festival and film industries office
Born: February 11 1954
Education: Forrester High School, Edinburgh
Higher education: Telford College; Napier Polytechnic, Edinburgh
Constituency: traditional, sought-after Edinburgh suburbs plus city's airport

Barron, Kevin
Labour MP for Rother Valley since 1983

Majority: 14,882 (40.4%)
Turnout: 53.2%

	Votes	Share %	Change %
Kevin Barron, Labour	22,851	62.1	−5.5
James Duddridge, Conservative	7,969	21.7	5
Ms Win Knight, Liberal Democrat	4,603	12.5	0.9
David Cutts, UK Independence party	1,380	3.8	n/a

Andrew Roth says: "shrewd, balanced energy and health specialist with a deep soft spot for fellow ex-miners and their shrunken industry"

Recent parliamentary career: intelligence and security committee (2001–); opposition spokesperson, Health (1995–97)
Background: worked for National Coal Board for 21 years; member of General Medical Council
Born: October 26 1946 in Tadcaster, Yorks
Education: Maltby Hall Secondary School
Higher education: Oxford, Ruskin

Constituency: south-eastern part of Rotherham borough, many small rural, mining and agricultural villages

Battle, John
Labour MP for Leeds West since 1987

Majority: 14,935 (46.5%)
Turnout: 50%

	Votes	Share %	Change %
John Battle, Labour	19,943	62.1	−4.6
John Robertshaw, Conservative	5,008	15.6	−1.9
Darren Finlay, Liberal Democrat	3,350	10.4	1.4
David Blackburn, Green party	2,573	8	n/a
Bill Finley, UK Independence party	758	2.4	n/a
Noel Nowosielski, Liberal	462	1.4	−0.2

Andrew Roth says: "one of the rare politicians who is both computer-literate and reads poetry"

Recent parliamentary career: international development committee (2001–); minister of state, FCO (1999–2001); minister of state, DTI (1997–99)
Background: national coordinator, Church Action on Poverty; Leeds councillor
Born: April 26 1951 in Bradford
Education: St Michael's College; Upholland College, Liverpool
Higher education: Leeds University
Constituency: on the River Aire, economy shifting from manufacturing to service industries

Bayley, Hugh
Labour MP for City of York since 1997; York (1992–97)

Majority: 13,779 (28.8%)
Turnout: 59.7%

	Votes	Share %	Change %
Hugh Bayley, Labour	25,072	52.3	−7.6
Michael McIntyre, Conservative	11,293	23.5	−1.2
Andrew Waller, Liberal Democrat	8,519	17.8	6.6
Bill Shaw, Green party	1,465	3.1	1.6
Frank Ormston, Socialist Alliance	674	1.4	n/a
Richard Bate, UK Independence party	576	1.2	n/a
Graham Cambridge, Official Monster Raving Loony party	381	0.8	n/a

Andrew Roth says: "worthy rather than exciting"

Recent parliamentary career: international development committee (2001–); junior minister, DSS (1999–2001); PPS to Frank Dobson (1997–99)
Background: social policy lecturer and academic; Camden councillor; NALGO official
Born: January 9 1952 in Oxford
Education: Haileybury
Higher education: Bristol University; York University
Constituency: elegant town with medieval history; railway centre and manufacturing industry, plus tourism and university

Beard, Nigel
Labour MP for Bexleyheath and Crayford since 1997

Majority: 1,472 (3.7%)
Turnout: 63.5%

	Votes	Share %	Change %
Nigel Beard, Labour	17,593	43.6	–1.9
David Evennett, Conservative	16,121	39.9	1.5
Nickolas O'Hare, Liberal Democrat	4,476	11.1	–0.1
Colin Smith, British National party	1,408	3.5	2.6
John Dunford, UK Independence party	780	1.9	n/a

Andrew Roth says: "an industrial intellectual straight from the laboratories of big business"

Recent parliamentary career: Treasury committee (2000–); Treasury subcommittee (2000–); unopposed bills panel (1998–)
Background: research and development manager, Zeneca; chief planner, Greater London Council
Born: October 10 1936 in Leeds
Education: Castleford Grammar School, Yorkshire
Higher education: University College, London
Constituency: outer south-east London, suburban, commuting, heavily owner-occupied

Beckett, Rt Hon Margaret
Labour MP for Derby South since 1983; Lincoln (1974–79)

Majority: 13,855 (32.1%)
Turnout: 55.7%

	Votes	Share %	Change %
Margaret Beckett, Labour	24,310	56.4	0.1
Simon Spencer, Conservative	10,455	24.3	–0.9
Anders Hanson, Liberal Democrat	8,310	19.3	4.9
Richard Fellowes, UK Independence party	n/a		

Andrew Roth says: "logical, numerate, technocratic mind who fights her ideological corner"

Recent parliamentary career: secretary of state, DEFRA (2001–); leader of House of Commons (1998–2001); president of board of trade (1997–98); acting Labour leader after John Smith's death (1994); stood for Labour leader and deputy leader but came third and second (1994); deputy leader, Labour party (1992–94)
Background: metallurgist; researcher for Labour party and Granada Television
Born: January 15 1943 in Ashton-under-Lyne
Education: Notre Dame High School, Norwich
Higher education: Manchester College of Science and Technology
Constituency: Derby's railway works, Rolls-Royce aero-factory and large Asian community

Begg, Anne
Labour MP for Aberdeen South since 1997

Majority: 4,388 (11.9%)
Turnout: 62.6%

	Votes	Share %	Change %
Anne Begg, Labour	14,696	39.8	4.5
Ian Yuill, Liberal Democrat	10,308	27.9	0.3
Moray Macdonald, Conservative	7,098	19.2	–7.2
Ian Angus, Scottish National party	4,293	11.6	1.8
Dave Watt, Scottish Socialist party	495	1.3	n/a

Andrew Roth says: "Blair-loyal, pro-EU, strong homeruler who has decided to stay in Westminster"

Recent parliamentary career: work and pensions committee (2001–); Scottish affairs committee (1997–2001)
Background: English teacher; member of Scottish General Teaching Council; wheelchair user
Born: December 6 1955 in Forfar, Angus
Education: Brechin High School
Higher education: Aberdeen University; Aberdeen College of Education
Constituency: situated on both sides of the River Dee in Aberdeen's affluent suburbs

Beggs, Roy
Ulster Unionist MP for East Antrim since 1983

Majority: 128 (0.4%)
Turnout: 59.1%

	Votes	Share %	Change %
Roy Beggs, Ulster Unionist party	13,101	36.4	–2.4
Sammy Wilson, Democratic Unionist party	12,973	36	16.5
John Mathews, Alliance party of Northern Ireland	4,483	12.5	–7.7
Danny O'Connor, Social Democratic and Labour Party	2,641	7.3	2.7
Robert Mason, Independent	1,092	3	n/a
Ms Jeanette Graffin, Sinn Fein	903	2.5	0.9
Alan Greer, Conservative	807	2.2	–4.6

Andrew Roth says: "vehement but not overly articulate"

Recent parliamentary career: UUP chief whip (2000–); Northern Ireland affairs committee (1997–); Ulster Unionist spokesperson, education and employment, culture (1997–2000)
Background: teacher and vice principal, Larne High School (1957–82); Larne Borough councillor; mayor of Larne; arrested in 1995 for participating in Orange Order road blockade; member NIA (1998– , 1982–86)
Born: February 20 1936 in Belfast
Education: Ballyclare High School
Higher education: Stranmillis Training College, Belfast
Constituency: coastal, eastern end of Northern Ireland, agricultural and some engineering industry, includes port of Larne

Beith, Rt Hon Alan James
Liberal Democrat MP for Berwick-upon-Tweed since 1973

Majority: 8,458 (23.3%)
Turnout: 63.8%

	Votes	Share %	Change %
Alan Beith, Liberal Democrat	18,651	51.4	5.9
Glen Sanderson, Conservative	10,193	28.1	4
Martin Walker, Labour	6,435	17.7	–8.5
John Pearson, UK Independence party	1,029	2.8	n/a

Andrew Roth says: "conscientious deputy headmaster type"

Recent parliamentary career: intelligence and security committee (2001–); Lib Dem deputy leader (1992–); procedure committee (2000–2001); Lib Dem spokesperson, home affairs (1997–99); Lib Dem Treasury spokesperson (1989–94); stood for party leadership (1988)
Background: politics lecturer; Tynedale councillor
Born: April 20 1943 in Poynton, Cheshire
Education: King's School, Macclesfield
Higher education: Oxford, Balliol; Oxford, Nuffield
Constituency: large, hilly borders seat, small towns, economy based on agriculture, fishing, and tourism

Bell, Stuart
Labour MP for Middlesbrough since 1983

Majority: 16,330 (48.5%)
Turnout: 49.8%

	Votes	Share %	Change %
Stuart Bell, Labour	22,783	67.6	–3.8
Alex Finn, Conservative	6,453	19.1	1.9
Keith Miller, Liberal Democrat	3,512	10.4	1.9
Geoff Kerr-Morgan, Socialist Alliance	577	1.7	n/a
Kai Andersen, Socialist Labour Party	392	1.2	n/a

Andrew Roth says: "able, courageous, but overly sectarian-immoderate"

Recent parliamentary career: chair, finance and services committee (2000–); second church estates commissioner (1997–)
Background: barrister; reporter; novelist; son of Durham miner
Born: May 16 1938 in High Spen, County Durham
Education: Hookergate Grammar School, Durham
Higher education: Council of Legal Education, Gray's Inn; Pitman's College
Constituency: urban steel city, predominantly working-class, high unemployment

Bellingham, Henry
Conservative MP for North West Norfolk since 2001; North West Norfolk (1983–97)

Majority: 3,485 (6.8%)
Turnout: 66.2%

	Votes	Share %	Change %
Henry Bellingham, Conservative	24,846	48.5	7
George Turner, Labour	21,361	41.7	–2.1
Ian Mack, Liberal Democrat	4,292	8.4	–1.2
Ian Durrant, UK Independence party	704	1.4	n/a

Andrew Roth says: "scion of local landowning gentry, superloyal and hardworking"

Recent parliamentary career: re-entered parliament 2001; Northern Ireland affairs committee (2001–)
Background: barrister; business consultant
Born: March 29 1955
Education: Eton College
Higher education: Magdalene, Cambridge; Council of Legal Education, Gray's Inn
Constituency: mainly rural, but not all rich or smart, includes King's Lynn

Benn, Hilary
Labour MP for Leeds Central since 1999

Majority: 14,381 (52.6%)
Turnout: 41.7%

	Votes	Share %	Change %
Hilary Benn, Labour	18,277	66.9	19.6
Victoria Richmond, Conservative	3,896	14.3	2.3
Stewart Arnold, Liberal Democrat	3,607	13.2	–17
David Burgess, UK Independence party	775	2.8	n/a
Stephen Johnston, Socialist Alliance	751	2.8	n/a

Hilary Benn says: "I am a Benn, and proud of it, but not a Bennite"

Recent parliamentary career: junior minister, DFID (2001–); environment, transport and regional affairs committee (1999–2001); environment subcommittee (1999–2001)
Background: head of policy and communication, MSF trade union; David Blunkett's special adviser; son of retired MP Tony Benn
Born: November 26 1953 in London
Education: Holland Park Comprehensive School
Higher education: Sussex University
Constituency: innercity Leeds, commercial centre and universities; lowest postwar turnout – 19.5% in 1999 byelection

Bennett, Andrew
Labour MP for Denton and Reddish since 1983; Stockport North (1974–83)
Majority: 15,330 (45.6%)
Turnout: 48.5%

	Votes	Share %	Change %
Andrew Bennett, Labour	21,913	65.2	–0.2
Paul Newman, Conservative	6,583	19.6	–1.7
Roger Fletcher, Liberal Democrat	4,152	12.4	–0.9
Alan Cadwallader, UK Independence party	945	2.8	n/a

Andrew Roth says: "civil libertarian sensitive to the rights of British ramblers and Irish dissidents"

Recent parliamentary career: joint chair, transport, local government, and the regions committee (2001–); joint committee on statutory instruments (2001–); chair, environment, transport and regional affairs committee (1997–2001)
Background: geography teacher; Oldham councillor; interest in the environment
Born: March 1 1939 in Manchester
Education: Hulme Grammar School, Manchester
Higher education: Birmingham University
Constituency: south-east Greater Manchester, urban, skilled manual, high unemployment

Benton, Joe
Labour MP for Bootle since 1990

Majority: 19,043 (69.1%)
Turnout: 49%

	Votes	Share %	Change %
Joe Benton, Labour	21,400	77.6	–5.3
Jim Murray, Liberal Democrat	2,357	8.5	2.8
Judith Symes, Conservative	2,194	8	–0.5
Dave Flynn, Socialist Labour Party	971	3.5	n/a
Peter Glover, Socialist Alliance	672	2.4	n/a

Andrew Roth says: "a rare, one-note voice always demanding a better stake for Merseyside"

Recent parliamentary career: secretary, all-party parliamentary pro-life group; opposition whip (1994–97)
Background: apprenticed fitter and turner; personnel manager; Roman Catholic; anti-abortion
Born: September 28 1933 in Bootle
Education: St Monica's Roman Catholic School, Bootle
Higher education: Bootle Technical College
Constituency: innercity Lancashire dockland town comprising the southern part of the Borough of Sefton; includes well-off areas such as Formby and Southport; safest Labour seat in the 2001 election

Bercow, John
Conservative MP for Buckingham since 1997

Majority: 13,325 (29.5%)
Turnout: 69.4%

	Votes	Share %	Change %
John Bercow, Conservative	24,296	53.7	3.9
Mark Seddon, Labour	10,971	24.2	–0.5
Isobel Wilson, Liberal Democrat	9,037	20	–4.6
Christopher Silcock, UK Independence Party	968	2.1	n/a

Andrew Roth says: "a jack-in-the-box who hardly lets a day pass without interventions"

Recent parliamentary career: shadow chief secretary (2001–); opposition spokesperson, home affairs (2000–01); opposition spokesperson, education and employment (1999–2000)
Background: PR consultant; credit analyst; Lambeth councillor; special adviser to Jonathan Aitken (1995) and Virginia Bottomley (1995–96)
Born: January 19 1963 in Edgware
Education: Manorhill School, Finchley

Higher education: Essex University
Constituency: affluent, rural villages, largest seat in Buckinghamshire; once elected Robert Maxwell

Beresford, Sir Paul
Conservative MP for Mole Valley since 1997; Croydon Central (1992–97)

Majority: 10,153 (21.5%)
Turnout: 69.5%

	Votes	Share %	Change %
Sir Paul Beresford, Conservative	23,790	50.5	2.5
Celia Savage, Liberal Democrat	13,637	29	–0.3
Dan Redford, Labour	7,837	16.7	1.9
Ron Walters, UK Independence party	1,333	2.8	n/a
William Newton, ProLife Alliance	475	1	n/a

Andrew Roth says: "right-wing pioneer of the privatisation of local services"

Recent parliamentary career: transport, local government, and the regions committee (2001–); procedure committee (1997–2001); junior minister, environment (1994–97)
Background: New Zealand-born dentist who continued to practise when a minister; Wandsworth Council leader(1983–92); famous as a cost-cutting Thatcher favourite; knighted in 1990
Born: April 6 1946 in New Zealand
Education: Richmond Primary Scotland, New Zealand
Higher education: Otago University, Dunedin; Eastman Dental Hospital, London University
Constituency: upmarket Surrey, mainly rural, middle class, includes Leith and Box Hill

Berry, Roger
Labour MP for Kingswood since 1992

Majority: 13,962 (26.5%)
Turnout: 65.4%

	Votes	Share %	Change %
Roger Berry, Labour	28,903	54.9	1.2
Robert Marven, Conservative	14,941	28.4	–1.5
Christopher Greenfield, Liberal Democrat	7,747	14.7	1.9
David Smith, UK Independence party	1,085	2.1	n/a

Andrew Roth says: "skilful defender of disability rights with an ironic, populist attacking style"

Recent parliamentary career: trade and industry committee (1997–)
Background: economics lecturer, University of Papua New Guinea, Sussex and Bristol Universities; Avon councillor
Born: July 4 1948 in Huddersfield
Education: Huddersfield New College
Higher education: Bristol University; Sussex University
Constituency: mixed urban and rural seat just east of Bristol

Best, Harold
Labour MP for Leeds North West since 1997

Majority: 5,236 (12.3%)
Turnout: 58.2%

	Votes	Share %	Change %
Harold Best, Labour	17,794	41.9	2
Adam Pritchard, Conservative	12,558	29.6	–2.5
David Hall-Matthews, Liberal Democrat	11,431	26.9	3.2
Andrew Spence, UK Independence party	668	1.6	n/a

Andrew Roth says: "said to work on two levels: as an ideological near-Marxist, or a practical political fixer"

Recent parliamentary career: accommodation and works committee (2001–); environmental audit committee (2001–); joint committee on statutory instruments (2001–); trade and industry committee (1997–2001)
Background: electrical engineer; trade union official; Yorkshire councillor; executive committee member, Liberty
Born: December 18 1939 in Leeds
Education: Meanwood County Secondary School
Higher education: technical college
Constituency: outer Leeds suburbs, professional middle class and students

Betts, Clive
Labour MP for Sheffield Attercliffe since 1992

Majority: 18,844 (52.6%)
Turnout: 52.4%

	Votes	Share %	Change %
Clive Betts, Labour	24,287	67.8	2.5
John Perry, Conservative	5,443	15.2	−0.9
Gail Smith, Liberal Democrat	5,092	14.2	−1.5
Pauline Arnott, UK Independence party	1,002	2.8	n/a

Andrew Roth says: "shy and self contained, 'his most conspicuous characteristics are caution and commitment'"

Recent parliamentary career: transport, local government, and the regions committee (2001–); committee of selection (1997–98); assistant government whip (1997–98)
Background: locally born; Sheffield councillor for 18 years; local government economist
Born: January 13 1950 in Sheffield
Education: King Edward VII School, Sheffield
Higher education: Cambridge, Pembroke
Constituency: ex-steelworking, skilled manual communities in south-east Sheffield

Blackman, Liz
Labour MP for Erewash since 1997

Majority: 6,932 (14.2%)
Turnout: 61.9%

	Votes	Share %	Change %
Liz Blackman, Labour	23,915	49.2	−2.5
Gregor MacGregor, Conservative	16,983	35	−1.6
Martin Garnett, Liberal Democrat	5,586	11.5	2.9
Louise Smith, UK Independence party	692	1.4	n/a
Steve Belshaw, British National party	591	1.2	n/a
RU Serious Brewer, Official Monster Reving Loony party	428	0.9	n/a
Peter Waldock, Socialist Labour party	401	0.8	0

Andrew Roth says: "fast climbing professional"

Recent parliamentary career: PPS to Geoff Hoon (2000–); Treasury committee (1997–2001); Treasury subcommittee (1998–2001)
Background: teacher and head teacher (1972–97); deputy leader, Broxtowe Council
Born: September 28 1949 in Carlisle
Education: Carlisle County High School for Girls; Prince Henry's Grammar School, Otley; Clifton College of Further Education
Constituency: mixed urban and rural area centred on Long Eaton, south of Derby

Blair, Rt Hon Tony
Labour MP for Sedgefield since 1983

Majority: 17,713 (44.0%)
Turnout: 62%

	Votes	Share %	Change %
Tony Blair, Labour	26,110	64.9	−6.3
Douglas Carswell, Conservative	8,397	20.9	3.1
Andrew Duffield, Liberal Democrat	3,624	9	.5
Andrew Spence, UK Independence party	974	2.4	n/a
Brian Gibson, Socialist Labour Party	518	1.3	0.3
Christopher Driver, R & R Loony	375	0.9	n/a
Helen John, WFLOE	260	0.7	n/a

Andrew Roth says: "a genius for reaching out to formerly Tory-voting middle England while showing the insensitivity of a tone-deaf orchestra leader to trade unionists and leftish activists"

Recent parliamentary career: prime minister (1997–); leader, Labour party (1994–)
Background: barrister, specialising in trade union and industrial law; sponsored by TGWU until 1996
Born: May 6 1953 in Edinburgh
Education: Durham Choristers' School; Fettes College, Edinburgh
Higher education: Oxford, St John's
Constituency: rural small towns and old mining villages in south-eastern County Durham surrounding Darlington

Blears, Hazel
Labour MP for Salford since 1997

Majority: 11,012 (48.9%)
Turnout: 41.6%

	Votes	Share %	Change %
Hazel Blears, Labour	14,649	65.1	−3.9
Norman Owen, Liberal Democrat	3,637	16.2	5.9
Chris King, Conservative	3,446	15.3	−2.1
Peter Grant, Socialist Alliance	414	1.8	n/a
Hazel Wallace, Independent	216	1	n/a
Roy Masterson, Ind Masters	152	0.7	n/a

Andrew Roth says: "former left-wing tigress turned Blairite pussycat"

Recent parliamentary career: junior minister, DoH (2001–); PPS to Alan Milburn (1997–99)
Background: solicitor; Salford councillor
Born: May 14 1956 in Salford
Education: Wardley Grammar School, Swinton; Eccles Sixth Form College
Higher education: Trent Polytechnic; Chester College of Law
Constituency: inner-city area north-east of Manchester city centre; new development including Lowrey Centre

Blizzard, Bob
Labour MP for Waveney since 1997

Majority: 8,553 (18.1%)
Turnout: 61.6%

	Votes	Share %	Change %
Bob Blizzard, Labour	23,914	50.7	−5.3
Lee Scott, Conservative	15,361	32.6	−1.9
David Young, Liberal Democrat	5,370	11.4	2.4
Brian Aylett, UK Independence party	1,097	2.3	n/a
Graham Elliot, Green party	983	2.1	n/a
Rupert Mallin, Socialist Alliance	442	0.9	n/a

Andrew Roth says: "loyal, extremely practical local improver"

Recent parliamentary career: PPS to Nick Brown (2001–); PPS to Baroness Hayman (1999–2001)
Background: English teacher (1972–97); Waveney council leader
Born: May 31 1950 in Bury St Edmunds
Education: Culford School, Bury St Edmunds
Higher education: Birmingham University
Constituency: most easterly point in Britain, coastal, fishing industry, shipbuilding, engineering, and industrial

Blunkett, Rt Hon David

Labour MP for Sheffield Brightside since 1987

Majority: 17,049 (66.7%)
Turnout: 46.7%

	Votes	Share %	Change %
David Blunkett, Labour	19,650	76.9	3.4
Matthew Wilson, Conservative	2,601	10.2	1.8
Alison Firth, Liberal Democrat	2,238	8.8	−5.8
Brian Wilson, Socialist Alliance	361	1.4	n/a
Robert Morris, Socialist Labour Party	354	1.4	0
Mark Suter, UK Independence party	348	1.4	n/a

Andrew Roth says: "trying to keep a foot in every camp moving his way"

Recent parliamentary career: home secretary (2001–); secretary of state, DFEE (1997–2001)
Background: politics tutor; clerk; shop assistant, councillor and leader of Sheffield council for 17 years
Born: June 6 1947 in Sheffield
Education: Sheffield School for the Blind
Higher education: Sheffield University; Shrewsbury Technical College; Royal Normal College for the Blind; Huddersfield College of Education
Constituency: north-east Sheffield, working-class, high unemployment and many council estates

Blunt, Crispin

Conservative MP for Reigate since 1997

Majority: 8,025 (20.3%)
Turnout: 60.7%

	Votes	Share %	Change %
Crispin Blunt, Conservative	18,875	47.8	4
Simon Charleton, Labour	10,850	27.5	−0.3
Jane Kulka, Liberal Democrat	8,330	21.1	1.1
Stephen Smith, UK Independence party	1,062	2.7	n/a
Harold Green, Ref UK	357	0.9	n/a

Andrew Roth says: "treats Labour ministers as though they are muddle-brained other ranks who mistakenly think they are in command"

Recent parliamentary career: opposition spokesperson, NIO (2001–); environment, transport and regional affairs committee (2000–2001); environment subcommittee (2000–2001)
Background: Sandhurst graduate; army officer for 11 years; worked for Forum of Private Business; special adviser to Malcolm Rifkind (1993–97)
Born: July 15 1960 in British Military Hospital Rinteln
Education: Wellington College
Higher education: Durham University; Royal Military Academy, Sandhurst; Cranfield School of Management
Constituency: mixed town in prosperous Surrey

Boateng, Rt Hon Paul
Labour MP for Brent South since 1987

Majority: 17,380 (60.7%)
Turnout: 51.2%

	Votes	Share %	Change %
Paul Boateng, Labour	20,984	73.3	0.3
Carupiah Selvarajah, Conservative	3,604	12.6	−3.3
Havard Hughes, Liberal Democrat	3,098	10.8	3.1
Mike McDonnell, Socialist Alliance	491	1.7	n/a
Thomas Mac Stiofain, Res Motor	460	1.6	n/a

Andrew Roth says: "deft, witty, formerly radical lawyer"

Recent parliamentary career: financial secretary, Treasury (2001–); public accounts committee (2001–); minister of state, HO (1998–2001); junior minister, DoH (1997–98)
Background: barrister; member of GLC; sat on several committees on race relations and crime and policing
Born: June 14 1951 in Hackney
Education: Accra Academy; Apsley Grammar School, Hemel Hempstead
Higher education: Bristol University
Constituency: southern strip on Brent border, majority ethnic-minority population

Borrow, David
Labour MP for South Ribble since 1997

Majority: 3,792 (8.3%)
Turnout: 62.5%

	Votes	Share %	Change %
David Borrow, Labour	21,386	46.4	−0.4
Adrian Owens, Conservative	17,594	38.1	0.5
Mark Alcock, Liberal Democrat	7,150	15.5	4.9

Andrew Roth says: "rectangular face, slightly funereal manner"

Recent parliamentary career: environment, food, and rural affairs committee (2001–); agriculture committee (1999–2001)
Background: clerk to Merseyside valuation tribunal for 14 years
Born: August 2 1952 in Huddersfield
Education: Mirfield Grammar School
Higher education: Manchester Polytechnic
Constituency: north-west seat on River Ribble, includes Leyland truck factory, suburban

Boswell, Tim
Conservative MP for Daventry since 1987

Majority: 9,649 (17.0%)
Turnout: 65.5%

	Votes	Share %	Change %
Timothy Boswell, Conservative	27,911	49.2	2.9
Kevin Quigley, Labour	18,262	32.2	−2.2
Jamie Calder, Liberal Democrat	9,130	16.1	1.1
Peter Baden, UK Independence party	1,381	2.4	n/a

Andrew Roth says: "a pleasant, civilised, low-profiled, not overly-partisan one nation type"

Recent parliamentary career: opposition spokesperson, DWP (2001–); spokesperson, education and employment (1999–); spokesperson, Treasury (1997); spokesperson, DTI (1997–99); junior minister, MAFF (1995–97)
Background: special adviser, MAFF; farmer
Born: December 2 1942 in Brentwood, Essex

Education: Marlborough College
Higher education: Oxford, New College
Constituency: large rural seat in south Northamptonshire; a few towns and many villages

Bottomley, Peter
Conservative MP for Worthing West since 1997; Eltham (1983–1997); Greenwich, Woolwich West (1975–83)

Majority: 9,037 (20.9%)
Turnout: 59.7%

	Votes	Share %	Change %
Peter Bottomley, Conservative	20,508	47.5	1.4
James Walsh, Liberal Democrat	11,471	26.6	–4.5
Alan Butcher, Labour	9,270	21.5	5.3
Tim Cross, UK Independence party	1,960	4.5	n/a

Andrew Roth says: "candidate-saint of the pro-European Tory wets"

Recent parliamentary career: unopposed bills panel (1997–); standards and privileges committee (1997–)
Background: industrial economist; former transport minister; IT enthusiast and trade union sympathiser; parliamentary swimming and dinghy sailing champion
Born: July 30 1944 in Newport, Salop
Education: Westminster School; Gordon Junior High School, Washington DC
Higher education: Cambridge, Trinity
Constituency: West Sussex seaside town, 30% of residents are OAPs

Bottomley, Rt Hon Virginia
Conservative MP for South West Surrey since 1984

Majority: 861 (1.7%)
Turnout: 66.9%

	Votes	Share %	Change %
Virginia Bottomley, Conservative	22,462	45.3	0.7
Simon Cordon, Liberal Democrat	21,601	43.6	3.8
Martin Whelton, Labour	4,321	8.7	–0.7
Timothy Clark, UK Independence party	1,208	2.4	n/a

Andrew Roth says: "continued to lead with her chin from the backbenches after most ex-ministers who survived the 1997 Labour flood had retreated to boardroom bunkers"

Recent parliamentary career: secretary of state, National Heritage (1995–97); secretary of state, DoH (1992–95)
Background: researcher; psychiatric social worker; social policy tutor; company director; magistrate
Born: March 12 1948 in Dunoon
Education: Putney High School
Higher education: London School of Economics; Essex University
Constituency: affluent countryside and residential Surrey; some industry, many London commuters

Bradley, Rt Hon Keith
Labour MP for Manchester Withington since 1987

Majority: 11,524 (32.9%)
Turnout: 51.9%

	Votes	Share %	Change %
Keith Bradley, Labour	19,239	54.9	–6.7
Yasmin Zalzala, Liberal Democrat	7,715	22	8.4
Julian Samways, Conservative	5,349	15.3	–4.1
Michelle Valentine, Green party	1,539	4.4	n/a
John Clegg, Socialist Alliance	1,208	3.5	n/a

Andrew Roth says: "persuasive but low-key Mancunian"

Recent parliamentary career: minister of state, HO (2001–); government whip (1998–2001); junior minister, DSS (1997–98)
Background: worked for accountancy firm; research officer, Manchester Council; Manchester councillor
Born: May 17 1950 in Birmingham
Education: Bishop's Vesey's Grammar School
Higher education: York University; Manchester Polytechnic
Constituency: gentrifying Manchester suburbs, ageing population and many public sector workers

Bradley, Peter
Labour MP for The Wrekin since 1997

Majority: 3,587 (8.7%)
Turnout: 63%

	Votes	Share %	Change %
Peter Bradley, Labour	19,532	47.1	0.2
Jacob Rees Mogg, Conservative	15,945	38.4	−1.8
Ian Jenkins, Liberal Democrat	4,738	11.4	−1.4
Denis Brookes, UK Independence party	1,275	3.1	n/a

Andrew Roth says: "Labour loyalist with strong anti-establishment instincts"

Recent parliamentary career: PPS to Alun Michael (2001–)
Background: public affairs consultant; Westminster councillor; led the campaign against Shirley Porter's Conservative leadership of Westminster Council
Born: April 12 1953 in Birmingham
Education: New College Prep School, Oxford; Abingdon School
Higher education: Sussex University; Occidental College, USA
Constituency: Shropshire, surrounds Telford new town, part rural

Bradshaw, Rt Hon Ben
Labour MP for Exeter since 1997

Majority: 11,759 (22.4%)
Turnout: 64.2%

	Votes	Share %	Change %
Ben Bradshaw, Labour	26,194	49.8	2.3
Anne Jobson, Conservative	14,435	27.4	−1.2
Richard Copus, Liberal Democrat	6,512	12.4	−5.6
David Morrish, Liberal	2,596	4.9	1.6
Paul Edwards, Green party	1,240	2.4	n/a
John Stuart, UK Independence party	1,109	2.1	n/a
Francis Choules, Socialist Alliance	530	1	n/a

Andrew Roth says: "assiduous self-publicist"

Recent parliamentary career: junior minister, FCO (2001–); European scrutiny committee (1998–2001)
Background: award-winning BBC radio journalist; openly gay
Born: August 30 1960 in London
Education: Thorpe St Andrew School, Norwich
Higher education: Sussex University
Constituency: Devon's prosperous city and county town, market and commercial centre

Brady, Graham
Conservative MP for Altrincham and Sale West since 1997

Majority: 2,941 (6.8%)
Turnout: 60.7%

	Votes	Share %	Change %
Graham Brady, Conservative	20,113	46.2	3
Janet Baugh, Labour	17,172	39.4	−0.9
Christopher Gaskell, Liberal Democrat	6,283	14.4	1.8

Andrew Roth says: "lucky middlebrow PR man"

Recent parliamentary career: opposition spokesperson, DFES (2001–); opposition whip (2000–01); spokesperson, education and employment (2000–01); PPS to Michael Ancram (2000–01)
Background: locally-born public affairs director
Born: May 20 1967 in Salford
Education: Altrincham Grammar School
Higher education: Durham University
Constituency: Cheshire middle class area, at end of Manchester tramline, more than just commuter belt

Brake, Tom
Liberal Democrat MP for Carshalton and Wallington since 1997

Majority: 4,547 (11.2%)
Turnout: 60.3%

	Votes	Share %	Change %
Tom Brake, Liberal Democrat	18,289	45	6.8
Ken Andrew, Conservative	13,742	33.8	0.3
Maggie Cooper, Labour	7,466	18.4	−5.5
Simon Dixon, Green party	614	1.5	n/a
Martin Haley, UK Independence party	501	1.2	n/a

Andrew Roth says: "thoughtful and enthusiastic, quiet and sensible computer buff who loves fighting elections"

Recent parliamentary career: Lib Dem spokesperson, DTLGR (2001–); accommodation and works committee (2001–); spokesperson, DETR and social justice (1999–2001); environment, transport and regional affairs committee (1997–2001)
Background: IT consultant, Cap Gemini; member of Greenpeace, Friends of the Earth, Oxfam, Amnesty
Born: May 6 1962 in Melton Mowbray, Leicestershire
Education: Lycee International, Paris
Higher education: London, Imperial College
Constituency: suburban outer London; top residential areas and giant council estates

Brazier, Julian
Conservative MP for Canterbury since 1987

Majority: 2,069 (4.6%)
Turnout: 60.9%

	Votes	Share %	Change %
Julian Brazier, Conservative	18,711	41.5	2.9
Emily Thornberry, Labour	16,642	36.9	5.6
Peter Wales, Liberal Democrat	8,056	17.9	−5.9
Hazel Dawe, Green party	920	2	n/a
Lisa Moore, UK Independence party	803	1.8	n/a

Andrew Roth says: "transparently honest and only occasionally cranky"

Recent parliamentary career: opposition whip (2001–); defence committee (1997–2001)
Background: management consultant; served in Territorial Army for 20 years
Born: July 24 1953 in Dartford, Kent
Education: Wellington College
Higher education: Oxford, Brasenose
Constituency: mainly rural, university, cathedral, middle class

Breed, Colin
Liberal Democrat MP for South East Cornwall since 1997

Majority: 5,375 (10.4%)
Turnout: 65.4%

	Votes	Share %	Change %
Colin Breed, Liberal Democrat	23,756	45.9	–1.2
Ashley Gray, Conservative	18,381	35.5	–0.3
Bill Stevens, Labour	6,429	12.4	–0.4
Graham Palmer, UK Independence party	1,978	3.8	n/a
Ken George, Mebyon Kernow	1,209	2.3	1.3

Andrew Roth says: "agreeable, ambitious London-born businessman"

Recent parliamentary career: Lib Dem spokesperson, DEFRA (2001–); environment, food, and rural affairs committee (2001–); European scrutiny committee (2001–); spokesperson, MAFF (1999–2001); competition and consumer affairs committee (1997–99)
Background: banker; company director
Born: May 4 1947 in London
Education: Torquay Grammar School
Constituency: remote southern corner of Cornwall; rural, pretty sea ports

Brennan, Kevin
Labour MP for Cardiff West since 2001

Majority: 11,321 (33.3%)
Turnout: 58.4%

	Votes	Share %	Change %
Kevin Brennan, Labour	18,594	54.6	–5.7
Andrew Davies, Conservative	7,273	21.3	–0.2
Jacqui Gasson, Liberal Democrat	4,458	13.1	2.3
Delme Bowen, Plaid Cymru	3,296	9.7	4.9
Joyce Jenking, UK Independence party	462	1.4	n/a

Maiden speech: "The voters whom I met want us to govern on the strong values of Labour: fair play, or chwarae teg, as we say in Wales; looking after one's neighbour; giving a fair chance in life to everyone"

Recent parliamentary career: elected to parliament 2001; public administration committee (2001–)
Background: economics and business studies teacher; Cardiff councillor for 10 years
Born: January 1 1960
Education: St Albans RC Comprehensive School, Pontypool
Higher education: Oxford, Pembroke College; University College, Cardiff University
Constituency: innercity, massive council estates, docks, high crime and racial tension

Brooke, Annette
Liberal Democrat MP for Mid Dorset and North Poole since 2001

Majority: 384 (0.9%)
Turnout: 65.6%

	Votes	Share %	Change %
Annette Brooke, Liberal Democrat	18,358	42	2.7
Christopher Fraser, Conservative	17,974	41.1	0.4
James Selby-Bennett, Labour	6,765	15.5	−0.3
Jeff Mager, UK Independence party	621	1.4	n/a

Maiden speech: "most of us would agree that we cannot improve public services just by throwing money at the problems"

Recent parliamentary career: entered parliament 2001, taking seat from Conservative; public administration committee (2001–)
Background: partner in small business; economics teacher; worked for Open University for 20 years; Poole councillor and mayor
Born: June 7 1947
Education: Romford Technical School
Higher education: London School of Economics; Cambridge, Hughes Hall
Constituency: part old world Dorset villages and part new suburbs

Brown, Rt Hon Gordon
Labour MP for Dunfermline East since 1983

Majority: 15,063 (50.1%)
Turnout: 57%

	Votes	Share %	Change %
Gordon Brown, Labour	19,487	64.8	−2
John Mellon, Scottish National party	4,424	14.7	−0.9
Stuart Randall, Conservative	2,838	9.4	−0.6
John Mainland, Liberal Democrat	2,281	7.6	1.7
Andy Jackson, Scottish Socialist party	770	2.6	n/a
Tom Dunsmore, UK Independence party	286	1	n/a

Andrew Roth says: "possesses the evangelical sincerity of a Scottish puritan and at times resembles a latterday John Knox"

Recent parliamentary career: chancellor of the exchequer (1997–); shadow chancellor (1992–97)
Background: rector of Edinburgh University; politics lecturer; television journalist; keen sportsman, blinded in left eye by rugby accident
Born: February 20 1951 in Glasgow
Education: Kirkcaldy High School
Higher education: Edinburgh University
Constituency: Fife towns including Rosyth naval yard

Brown, Rt Hon Nicholas
Labour MP for Newcastle upon Tyne East and Wallsend since 1997; Newcastle upon Tyne East (1983–97)

Majority: 14,223 (43.5%)
Turnout: 53.2%

	Votes	Share %	Change %
Nick Brown, Labour	20,642	63.1	−8.1
David Ord, Liberal Democrat	6,419	19.6	9
Tim Troman, Conservative	3,873	11.9	−2
Andrew Gray, Green party	651	2	n/a
Dr Harash Narang, Independent	563	1.7	n/a
B Carpenter, Socialist Labour Party	420	1.3	−0.2
Martin Levy, Communist party	126	0.4	0

Andrew Roth says: "sensible, witty, locally-based trade unionist"

Recent parliamentary career: minister of state, DWP (2001–); minister of state, MAFF (1998–2001); government chief whip (1997–98)

Background: worked for Proctor and Gamble; ran MAFF during foot and mouth crisis
Born: June 13 1950 in Kent
Education: Swatenden Secondary Modern School; Tunbridge Wells Technical High School
Higher education: Manchester University
Constituency: mixed Newcastle seat; powerplant manufacturing, includes Byker and river

Brown, Russell
Labour MP for Dumfries since 1997

Majority: 8,834 (20.7%)
Turnout: 67.7%

	Votes	Share %	Change %
Russell Brown, Labour	20,830	48.9	1.4
John Charteris, Conservative	11,996	28.2	0.2
John Ross Scott, Liberal Democrat	4,955	11.6	0.5
Robert Fairbairn, Scottish National party	4,103	9.6	−2.5
John Dennis, Scottish Socialist party	702	1.7	n/a

Andrew Roth says: "local government stalwart, who, on his first parliamentary attempt, rode the anti-Conservative tide into a hitherto-unbreachable fortress"

Recent parliamentary career: standards and privileges committees (2001–); deregulation committee (1999–); Scottish affairs committee (1999–2001)
Background: locally born councillor; worked for ICI for 23 years
Born: September 17 1951 in Annan
Education: Annan Academy
Constituency: southern Scottish seat, includes Gretna Green and Borders hills

Browne, Desmond
Labour MP for Kilmarnock and Loudoun since 1997

Majority: 10,334 (27.4%)
Turnout: 61.7%

	Votes	Share %	Change %
Desmond Browne, Labour	19,926	52.9	3.1
John Brady, Scottish National party	9,592	25.5	−9
Donald Reece, Conservative	3,943	10.5	−0.3
John Stewart, Liberal Democrat	3,177	8.4	4.4
Jason Muir, Scottish Socialist party	1,027	2.7	n/a

Andrew Roth says: "able, well-connected, socially-sensitive party loyalist"

Recent parliamentary career: junior minister, NIO (2001–); PPS to Donald Dewar (1998–99)
Background: solicitor advocate; member of Scottish Council for Civil Liberties; chair, Scottish Child Law Centre; member of all-party Scotch whisky parliamentary group
Born: March 22 1952 in Kilwinning, Ayrshire
Education: St Michael's Academy, Kilwinning
Higher education: Glasgow University
Constituency: industrial, self-contained area south-west of Glasgow

Browning, Angela
Conservative MP for Tiverton and Honiton since 1997; Tiverton (1992–97)

Majority: 6,284 (11.3%)
Turnout: 69.2%

	Votes	Share %	Change %
Angela Browning, Conservative	26,258	47.1	5.8
Jim Barnard, Liberal Democrat	19,974	35.8	−2.7
Isabel Owen, Labour	6,647	11.9	−0.9
Alan Langmaid, UK Independence party	1,281	2.3	n/a
Matthew Burgess, Green party	1,030	1.9	1.1
Mrs Jennifer Roach, Liberal	594	1.1	0

Andrew Roth says: "more interested in solving real problems in a one nation spirit than partisan posturing"

Recent parliamentary career: modernisation of the House of Commons committee (2001–); shadow leader of House of Commons and constitutional affairs (2000–01); shadow secretary of state, DTI (1999–2000)
Background: sales and training manager; adviser to DFEE; management consultant; worked in charity sector
Born: December 4 1946 in Reading
Education: Westwood Girls' Grammar School
Higher education: Bournemouth College of Technology; Reading College of Technology
Constituency: rolling rural mid Devon plus east Devon around Honiton

Bruce, Malcolm
Liberal Democrat MP for Gordon since 1983

Majority: 7,879 (22.5%)
Turnout: 58.3%

	Votes	Share %	Change %
Malcolm Bruce, Liberal Democrat	15,928	45.5	2.9
Nanette Milne, Conservative	8,049	23	−3
Rhona Kemp, Scottish National party	5,760	16.5	−3.5
Ellis Thorpe, Labour	4,730	13.5	3.2
John Sangster, Scottish Socialist party	534	1.5	n/a

Andrew Roth says: "shrewd, fair-minded regionally-based vote winner"

Recent parliamentary career: Lib Dem spokesperson, DEFRA (2001–); standards and privileges committee (1999–2001); chairman, parliamentary party (1999–2001); Lib Dem spokesperson, Treasury (1994–99)
Background: barrister; researcher; journalist and publisher; conversant in sign language
Born: November 17 1944 in Birkenhead
Education: Wrekin College, Shropshire
Higher education: St Andrews University, Dundee campus; Strathclyde University
Constituency: large rural seat in north-east Scotland with few towns

Bryant, Chris
Labour MP for Rhondda since 2001

Majority: 16,047 (47.2%)
Turnout: 60.7%

	Votes	Share %	Change %
Chris Bryant, Labour	23,230	68.3	−6.2
Leanne Wood, Plaid Cymru	7,183	21.1	7.7
Peter Hobbins, Conservative	1,557	4.6	0.8
Gavin Cox, Liberal Democrat	1,525	4.5	−1.2
Glyndwr Summers, Independent	507	1.5	n/a

Maiden speech: "I am scarcely the stereotypical MP for the Rhondda, with its macho image and non-conformist tradition"

Recent parliamentary career: entered parliament 2001; culture, media and sport committee (2001–)

Background: Frank Dobson's election agent; BBC head of European affairs; Anglican priest who served as a curate in High Wycombe for three years; chair, Christian Socialist Movement; author of books on Christian socialism; openly gay
Born: January 11 1962
Education: Cheltenham College
Higher education: Mansfield College, Oxford
Constituency: the most famous Welsh valley of them all, ex-mining communities famous for chapels and choirs

Buck, Karen
Labour MP for Regent's Park and Kensington North since 1997

Majority: 10,266 (27.7%)
Turnout: 48.8%

	Votes	Share %	Change %
Karen Buck, Labour	20,247	54.6	−5.3
Peter Wilson, Conservative	9,981	26.9	−2.1
David Boyle, Liberal Democrat	4,669	12.6	4.1
Paul Miller, Green party	1,268	3.4	n/a
China Mieville, Socialist Alliance	459	1.2	n/a
Alan Crisp, UK Independence party	354	1	n/a
Ms Charlotte Regan, Independent	74	0.2	n/a

Andrew Roth says: "one of Labour's brightest feminist insiders"

Recent parliamentary career: turned down job as government whip (2001); work and pensions committee (2001–); committee of selection (1999–); social security committee (1997–2001)
Background: officer in disabled employment; officer, Hackney council; public health officer; worked for the Labour party campaigns department in the 1990s
Born: August 30 1958 in Northern Ireland
Education: Chelmsford County High School
Higher education: London School of Economics
Constituency: diverse seat in central west London; some parts are affluent, other parts are very poor

Burden, Richard
Labour MP for Birmingham Northfield since 1992

Majority: 7,798 (26.4%)
Turnout: 52.8%

	Votes	Share %	Change %
Richard Burden, Labour	16,528	56	−1.4
Nils Purser, Conservative	8,730	29.6	1.6
Trevor Sword, Liberal Democrat	3,322	11.3	0.8
Steve Rogers, UK Independence party	550	1.9	n/a
Clive Walder, Socialist Alliance	193	0.7	n/a
Zane Carpenter, Socialist Labour party	151	0.5	n/a
Andrew Chaffer, Communist party	60	0.2	n/a

Andrew Roth says: "hyperactive, publicity-seeking multi-cause groupie"

Recent parliamentary career: trade and industry committee (2001–); PPS to Jeff Rooker (1997–2001); chair, all-party group on electoral reform
Background: Unison official, member of Labour campaign for electoral reform
Born: September 1 1954 in Liverpool
Education: Wallasey Technical Grammar School; Bramhall Comprehensive School
Higher education: York University; Warwick University; St John's College of Education, Manchester
Constituency: home of Cadbury's chocolate and Rover's huge and troubled plant at Longbridge

Burgon, Colin
Labour MP for Elmet since 1997

Majority: 4,171 (9.1%)
Turnout: 65.6%

	Votes	Share %	Change %
Colin Burgon, Labour	22,038	48	−4.4
Michael Hayman, Conservative	17,867	38.9	2.7
Madeleine Kirk, Liberal Democrat	5,001	10.9	2.2
Simon Jones, UK Independence party	1,031	2.2	n/a

Andrew Roth says: "locally-based union-backed teacher turned local government officer"

Recent parliamentary career: Northern Ireland affairs committee (2000–2001); procedure committee (1999–2001)
Background: local government policy and research officer; secondary school teacher; for 16 years; football coach
Born: April 22 1948 in Leeds
Education: St Michael's College, Leeds
Higher education: Huddersfield Polytechnic; Carnegie College, Leeds
Constituency: Leeds far eastern outer suburbs, market towns and council estates

Burnett, John
Liberal Democrat MP for Torridge and West Devon since 1997

Majority: 1,194 (2.2%)
Turnout: 70.5%

	Votes	Share %	Change %
John Burnett, Liberal Democrat	23,474	42.2	0.4
Geoffrey Cox, Conservative	22,280	40	1.5
David Brenton, Labour	5,959	10.7	−1.7
Bob Edwards, UK Independence party	2,674	4.8	n/a
Martin Quinn, Green party	1,297	2.3	n/a

Andrew Roth says: "slightly unpredictable maverick and colourful eccentric"

Recent parliamentary career: Lib Dem spokesperson, HO (2001–); Northern Ireland affairs committee (2000–2001); procedure committee (1999–2001)
Background: Royal Marine commando; solicitor; breeder of Devon cattle; member of National Farmers' union
Born: September 19 1945 in Oswestry
Education: Ampleforth
Higher education: College of Law, London
Constituency: largest seat in the county, Dartmoor and surrounding villages

Burnham, Andy
Labour MP for Leigh since 2001

Majority: 16,362 (46.3%)
Turnout: 49.7%

	Votes	Share %	Change %
Andy Burnham, Labour	22,783	64.5	−4.4
Andrew Oxley, Conservative	6,421	18.2	2.6
Ray Atkins, Liberal Democrat	4,524	12.8	1.6
William Kelly, Socialist Labour Party	820	2.3	n/a
Chris Best, UK Independence party	750	2.1	n/a

Maiden speech: "I aim to give the house an authentic voice from my home area in years to come"

Recent parliamentary career: entered parliament 2001; health committee (2001–)

Background: worked for health think-tank; administrator of football task force; special adviser to Chris Smith at the DCMS
Born: January 7 1970
Education: St Aelred's RC High School
Higher education: Fitzwilliam College, Cambridge
Constituency: Wigan borough wards; ex-mining, now a light industrial seat

Burns, Simon
Conservative MP for Chelmsford West since 1997; Chelmsford (1987–97)

Majority: 6,261 (13.0%)
Turnout: 61.5%

	Votes	Share %	Change %
Simon Burns, Conservative	20,446	42.5	1.9
Adrian Longden, Labour	14,185	29.5	3.1
Stephen Robinson, Liberal Democrat	11,197	23.3	–5.9
Mrs Eleanor Burgess, Green party	837	1.7	n/a
Ken Wedon, UK Independence party	785	1.6	n/a
Christopher Philbin, LCA	693	1.4	n/a

Andrew Roth says: "a wind-sensitive political weathervane"

Recent parliamentary career: opposition spokesperson, DOH (2001–); health committee (2001–); opposition spokesperson, environment (1998–99); opposition spokesperson, social security (1997–98)
Background: political adviser; journalist; company director; secretary, Oxford University Conservative Association
Born: September 6 1952 in Nottingham
Education: Stamford School
Higher education: Oxford, Worcester
Constituency: centre of Essex town; suburban villages and rural areas

Burnside, David
Ulster Unionist MP for South Antrim since 2001

Majority: 1,011 (2.3%)
Turnout: 62.5%

	Votes	Share %	Change %
David Burnside, Ulster Unionist party	16,366	37.1	1.8
William McCrea, Democratic Unionist party	15,355	34.8	–3.2
Sean Mckee, Social Democratic and Labour party	5,336	12.1	0.7
Martin Meehan, Sinn Fein	4,160	9.4	0.9
David Ford, Alliance party of Northern Ireland	1,969	4.5	–2.1
Norman Boyd, NI Unionist	972	2.2	n/a

Nicholas Watt, the *Guardian*: "the gruff face of Ulster Unionism"

Recent parliamentary career: entered parliament in 2001, taking seat from Democratic Unionist party; environment, food, and rural affairs committee (2001–)
Background: PR consultant, British Airways; director, UUP information office; Vanguard Unionist party member in the 1970s
Born: August 24 1951
Education: Cookstown High School; Paisley Theological College
Higher education: Queen's University, Belfast
Constituency: stretches from Lough Neagh and River Bann to Belfast borders, urban, industrial and agricultural, includes Aldergrove Airport

Burstow, Paul
Liberal Democrat MP for Sutton and Cheam since 1997

Majority: 4,304 (10.8%)
Turnout: 62.4%

	Votes	Share %	Change %
Paul Burstow, Liberal Democrat	19,382	48.8	6.5
Olga Maitland, Conservative	15,078	38	0.2
Lisa Homan, Labour	5,263	13.3	−2.2
Simon McKie, UK Independence party			n/a

Andrew Roth says: "hyperactive member of the social democratic wing of his party, inclined to sympathetic but firm pressure on Labour"

Recent parliamentary career: Lib Dem spokesperson, older people (2001–); spokesperson, social security (1999–2001)
Background: retail buyer; worked for Sutton Council; organising secretary, Association of Social Democrat councillors
Born: May 13 1962 in Carshalton
Education: Glastonbury High School, Carshalton
Higher education: South Bank Polytechnic
Constituency: middle class suburbs in outer south-west London

Burt, Alistair
Conservative MP for North East Bedfordshire since 2001; Bury North (1983-97)

Majority: 8,577 (18.9%)
Turnout: 65.2%

	Votes	Share %	Change %
Alastair Burt, Conservative	22,586	49.9	5.6
Philip Ross, Labour	14,009	31	−1.6
Dan Rogerson, Liberal Democrat	7,409	16.4	2.2
Ros Hill, UK Independence party	1,242	2.7	n/a

Andrew Roth says: "highly-intelligent churchy moderate"

Recent parliamentary career: opposition spokesperson, DFES (2001–); re-elected to parliament 2001; procedure committee (2001); international development committee (2001); social security minister (1995–97)
Background: solicitor; board member: Habitat for Humanity (low income housing charity), and Council of the Evangelical Alliance; has run five London marathons
Born: May 25 1955
Education: Bury Grammar School
Higher education: Oxford, St John's
Constituency: mainly rural, professional, main towns are Biggleswade and Sandy

Butterfill, John
Conservative MP for Bournemouth West since 1983

Majority: 4,718 (14.1%)
Turnout: 54.2%

	Votes	Share %	Change %
John Butterfill, Conservative	14,417	42.9	1.2
David Stokes, Labour	9,699	28.8	4.2
Fiona Hornby, Liberal Democrat	8,468	25.2	−2.6
Cynthia Blake, UK Independence party	1,064	3.2	n/a

Andrew Roth says: "the conscientious strongly pro-EU right-wing voice of the investment community"

Recent parliamentary career: stood for 1922 committee chair (2001); stood for House of Commons speakership (2000); unopposed bills panel (1997–); trade and industry committee (1997–2001)
Background: company director; surveyor and valuer; chair of several Conservative groups

Born: February 14 1941 in Kingston-upon-Thames
Education: Caterham School
Higher education: College of Estate Management, London
Constituency: western part of seaside resort, includes town's largest council estate and many pensioners

Byers, Rt Hon Stephen
Labour MP for North Tyneside since 1997; Wallsend (1992–97)

Majority: 20,668 (55.0%)
Turnout: 57.9%

	Votes	Share %	Change %
Stephen Byers, Labour	26,127	69.5	–3.2
Mark Ruffell, Conservative	5,459	14.5	n/a
Simon Reed, Liberal Democrat	4,649	12.4	1.8
Alan Taylor, UK Independence party	770	2.1	n/a
Pete Burnett, Socialist Alliance	324	0.9	n/a
Ken Capstick, Socialist Labour party	240	0.6	n/a

Andrew Roth says: "Blair-approved rising politician"

Recent parliamentary career: secretary of state, DTLGR (2001–); secretary of state, DTI (1998–2001); chief secretary to the Treasury (1998); minister of state, DFEE (1997–98)
Background: law lecturer, Newcastle Polytechnic; North Tyneside councillor
Born: April 13 1953 in Wolverhampton
Education: Chester City Grammar School
Higher education: Liverpool Polytechnic
Constituency: inner-city Newcastle, former pit villages, working-class

C

Cable, Dr Vincent
Liberal Democrat MP for Twickenham since 1997

Majority: 7,655 (15.4%)
Turnout: 67.4%

	Votes	Share %	Change %
Dr Vincent Cable, Liberal Democrat	24,344	48.8	3.7
Nick Longworth, Conservative	16,689	33.4	–4.4
Dean Rogers, Labour	6,903	13.8	–1.8
Ms Judy Maciejowska, Green party	1,423	2.9	n/a
Ray Hollebone, UK Independence party	579	1.2	n/a

Andrew Roth says: "academic intellectual economist who has won party plaudits despite his tendency to discursive economics lectures rather than sharp political points"

Recent parliamentary career: introduced private member's bill on copyright (2001); Lib Dem spokesperson, trade and industry (1999–); spokesperson, Treasury (1997–99); spokesperson, foreign affairs and defence (1997–97);
Background: economics lecturer; worked for Kenyan government, FCO, Overseas Development Institute; chief economist, Shell Oil; author of books on globalisation and economics
Born: May 9 1943
Education: Nunthorpe Grammar School, York
Higher education: Glasgow University; Cambridge, Fitzwilliam
Constituency: leafy outer London, middle class and suburban

Caborn, Rt Hon Richard
Labour MP for Sheffield Central since 1983

Majority: 12,544 (41.8%)
Turnout: 48.5%

	Votes	Share %	Change %
Richard Caborn, Labour	18,477	61.5	–2.1
Ali Qadar, Liberal Democrat	5,933	19.7	2.5
Noelle Brelsford, Conservative	3,289	10.9	–1
Bernard Little, Green party	1,008	3.4	0.8
Nick Riley, Socialist Alliance	754	2.5	n/a
David Hatfield, Socialist Labour party	289	1	n/a
Charlotte Schofield, UK Independence party	257	0.9	n/a
Michael Driver, Workers' Revolutionary party	62	0.2	0

Patrick Wintour, the *Guardian*: "One of Prescott's closest allies"

Recent parliamentary career: sports minister, DCMS (2001–); minister of state, DTI (1999–2001)
Background: engineering worker; convener of shop stewards; ran John Prescott's leadership campaign (1995); supporter of regional government; set up regional development agencies (1999); MEP (1979–84)
Born: October 6 1943 in Sheffield
Education: Hurfield Comprehensive School
Higher education: Sheffield Polytechnic; Granville College of Education
Constituency: innercity, high unemployment

Cairns, David
Labour MP for Greenock and Inverclyde since 2001

Majority: 9,890 (34.8%)
Turnout: 59.4%

	Votes	Share %	Change %
David Cairns, Labour	14,929	52.5	–3.7
Chic Brodie, Liberal Democrat	5,039	17.7	3.9
Andrew Murie, Scottish National party	4,248	15	–3.6
Alister Haw, Conservative	3,000	10.6	–0.9
Davie Landels, Scottish Socialist party	1,203	4.2	n/a

Maiden speech: "I have the honour to be the first member for Greenock and Inverclyde to come from Greenock and Inverclyde. I am also the first for almost 50 years not to possess a doctorate, although whether that is an advantage only time will tell"

Recent parliamentary career: entered parliament 2001
Background: a priest for three years; director, Christian Socialist Movement; campaigned against disqualification of ex-Roman Catholic priests from becoming MPs (law changed February 2001); parliamentary assistant to Siobhan MacDonagh
Born: July 8 1966
Education: Notre Dame High School
Higher education: Gregnor University, Italy
Constituency: industrial Scotland (especially electronics), some hills

Calton, Patsy
Liberal Democrat MP for Cheadle since 2001

Majority: 33 (0.1%)
Turnout: 63.2%

	Votes	Share %	Change %
Patsy Calton, Liberal Democrat	18,477	42.4	4.7
Stephen Day, Conservative	18,444	42.3	–1.4
Howard Dawber, Labour	6,086	14	–1.8
Vincent Cavanagh, UK Independence party	599	1.4	n/a

Maiden speech: "Those on low incomes should be remembered first by a government who put social inclusion high on their agenda"
Recent parliamentary career: entered parliament 2001, taking seat from Conservative; administration committee (2001–)
Background: chemistry and human biology teacher; deputy leader of Stockport Council
Born: September 19 1948
Education: Wymondham College, Norfolk
Higher education: UMIST
Constituency: upmarket, commuting belt of Manchester, now UK's most marginal seat

Cameron, David
Conservative MP for Witney since 2001

Majority: 7,973 (16.2%)
Turnout: 65.9%

	Votes	Share %	Change %
David Cameron, Conservative	22,153	45	1.9
Mike Bartlet, Labour	14,180	28.8	–1.8
Gareth Epps, Liberal Democrat	10,000	20.3	0.4
Mark Stevenson, Green party	1,100	2.2	1.1
Barry Beadle, Independent	1,003	2	n/a
Kenneth Dukes, UK Independence party	767	1.6	n/a

Maiden speech: "[Shaun Woodward] remains a constituent, and a not insignificant local employer – not least in the area of domestic service. We are, in fact, quite close neighbours. On a clear day, from the hill behind my cottage, I can almost see some of the glittering spires of his great house"

Recent parliamentary career: entered parliament 2001, taking seat from retiring Tory-turned-Labour MP Shaun Woodward; home affairs committee (2001–)
Background: adviser, Treasury and HO; head of corporate affairs, Carlton Television; great-great-grandfather and great-grandfather were Conservative MPs
Born: October 9 1966 in London
Education: Eton College
Higher education: Brasenose College, Oxford
Constituency: rambling Cotswold fringes, includes mansions, market towns, and council estates

Campbell, Alan
Labour MP for Tynemouth since 1997

Majority: 8,678 (19.7%)
Turnout: 67.4%

	Votes	Share %	Change %
Alan Campbell, Labour	23,364	53.2	–2.2
Karl Poulsen, Conservative	14,686	33.5	0.2
Penny Reid, Liberal Democrat	5,108	11.6	2.8
Michael Rollings, UK Independence party	745	1.7	0.8

Andrew Roth says: "another pro-European Labour recruit from the chalkface"

Recent parliamentary career: PPS to Lord Macdonald (2001–); public accounts committee (1997–2001)
Background: teacher (1980–96); head of sixth form, Whitley Bay High School
Born: July 8 1957 in Northumberland
Education: Hirst High School, Ashington
Higher education: Lancaster University; Leeds University; Northumbria University
Constituency: Tyne and Wear heavy industry and smart seaside towns

Campbell, Anne
Labour MP for Cambridge since 1992

Majority: 8,579 (20.0%)
Turnout: 60.6%

	Votes	Share %	Change %
Anne Campbell, Labour	19,316	45.1	−8.3
David Howarth, Liberal Democrat	10,737	25.1	9
Graham Stuart, Conservative	9,829	23	−2.9
Stephen Lawrence, Green party	1,413	3.3	n/a
Howard Senter, Socialist Alliance	716	1.7	n/a
Len Baynes, UK Independence party	532	1.2	n/a
Clare Underwood, ProLife Alliance	232	0.5	0.1
Ms Margaret Courtney, Workers' Revolutionary party	61	0.1	−0.1

Andrew Roth says: "widely-respected, cerebrally-cool, pro-EU Blair-worshipper"

Recent parliamentary career: PPS to Patricia Hewitt (1999–)
Background: statistician; lecturer in statistics and data processing; IT expert; Cambridgeshire councillor
Born: April 6 1940 in Dewsbury
Education: Penistone Grammar School
Higher education: Cambridge, Newnham
Constituency: university and city of Cambridge

Campbell, Gregory
Democratic Unionist party MP for East Londonderry since 2001

Majority: 1,901 (4.8%)
Turnout: 66.1%

	Votes	Share %	Change %
Gregory Campbell, Democratic Unionist party	12,813	32.1	6.5
Willie Ross, Ulster Unionist party	10,912	27.4	−8.2
John Dallat, Social Democratic and Labour party	8,298	20.8	−0.9
Francie Brolly, Sinn Fein	6,221	15.6	6.5
Yvonne Boyle, Alliance party of Northern Ireland	1,625	4.1	−2.3

Maiden speech: "my community is angry, disillusioned, discriminated against and marginalised, not only since the Belfast agreement but for decades before. I am here to work for the revitalisation of that community"

Recent parliamentary career: entered parliament 2001, taking seat from Ulster Unionist party; transport, local government, and the regions committee (2001–)
Background: self-employed businessman; responsible for transport in the Northern Ireland Executive
Born: February 15 1953
Education: Londonderry Technical College
Higher education: Magee University College
Constituency: predominantly rural, scenic north coast of Northern Ireland

Campbell, Menzies
Liberal Democrat MP for North East Fife since 1987

Majority: 9,736 (28.1%)
Turnout: 56.1%

	Votes	Share %	Change %
Menzies Campbell, Liberal Democrat	17,926	51.7	0.5
Mike Scott-Hayward, Conservative	8,190	23.6	−2.9
Claire Brennan, Labour	3,950	11.4	1.1
Kris Murray-Browne, Scottish National party	3,596	10.4	−0.5
Keith White, Scottish Socialist party	610	1.8	n/a
Leslie Von Goetz, LCA	420	1.2	n/a

Andrew Roth says: "active, mainstream Scots QC who recaptured Asquith's old seat for the Liberals ... tall, balding, well-dressed and grand'"

Recent parliamentary career: Lib Dem shadow foreign secretary (2001–); Lib Dem spokesperson, foreign affairs and defence (1988–2001); candidate for speaker (2000); considered running for party leader (1999)
Background: Glasgow-born lawyer; law student contemporary of Donald Dewar and John Smith; Olympic athlete (1964); known as "Ming"
Born: May 22 1941 in Glasgow
Education: Hillhead High School, Glasgow
Higher education: Glasgow University; Stanford University, California
Constituency: smart, rural east Scotland, includes St Andrews golf courses

Campbell, Ronnie
Labour MP for Blyth Valley since 1987

Majority: 12,188 (35.3%)
Turnout: 54.6%

	Votes	Share %	Change %
Ronnie Campbell, Labour	20,627	59.7	–4.5
Jeffrey Reid, Liberal Democrat	8,439	24.4	1.9
Wayne Daley, Conservative	5,484	15.9	2.6

Andrew Roth says: "hard-left Campaign Group member who rebels against the Labour whip"

Recent parliamentary career: catering committee (2001–)
Background: miner for 27 years, made redundant a year before he became an MP; Blyth Valley councillor
Born: August 14 1943 in Blyth Valley
Education: Ridley High School, Blyth
Constituency: ex-mining seat in north-east, industrial, power station, and dockyards, part new town

Cann, Jamie
Labour MP for Ipswich since 1992

Majority: 8,081 (20.8%)
Turnout: 57%

	Votes	Share %	Change %
Jamie Cann, Labour	19,952	51.3	–1.4
Edward Wild, Conservative	11,871	30.5	–0.6
Terry Gilbert, Liberal Democrat	5,904	15.2	3
William Vinyard, UK Independence party	624	1.6	n/a
Peter Leech, Socialist Alliance	305	0.8	n/a
Shaun Gratton, Socialist Labour party	217	0.6	n/a

Andrew Roth says: "shows refreshing modesty about his knowledge and argues his cases factually and with restraint and humour"

Recent parliamentary career: defence committee (1997–2001)
Background: primary school teacher and deputy head teacher (1967–92); Ipswich councillor for 19 years, 12 of them as council leader
Born: June 28 1946 in Barton on Humber
Education: Barton on Humber Grammar School
Higher education: Kesteven College of Education, Edinburgh
Constituency: mixed coastal town on east Anglian coast, includes growing port

Caplin, Ivor
Labour MP for Hove since 1997

Majority: 3,171 (7.6%)
Turnout: 59.2%

	Votes	Share %	Change %
Ivor Caplin, Labour	19,253	45.9	1.3
Jenny Langston, Conservative	16,082	38.3	1.9
Harold de Souza, Liberal Democrat	3,823	9.1	−0.6
Anthea Ballam, Green party	1,369	3.3	n/a
Andy Richards, Socialist Alliance	531	1.3	n/a
Franklin Richard, UK Independence party	358	0.9	n/a
Nigel Donovan, Liberal	316	0.8	n/a
Simon Dobbshead, Free	196	0.5	n/a
Thomas Major, Independent	60	0.1	n/a

Andrew Roth says: "completely loyal, on-message Blairite"

Recent parliamentary career: assistant whip (2001–); PPS to Margaret Beckett (1998–2001); modernisation of the House of Commons committee (1998–2001)
Background: locally-born Brighton and Hove councillor; Hove's first Labour MP; supports electoral reform and animal rights
Born: November 8 1958 in Brighton
Education: King Edward's School, Witley
Higher education: Brighton College of Technology
Constituency: grand, old-fashioned town next to Brighton, no longer a byword for Tory values

Carmichael, Alistair
Liberal Democrat MP for Orkney and Shetland since 2001

Majority: 3,475 (20.8%)
Turnout: 52.4%

	Votes	Share %	Change %
Alistair Carmichael, Liberal Democrat	6,919	41.4	−10.6
Robert Mochrie, Labour	3,444	20.6	2.3
John Firth, Conservative	3,121	18.7	6.5
John Mowat, Scottish National party	2,473	14.8	2.1
Peter Andrews, Scottish Socialist party	776	4.6	n/a

Maiden speech: "It is my privilege to represent in the House a constituency that is independently-minded and deeply self-reliant. I am here merely to ask that my constituents be allowed the opportunities to develop the potential of their communities"

Recent parliamentary career: entered parliament 2001; Scottish affairs committee (2001–)
Background: solicitor; deputy procurator fiscal; director, Aberdeenshire Women's Aid; elder of Church of Scotland
Born: July 15 1965
Education: Islay High School, Argyll
Higher education: Aberdeen University
Constituency: second-smallest number of votes needed to become an MP; remote, diverse northern islands; hardly part of Scotland

Casale, Roger
Labour MP for Wimbledon since 1997

Majority: 3,744 (9.2%)
Turnout: 64.3%

	Votes	Share %	Change %
Roger Casale, Labour	18,806	45.8	3
Stephen Hammond, Conservative	15,062	36.6	0
Martin Pierce, Liberal Democrat	5,341	13	−3.6
Rajeev Thacker, Green party	1,007	2.5	1.5
Roger Glencross, CPA	479	1.2	n/a
Mariana Bell, UK Independence party	414	1	n/a

Andrew Roth says: "over-idealist, over-eager and over-loyal"

Recent parliamentary career: European scrutiny committee (1998–)
Background: European studies lecturer; policy adviser to Tony Blair and John Prescott; head of training institute in Germany
Born: May 22 1960 in Wimbledon
Education: Hurstpierpoint College, Sussex
Higher education: London School of Economics; Maximillian University, Munich; John Hopkins University; Oxford, Brasenose
Constituency: expensive London suburb famous for tennis and Wombles

Cash, William
Conservative MP for Stone since 1997; Stafford (1984–97)

Majority: 6,036 (13.3%)
Turnout: 66.3%

	Votes	Share %	Change %
William Cash, Conservative	22,395	49.1	2.3
John Palfreyman, Labour	16,359	35.8	–3.8
Brendan McKeown, Liberal Democrat	6,888	15.1	3.1

Andrew Roth says: "belatedly transformed into the de facto rebel leader by his constitutional opposition to federalism"

Recent parliamentary career: shadow attorney general (2001–); supporter of Iain Duncan Smith (2001); outspoken opponent of Maastricht Treaty (1992–93); lost Conservative whip (1994–95) for rebellion over Europe; European scrutiny committee (1998–)
Background: solicitor; legal adviser to Libarary Association and other organisations
Born: May 10 1940 in London
Education: Stonyhurst College
Higher education: Oxford, Lincoln
Constituency: rural seat in Staffordshire, several villages, includes Alton Towers

Caton, Martin
Labour MP for Gower since 1997

Majority: 7,395 (19.8%)
Turnout: 63.4%

	Votes	Share %	Change %
Martin Caton, Labour	17,676	47.3	–6.5
John Bushell, Conservative	10,281	27.5	3.7
Sheila Waye, Liberal Democrat	4,507	12.1	–0.9
Sian Caiach, Plaid Cymru	3,865	10.4	5.3
Tina Shrewsbury, Green party	607	1.6	n/a
Darran Hickery, Socialist Labour party	417	1.1	n/a

Andrew Roth says: "pleasant, articulate and original-minded"

Recent parliamentary career: Welsh affairs committee (1997–)
Background: political researcher for David Morris MEP (1984–97); agricultural researcher; Swansea councillor
Born: June 15 1951 in Bishop's Stortford
Education: Newport Grammar School, Essex; Aberystwyth College of Further Education
Higher education: Norfolk School of Agriculture
Constituency: partly Welsh-speaking seat, includes Gower Peninsula and Swansea suburb of Mumbles

Cawsey, Ian
Labour MP for Brigg and Goole since 1997

Majority: 3,961 (9.7%)
Turnout: 64.6%

	Votes	Share %	Change %
Ian Cawsey, Labour	20,066	48.9	−1.3
Donald Stewart, Conservative	16,105	39.2	2.7
David Nolan, Liberal Democrat	3,796	9.3	−0.7
Godfrey Bloom, UK Independence party	688	1.7	n/a
Michael Kenny, Socialist Labour party	399	1	n/a

Andrew Roth says: "one of the 'cheeky chappie' interjectors"

Recent parliamentary career: PPS to Lord Williams (2001–); introduced private member's bill on animal sanctuaries (2001); home affairs committee (1999–2001)
Background: systems analyst; IT consultant; parliamentary researcher (1987–97)
Born: April 14 1960 in Grimsby
Education: Wintringham School
Constituency: Humberside towns dominated by docks

Challen, Colin
Labour MP for Morley and Rothwell since 2001

Majority: 12,090 (31.4%)
Turnout: 53.5%

	Votes	Share %	Change %
Colin Challen, Labour	21,919	57	−1.5
David Schofield, Conservative	9,829	25.6	−0.7
Stewart Golton, Liberal Democrat	5,446	14.2	3.1
John Bardsley, UK Independence party	1,248	3.3	n/a

Maiden speech: "whether we use the word 'inclusive' or not, let us show it in our actions and deliver it in practice"

Recent parliamentary career: entered parliament 2001
Background: printer and publisher; marketing development worker; Labour party organiser; Hull City councillor
Born: June 12 1953
Education: Malton Grammar School
Higher education: Hull University
Constituency: south of Leeds, industrial, towns include Middleton

Chapman, Ben
Labour MP for Wirral South since 1997

Majority: 5,049 (12.6%)
Turnout: 65.7%

	Votes	Share %	Change %
Ben Chapman, Labour	18,890	47.4	−3.5
Tony Millard, Conservative	13,841	34.8	−1.6
Phillip Gilchrist, Liberal Democrat	7,087	17.8	7.4

Andrew Roth says: "self-effacing byelection phenomenon who momentarily illuminated the whole political sky, revealing middle class disillusion with the Tories"

Recent parliamentary career: PPS to Richard Caborn (1999–); won Wirral South byelection (1997) signalling impending landslide against Conservative party
Background: civil servant; commercial attaché in the Diplomatic Service; businessman
Born: July 8 1940 in Appleby-in-Westmorland
Education: Westmorland Grammar School, Appleby
Constituency: Merseyside, mainly middle class residential, classic suburban seat

Chapman, Sir Sydney
Conservative MP for Chipping Barnet since 1979; Birmingham Handsworth (1970–74)

Majority: 2,701 (6.4%)
Turnout: 60.5%

	Votes	Share %	Change %
Sydney Chapman, Conservative	19,702	46.4	3.4
Damien Welfare, Labour	17,001	40	–0.9
Sean Hooker, Liberal Democrat	5,753	13.6	1.3

Andrew Roth says: "pleasantly cheerful, genial smiler, self-mocking"

Recent parliamentary career: finance and services committee (1997–); chair, accommodation and works committee (1997–2001); government whip (1988–95)
Background: architect and surveyor; chartered town and country planner; environmentalist and Europhile
Born: October 17 1935 in Macclesfield
Education: Rugby School
Higher education: Manchester University
Constituency: outer north-east London, commuting, middle class seat

Chaytor, David
Labour MP for Bury North since 1997

Majority: 6,532 (14.5%)
Turnout: 63%

	Votes	Share %	Change %
David Chaytor, Labour	22,945	51.2	–0.6
John Walsh, Conservative	16,413	36.7	–0.8
Bryn Hackley, Liberal Democrat	5,430	12.1	3.9

Andrew Roth says: "major contributor to the environment debate"

Recent parliamentary career: education and skills committee (2001–); deregulation committee (1997–); introduced private member's bill on environmental audit (2001); environmental audit committee (2000–2001)
Background: lecturer and head of continuing education; Calderdale councillor
Born: August 3 1949 in Lancashire
Education: Bury Grammar School
Higher education: Huddersfield Polytechnic; Leeds University; London University
Constituency: residential, traditional north-west seat, borders Irwell Valley to north

Chidgey, David
Liberal Democrat MP for Eastleigh since 1994

Majority: 3,058 (6.4%)
Turnout: 63.8%

	Votes	Share %	Change %
David Chidgey, Liberal Democrat	19,360	40.7	5.6
Conor Burns, Conservative	16,302	34.3	0.6
Sam Jaffa, Labour	10,426	21.9	–4.9
Stephen Challis, UK Independence party	849	1.8	n/a
Martha Lyn, Green party	636	1.3	n/a

Andrew Roth says: "calm, measured, has common sense"

Recent parliamentary career: standards and privileges committees (2001–); foreign affairs committee (1999–); Lib Dem spokesperson, trade and industry (1997–99); spokesperson, transport (1995–97)
Background: mechanical and aeronautical engineer in Bangladesh, Brazil, Middle East and West Africa

Born: July 9 1942 in Basingstoke
Education: Brunel Park County High School
Higher education: Portsmouth Naval College; Portsmouth Polytechnic; Royal Navy College
Constituency: suburbs, airport and former railworks outside Southampton

Chope, Christopher

Conservative MP for Christchurch since 1997; Southampton Itchen (1983–92)

Majority: 13,544 (27.3%)
Turnout: 67.4%

	Votes	Share %	Change %
Christopher Chope, Conservative	27,306	55.1	8.7
Dorothy Webb, Liberal Democrat	13,762	27.8	−14.8
Judith Begg, Labour	7,506	15.1	8.2
Margaret Strange, UK Independence party	993	2	n/a

Andrew Roth says: "would-be hardhitter whose muscles are bound to right-wing ideology"

Recent parliamentary career: opposition spokesperson, Treasury (2001–); trade and industry committee (1999–2001); opposition spokesperson, trade and industry (1998–99)
Background: barrister; consultant, Ernst & Young; member of Local Government Commission for England; member, Health and Safety Commission
Born: May 19 1947 in Eastbourne
Education: Marlborough College; St Andrew's, Eastbourne
Higher education: St Andrews University
Constituency: east and north of Bournemouth, seaside plus recently built suburbs, many pensioners

Clapham, Michael

Labour MP for Barnsley West and Penistone since 1992

Majority: 12,352 (35.8%)
Turnout: 52.9%

	Votes	Share %	Change %
Michael Clapham, Labour	20,244	58.6	−0.7
William Rowe, Conservative	7,892	22.8	4.4
Miles Crompton, Liberal Democrat	6,428	18.6	0.6
David Barley, UK Independence	n/a		

Andrew Roth says: "union loyalist, locally-popular"

Recent parliamentary career: PPS to Alan Milburn (1997–97)
Background: miner; college lecturer in trade union studies; trade unionist (NUM)
Born: May 15 1943 in Barnsley
Education: Darton Secondary Modern School
Higher education: Leeds Polytechnic; Leeds University; Bradford University; Barnsley Technical College
Constituency: home of Arthur Scargill; Pennine uplands, sheep farming, small towns

Clappison, James

Conservative MP for Hertsmere since 1992

Majority: 4,902 (11.8%)
Turnout: 60.3%

	Votes	Share %	Change %
James Clappison, Conservative	19,855	47.8	3.5
Hilary Broderick, Labour	14,953	36	−2.2
Paul Thompson, Liberal Democrat	6,300	15.2	2.4
James Dry, Socialist Labour party	397	1	n/a

Andrew Roth says: "transformed into a moderate and sensible spokesman, replacing the former combative young superloyalist"

Recent parliamentary career: opposition spokesperson, DWP (2001–); shadow Treasury spokesperson (2000–01); opposition spokesperson, education and employment (1999–2000); opposition spokesperson, home affairs (1997–99)
Background: barrister; member of the National Trust, English Heritage, and NSPCC
Born: September 14 1956 in Beverley, Yorkshire
Education: St Peter's School, York
Higher education: Oxford, Queen's
Constituency: just outside London, wealthy Thameslink commuters

Clark, Helen
Labour MP for Peterborough since 1997

Majority: 2,854 (7.2%)
Turnout: 61.3%

	Votes	Share %	Change %
Helen Brinton (now Clark), Labour	17,975	45.2	–5.1
Stewart Jackson, Conservative	15,121	38	2.8
Nick Sandford, Liberal Democrat	5,761	14.5	3.8
Julian Fairweather, UK Independence party	955	2.4	n/a

Andrew Roth says: "constituency worshipper of the 'I love Basildon' intensity'"

Recent parliamentary career: broadcasting committee (2001–); unopposed bills panel (1998–); environmental audit committee (1997–)
Background: English teacher and lecturer; freelance examiner for exam boards; until married (2001) was known as Helen Brinton
Born: December 23 1954 in Derby
Education: Spondon Park Grammar School
Higher education: Bristol University
Constituency: much-expanded cathedral city north of London

Clark, Dr Lynda
Labour MP for Edinburgh Pentlands since 1997

Majority: 1,742 (4.5%)
Turnout: 65.1%

	Votes	Share %	Change %
Lynda Clark, Labour	15,797	40.6	–2.4
Malcolm Rifkind, Conservative	14,055	36.1	3.7
David Walker, Liberal Democrat	4,210	10.8	0.8
Stuart Crawford, Scottish National party	4,210	10.8	–2.2
Jimmy Mearns, Scottish Socialist party	555	1.4	n/a
William McMurdo, UK Independence party	105	0.3	n/a

Andrew Roth says: "most senior woman advocate practising at the Scottish bar, from a poor, working-class, Dundonian background"

Recent parliamentary career: advocate general for Scotland (1999–)
Background: advocate; law lecturer; interest in constitutional reform
Born: February 26 1949 in Dundee
Education: Lawside Academy, Dundee
Higher education: Edinburgh University; St Andrews University
Constituency: mix of council estates and smart suburbs, Malcolm Rifkind failed to retake (2001)

Clark, Paul
Labour MP for Gillingham since 1997

Majority: 2,272 (5.4%)
Turnout: 59.5%

	Votes	Share %	Change %
Paul Clark, Labour	18,782	44.5	4.7
Tim Butcher, Conservative	16,510	39.1	3.2
Jonathan Hunt, Liberal Democrat	5,755	13.6	−5.4
Tony Scholefield, UK Independence party	933	2.2	n/a
Wynford Thomas, Socialist Alliance	232	0.6	n/a

Andrew Roth says: "retreating forehead, heart-shaped face, estuarial cockney"

Recent parliamentary career: PPS to Lord Falconer (2001–); PPS to Lord Irvine (1999–2001)
Background: manager, TUC (1986–97); assistant to president of AEU (1980–86); Gillingham councillor and leader
Born: April 29 1957 in Gillingham
Education: Gillingham Grammar School
Higher education: Keele University
Constituency: residential seat centred on Medway town of Gillingham

Clarke, Rt Hon Charles
Labour MP for Norwich South since 1997

Majority: 8,816 (20.7%)
Turnout: 64.7%

	Votes	Share %	Change %
Charles Clarke, Labour	19,367	45.5	−6.2
Andrew French, Conservative	10,551	24.8	1.1
Andrew Aalders Dunthorne, Liberal Democrat	9,640	22.6	4
Adrian Holmes, Green party	1,434	3.4	2
Alun Buffrey, LCA	620	1.5	n/a
Dave Manningham, Socialist Alliance	507	1.2	n/a
Tarquin Mills, UK Independence party	473	1.1	n/a

Andrew Roth says: "shrewd and able politician who has finally come out of the backroom"

Recent parliamentary career: minister without portfolio and party chair (2001–); minister of state, HO (1999–2001); junior minister, DFEE (1998–99)
Background: maths lecturer; Hackney councillor; member of Labour party NEC (2001–); researcher, then chief of staff to Neil Kinnock as Labour leader (1983–92)
Born: September 21 1950 in London
Education: Highgate School
Higher education: Cambridge, King's
Constituency: Norwich city centre and university

Clarke, Rt Hon Kenneth
Conservative MP for Rushcliffe since 1970

Majority: 7,357 (13.5%)
Turnout: 66.5%

	Votes	Share %	Change %
Kenneth Clarke, Conservative	25,869	47.5	3.1
Paul Fallon, Labour	18,512	34	−2.2
Jeremy Hargreaves, Liberal Democrat	7,395	13.6	−0.7
Ken Browne, UK Independence party	1,434	2.6	n/a
Ashley Baxter, Green party	1,236	2.3	n/a

Andrew Roth says: "Mr Clarke not only knows where all the Tory bodies are buried, he buried a few himself"

Recent parliamentary career: defeated for party leadership (2001) winning 39% of membership vote; challenged for party leadership (1997); chancellor of the exchequer (1993–97); home secretary (1992–93); secretary of state, education (1990–92); secretary of state, health (1988–90)
Background: barrister; deputy chairman of British American Tobacco; fond of single European currency
Born: July 2 1940 in Nottingham
Education: Nottingham High School
Higher education: Cambridge, Gonville & Caius
Constituency: commuting, middle-class seat on edge of Nottingham

Clarke, Tom
Labour MP for Coatbridge and Chryston since 1997; Monklands West (1983–97); Coatbridge and Airdrie (1982–3)

Majority: 15,314 (50.6%)
Turnout: 58.1%

	Votes	Share %	Change %
Tom Clarke, Labour	19,807	65.4	–2.9
Peter Kearney, Scottish National party	4,493	14.8	–2.2
Alistair Tough, Liberal Democrat	2,293	7.6	2.2
Patrick Ross-Taylor, Conservative	2,171	7.2	–1.4
Lynn Sheridan, Scottish Socialist party	1,547	5.1	n/a

Andrew Roth says: "centre-right moderate at home, radical on self-determination and on the third world"

Recent parliamentary career: minister of state, DCMS (1997–98)
Background: assistant director, Scottish Film Council; director of award-winning amateur film Give us a Goal
Born: January 10 1941 in Coatbridge
Education: Columba High School, Coatbridge
Higher education: Scottish College of Commerce
Constituency: once a steel town in central Scotland, now much deprivation

Clarke, Tony
Labour MP for Northampton South since 1997

Majority: 885 (1.7%)
Turnout: 59.8%

	Votes	Share %	Change %
Tony Clarke, Labour	21,882	42.9	0.5
Shailesh Vara, Conservative	20,997	41.2	0.1
Andrew Simpson, Liberal Democrat	6,355	12.5	1.4
Derek Clark, UK Independence party	1,237	2.4	n/a
Miss Tina Harvey, LP	362	0.7	n/a
Clare Johnson, ProLife Alliance	196	0.4	n/a

Andrew Roth says: "young, local councillor and a committed environmentalist, led many local green initiatives"

Recent parliamentary career: Northern Ireland affairs committee (1999–); joint committee on consolidation of bills (1997–)
Background: social work trainer (1984–97); Northampton councillor
Born: September 6 1963 in Northampton
Education: Lings Upper School, Northampton
Higher education: Institute of Training and Development; Institute of Safety and Health
Constituency: partly rural villages, many affluent commuters around Northampton

Clelland, David
Labour MP for Tyne Bridge since 1985

Majority: 14,889 (57.2%)
Turnout: 44.2%

	Votes	Share %	Change %
David Clelland, Labour	18,345	70.5	–6.3
James Cook, Conservative	3,456	13.3	2.2
Jonathan Wallace, Liberal Democrat	3,213	12.3	4.3
James Fitzpatrick, Socialist Labour party	533	2.1	n/a
Sam Robson, Socialist Alliance	485	1.9	n/a

Andrew Roth says: "assiduous but low-profiled, displays a dry Geordie sense of humour"

Recent parliamentary career: government whip (1997–2001)
Background: electrical fitter (1964–81); secretary, Local Government Association
Born: July 27 1943 in Gateshead
Education: Kelvin Grove Boys School, Gateshead
Higher education: Gateshead Technical College, Hebburn Technical College
Constituency: crosses River Tyne to include centre of Newcastle and Gateshead

Clifton-Brown, Geoffrey
Conservative MP for Cotswold since 1997; Cirencester and Tewkesbury (1992–97)

Majority: 11,983 (26.0%)
Turnout: 67.5%

	Votes	Share %	Change %
Geoffrey Clifton-Brown, Conservative	23,133	50.3	3.9
Angela Lawrence, Liberal Democrat	11,150	24.3	1.3
Richard Wilkins, Labour	10,383	22.6	–0.1
Jill Stopps, UK Independence party	1,315	2.9	n/a

Andrew Roth says: "keen to bait Labour, whether in opposition or in government"

Recent parliamentary career: opposition spokesperson, DEFRA (2001–); administration committee (2001); opposition whip (1999–2001)
Background: company director; farmer; chartered surveyor; joined Conservatives at 15; five of his ancestors were MPs
Born: March 23 1953 in Cambridge
Education: Eton College
Higher education: Royal Agricultural College, Cirencester
Constituency: heart of the Cotswolds, rural, professional, contains Cirencester, Tewkesbury

Clwyd, Ann
Labour MP for Cynon Valley since 1984

Majority: 12,998 (48.2%)
Turnout: 55.5%

	Votes	Share %	Change %
Ann Clwyd, Labour	17,685	65.6	–4.1
Steven Cornelius, Plaid Cymru	4,687	17.4	6.8
Ian Parry, Liberal Democrat	2,541	9.4	–0.9
Julian Waters, Conservative	2,045	7.6	0.8

Andrew Roth says: "senior woman in the awkward squad, her high intelligence and foresight can be obscured by quarrels with colleagues"

Recent parliamentary career: international development committee (1997–)
Background: broadcaster and journalist; Welsh correspondent for Guardian and Observer; BBC studio manager; MEP (1979–84); interest in human rights
Born: March 21 1937 in Denbigh
Education: Holywell Grammar School; Queen's School, Chester
Higher education: Bangor University
Constituency: small valleys seat, ex-mining, working-class

Coaker, Vernon
Labour MP for Gedling since 1997

Majority: 5,598 (12.8%)
Turnout: 63.9%

	Votes	Share %	Change %
Vernon Coaker, Labour	22,383	51.1	4.3
Jonathan Bullock, Conservative	16,785	38.3	−1.2
Tony Gillam, Liberal Democrat	4,648	10.6	0.7

Andrew Roth says: "loyal intervener who was the archetypal teacher-councillor"

Recent parliamentary career: PPS to Stephen Timms (1999–)
Background: deputy headteacher; Rushcliffe councillor; member of League Against Cruel Sports, Greenpeace
Born: June 17 1953 in London
Education: Drayton Manor Grammar School
Higher education: Warwick University; Nottingham Trent University
Constituency: suburban, middle class commuters to Nottingham

Coffey, Ann
Labour MP for Stockport since 1992

Majority: 11,569 (32.7%)
Turnout: 53.3%

	Votes	Share %	Change %
Ann Coffey, Labour	20,731	58.6	−4.3
John Allen, Conservative	9,162	25.9	3.6
Mark Hunter, Liberal Democrat	5,490	15.5	4.9

Andrew Roth says: "has a practical approach to trying to solve well-anticipated problems with realism"

Recent parliamentary career: modernisation of the House of Commons committee (2001–); PPS to Alistair Darling (1998–); PPS to Tony Blair (1997–98)
Background: social worker; Stockport councillor
Born: August 31 1946 in Inverness
Education: Nairn Academy; Bodmin Grammar School; Bushey Grammar School
Higher education: Manchester University; South Bank Polytechnic; Walsall College of Education
Constituency: western part of Stockport, engineering and foodstuffs

Cohen, Harry
Labour MP for Leyton and Wanstead since 1997; Leyton (1983–97)

Majority: 12,904 (38.3%)
Turnout: 54.8%

	Votes	Share %	Change %
Harry Cohen, Labour	19,558	58	−2.8
Edward Heckels, Conservative	6,654	19.7	−2.5
Alex Wilcock, Liberal Democrat	5,389	16	0.9
Ashley Gunstock, Green party	1,030	3.1	n/a
Sally Labern, Socialist Alliance	709	2.1	n/a
Michael d'Ingerthorpe, UK Independence party	378	1.1	n/a

Andrew Roth says: "pacifist prober of nuclear and government computer secrets with a sharp eye for emperors without clothes"

Recent parliamentary career: defence committee (1997–2001)
Background: accountant and auditor; member of UK delegation to North Atlantic Assembly (1992–); vice president of Royal College of Midwives

Born: December 10 1949 in Hackney
Education: George Gascoigne Secondary Modern School
Higher education: Birkbeck College, London
Constituency: inner East End London seat, large ethnic-minority population

Coleman, Iain
Labour MP for Hammersmith and Fulham since 1997

Majority: 2,015 (4.5%)
Turnout: 56.4%

	Votes	Share %	Change %
Iain Coleman, Labour	19,801	44.3	−2.5
Matthew Carrington, Conservative	17,786	39.8	0.2
Jon Burden, Liberal Democrat	5,294	11.8	3
Daniel Lopez Dias, Green party	1,444	3.2	n/a
Gerald Roberts, UK Independence party	375	0.8	n/a

Andrew Roth says: "the leftish leader of Hammersmith and Fulham council"

Recent parliamentary career: vice chair, London regional group of Labour MPs (1999–)
Background: local government officer; leader of Hammersmith and Fulham Borough Council; supports Arsenal FC
Born: January 18 1958 in London
Education: Tonbridge School
Constituency: gentrified residential West London plus council estates

Collins, Tim
Conservative MP for Westmorland and Lonsdale since 1997

Majority: 3,147 (6.5%)
Turnout: 67.8%

	Votes	Share %	Change %
Tim Collins, Conservative	22,486	46.9	4.6
Tim Farron, Liberal Democrat	19,339	40.4	7
John Bateson, Labour	5,234	10.9	−9.7
Robert Gibson, UK Independence party	552	1.2	n/a
Tim Bell, Independent	292	0.6	n/a

Andrew Roth says: "ultimate former backroom whizzkid who made a delayed start as an able counter-propagandist"

Recent parliamentary career: shadow secretary of state, CO (2001–); vice chairman, Conservative party (1999–2001); information committee (1998–2001); opposition whip (1998–99)
Background: director of communications, Conservative party (1992–95); press secretary to John Major (1992); special adviser, environment (1989–90); Conservative Research Department (1986–89)
Born: May 7 1964 in Epping
Education: Chigwell School
Higher education: London School of Economics; King's College, London
Constituency: southern Lake District, rural, many agricultural workers, tourists attracted to Windermere and Coniston

Colman, Tony
Labour MP for Putney since 1997

Majority: 2,771 (8.1%)
Turnout: 56.5%

	Votes	Share %	Change %
Tony Colman, Labour	15,911	46.5	0.8
Michael Simpson, Conservative	13,140	38.4	-0.5
Anthony Burrett, Liberal Democrat	4,671	13.6	2.8
Pat Wild, UK Independence party	347	1	n/a
Yvonne Windsor, ProLife Alliance	185	0.5	n/a

Andrew Roth says: "rare example of a wealthy former captain of industry transformed into a Labour borough chieftain"

Recent parliamentary career: international development committee (2000–); PPS to Adam Ingram (1998–2000)
Background: businessman working for Unilever, Associated Fisheries, and Burton Group; Merton councillor
Born: July 24 1943 in Upper Sheringham, Norfolk
Education: Paston Grammar School, North Walsham
Higher education: Cambridge, Magdalene
Constituency: smart south-west London riverside suburb

Connarty, Michael
Labour MP for Falkirk East since 1992

Majority: 10,712 (31.8%)
Turnout: 58.5%

	Votes	Share %	Change %
Michael Connarty, Labour	18,536	55	-1.1
Isobel Hutton, Scottish National party	7,824	23.2	-0.7
Bill Stevenson, Conservative	3,252	9.7	-4.3
Karen Utting, Liberal Democrat	2,992	8.9	3.7
Tony Weir, Scottish Socialist party	725	2.2	n/a
Raymond Stead, Socialist Labour party	373	1.1	n/a

Andrew Roth says: "former hyperactive left-winger who still looks back to his earlier incarnation in Commons debates"

Recent parliamentary career: information committee (1997–); European scrutiny committee (1998–); PPS to Tom Clarke (1997–98)
Background: special needs teacher; Stirling Council leader
Born: September 3 1947 in Coatbridge
Education: St Patrick's High School, Coatbridge
Higher education: Glasgow University; Stirling University; Jordanhill College of Education
Constituency: partly rural seat containing oil port of Grangemouth

Conway, Derek
Conservative MP for Old Bexley and Sidcup since 2001; Shrewsbury and Atcham (1983–97)

Majority: 3,345 (7.9%)
Turnout: 62.1%

	Votes	Share %	Change %
Derek Conway, Conservative	19,130	45.4	3.4
Jim Dickson, Labour	15,785	37.5	2.4
Belinda Ford, Liberal Democrat	5,792	13.8	-2.3
Janice Cronin, UK Independence party	1,426	3.4	n/a

Andrew Roth says: "quietly ambitious one-time folk guitarist"

Recent parliamentary career: re-elected to parliament (2001); chair, accommodation and works committee (2001–); government whip (1994–97)
Background: advertising executive; grocer; chief executive, Cats Protection League (1998–)
Born: February 15 1953 in Newcastle upon Tyne

Education: Beacon Hill Boys' School
Higher education: Newcastle Polytechnic
Constituency: outer south-east London, very suburban, sent Sir Edward Heath to parliament for 50 years

Cook, Frank
Labour MP for Stockton North since 1983

Majority: 14,647 (41.3%)
Turnout: 54.3%

	Votes	Share %	Change %
Frank Cook, Labour	22,470	63.4	−3.4
Amanda Vigar, Conservative	7,823	22.1	3.3
David Freeman, Liberal Democrat	4,208	11.9	1.1
Bill Wennington, Green party	926	2.6	n/a

Andrew Roth says: "mellowed veteran Catholic maverick"

Recent parliamentary career: defence committee (1992–97)
Background: schoolmaster; gravedigger; postman; Butlins redcoat
Born: November 3 1935 in West Hartlepool
Education: Corby School, Sunderland
Higher education: Institute of Education, Leeds; De La Salle College, Manchester
Constituency: north-east seat dominated by chemical plant at Billingham

Cook, Rt Hon Robin
Labour MP for Livingston since 1983; Edinburgh Central (1974–83)

Majority: 10,616 (29.4%)
Turnout: 55.6%

	Votes	Share %	Change %
Robin Cook, Labour	19,108	53	−1.9
Graham Sutherland, Scottish National party	8,492	23.6	−3.9
Gordon MacKenzie, Liberal Democrat	3,969	11	4.3
Ian Mowatt, Conservative	2,995	8.3	−1.1
Wendy Milne, Scottish Socialist party	1,110	3.1	n/a
Robert Kingdon, UK Independence party	359	1	n/a

Andrew Roth says: "arrogant but brilliant debater, tactician and strategist"

Recent parliamentary career: leader of House of Commons (2001–); chair, modernisation of the House of Commons committee (2001–); secretary of state, FCO (1997–2001)
Background: tutor for workers' educational association; journalist; Edinburgh councillor
Born: February 28 1946 in Bellshill
Education: Aberdeen Grammar School; Royal High School, Edinburgh
Higher education: Edinburgh University
Constituency: new town dominated by electronics industry, so-called 'Silicon Glen'

Cooper, Yvette
Labour MP for Pontefract and Castleford since 1997

Majority: 16,378 (52.1%)
Turnout: 49.7%

	Votes	Share %	Change %
Yvette Cooper, Labour	21,890	69.7	−6
Pamela Singleton, Conservative	5,512	17.6	4
Wesley Paxton, Liberal Democrat	2,315	7.4	0.1
John Burdon, UK Independence party	739	2.4	n/a
Trevor Bolderson, Socialist Labour party	605	1.9	n/a
John Gill, Socialist Alliance	330	1.1	n/a

Andrew Roth says: "golden girl of New Labour, a young journalist shoehorned into a super-safe West Yorkshire seat"

Recent parliamentary career: junior minister, DoH (1999–); the first minister to take maternity leave (2001)
Background: journalist, the *Independent* (leader writer and economics comentator) economist; married to Ed Balls, Gordon Brown's senior adviser; former adviser to John Smith (1991–92) and Gordon Brown (1993–94)
Born: March 20 1969 in Inverness
Education: Eggars Comprehensive School; Alton Sixth Form College
Higher education: London School of Economics; Harvard University; Oxford, Balliol
Constituency: West Yorkshire towns, with power stations and historic castle

Corbyn, Jeremy
Labour MP for Islington North since 1983

Majority: 12,958 (42.9%)
Turnout: 48.8%

	Votes	Share %	Change %
Jeremy Corbyn, Labour	18,699	61.9	–7.4
Laura Willoughby, Liberal Democrat	5,741	19	5.4
Neil Rands, Conservative	3,249	10.8	–2.1
Chris Ashby, Green party	1,876	6.2	n/a
Steve Cook, Socialist Labour party	512	1.7	n/a
Emine Hassan, Reform 2000	139	0.5	n/a

Andrew Roth says: "hyperactive quasi-Trotskyist and excellent constituency MP"

Recent parliamentary career: persistent rebel against government whip, including eight major rebellions in 1997 parliament; supporter of Irish nationalism; opponent of Gulf War; rare Labour Eurosceptic
Background: fulltime organiser for NUPE; Haringey councillor
Born: May 26 1949 in Chippenham
Education: Adams Grammar School, Newport
Higher education: North London Polytechnic
Constituency: north end of Islington away from smarter south; poor; many Cypriot voters

Cormack, Sir Patrick
Conservative MP for South Staffordshire since 1983; South West Staffordshire (1974–83); Cannock (1970–74)

Majority: 6,881 (16.3%)
Turnout: 60.3%

	Votes	Share %	Change %
Sir Patrick Cormack, Conservative	21,295	50.5	0.5
Paul Kalinauckas, Labour	14,414	34.2	–0.5
Jo Harrison, Liberal Democrat	4,891	11.6	0.3
Mike Lynch, UK Independence party	1,580	3.8	n/a

Andrew Roth says: "orotund of figure and speech"

Recent parliamentary career: foreign affairs committee (2001–); accommodation and works committee (1987–2001)
Background: industrial consultant; editor, *House Magazine*; history lecturer and teacher
Born: May 18 1939 in Grimsby
Education: St James' Choir School, Grimsby; Havelock School, Grimsby
Higher education: Hull University
Constituency: rural fringe of West Midlands

Corston, Jean
Labour MP for Bristol East since 1992

Majority: 13,392 (33.2%)
Turnout: 57.4%

	Votes	Share %	Change %
Jean Corston, Labour	22,180	55	−1.9
Jack Lo-Presti, Conservative	8,788	21.8	−1.6
Brian East, Liberal Democrat	6,915	17.1	2.3
Geoff Collard, Green party	1,110	2.8	n/a
Roger Marsh, UK Independence party	572	1.4	n/a
Mike Langley, Socialist Labour party	438	1.1	−0.5
Andy Prior, Socialist Alliance	331	0.8	n/a

Andrew Roth says: "has low-profiled significance as the interface between the leadership and backbenchers"

Recent parliamentary career: chair, parliamentary Labour party (2001–); chair, joint committee on human rights (2001–); PPS to David Blunkett (1997–2001); deputy chair PLP (1997–2001)
Background: barrister; activist for women's rights and legal reform; Labour party south-west regional organiser
Born: May 5 1942 in Hull
Education: Yeovil Girls' High School
Higher education: School of Law, Inns of Court; London School of Economics; Open University
Constituency: eastern end of Bristol, skilled working-class

Cotter, Brian
Liberal Democrat MP for Weston-Super-Mare since 1997

Majority: 338 (0.8%)
Turnout: 62.8%

	Votes	Share %	Change %
Brian Cotter, Liberal Democrat	18,424	39.5	−0.6
John Penrose, Conservative	18,086	38.7	1
Derek Kraft, Labour	9,235	19.8	1.9
Bill Lukins, UK Independence party	650	1.4	n/a
John Peverelle, Independent	206	0.4	n/a
Richard Sibley, Independent	79	0.2	n/a

Andrew Roth says: "capable if not spectacular"

Recent parliamentary career: Lib Dem spokesperson, trade and industry (1999–); deregulation committee (1997–); spokesperson, small business (1997–99);
Background: managing director; member of Charter 88; Amnesty; Green Lib Dems
Born: August 24 1938 in Ealing
Education: Downside School, Bath; St Benedict's, Ealing
Higher education: London Polytechnic
Constituency: seaside, retirement town south of Bristol

Cousins, Jim
Labour MP for Newcastle upon Tyne Central since 1987

Majority: 11,605 (33.3%)
Turnout: 51.3%

	Votes	Share %	Change %
Jim Cousins, Labour	19,169	55	−4.2
Stephen Psallidas, Liberal Democrat	7,564	21.7	6.7
Aidan Ruff, Conservative	7,414	21.3	−2.1
Gordon Potts, Socialist Labour Party	723	2.1	n/a

Andrew Roth says: "highly-intelligent low-profiled, rooted local fixer"

Recent parliamentary career: Treasury committee (1997-)
Background: researcher and lecturer in urban affairs; Tyne and Wear councillor
Born: February 23 1944 in Hammersmith
Education: City of London School
Higher education: London School of Economics; Oxford, New College
Constituency: Newcastle city centre with middle class suburbs to the north

Cox, Tom
Labour MP for Tooting since 1974; Wandsworth Central (1970–74)

Majority: 10,400 (27.7%)
Turnout: 54.9%

	Votes	Share %	Change %
Tom Cox, Labour	20,332	54.1	–5.6
Alexander Nicoll, Conservative	9,932	26.4	–0.7
Simon James, Liberal Democrat	5,583	14.9	5.5
Matthew Ledbury, Green party	1,744	4.6	3.5

Andrew Roth says: "partisan battler for social and international causes "

Recent parliamentary career: sits on committees of several European organisations
Background: electrical worker; Labour whip (1977–79)
Born: January 19 1930 in London
Education: London state schools
Higher education: London School of Economics
Constituency: southern part of Wandsworth, dense, old, and suburban

Cran, James
Conservative MP for Beverley and Holderness since 1997; Beverley (1987–97)

Majority: 781 (1.6%)
Turnout: 61.7%

	Votes	Share %	Change %
James Cran, Conservative	19,168	41.3	0.1
Philippa Langford, Labour	18,387	39.7	0.8
Stewart Willie, Liberal Democrat	7,356	15.9	–2.5
Stephen Wallis, UK Independence party	1,464	3.2	n/a

Andrew Roth says: "flinty Aberdonian Eurosceptic"

Recent parliamentary career: shadow deputy leader of the House of Commons (2001–);
opposition whip (1998–2001); committee of selection (1998–2001)
Background: chief executive, National Association of Pension Funds; northern director,
Confederation of British Industry
Born: January 28 1944 in Kintore, Aberdeen
Education: St Paul's School; Ruthrieston School, Aberdeen
Higher education: Heriot-Watt University; Aberdeen University
Constituency: remote south Yorkshire coast and county town of Beverley

Cranston, Ross
Labour MP for Dudley North since 1997

Majority: 6,800 (17.6%)
Turnout: 55.9%

	Votes	Share %	Change %
Ross Cranston, Labour	20,095	52.1	0.9
Andrew Griffiths, Conservative	13,295	34.5	3.1
Richard Burt, Liberal Democrat	3,352	8.7	0.5
Simon Darby, British National party	1,822	4.7	n/a

Andrew Roth says: "always eager to provide informed background and loyal support in any debate"

Recent parliamentary career: standards and privileges committees (2001–); solicitor general, Law Officers' Department (1998–2001)
Background: Australian-born barrister; parachuted into seat before 1997 election; close to Tony Blair
Born: July 23 1948 in Brisbane, Australia
Higher education: Queensland University, Australia; Harvard University; Oxford, Wolfson College
Constituency: busy large town on south-western edge of Black Country

Crausby, David
Labour MP for Bolton North East since 1997

Majority: 8,422 (21.6%)
Turnout: 56%

	Votes	Share %	Change %
David Crausby, Labour	21,166	54.3	–1.8
Michael Winstanley, Conservative	12,744	32.7	2.3
Tim Perkins, Liberal Democrat	4,004	10.3	0.4
Graeme McIver, Green party	629	1.6	n/a
Lynn Lowe, Socialist Labour Party	407	1	–0.4

Andrew Roth says: "low-profiled but sharp local politician and trade unionist"

Recent parliamentary career: defence committee (2001–); social security committee (1999–2001); administration committee (1997–2001)
Background: engineering turner; AEEU union organiser; Bury councillor
Born: June 17 1946 in Bury
Education: Derby Grammar School
Higher education: Bury Technical College
Constituency: industrial, urban town north-west of Greater Manchester

Cruddas, Jon
Labour MP for Dagenham since 2001

Majority: 8,693 (31.5%)
Turnout: 46.5%

	Votes	Share %	Change %
Jon Cruddas, Labour	15,784	57.2	–8.5
Michael White, Conservative	7,091	25.7	7.2
Adrian Gee-Turner, Liberal Democrat	2,820	10.2	2.7
David Hill, British National party	1,378	5	2.5
Berlyne Hamilton, Socialist Alliance	262	1	n/a
Robert Siggins, Socialist Labour party	245	0.9	n/a

Nicholas Watt, the *Guardian*: "the prime minister's former trade union fixer"

Recent parliamentary career: elected to parliament in 2001
Background: deputy political secretary to Tony Blair (1997–2001); chief assistant to party general secretary (1994–97); married to Labour official, Anna Healy
Born: April 7 1962
Education: Oaklands RC School, Portsmouth
Higher education: Warwick University
Constituency: hit by part-closure of Ford plant but will recover, on tube to city

Cryer, Ann
Labour MP for Keighley since 1997

Majority: 4,005 (9.2%)
Turnout: 63.4%

Votes	Share %	Change %
Ann Cryer, Labour	20,888	48.2	−2.4
Simon Cooke, Conservative	16,883	39	2.3
Mike Doyle, Liberal Democrat	4,722	10.9	1.1
Michael Cassidy, UK Independence party	840	1.9	n/a

Andrew Roth says: "seen as a decent honest person … a more restrained version of her widely popular, hard-left husband-MP"

Recent parliamentary career: attracted criticism for saying UK immigrants should be expected to speak English (2001); rebelled on four major occasions (1997–2001)
Background: secretary for MP and MEP husband until his death in a car accident (1994); mother to John Cryer MP; ICI clerk; involved in CND and Co-operative party
Born: December 12 1939 in St Anne's on Sea, Lewes
Education: Spring Bank Secondary Modern
Higher education: Bolton Technical College
Constituency: semi-rural West Yorkshire, scenic countryside, including the Brontës' parsonage at Haworth

Cryer, John
Labour MP for Hornchurch since 1997

Majority: 1,482 (4.1%)
Turnout: 58.3%

	Votes	Share %	Change %
John Cryer, Labour	16,514	46.4	−3.8
Robin Squire, Conservative	15,032	42.3	5
Sarah Lea, Liberal Democrat	2,928	8.2	0.4
Lawrence Webb, UK Independence party	893	2.5	n/a
David Durrant, Third Way	190	0.5	−0.1

Andrew Roth says: "one of the worries of whips and Blairites, 'has spoken well and sparingly in the House'"

Recent parliamentary career: deregulation committee (1997–); persistent rebel in 1997 parliament
Background: journalist; insurance underwriter; son of Ann and Robert Cryer, both MPs for Keighley
Born: April 11 1964 in Darwen, Lancashire
Education: Oakbank School, Keighley
Higher education: London College of Printing; Hatfield Polytechnic
Constituency: north-east outer London, close Essex ties, whitecollar

Cummings, John
Labour MP for Easington since 1987

Majority: 21,949 (66.5%)
Turnout: 53.7%

	Votes	Share %	Change %
John Cummings, Labour	25,360	76.8	−3.4
Philip Lovel, Conservative	3,411	10.3	1.7
Christopher Ord, Liberal Democrat	3,408	10.3	3.1
Dave Robinson, Socialist Labour party	831	2.5	n/a

Andrew Roth says: "an emotional style, especially when discussing the 'betrayed' mining industry"

Recent parliamentary career: environment, transport and regional affairs committee (1997–2001)
Background: worked at Murton Colliery for 29 years

Born: July 6 1943 in Newcastle upon Tyne
Education: Murton state schools
Higher education: Easington Technical College
Constituency: biggest numerical majority in Britain, ex-mining County Durham seat

Cunningham, Rt Hon Jack

Labour MP for Copeland since 1983; Whitehaven (1970–83)

Majority: 4,964 (14.3%)
Turnout: 64.9%

	Votes	Share %	Change %
Jack Cunningham, Labour	17,991	51.8	–6.4
Mike Graham, Conservative	13,027	37.5	8.3
Mark Gayler, Liberal Democrat	3,732	10.7	1.5

Andrew Roth says: "very bright, highly educated radical moderate"

Recent parliamentary career: minister of state, CO (1998–99); minister of state, chancellor of the Duchy of Lancaster (1998–99); secretary of state, MAFF (1997–98)
Background: chemistry research fellow; adviser to chemical companies; union official GMWU (now GMB)
Born: August 4 1939 in Felling, County Durham
Education: Jarrow Grammar School
Higher education: Durham University
Constituency: lakes and fells plus remote urban coast and nuclear power

Cunningham, Jim

Labour MP for Coventry South since 1997; Coventry South East (1992–97)

Majority: 8279 (20.7%)
Turnout: 55.3%

	Votes	Share %	Change %
Jim Cunningham, Labour	20,125	50.2	–0.7
Heather Wheeler, Conservative	11,846	29.5	0.5
Vincent McKee, Liberal Democrat	5,672	14.2	5
Rob Windsor, Socialist Alliance	1,475	3.7	n/a
Irene Rogers, Independent	564	1.4	n/a
Timothy Logan, Socialist Labour party	414	1	n/a

Andrew Roth says: "trade unionist loyalist addicted to reading his speeches"

Recent parliamentary career: trade and industry committee (1997–2001)
Background: engineer; trade unionist for over 27 years; spent 20 years on Coventry Council
Born: February 4 1941 in Coatbridge
Education: St Columba High School, Coatbridge
Higher education: Tillicoultry Trade Union College
Constituency: city centre and council estates, leafy suburbs, Warwick University campus

Cunningham, Tony

Labour MP for Workington since 2001

Majority: 10,850 (25.9%)
Turnout: 63.4%

	Votes	Share %	Change %
Tony Cunningham, Labour	23,209	55.5	–8.7
Tim Stoddart, Conservative	12,359	29.6	5.2
Ian Francis, Liberal Democrat	5,214	12.5	4.5
John Peacock, LCA	1,040	2.5	n/a

Maiden speech: "No matter how beautiful the constituency is, if people do not have jobs and do not

share in its prosperity, the beauty is not so obvious. Small businesses are important."
Recent parliamentary career: elected to parliament 2001; European scrutiny committee (2001–);
joint committee on human rights (2001–); catering committee (2001–)
Background: MEP (1994–99); secondary school teacher for 18 years; human rights organiser;
leader of Allerdale Council; mayor of Workington
Born: September 16 1952
Education: Workington Grammar School
Higher education: Liverpool University
Constituency: remote ex-mining industrial coast, very working-class

Curry, Rt Hon David
Conservative MP for Skipton and Ripon since 1987

Majority: 12,930 (26.3%)
Turnout: 65.3%

	Votes	Share %	Change %
David Curry, Conservative	25,736	52.4	5.9
Bernard Bateman, Liberal Democrat	12,806	26.1	0.9
Michael Dugher, Labour	8,543	17.4	–5
Nancy Holdsworth, UK Independence party	2,041	4.2	n/a

Andrew Roth says: "Europhile defector from William Hague's shadow cabinet, seen by Labour opponents as a decent type"

Recent parliamentary career: chair, environment, food, and rural affairs committee (2001–); chair, agriculture committee (2000–2001); introduced private member's bill on pensions (2001); shadow minister of agriculture (1997–97); minister of state, local government, housing, and urban regeneration (1993–97)
Background: studied international politics under Henry Kissinger; journalist; MEP (1979–89); noted Conservative Europhile
Born: June 13 1944 in Burton on Trent
Education: Ripon Grammar School
Higher education: Harvard; Oxford, Corpus Christi
Constituency: scenic southern edge of Yorkshire Dales, north of Harrogate

Curtis-Thomas, Claire
Labour MP for Crosby since 1997

Majority: 8,353 (22.6%)
Turnout: 64.3%

	Votes	Share %	Change %
Claire Curtis-Thomas, Labour	20,327	55.1	4
Robert Collinson, Conservative	11,974	32.5	–2.3
Tim Drake, Liberal Democrat	4,084	11.1	–0.4
Mark Holt, Socialist Labour Party	481	1.3	n/a

Andrew Roth says: "extremely able speaker and active animal rights defender"

Recent parliamentary career: science and technology committee (1997–)
Background: chartered engineer; strategic planner
Born: April 30 1958 in Neath
Education: Mynyddbach Comprehensive School for Girls, Swansea
Higher education: University College, Cardiff; Aston University
Constituency: Liverpool commuters north of city, middle class, shock Labour gain (1997)

D

Daisley, Paul
Labour MP for Brent East since 2001

Majority: 13,047 (45.0%)
Turnout: 49.9%

	Votes	Share %	Change %
Paul Daisley, Labour	18,325	63.2	−4.1
David Gauke, Conservative	5,278	18.2	−4.1
Nowsheen Bhatti, Liberal Democrat	3,065	10.6	2.8
Simone Aspis, Green party	1,361	4.7	n/a
Sarah Macken, ProLife Alliance	392	1.4	0.8
Iris Cremer, Socialist Labour Party	383	1.3	0
Ashwin Tanna, UK Independence party	188	0.7	n/a

Paul Daisley says: "Anyone who thinks we would allow a football club [such as Arsenal] to play at Wembley is living in cloud-cuckoo land"

Recent parliamentary career: entered parliament 2001
Background: accounting officer, Texaco; finance and administration director; Brent Council leader for five years, where he was involved in unsuccessful efforts to upgrade Wembley stadium
Born: July 20 1957
Education: Littlemore School, Oxfordshire; Abingdon College
Constituency: urban home of ex-Labour London mayor Ken Livingstone, large Irish population

Dalyell, Tam
Labour MP for Linlithgow since 1983; West Lothian (1962–83)

Majority: 9,129 (28.9%)
Turnout: 58%

	Votes	Share %	Change %
Tam Dalyell, Labour	17,207	54.4	0.3
Jim Sibbald, Scottish National party	8,078	25.5	−1.3
Gordon Lindhurst, Conservative	2,836	9	−3.5
Martin Oliver, Liberal Democrat	2,628	8.3	2.4
Eddie Cornock, Scottish Socialist party	695	2.2	n/a
Ms Helen Cronin, R & R Loony	211	0.7	n/a

Andrew Roth says: "Scotland's veteran political pillar… obsessional Etonian Cassandra"

Recent parliamentary career: father of the House (2001–)
Background: baronet; secondary school teacher; noted campaigner, especially against devolution; prone to rebellions against the party line; parliamentary columnist, *New Scientist*
Born: August 9 1932 in Edinburgh
Education: Eton College
Higher education: Cambridge, King's
Constituency: small towns, bleak ex-shale mines, struggling Bathgate plus ancient town of Linlithgow

Darling, Rt Hon Alistair
Labour MP for Edinburgh Central since 1987

Majority: 8,142 (23.7%)
Turnout: 52%

	Votes	Share %	Change %
Alistair Darling, Labour	14,495	42.2	−4.9
Andrew Myles, Liberal Democrat	6,353	18.5	5.4
Alastair Orr, Conservative	5,643	16.4	−4.8
Ian McKee, Scottish National party	4,832	14.1	−1.7
Graeme Farmer, Green party	1,809	5.3	n/a
Kevin Williamson, Scottish Socialist party	1,258	3.7	n/a

Andrew Roth says: "highly-competent product of the 'sensible left'"

Recent parliamentary career: secretary of state, DWP (2001–); secretary of state, DSS (1998–2001); chief secretary to Treasury (1997–98)
Background: Edinburgh solicitor and advocate
Born: November 28 1953 in London
Education: Loretto School
Higher education: Aberdeen University
Constituency: elegant city centre, top residential areas, professional

Davey, Edward
Liberal Democrat MP for Kingston and Surbiton since 1997

Majority: 15,676 (32.0%)
Turnout: 67.5%

	Votes	Share %	Change %
Edward Davey, Liberal Democrat	29,542	60.2	23.5
David Shaw, Conservative	13,866	28.2	–8.4
Phil Woodford, Labour	4,302	8.8	–14.2
Chris Spruce, Green party	572	1.2	n/a
Miss Amy Burns, UK Independence party	438	0.9	n/a
John Hayball, Socialist Labour Party	319	0.7	n/a
Jeremy Middleton, Unrep	54	0.1	n/a

Andrew Roth says: "one of the clever backroom boys transmuted into a rising star"

Recent parliamentary career: Lib Dem shadow chief secretary to the Treasury (2001–); Lib Dem whip (1998–2001); spokesperson, Treasury (1997–2001)
Background: Lib Dem economic researcher; management consultant; postal services expert
Born: December 25 1965 in Annersley-Woodhouse, Nottinghamshire
Education: Nottingham High School
Higher education: Birkbeck College, London; Oxford, Jesus
Constituency: deep suburbia in outer south-west London

Davey, Valerie
Labour MP for Bristol West since 1997

Majority: 4,426 (7.9%)
Turnout: 65.6%

	Votes	Share %	Change %
Valerie Davey, Labour	20,505	36.8	1.6
Stephen Williams, Liberal Democrat	16,079	28.9	0.9
Pamela Chesters, Conservative	16,040	28.8	–4
John Devaney, Green party	1,961	3.5	2.1
Bernard Kennedy, Socialist Labour party	590	1.1	0.7
Simon Muir, UK Independence party	490	0.9	n/a

Andrew Roth says: "education preoccupied, a forceful and accomplished speaker"

Recent parliamentary career: education and skills committee (2001–); education and employment committee (1997–2001)
Background: teacher in Tanzania and Wolverhampton; full-time Avon County councillor
Born: April 16 1940 in Sutton, Surrey
Education: state schools
Higher education: London University; Birmingham University
Constituency: elegant university and Clifton suburb, hilly residential Bristol

David, Wayne
Labour MP for Caerphilly since 2001
Majority: 14,425 (37.1%)
Turnout: 57.5%

	Votes	Share %	Change %
Wayne David, Labour	22,597	58.2	–9.6
Lindsay Whittle, Plaid Cymru	8,172	21.1	11.4
David Simmonds, Conservative	4,413	11.4	0.7
Rob Roffe, Liberal Democrat	3,649	9.4	1.2

Maiden speech: "I was a member of the European parliament for 10 years. That experience has made me a committed European and internationalist"

Recent parliamentary career: entered parliament 2001; European scrutiny committee (2001–)
Background: policy adviser for the youth service; WEA tutor organiser; MEP (1989–94); teacher; leader, European parliamentary Labour party (1994–98)
Born: July 1 1957
Education: Cynffig Comprehensive Schools
Higher education: Swansea University; Cardiff University
Constituency: remote ex-mining valleys north of Cardiff

Davidson, Ian
Labour MP for Glasgow Pollok since 1997; Glasgow Govan (1992–97)

Majority: 11,268 (44.6%)
Turnout: 51.4%

	Votes	Share %	Change %
Ian Davidson, Labour	15,497	61.3	1.4
David Ritchie, Scottish National party	4,229	16.7	–1.2
Keith Baldesarra, Scottish Socialist party	2,522	10	n/a
Isabel Nelson, Liberal Democrat	1,612	6.4	2.9
Rory O'Brien, Conservative	1,417	5.6	–0.4

Andrew Roth says: "'sharp tongued left-winger' quick and cutting in debate'"

Recent parliamentary career: public accounts committee (1997–); chair, trade union group of Labour MPs; Tribune group
Background: political researcher; community service volunteer
Born: September 8 1950 in Jedburgh
Education: Jedburgh Grammar School; Galashiels Academy
Higher education: Edinburgh University
Constituency: south-west Glasgow, sprawling council estates, troubled by crime and unemployment

Davies, Rt Hon Denzil
Labour MP for Llanelli since 1970

Majority: 6,403 (17.7%)
Turnout: 62.3%

	Votes	Share %	Change %
Denzil Davies, Labour	17,586	48.6	–9.3
Dyfan Jones, Plaid Cymru	11,183	30.9	11.9
Simon Hayes, Conservative	3,442	9.5	–2.6
Ken Rees, Liberal Democrat	3,065	8.5	–0.7
Ms January Cliff, Green party	515	1.4	n/a
John Willock, Socialist Labour Party	407	1.1	n/a

Andrew Roth says: "brilliant, witty Keynesian who represents the mating of Bill Cash and Tam Dalyell"

Recent parliamentary career: currently backbencher; various opposition roles (1979–88); minister of state, Treasury (1975–79)
Background: law lecturer at Chicago and Leeds Universities, barrister
Born: October 9 1938 in Carmarthen
Education: Queen Elizabeth Grammar School, Carmarthen
Higher education: Oxford, Pembroke
Constituency: rugby-playing town in south-west Wales

Davies, Geraint
Labour MP for Croydon Central since 1997

Majority: 3,984 (8.7%)
Turnout: 59.1%

	Votes	Share %	Change %
Geraint Davies, Labour	21,643	47.2	1.6
David Congdon, Conservative	17,659	38.5	–0.1
Paul Booth, Liberal Democrat	5,156	11.2	0.3
James Feisenberger, UK Independence party	545	1.2	n/a
Lynda Miller, British National party	449	1	n/a
John Cartwright, Official Monster Raving Loony party	408	0.9	n/a

Andrew Roth says: "clever, quick-witted Blairite intervener"

Recent parliamentary career: public accounts committee (1997–)
Background: marketing manager, Unilever, Colgate Palmolive
Born: May 3 1960 in Chester
Education: Llanishen Comprehensive School, Cardiff
Higher education: Oxford, Jesus
Constituency: white-collar commercial and shopping centre of outer south London

Davies, Quentin
Conservative MP for Grantham and Stamford since 1997; Stamford and Spalding (1987–97)

Majority: 4,518 (9.8%)
Turnout: 62.2%

	Votes	Share %	Change %
Quentin Davies, Conservative	21,329	46.1	3.3
John Robinson, Labour	16,811	36.3	–1.4
Jane Carr, Liberal Democrat	6,665	14.4	1.9
Marilyn Swain, UK Independence party	1,484	3.2	n/a

Andrew Roth says: "sophisticated, well-informed, normally loyal"

Recent parliamentary career: shadow secretary of state, NIO (2001–); opposition spokesperson, defence (2000–01)
Background: diplomat; director; financial consultant
Born: May 29 1944 in Oxford
Education: Dragon School, Oxford; Leighton Park School
Higher education: Harvard University; Cambridge, Gonville & Caius
Constituency: mainly rural plus small Lincolnshire towns including historic Stamford

Davis, Rt Hon David
Conservative MP for Haltemprice and Howden since 1997; Boothferry (1987–97)

Majority: 1,903 (4.3%)
Turnout: 65.5%

	Votes	Share %	Change %
David Davis, Conservative	18,994	43.2	–0.8
Jon Neal, Liberal Democrat	17,091	38.9	10.1
Leslie Howell, Labour	6,898	15.7	–7.9
Joanne Robinson, UK Independence party	945	2.2	n/a

Andrew Roth says: "shrewd, tough dynamic operator who cannily sidelined himself as chairman of the public accounts committee (1997–2001) away from the Tory civil war"

Recent parliamentary career: Conservative party chairman (2001–); challenged for party leadership before supporting Iain Duncan Smith(2001); chair, public accounts committee

(1997–2001); minister of state, FCO (1994–97); government whip (1990–93), where he secured passage of the Maastricht Treaty as a self-declared "Eurosceptic for Maastricht"; a sharp right-winger who puts loyalty above ideology and is widely respected
Background: finance director; managing director, Tate and Lyle
Born: December 23 1948 in York
Education: Bec Grammar School
Higher education: London University; Warwick University; Harvard University; London Business School
Constituency: main town is Beverley, home to Hull's middle class

Davis, Rt Hon Terry
Labour MP for Birmingham Hodge Hill since 1983; Birmingham Stechford (1979-83); Bromsgrove (1971–74)

Majority: 11,618 (43.9%)
Turnout: 47.9%

	Votes	Share %	Change %
Terry Davis, Labour	16,901	63.9	–1.7
Debbie Lewis, Conservative	5,283	20	–4
Tracey O'Brien, Liberal Democrat	2,147	8.1	–0.4
Lee Windridge, British National party	889	3.4	n/a
Parwez Hussain, PJP	561	2.1	n/a
Dennis Cridge, Socialist Labour Party	284	1.1	n/a
Vivian Harvey, UK Independence party	275	1	n/a
Ayub Khan, Muslim	125	0.5	n/a

Andrew Roth says: "disciplined old Labour workhorse"

Recent parliamentary career: European scrutiny committee (2001–); member of delegation to Council of Europe and Western EU Assembly (1992–)
Background: company executive; manager in motor industry
Born: January 5 1938 in Stourbridge
Education: King Edward VI, Stourbridge
Higher education: Michigan University, USA; London, University College
Constituency: innercity, skilled-manual, large Pakistani community

Dawson, Hilton
Labour MP for Lancaster and Wyre since 1997

Majority: 481 (0.9%)
Turnout: 66.3%

	Votes	Share %	Change %
Hilton Dawson, Labour	22,556	43.1	0.3
Steve Barclay, Conservative	22,075	42.2	1.6
Liz Scott, Liberal Democrat	5,383	10.3	–1.3
John Whitelegg, Green party	1,595	3.1	n/a
John Whittaker, UK Independence party	741	1.4	n/a

Andrew Roth says: "former child care social worker who feels 'we need to make this country child centred'"

Recent parliamentary career: administration committee (1997–2001)
Background: social work manager
Born: September 30 1953 in Stannington, Northumberland
Education: Ashington Grammar School
Higher education: Warwick University; Lancaster University
Constituency: Lancaster plus rural small towns and villages

Dean, Janet
Labour MP for Burton since 1997

Majority: 4,849 (10.4%)
Turnout: 61.8%

	Votes	Share %	Change %
Janet Dean, Labour	22,783	49	–2
Maggie Punyer, Conservative	17,934	38.6	–0.8
David Fletcher, Liberal Democrat	4,468	9.6	1.1
Ian Crompton, UK Independence party	984	2.1	n/a
John Roberts, ProLife Alliance	288	0.6	n/a

Andrew Roth says: "motherly, ultra-busy activist"

Recent parliamentary career: home affairs committee (1999–); catering committee (1997–)
Background: housewife; bank clerk; Staffordshire councillor
Born: January 28 1949 in Crewe
Education: Winsford Verdin Grammar School
Constituency: east Staffordshire brewing industry and JCB factories, high unemployment

Denham, Rt Hon John
Labour MP for Southampton Itchen since 1992

Majority: 11,223 (27.1%)
Turnout: 54%

	Votes	Share %	Change %
John Denham, Labour	22,553	54.5	–0.3
Caroline Nokes, Conservative	11,330	27.4	–1
Mark Cooper, Liberal Democrat	6,195	15	3.3
Kim Rose, UK Independence party	829	2	n/a
Gavin Marsh, Socialist Alliance	241	0.6	n/a
Michael Holmes, Socialist Labour party	225	0.5	–0.7

Andrew Roth says: "energetic, idealist internationalist who has outgrown his early flirtation with 'extra-parliamentary action'"

Recent parliamentary career: minister of state, HO (2001–); junior minister, Health (1999–2001); junior minister, Social Security (1997–99)
Background: campaigner for Friends of the Earth, British Youth Council, War on Want
Born: July 15 1953 in Seaton, Devon
Education: Woodroffe Comprehensive School
Higher education: Southampton University
Constituency: eastern half of south coast port city, urban and working-class

Dhanda, Parmjit
Labour MP for Gloucester since 2001

Majority: 3,880 (8.1%)
Turnout: 59.4%

	Votes	Share %	Change %
Parmjit Dhanda, Labour	22,067	45.8	–4.2
Paul James, Conservative	18,187	37.7	2
Tim Bullamore, Liberal Democrat	6,875	14.3	3.8
Terry Lines, UK Independence party	822	1.7	n/a
Stewart Smyth, Socialist Alliance	272	0.6	n/a

Maiden speech: "I stand here as the very proud MP for Gloucester and I shall do my best to deliver a city that is fit for the twenty-first century"

Recent parliamentary career: entered parliament 2001

Background: assistant national organiser, Connect trade union; Hillingdon councillor; Labour party agent; TV newspaper reviewer
Born: September 17 1971 in London
Education: Mellow Lane Comprehensive School
Higher education: Nottingham University
Constituency: diverse industry including huge ice-cream factory, mixed council and private housing

Dismore, Andrew
Labour MP for Hendon since 1997

Majority: 7,417 (18.2%)
Turnout: 52.2%

	Votes	Share %	Change %
Andrew Dismore, Labour	21,432	52.5	3.2
Richard Evans, Conservative	14,015	34.3	−2.7
Wayne Casey, Liberal Democrat	4,724	11.6	0.8
Craig Crosbie, UK Independence party	409	1	n/a
Ms Stella Taylor, Workers' Revolutionary party	164	0.4	0.1
Michael Stewart, Prog Dem	107	0.3	n/a

Andrew Roth says: "hardworking, dogged campaigner with a bright legal mind"

Recent parliamentary career: work and pensions committee (2001–); standards and privileges committee (2001–); social security committee (1998–2001)
Background: solicitor, Westminster councillor
Born: September 2 1954 in Bridlington
Education: Bridlington Grammar School
Higher education: London School of Economics; Warwick University; College of Law, Guildford
Constituency: mixed suburbs in outer north London; classic Tory seat, now Labour

Djanogly, Jonathan
Conservative MP for Huntingdon since 2001

Majority: 12,792 (26.0%)
Turnout: 62.5%

	Votes	Share %	Change %
Jonathan Djanogly, Conservative	24,507	49.9	−5.4
Michael Pope, Liberal Democrat	11,715	23.9	9.2
Takki Sulaiman, Labour	11,211	22.8	−0.7
Derek Norman, UK Independence party	1,656	3.4	n/a

Maiden speech: "In the towns of Huntingdonshire there is hardly a cul-de-sac that has not been opened up for development in recent years … what is needed is a balance"

Recent parliamentary career: entered parliament 2001; trade and industry committee (2001–); joint committee on statutory instruments (2001–)
Background: solicitor specialising in commercial law; cofounded mail order cassette business with his wife; Westminster councillor
Born: June 3 1965
Education: University College School
Higher education: Oxford Brookes Polytechnic; Guildford College of Law
Constituency: thriving, flat farmland and developments by A1

Dobbin, Jim
Labour MP for Heywood and Middleton since 1997

Majority: 11,670 (30.1%)
Turnout: 53.1%

	Votes	Share %	Change %
Jim Dobbin, Labour	22,377	57.7	0
Marilyn Hopkins, Conservative	10,707	27.6	4.6
Ian Greenhalgh, Liberal Democrat	4,329	11.2	−4.4
Philip Burke, Liberal	1,021	2.6	1.1
Ms Christine West, Christian Democrat	345	0.9	n/a

Andrew Roth says: "Scottish born local political fixer, self-effacing, but 'doesn't miss a trick'"

Recent parliamentary career: European scrutiny committee (1998–)
Background: microbiologist with NHS for 33 years; Rochdale councillor
Born: May 26 1941 in Kincardine, Fife
Education: St Columba's High School, Cowdenbeath; St Andrew's High School, Fife
Higher education: Napier College, Edinburgh
Constituency: outer Rochdale, suburbs north-west of Manchester

Dobson, Rt Hon Frank
Labour MP for Holborn and St Pancras since 1979

Majority: 11,175 (35.9%)
Turnout: 49.6%

	Votes	Share %	Change %
Frank Dobson, Labour	16,770	53.9	−11.1
Nathaniel Green, Liberal Democrat	5,595	18	5.5
Roseanne Serelli, Conservative	5,258	16.9	−1
Rob Whitley, Green party	1,875	6	n/a
Candy Udwin, Socialist Alliance	971	3.1	n/a
Joti Brar, Socialist Labour party	359	1.2	n/a
Magnus Nielsen, UK Independence party	301	1	n/a

Andrew Roth says: "rumbustious, aggressively partisan leftist with bluff common sense"

Recent parliamentary career: introduced private member's bill on tobacco sales (2001); secretary of state, DoH (1997–99)
Background: office of the local ombudsman; Camden councillor; Labour's candidate in London mayoral race (2000)
Born: March 15 1940 in York
Education: Archbishop Holgate Grammar School
Higher education: London School of Economics
Constituency: typical innercity London, trendy Camden plus West End fringe

Dodds, Nigel
Democratic Unionist party MP for Belfast North since 2001

Majority: 6,387 (15.6%)
Turnout: 67.2%

	Votes	Share %	Change %
Nigel Dodds, Democratic Unionist party	16,718	40.8	n/a
Gerry Kelly, Sinn Fein	10,331	25.2	5
Alban Maginness, Social Democratic and Labour party	8,592	21	0.6
Cecil Walker, Ulster Unionist party	4,904	12	−39.8
Ms Marcella Delaney, Workers' party	253	0.6	−0.1
Rainbow George Weiss, Ind Vote	134	0.3	n/a

Maiden speech: "I come to the house with a clear mandate not only as a Unionist – which I am and I am proud to be – but as a campaigning member of the house, to work for the social and economic betterment of all my constituents"

Recent parliamentary career: entered parliament 2001, taking seat from Ulster Unionist party
Background: barrister; lord mayor of Belfast; member of NIA (1999–)

Born: August 20 1958
Education: Portora Royal School, Enniskillen
Higher education: Cambridge, St John's College
Constituency: includes Protestant Shankill and substantial Catholic minority, pleasant residential to slum housing

Doherty, Pat
Sinn Fein MP for West Tyrone since 2001

Majority: 5,040 (12%)
Turnout: 79.9%

	Votes	Share %	Change %
Pat Doherty, Sinn Fein	19,814	40.8	10
Willie Thompson, Ulster Unionist party	14,774	30.4	−4.1
Brid Rodgers, SDLP	13,942	28.7	−3.3

Pat Doherty says: "Mr Blair must face down his generals and remove the apparatus of war from our country"

Recent parliamentary career: entered parliament 2001, taking seat from Ulster Unionist party; has not taken his seat in Parliament
Background: Glasgow-born site engineer; Sinn Fein activist and vice president (1988–); member of NIA and chair of NIA's economic development committee
Born: July 18 1945 in Glasgow
Constituency: scenic rural seat centred on Omagh

Donaldson, Jeffrey
Ulster Unionist party MP for Lagan Valley since 1997

Majority: 18,342 (39.9%)
Turnout: 63.2%

	Votes	Share %	Change %
Jeffrey Donaldson, Ulster Unionist party	25,966	56.5	1.1
Seamus Close, Alliance party of Northern Ireland	7,624	16.6	−0.6
Edwin Poots, Democratic Unionist party	6,164	13.4	−0.2
Patricia Lewsley, Social Democratic and Labout party	3,462	7.5	−0.3
Paul Butler, Sinn Fein	2,725	5.9	3.4

Andrew Roth says: "'no man' who broke ranks over the Good Friday Agreement"

Recent parliamentary career: Ulster Unionist spokesperson, DTLGR (2001–); joint committee on statutory instruments (2001–); deregulation committee (2001–); environment, transport and regional affairs committee (2000–2001); transport subcommittee (2000–2001); spokesperson, Treasury, work and pensions; spokesperson, DTI (1997–2001)
Background: Ulster Defence Regiment; agent to Enoch Powell MP; member, Ulster Unionist Council; partner, financial services and estate agency business; member of Care and the Evangelical Alliance
Born: December 7 1962 in Kilkeel, County Down
Education: Kilkeel High School
Higher education: Castlereagh College of Education
Constituency: strong Unionist seat, mainly urban, fast-growing

Donohoe, Brian
Labour MP for Cunninghame South since 1992

Majority: 11,230 (40.1%)
Turnout: 56%

	Votes	Share %	Change %
Brian Donohoe, Labour	16,424	58.6	–4.1
Bill Kidd, Scottish National party	5,194	18.5	–2.3
Eveline Archer, Conservative	2,682	9.6	–0.5
John Boyd, Liberal Democrat	2,094	7.5	3
Rosemary Byrne, Scottish Socialist party	1,233	4.4	n/a
Bobby Cochrane, Socialist Labour Party party	382	1.4	0

Andrew Roth says: "quiet, low-profile Scots loyalist, politically ambitious"

Recent parliamentary career: environment, transport and regional affairs committee (1997–2001); transport subcommittee (1997–2001); environment subcommittee (1997–2001)
Background: power station engineer and draughtsman
Born: September 10 1948 in Kilmarnock
Education: Irvine Royal Academy
Higher education: Kilmarnock Technical College
Constituency: Ayrshire industrial including giant paper mill, new and old towns, working-class

Doran, Frank
Labour MP for Aberdeen Central since 1997; Aberdeen South (1987–92)

Majority: 6,646 (25.1%)
Turnout: 52.8%

	Votes	Share %	Change %
Frank Doran, Labour	12,025	45.5	–4.3
Wayne Gault, Scottish National party	5,379	20.4	4.2
Eleanor Anderson, Liberal Democrat	4,547	17.2	4
Stewart Whyte, Conservative	3,761	14.2	–5.3
Andy Cumbers, Scottish Socialist party	717	2.7	n/a

Andrew Roth says: "cautious, rightward-moving former semi-hard left-winger"

Recent parliamentary career: culture, media and sport committee (2001–); PPS to Ian McCartney (1997–2001)
Background: solicitor; founding member of Scottish Legal Action Group
Born: April 13 1949 in Edinburgh
Education: Ainslie Park Secondary School; Leith Academy
Higher education: Dundee University
Constituency: city centre plus north and South Aberdeen, council estates and fashionable areas

Dorrell, Rt Hon Stephen
Conservative MP for Charnwood since 1997; Loughborough (1979–97)

Majority: 7,739 (16.0%)
Turnout: 64.5%

	Votes	Share %	Change %
Stephen Dorrell, Conservative	23,283	48.2	1.7
Sean Sheahan, Labour	15,544	32.2	–3.8
Susan King, Liberal Democrat	7,835	16.2	3.3
Jamie Bye, UK Independence party	1,603	3.3	n/a

Andrew Roth says: "one-man thinktank with a well-endowed analytical mind but dubious judgement"

Recent parliamentary career: shadow secretary of state, DFEE (1997–98); secretary of state, DoH (1995–97); secretary of state for National Heritage (1994–95)
Background: director, family industrial clothing firm; chair of Millennium Commission; noted Tory wet who ran for party leader (1997) and subsided from the front rank shortly after
Born: March 25 1952 in Worcester
Education: Uppingham School
Higher education: Oxford, Brasenose
Constituency: commuting, managerial, between Leicester and Loughborough

Doughty, Sue
Liberal Democrat MP for Guildford since 2001

Majority: 538 (1.2%)
Turnout: 62.9%

	Votes	Share %	Change %
Sue Doughty, Liberal Democrat	20,358	42.6	8.5
Nicholas St Aubyn, Conservative	19,820	41.4	−1.1
Joyce Still, Labour	6,558	13.7	−3.8
Sonya Porter, UK Independence party	736	1.5	n/a
John Morris, Pacifist	370	0.8	n/a

Maiden speech: "Guildford is more than a pretty town and a shopping centre. It is a thriving cultural, academic and social hub."

Recent parliamentary career: entered parliament 2001, taking seat from Conservative in an unexpected victory; environmental audit committee (2001–)
Background: management consultant; project manager for Thames Water; teacher; interest in the environment, member of Green Lib Dems
Born: April 13 1948 in York
Education: Mill Mount Grammar School, York; Northumberland College
Constituency: large Surrey commercial centre, mixed housing but mainly middle class

Dowd, Jim
Labour MP for Lewisham West since 1992

Majority: 11,920 (38.7%)
Turnout: 50.6%

	Votes	Share %	Change %
Jim Dowd, Labour	18,816	61.1	−0.9
Gary Johnson, Conservative	6,896	22.4	−1.4
Richard Thomas, Liberal Democrat	4,146	13.5	3.7
Frederick Pearson, UK Independence party	485	1.6	n/a
Nick Long, Independent	472	1.5	n/a

Andrew Roth says: "witty, locally-active mainstream councillor"

Recent parliamentary career: health committee (2001–); government whip (1997–2001)
Background: telecommunications engineer; Lewisham councillor, deputy leader and mayor; member of Greenpeace, CND, RSPB, National Trust
Born: March 5 1951 in Bad Eilsen, Germany
Education: Sedgehill Comprehensive School; London Nautical School
Constituency: suburban south-east London, large Afro-Caribbean population

Drew, David
Labour MP for Stroud since 1997

Majority: 5,039 (9.2%)
Turnout: 70%

	Votes	Share %	Change %
David Drew, Labour	25,685	46.6	3.9
Neil Carmichael, Conservative	20,646	37.4	−0.5
Janice Beasley, Liberal Democrat	6,036	10.9	−4.6
Kevin Cranston, Green party	1,913	3.5	−0.4
Adrian Blake, UK Independence party	895	1.6	n/a
Adrian Blake, 21st Century Independent Foresters	n/a		

Andrew Roth says: "sensible contributions are somewhat undermined by a portentous manner"

Recent parliamentary career: environment, food, and rural affairs committee (2001–); procedure committee (1997–); agriculture committee (1999–2001)

Background: teacher and lecturer in education for 21 years; councillor for Stevenage, Stroud, Stonehouse and Gloucestershire; member of Friends of the Earth, Greenpeace, Charter 88, Age Concern
Born: April 13 1952 in Gloucestershire
Education: Kingsfield Comprehensive School
Higher education: Nottingham University; Birmingham University; Bristol Polytechnic
Constituency: prosperous mainly urban seat by M5, south of Gloucester

Drown, Julia
Labour MP for South Swindon since 1997

Majority: 7,341 (16.9%)
Turnout: 61%

	Votes	Share %	Change %
Julia Drown, Labour	22,260	51.3	4.5
Simon Coombs, Conservative	14,919	34.4	−1.4
Geoff Brewer, Liberal Democrat	5,165	11.9	−2.5
Vicki Sharp, UK Independence party	713	1.6	n/a
Roly Gillard, R & R Loony	327	0.8	n/a

Andrew Roth says: "NHS high flyer and multiple-cause groupie"

Recent parliamentary career: information committee (2001–); health committee (2001–)
Background: NHS finance director; member of Greenpeace, Friends of the Earth, CND, Amnesty
Born: August 23 1962 in London
Education: Hampstead Comprehensive School
Higher education: Oxford, University College
Constituency: industrial Wiltshire boom town plus rural village wards, posh residential

Duncan, Alan
Conservative MP for Rutland and Melton since 1992

Majority: 8,612 (18.3%)
Turnout: 65%

	Votes	Share %	Change %
Alan Duncan, Conservative	22,621	48.1	2.3
Matthew O'Callaghan, Labour	14,009	29.8	0.8
Kim Lee, Liberal Democrat	8,386	17.8	−1.4
Peter Baker, UK Independence party	1,223	2.6	n/a
Christopher Davies, Green party	817	1.7	n/a

Andrew Roth says: "economic libertarian who rushes in where more prudent Tories fear to tread"

Recent parliamentary career: opposition spokesperson, FO (2001–); opposition spokesperson, DTI (1999–2001); opposition spokesperson, DoH (1998–99); helped secure William Hague's election as leader (1997); called for legislation of drugs (1994)
Background: oil trader and adviser; author of books on politics
Born: March 31 1957 in Rickmansworth
Education: Merchant Taylors' School, Northwood
Higher education: Harvard University; Oxford, St John's
Constituency: revived independent county of Rutland plus surrounds, almost entirely rural

Duncan, Peter
Conservative MP for Galloway and Upper Nithsdale since 2001

Majority: 74 (0.2%)
Turnout: 68.1%

	Votes	Share %	Change %
Peter Duncan, Conservative	12,222	34	3.5
Malcolm Fleming, Scottish National party	12,148	33.8	−10.1
Thomas Sloan, Labour	7,258	20.2	3.9
Neil Wallace, Liberal Democrat	3,698	10.3	3.9
Andy Harvey, Scottish Socialist party	588	1.6	n/a

Maiden speech: "my particular accent has not emanated much from the Conservative benches in recent times. I am happy to be the advance party for others who will surely follow"

Recent parliamentary career: entered parliament 2001 taking seat from SNP; first Conservative MP elected in Scotland since 1992; Scottish affairs committee (2001–)
Background: locally-born freelance business consultant; runs family textile business; liberal Eurosceptic
Born: July 10 1965
Education: Ardossan Academy
Higher education: Birmingham University
Constituency: south Scotland isolated, scenic lowlands, most agricultural constituency in Britain

Duncan Smith, Iain
Conservative MP for Chingford and Woodford Green since 1997; Chingford (1992–7)

Majority: 5,487 (14.8%)
Turnout: 58.5%

	Votes	Share %	Change %
Iain Duncan Smith, Conservative	17,834	48.2	0.7
Jessica Webb, Labour	12,347	33.4	−1.2
John Beanse, Liberal Democrat	5,739	15.5	0
Jean Griffin, British National party	1,062	2.9	0.5

Andrew Roth says: "the right-wing Tory Eurosceptic's top sane intellectual ... a representative of the political squirearchy, bone dry on the economy, strong on defence"

Recent parliamentary career: elected leader, Conservative party (2001) with 61% of membership vote; shadow secretary of state, MoD (1999–2001); shadow secretary of state, DSS (1997–99); well-connected and respected in US, especially in defence circles
Background: Sandhurst-educated Scots Guard captain; worked for GEC Marconi; Jane's Information Group; author and novelist; company director; his great-grandmother was Japanese; his wife comes from aristocratic Buckinghamshire family
Born: April 9 1954 in Edinburgh
Education: HMS Conway; Royal Military Academy, Sandhurst
Higher education: Perugia University, Italy
Constituency: centred on mainstream Essex town of Chingford, runs through Epping Forest to Upper Walthamstow

Dunwoody, Rt Hon Gwyneth
Labour MP for Crewe and Nantwich since 1983; Crewe (1974–83); Exeter (1966–70)

Majority: 9,906 (23.8%)
Turnout: 60.2%

	Votes	Share %	Change %
Gwyneth Dunwoody, Labour	22,556	54.3	−3.9
Donald Potter, Conservative	12,650	30.5	3.5
David Cannon, Liberal Democrat	5,595	13.5	1.8
Roger Croston, UK Independence party	746	1.8	n/a

Andrew Roth says: "a brave, bouncy, centre-right radical, Labour's longest-serving woman MP ... once the battle-hammer of the hard left'"

Recent parliamentary career: joint chair, transport, local government and the regions committee (2001–); chair, environment, transport and regional affairs committee (1997–2001); environment sub-committee (1997–2001); chair, transport subcommittee (1997–2001); challenged for speakership (1999)

Background: parliamentary consultant; Labour's longest-serving female MP; speaks Dutch, French and Italian; daughter of Labour general secretary, Morgan Philips

Born: December 12 1930 in Fulham
Education: Fulham County Secondary School
Constituency: socially and politically divided seat in Cheshire: working-class Crewe plus affluent Nantwich

E

Eagle, Angela
Labour MP for Wallasey since 1992

Majority: 12,276 (32.8%)
Turnout: 57.6%

	Votes	Share %	Change %
Angela Eagle, Labour	22,718	60.8	–3.8
Lesley Rennie, Conservative	10,442	28	4.1
Peter Reisdorf, Liberal Democrat	4,186	11.2	2.9

Andrew Roth says: "tough-minded and hardworking though marred by a droning, monotonous presentation and her caution as a left-winger in a Blair government"

Recent parliamentary career: junior minister, HO (2001–); junior minister, DSS (1998–2001)
Background: researcher, press officer, parliamentary officer for COHSE trade union; columnist for Tribune; twin sister is also an MP; openly lesbian
Born: February 17 1961 in Bridlington
Education: Formby High School
Higher education: Oxford, St John's
Constituency: outer Wirral suburbs astride the Mersey, in economic decline

Eagle, Maria
Labour MP for Liverpool Garston since 1997

Majority: 12,494 (38.3%)
Turnout: 50.2%

	Votes	Share %	Change %
Maria Eagle, Labour	20,043	61.4	0.1
Paula Keaveney, Liberal Democrat	7,549	23.1	4.1
Helen Sutton, Conservative	5,059	15.5	–0.2

Andrew Roth says: "is considered more radical, less cautious and more witty [than her MP twin sister]"

Recent parliamentary career: junior minister, DWP (2001–); PPS to John Hutton (1999–2001)
Background: solicitor; played junior cricket for Lancashire, chess for Lancashire and England; twin sister is also an MP
Born: February 17 1961 in Bridlington
Education: Formby High School
Higher education: College of Law, Lancaster Gate; Oxford, Pembroke
Constituency: divided suburban south-east Liverpool, mixed attractive residential and huge Speke council estate

Edwards, Huw
Labour MP for Monmouth since 1997; Monmouth (1991–92)

Majority: 384 (0.9%)
Turnout: 71.5%

	Votes	Share %	Change %
Huw Edwards, Labour	19,021	42.8	−4.9
Roger Evans, Conservative	18,637	41.9	2.7
Neil Parker, Liberal Democrat	5,080	11.4	1.8
Marc Hubbard, Plaid Cymru	1,068	2.4	1.3
David Rowlands, UK Independence party	656	1.5	n/a

Andrew Roth says: "thoughtful, restrained Christian Fabian loyalist"

Recent parliamentary career: Welsh affairs committee (1997–2001)
Background: lecturer in social policy; research consultant; member of Amnesty, One World Action, Shelter, Gwalia male choir
Born: April 12 1953 in Carshalton
Education: Eastfields High School, Mitchum
Higher education: York University; Manchester Polytechnic
Constituency: border valleys between England and Wales, rural small towns and villages

Efford, Clive
Labour MP for Eltham since 1997

Majority: 6,996 (20.7%)
Turnout: 58.8%

	Votes	Share %	Change %
Clive Efford, Labour	17,855	52.8	−1.8
Sharon Massey, Conservative	10,859	32.1	0.9
Martin Morris, Liberal Democrat	4,121	12.2	3.7
Terry Jones, UK Independence party	706	2.1	n/a
Andrew Graham, Independent	251	0.7	n/a

Andrew Roth says: "local municipal politician with a long record as a caring campaigner"

Recent parliamentary career: procedure committee (1997–2001)
Background: licensed London taxi driver; Greenwich councillor; supports Millwall FC
Born: July 10 1958 in London
Education: Walworth Comprehensive School
Constituency: south part of Greenwich, almost wholly white middle class and suburban

Ellman, Louise
Labour MP for Liverpool Riverside since 1997

Majority: 13,950 (54.7%)
Turnout: 34.1%

	Votes	Share %	Change %
Louise Ellman, Labour	18,201	71.4	1
Richard Marbrow, Liberal Democrat	4,251	16.7	3.4
Judith Edwards, Conservative	2,142	8.4	−1.1
Cathy Wilson, Socialist Alliance	909	3.6	n/a

Andrew Roth says: "one of the Blair government's most loyal cheerleaders"

Recent parliamentary career: transport, local government, and the regions committee (2001–); environment, transport and regional affairs committee (1997–2001); environment subcommittee (1997–2001)
Background: lecturer in further education; Open University counsellor; Lanacashire councillor and leader
Born: November 14 1945 in Manchester
Education: Manchester High School for Girls
Higher education: York University; Hull University
Constituency: Liverpool city centre, high unemployment, UK's worst turnout in 2001 (34.1%)

Ennis, Jeff
Labour MP for Barnsley East and Mexborough since 1997; Barnsley East (1996–97)

Majority: 16,789 (51.6%)
Turnout: 49.5%

	Votes	Share %	Change %
Jeff Ennis, Labour	21,945	67.5	–5.6
Sharron Brook, Liberal Democrat	5,156	15.9	5.5
Matthew Offord, Conservative	4,024	12.4	1
Terry Robinson, Socialist Labour party	722	2.2	–0.6
George Savage, UK Independence party	662	2	n/a

Andrew Roth says: "physically enormous but a local rather than a national big wheel"

Recent parliamentary career: education and skills committee (2001–); PPS to Tessa Jowell (1997–2001)
Background: primary and middle-school teacher; Barnsley councillor and leader
Born: November 13 1952 in Grimethorpe
Education: Hemsworth Grammar School; Redland College, Bristol
Constituency: South Yorkshire, ex-mining seat outside Rotherham, mostly made up of old Hemsworth seat, very white

Etherington, Bill
Labour MP for Sunderland North since 1992

Majority: 13,354 (44.8%)
Turnout: 49%

	Votes	Share %	Change %
Bill Etherington, Labour	18,685	62.7	–5.5
Michael Harris, Conservative	5,331	17.9	1.2
John Lennox, Liberal Democrat	3,599	12.1	1.7
Neil Herron, Independent	1,518	5.1	n/a
Dave Guynan, British National party	687	2.3	n/a

Andrew Roth says: "highly-conscientious and thoughtful left-fundamentalist"

Recent parliamentary career: rebelled three times in 1997 parliament
Background: shipyard fitter; mine fitter; NUM official
Born: July 17 1941
Education: Redby Infant and Junior School; Monkwearmouth Grammar School
Constituency: innercity north-east seat on coast, skilled manual, new industry but high unemployment

Evans, Nigel
Conservative MP for Ribble Valley since 1992

Majority: 11,238 (22.9%)
Turnout: 66.2%

	Votes	Share %	Change %
Nigel Evans, Conservative	25,308	51.5	4.8
Mike Carr, Liberal Democrat	14,070	28.6	–6.5
Marcus Johnstone, Labour	9,793	19.9	4.1

Andrew Roth says: "super-ambitious India-rubber bantamweight"

Recent parliamentary career: opposition spokesperson, constitutional affairs (1997–); introduced private member's bill on planning appeals (2001)
Background: ran family newsagent's for 11 years; West Glamorgan councillor; worked on three US presidential elections
Born: November 10 1957 in Swansea
Education: Dyvenor School, Swansea

Higher education: Swansea University
Constituency: scenic uplands in rural north Lancashire, affluent towns and villages

Ewing, Annabelle
Scottish National party MP for Perth since 2001

Majority: 48 (0.1%)
Turnout: 61.5%

	Votes	Share %	Change %
Annabelle Ewing, Scottish National party	11,237	29.7	–6.7
Elizabeth Smith, Conservative	11,189	29.6	0.3
Marion Dingwall, Labour	9,638	25.5	0.7
Ms Vicki Harris, Liberal Democrat	4,853	12.8	4.8
Frank Byrne, Scottish Socialist party	899	2.4	n/a

Maiden speech: "the Union is not working for Scotland… it is only with independence that Scotland can move forward"

Recent parliamentary career: entered parliament 2001
Background: solicitor; worked for EU legal services; daughter of president of SNP, Winnie Ewing
Born: January 1 1960
Education: Craigholme School, Glasgow
Higher education: Amsterdam University Europa Instituut; Johns Hopkins University
Constituency: big, scenic seat in lowland Scotland

F

Fabricant, Michael
Conservative MP for Lichfield since 1997; Mid Staffordshire (1992–97)

Majority: 4,426 (10.6%)
Turnout: 65.3%

	Votes	Share %	Change %
Michael Fabricant, Conservative	20,480	49.1	6.2
Martin Machray, Labour	16,054	38.5	–3.9
Phillip Bennion, Liberal Democrat	4,462	10.7	–0.6
John Phazey, UK Independence party	684	1.6	n/a

Andrew Roth says: "bright, thrusting right-wing Tory Eurosceptic, sketchwriters find it impossible to avoid referring to his strange hair"

Recent parliamentary career: culture, media and sport committee (2001–); information committee (2001–); home affairs committee (1999–2001); catering committee (1999–2001)
Background: economist; chartered electronics engineer; radio broadcaster; cochairman of all-party internet group
Born: June 12 1950 in Brighton
Education: Hove and Sussex Grammar School, Brighton
Higher education: London University; Oxford, Sussex; Loughborough University; University of Southern California, USA
Constituency: pleasant cathedral city on border of West Midlands and the Potteries

Fallon, Michael
Conservative MP for Sevenoaks since 1997; Darlington (1983–92)

Majority: 10,154 (23.8%)
Turnout: 63.9%

	Votes	Share %	Change %
Michael Fallon, Conservative	21,052	49.4	4
Caroline Humphreys, Labour	10,898	25.6	1
Clive Gray, Liberal Democrat	9,214	21.6	-2.5
Lisa Hawkins, UK Independence party	1,155	2.7	n/a
Mark Ellis, Pathfinders	295	0.7	0.2

Andrew Roth says: "hard-right fundamentalist and leading innovative intellectual"

Recent parliamentary career: Treasury committee (1999–); Treasury subcommittee (1999–); opposition spokesperson, Treasury (1997–98)
Background: company director and adviser; Conservative Research Department (1975–78)
Born: May 14 1952 in Perth
Education: Epsom College; Craigflower School, Fife
Higher education: St Andrews University
Constituency: affluent middle class commuter belt in West Kent

Farrelly, Paul
Labour MP for Newcastle-under-Lyme since 2001

Majority: 9,986 (25.8%)
Turnout: 58.8%

	Votes	Share %	Change %
Paul Farrelly, Labour	20,650	53.4	-3.1
Mike Flynn, Conservative	10,664	27.6	6.2
Jerry Roodhouse, Liberal Democrat	5,993	15.5	1.5
Robert Fyson, Independent	773	2	n/a
Paul Godfrey, UK Independence party	594	1.5	n/a

Maiden speech: "I can safely say that I am the only new Labour member of parliament to be the grandson of a rabbit trapper from County Meath"

Recent parliamentary career: entered parliament 2001
Background: journalist; most recently city editor of the *Observer*; previously *Independent on Sunday* and Reuters; corporate financier
Born: March 2 1962
Education: Wolstanton Grammar School
Higher education: Oxford, St Edmund Hall
Constituency: ex-mining and Potteries, plus new industries and Keele University

Field, Rt Hon Frank
Labour MP for Birkenhead since 1979

Majority: 15,591 (53.8%)
Turnout: 47.7%

	Votes	Share %	Change %
Frank Field, Labour	20,418	70.5	-0.3
Brian Stewart, Conservative	4,827	16.7	1.5
Roy Wood, Liberal Democrat	3,722	12.9	3.9

Andrew Roth says: "relentless and priest-like maverick crusader against poverty and social inequality"

Recent parliamentary career: minister of state, DSS (1997–98)
Background: director, Child Poverty Action Group and Low Pay Unit; further education lecturer; columnist for Catholic Herald; Hounslow councillor; author of several books on welfare
Born: July 16 1942 in London
Education: St Clements Danes Grammar School
Higher education: Hull University
Constituency: innercity seat across the Mersey from Liverpool

Field, Mark
Conservative MP for Cities of London and Westminster since 2001

Majority: 4,499 (13.2%)
Turnout: 47.2%

	Votes	Share %	Change %
Mark Field, Conservative	15,737	46.3	−1
Mike Katz, Labour	11,238	33.1	−2
Martin Horwood, Liberal Democrat	5,218	15.4	3.1
Hugo Charlton, Green party	1,318	3.9	n/a
Colin Merton, UK Independence party	464	1.4	n/a

Maiden speech: "We need low income tax and a low capital gains tax regime to ensure that entrepreneurs are not persuaded to leave these shores in a brain drain"

Recent parliamentary career: entered parliament 2001
Background: solicitor; consultant; runs own publishing and recruitment agency; Kensington and Chelsea councillor
Born: October 6 1964
Education: Reading School
Higher education: St Edmund Hall, Oxford
Constituency: rare innercity safe Conservative seat, famous London sights

Fisher, Mark
Labour MP for Stoke-on-Trent Central since 1983

Majority: 11,845 (41.9%)
Turnout: 47.4%

	Votes	Share %	Change %
Mark Fisher, Labour	17,170	60.7	−5.5
Jill Clark, Conservative	5,325	18.8	2.1
Gavin Webb, Liberal Democrat	4,148	14.7	2.8
Richard Wise, Independent	1,657	5.9	n/a

Andrew Roth says: "realistic voice of sweet cultural reason"

Recent parliamentary career: junior minister, DCMS (1997–98)
Background: documentary and film producer; scriptwriter; headteacher; cultural administrator
Born: October 29 1944 in Woking
Education: Eton College
Higher education: Cambridge, Trinity
Constituency: pottery industry, skilled manual

Fitzpatrick, Jim
Labour MP for Poplar and Canning Town since 1997

Majority: 14,104 (41.4%)
Turnout: 45.4%

	Votes	Share %	Change %
Jim Fitzpatrick, Labour	20,862	61.2	−2
Robert Marr, Conservative	6,758	19.8	4.8
Alexi Sugden, Liberal Democrat	3,795	11.1	0.7
Paul Borg, British National party	1,743	5.1	−2.2
Kambiz Boomla, Socialist Alliance	950	2.8	n/a

Andrew Roth says: "assiduous Scots-born, internationally-focussed multi-cause groupie"

Recent parliamentary career: PPS to Alan Milburn (1999–)
Background: award-winning fireman for 23 years; trade union activist (FBU); member of Amnesty, War on Want, Greenpeace
Born: April 4 1952 in Glasgow

Education: Holyrood Senior Secondary Modern School, Glasgow
Constituency: changing London Docklands, some costly houses, much poverty too

Fitzsimons, Lorna
Labour MP for Rochdale since 1997

Majority: 5,655 (14.3%)
Turnout: 56.7%

	Votes	Share %	Change %
Lorna Fitzsimons, Labour	19,406	49.2	–0.2
Paul Rowan, Liberal Democrat	13,751	34.9	–5.1
Elaina Cohen, Conservative	5,274	13.4	4.6
Nick Harvey, Green party	728	1.9	n/a
Mohammed Salim, Independent	253	0.6	n/a

Andrew Roth says: "young, very ambitious former lobbyist"

Recent parliamentary career: PPS to Robin Cook (2001–); modernisation of the House of Commons committee (1999–); procedure committee (1997–2001)
Background: artist; lobbyist; president of NUS; pro-PR member of Labour campaign for electoral reform; Young Communicator of the Year (1995–96)
Born: August 6 1967 in Wardle
Education: Wardle High School
Higher education: Loughborough College of Art and Design
Constituency: changing ex mill town in Greater Manchester, large Asian community

Flight, Howard
Conservative MP for Arundel and South Downs since 1997

Majority: 13,704 (29.8%)
Turnout: 64.7%

	Votes	Share %	Change %
Howard Flight, Conservative	23,969	52.2	–0.9
Derek Deedman, Liberal Democrat	10,265	22.4	–3.3
Charles Taylor, Labour	9,488	20.7	2.4
Robert Perrin, UK Independence party	2,167	4.7	n/a

Andrew Roth says: "thoughtful and assiduous self-described 'Essex man'"

Recent parliamentary career: opposition spokesperson, Treasury (2001–); opposition spokesperson, Treasury (1999–2001)
Background: investment adviser and manager; merchant banker
Born: June 16 1948 in London
Education: Brentwood School
Higher education: University of Michigan, USA; Cambridge, Magdalene
Constituency: West Sussex, rich, rural, and retired

Flint, Caroline
Labour MP for Don Valley since 1997

Majority: 9,520 (26.0%)
Turnout: 55.3%

	Votes	Share %	Change %
Caroline Flint, Labour	20,009	54.6	–3.7
James Browne, Conservative	10,489	28.6	4
Philip Smith, Liberal Democrat	4,089	11.2	1.5
Terry Wilde, Independent	800	2.2	n/a
David Cooper, UK Independence party	777	2.1	n/a
Nigel Ball, Socialist Labour Party	466	1.3	–1.1

Andrew Roth says: "loyal Blairite with a soft line in stooge questions"

Recent parliamentary career: PPS to Peter Hain (2001–); administration committee (2001–)
Background: policy officer; senior researcher; trade union activist (GMB)
Born: September 20 1961 in St John's Wood
Education: Twickenham Girls' School
Higher education: Richmond Tertiary College; East Anglia University
Constituency: curls around edge of Doncaster, has lost most of its pits

Flook, Adrian
Conservative MP for Taunton since 2001

Majority: 235 (0.4%)
Turnout: 67.6%

	Votes	Share %	Change %
Adrian Flook, Conservative	23,033	41.7	3
Jackie Ballard, Liberal Democrat	22,798	41.3	–1.4
Andrew Govier, Labour	8,254	15	1.5
Michael Canton, UK Independence party	1,140	2.1	n/a

Maiden speech: "If I have one long-term aim as a MP, it is to help the rural and urban elements of my constituency to understand that they rely heavily on each other"

Recent parliamentary career: entered parliament 2001, taking seat from Lib Dem; culture, media and sport committee (2001–)
Background: merchant banker; PR; involved in cancer charities; Wandsworth councillor
Born: July 9 1963
Education: King Edward School, Bath
Constituency: west Somerset to Devon border, light industry, council estates and surrounding farmland

Flynn, Paul
Labour MP for Newport West since 1987

Majority: 9,304 (26.5%)
Turnout: 58.7%

	Votes	Share %	Change %
Paul Flynn, Labour	18,489	52.7	–7.8
William Morgan, Conservative	9,185	26.2	1.8
Veronica Watkins, Liberal Democrat	4,095	11.7	2
Anthony Salkeld, Plaid Cymru	2,510	7.2	5.6
Hugh Moelwyn-Hughes, UK Independence party	506	1.4	n/a
Terry Cavill, British National party	278	0.8	n/a

Andrew Roth says: "verbally resourceful pixie who can take the skin off opponents with a light whip tipped with barbs from his well-furnished bilingual mind"

Recent parliamentary career: noted campaigner, especially on drug-law reform; member, UK Delegation Council of Europe; secretary, Welsh Group Labour MPs (1997–)
Background: chemist in steel industry; research officer; MEP (1984–87); author
Born: February 9 1935 in Cardiff
Education: St Llityd's School, Cardiff
Higher education: Cardiff University
Constituency: first town in Wales on the M4, middle class residential plus rural surround

Follett, Barbara
Labour MP for Stevenage since 1997

Majority: 8,566 (20.2%)
Turnout: 61.4%

	Votes	Share %	Change %
Barbara Follett, Labour	22,025	51.9	–3.4
Graeme Quar, Conservative	13,459	31.7	–1.1
Harry Davies, Liberal Democrat	6,027	14.2	5.3
Steve Glennon, Socialist Alliance	449	1.1	n/a
Antal Losonczi, Independent	320	0.8	n/a
Sarah Bell, ProLife Alliance	173	0.4	0

Andrew Roth says: "left-of-centre Kinnockite, over-publicised for her roles as a political feminist and as wife of millionaire Labour-supporting Ken Follett"

Recent parliamentary career: modernisation of the House of Commons committee (2001–); international development committee (1997–2001); her husband Ken criticised Tony Blair in a much-publicised article (2000)
Background: lecturer in cross-cultural communications; research associate; director of Emily's list (supporting women parliamentary candidates); married to novelist Ken Follett; formerly married to South African anti-apartheid activist, murdered (1978)
Born: December 25 1942 in Jamaica
Education: Sandford School, Ethiopia; Ellerslie Girls' High, South Africa
Higher education: London School of Economics; Open University; Cape Town University
Constituency: new town north of London

Forth, Rt Hon Eric
Conservative MP for Bromley and Chislehurst since 1997; Mid Worcestershire (1983–97)

Majority: 9,037 (20.9%)
Turnout: 62.9%

	Votes	Share %	Change %
Eric Forth, Conservative	21,412	49.5	3.2
Sue Polydorou, Labour	12,375	28.6	3.4
Geoff Payne, Liberal Democrat	8,180	18.9	–4.9
Rob Bryant, UK Independence party	1,264	2.9	n/a

Andrew Roth says: "hard-headed, independent-minded 'rogue parliamentarian' and described as 'one of the least popular men in British politics'"

Recent parliamentary career: shadow leader of the House of Commons (2001–); standards and privileges committee (1999–2001); minister of state, DFEE (1995–97)
Background: manager in industry; Brentwood councillor
Born: September 9 1944 in Glasgow
Education: Jordanhill College School, Glasgow
Higher education: Glasgow University; Jordanhill College of Education
Constituency: outer London suburbs, mainly affluent middle class

Foster, Rt Hon Derek
Labour MP for Bishop Auckland since 1979

Majority: 13,926 (36.1%)
Turnout: 57.2%

	Votes	Share %	Change %
Derek Foster, Labour	22,680	58.8	–7.1
Fiona McNish, Conservative	8,754	22.7	2.5
Chris Foote Wood, Liberal Democrat	6,073	15.8	6.5
Carl Bennett, Green party	1,052	2.7	n/a

Andrew Roth says: "now seriously disaffected former centre-right Kinnockite"

Recent parliamentary career: chair, education and employment committee (1997–2001); chair, employment subcommittee (1997–2001); education subcommittee (1997–2001)
Background: education administrator; Tyne and Wear councillor
Born: June 25 1937 in Sunderland
Education: Bede Grammar School, Sunderland
Higher education: Oxford University, St Catherine's
Constituency: south-west Durham, ex-mining, working-class, unexpectedly rural in parts

Foster, Don
Liberal Democrat MP for Bath since 1992

Majority: 9,894 (21.4%)
Turnout: 64.9%

	Votes	Share %	Change %
Don Foster, Liberal Democrat	23,372	50.5	2
Ashley Fox, Conservative	13,478	29.1	–2.1
Marilyn Hawkings, Labour	7,269	15.7	–0.7
Mike Boulton, Green party	1,469	3.2	n/a
Andrew Tettenborn, UK Independence party	708	1.5	n/a

Andrew Roth says: "gruffly-reasonable, strongly-motivated but moderate education reformer"

Recent parliamentary career: Lib Dem spokesperson, DTLGR (2001–); spokesperson, DETR (1999–2001); spokesperson, DFEE (1995–99)
Background: science teacher and lecturer; author of science textbooks; Avon councillor
Born: March 31 1947 in Preston
Education: Lancaster Royal Grammar School
Higher education: Keele University; Bath University
Constituency: elegant, rich spa and tourist town

Foster, Michael Jabez
Labour MP for Hastings and Rye since 1997

Majority: 4,308 (10.5%)
Turnout: 58.4%

	Votes	Share %	Change %
Michael Foster, Labour	19,402	47.1	12.7
Mark Coote, Conservative	15,094	36.6	7.4
Graeme Peters, Liberal Democrat	4,266	10.4	–17.6
Alan Coomber, UK Independence party	911	2.2	n/a
Sally Phillips, Green party	721	1.8	n/a
Mrs Gillian Bargery, Independent	486	1.2	n/a
John Ord-Clarke, Official Monster Raving Loony party	198	0.5	0.2
Brett McLean, R & R Loony	140	0.3	n/a

Andrew Roth says: "Christian socialist native son who protects local fishermen"

Recent parliamentary career: PPS to Lord Goldsmith and Harriet Harman (2001–); standards and privileges committee (1997–)
Background: solicitor, specialising in employment law; legal adviser to GMB trade union
Born: February 26 1946 in Hastings
Education: Hastings Grammar School; Hastings Secondary Boys' School
Higher education: Leicester University
Constituency: declining seaside town in East Sussex, unemployment and rejected bypass are key issues

Foster, Michael John
Labour MP for Worcester since 1997

Majority: 5,766 (13.1%)
Turnout: 62%

	Votes	Share %	Change %
Michael Foster, Labour	21,478	48.6	−1.5
Richard Adams, Conservative	15,712	35.5	−0.2
Paul Chandler, Liberal Democrat	5,578	12.6	0.1
Richard Chamings, UK Independence party	1,442	3.3	n/a

Andrew Roth says: "another on-message loyal Labour recruit from the chalkface"

Recent parliamentary career: PPS to Margaret Hodge (2001–); proposed private member's bill to ban foxhunting (1998)
Background: accountancy lecturer; management accountant; financial planner, Jaguar cars
Born: March 14 1963 in Oswestry
Education: Great Wyrley High School, Staffordshire
Higher education: Wolverhampton Polytechnic and University
Constituency: self-confident south Midlands town

Foulkes, George
Labour MP for Carrick, Cumnock, and Doon Valley since 1983; South Ayrshire (1979–83)

Majority: 14,856 (37.0%)
Turnout: 61.8%

	Votes	Share %	Change %
George Foulkes, Labour	22,174	55.3	−4.5
Gordon Miller, Conservative	7,318	18.3	1.3
Tom Wilson, Scottish National party	6,258	15.6	−1.1
Amy Roger, Liberal Democrat	2,932	7.3	2
Amanda McFarlane, Scottish Socialist party	1,058	2.6	n/a
James McDaid, Socialist Labour party	367	0.9	n/a
Martyn Davidson, UK Independence party	n/a		

Andrew Roth says: "chastened, volatile and extrovert soft-left internationalist"

Recent parliamentary career: minister of state, SO (2001–); junior minister, DFID (1997–2001)
Background: director of voluntary organisations, including Age Concern Scotland; Lothian councillor
Born: January 21 1942 in Oswestry
Education: Keith Grammar School, Banffshire; Haberdashers' Askes School, Hertfordshire
Higher education: Edinburgh University
Constituency: coastal south Ayrshire, ex-mining, industrial, seaside resorts and farmland

Fox, Dr Liam
Conservative MP for Woodspring since 1992

Majority: 8,798 (18.1%)
Turnout: 68.7%

	Votes	Share %	Change %
Dr Liam Fox, Conservative	21,297	43.7	−0.7
Chanel Stevens, Labour	12,499	25.6	4.9
Colin Eldridge, Liberal Democrat	11,816	24.2	−6.2
David Shopland, Independent	1,412	2.9	n/a
Dr Richard Lawson, Green party	1,282	2.6	1.4
Fraser Crean, UK Independence party	452	0.9	n/a

Andrew Roth says: "assiduous, articulate, displaced partisan"

Recent parliamentary career: opposition spokesperson, DoH (1999–); opposition spokesperson, constitutional affairs (1997–99)
Background: Scottish-born GP; medical lecturer; Catholic opponent of abortion
Born: September 22 1961 in Lanarkshire
Education: St Bride's High School, East Kilbride
Higher education: Glasgow University
Constituency: prosperous commuters on coast south of Bristol

Francis, Hywel
Labour MP for Aberavon since 2001

Majority: 16,108 (53.3%)
Turnout: 60.8%

	Votes	Share %	Change %
Hywel Francis, Labour	19,063	63.1	–8.2
Lisa Turnbull, Plaid Cymru	2,955	9.8	4
Chris Davies, Liberal Democrat	2,933	9.7	–1.6
Ali Miraj, Conservative	2,296	7.6	–0.3
Andrew Tutton, RP	1,960	6.5	n/a
Captain Beany, Bean	727	2.4	n/a
Martin Chapman, Socialist Alliance	256	0.9	n/a

Maiden speech: "I want to focus specifically on the citizenship rights of disabled people and their carers in relation to the economy and to the whole of society"

Recent parliamentary career: entered parliament 2001; Welsh affairs committee (2001–)
Background: adviser to Welsh secretary Paul Murphy; professor of continuing education at Swansea University; vice president, Welsh Labour history society; son of Dai Francis – former Welsh miners' leader and chair of Wales TUC
Born: June 6 1946
Education: Whitchurch Grammar School, Cardiff
Higher education: University of Wales, Swansea (UWS)
Constituency: really Port Talbot, very working-class, threat to local steel industry

Francois, Mark
Conservative MP for Rayleigh since 2001

Majority: 8,290 (19.4%)
Turnout: 61%

	Votes	Share %	Change %
Mark Francois, Conservative	21,434	50.1	0.4
Paul Clark, Labour	13,144	30.7	1.8
Geoff Williams, Liberal Democrat	6,614	15.5	–4.3
Colin Morgan, UK Independence party	1,581	3.7	n/a

Maiden speech: "We are a historically tolerant people, and we are willing to negotiate and cooperate, but we will not be subsumed by a foreign superstate that ignores our traditions and undermines our laws"

Recent parliamentary career: entered parliament 2001; environmental audit committee (2001–)
Background: Essex-born, director of lobbying firm; Basildon councillor; member of Territorial Army
Born: August 14 1965 in London
Education: Nicholas Comprehensive School, Basildon
Higher education: Bristol University; London University
Constituency: Essex suburbs north-west of Southend-on-Sea

G

Gale, Roger
Conservative MP for North Thanet since 1983

Majority: 6,650 (15.9%)
Turnout: 59.3%

	Votes	Share %	Change %
Roger Gale, Conservative	21,050	50.3	6.2
James Stewart Laing, Labour	14,400	34.4	–4
Seth Thanet, Liberal Democrat	4,603	11	–0.4
John Moore, UK Independence party	980	2.3	n/a
David Short, Independent	440	1.1	n/a
Thomas Holmes, National Front	395	0.9	n/a

Andrew Roth says: "seemingly contradictory because he is socially more liberal than his occasionally bellicose partisan language allows"

Recent parliamentary career: Conservative party vice-chairman (2001–);broadcasting committee (1997–2001)
Background: television producer, director, and broadcaster; produced Newsbeat, Radio 4's Today programme and Blue Peter
Born: August 20 1943 in Poole, Dorset
Education: Hardye's School, Dorchester
Higher education: Guildhall School of Music and Drama
Constituency: Kent coast around Margate, includes Herne Bay

Galloway, George
Labour MP for Glasgow Kelvin since 1997; Glasgow Hillhead (1987–97)

Majority: 7,260 (27.1%)
Turnout: 43.6%

	Votes	Share %	Change %
George Galloway, Labour	12,014	44.8	–6.2
Tasmin Mayberry, Liberal Democrat	4,754	17.7	3.5
Frank Rankin, Scottish National party	4,513	16.8	–4.6
Davina Rankin, Conservative	2,388	8.9	–1.9
Heather Ritchie, Scottish Socialist party	1,847	6.9	n/a
Tim Shand, Green party	1,286	4.8	n/a

Andrew Roth says: "suffers from shin kicking of leaders, over-the-toppism and pariah worship; glories in his ability to rub more people the wrong way faster than anyone else"

Recent parliamentary career: attacked UK strikes on Iraq (1998 and 1999); sympathetic to Arab causes
Background: Labour party organiser; general secretary, War on Want; Kashmir Award 1998; Hilal-I-Quaid-Azam for services to democracy in Pakistan
Born: August 16 1954 in Dundee
Education: Charleston Primary; Harris Academy, Dunfermline
Constituency: grand inner and West End of Glasgow, includes Hillhead

Gapes, Mike
Labour MP for Ilford South since 1992

Majority: 13,997 (33.9%)
Turnout: 54.3%

	Votes	Share %	Change %
Mike Gapes, Labour	24,619	59.6	1.1
Suresh Kumar, Conservative	10,622	25.7	–4.4
Ralph Scott, Liberal Democrat	4,647	11.3	5
Harun Khan, UK Independence party	1,407	3.4	n/a

Andrew Roth says: "cautious, knowledgeable, left-of-centre intellectual"

Recent parliamentary career: PPS to Lord Rooker (2001–); defence committee (1999–2001), PPS to Paul Murphy (1997–99)
Background: research officer, Labour party; Labour party student organiser
Born: September 4 1952 in Wanstead

Education: Manford Primary School; Buckhurst Hill County High School, Essex
Higher education: Middlesex Polytechnic; Cambridge, Fitzwilliam
Constituency: commercial shopping centre in north-east London, large Asian community

Gardiner, Barry
Labour MP for Brent North since 1997

Majority: 10,205 (30.1%)
Turnout: 57.7%

	Votes	Share %	Change %
Barry Gardiner, Labour	20,149	59.4	8.7
Philip Allott, Conservative	9,944	29.3	−10.8
Paul Lorber, Liberal Democrat	3,846	11.3	3.2

Andrew Roth says: "one of the best-educated and most internationally experienced MPs"

Recent parliamentary career: public accounts committee (1999–); broadcasting committee (1998–2001); procedure committee (1997–2001);
Background: company partner; international loss adjuster; lecturer at Moscow Academy of National Economy; Cambridge councillor and mayor
Born: March 10 1957 in Glasgow
Education: Haileybury College; Glasgow High School
Higher education: St Andrews University; Harvard University (JF Kennedy scholarship); Cambridge, Corpus Christi
Constituency: outer north-west London, middle class residential, significant Asian population

Garnier, Edward QC
Conservative MP for Harborough since 1992

Majority: 5,252 (11.3%)
Turnout: 63.3%

	Votes	Share %	Change %
Edward Garnier, Conservative	20,748	44.7	2.9
Jill Hope, Liberal Democrat	15,496	33.4	3.9
Raj Jethwa, Labour	9,271	20	−5.2
David Knight, UK Independence party	912	2	n/a

Andrew Roth says: "too sophisticated for simple fanaticism; otherwise a loyal, fairly orthodox partisan"

Recent parliamentary career: shadow attorney general (1999–2001); opposition spokesperson, LCD (1997–99)
Background: barrister; coauthor of three books and contributor to Halsbury's Laws of England; noted Eurosceptic
Born: October 26 1952 in Germany
Education: Wellington College
Higher education: College of Law, London; Oxford, Jesus
Constituency: centred on busy town of Market Harborough, some countryside too

George, Andrew
Liberal Democrat MP for St Ives since 1997

Majority: 10,053 (20.4%)
Turnout: 66.4%

	Votes	Share %	Change %
Andrew George, Liberal Democrat	25,413	51.6	7.1
Joanna Richardson, Conservative	15,360	31.2	0
William Morris, Labour	6,567	13.3	−1.9
Mick Faulkner, UK Independence party	1,926	3.9	n/a

Andrew Roth says: "puts himself across as a local yokel in a rather Penhaligonesque way"
Recent parliamentary career: PPS to Charles Kennedy (2001–); spokesperson, DSS (1999–2001); spokesperson, fishing (1997–99)
Background: charity worker; rural development worker, Nottinghamshire and Cornwall; member of Friends of the Earth, World Development Movement, Cornwall Racial Equality Council
Born: December 2 1958 in Mullion, Cornwall
Education: Helston Grammar School
Higher education: Sussex University; Oxford, University College
Constituency: Land's End and Scilly Isles, Penzance is main town

George, Rt Hon Bruce
Labour MP for Walsall South since 1974

Majority: 9,931 (28.5%)
Turnout: 55.7%

	Votes	Share %	Change %
Bruce George, Labour	20,574	59	1.1
Mike Bird, Conservative	10,643	30.5	−1.2
Bill Tomlinson, Liberal Democrat	2,365	6.8	0.6
Derek Bennett, UK Independence party	974	2.8	n/a
Pete Smith, Socialist Alliance	343	1	n/a

Andrew Roth says: "pragmatic centre-left, considered right-wing on defence"

Recent parliamentary career: chair, defence committee (1997–)
Background: politics lecturer at several universities; author of books on defence
Born: June 1 1942 in Mountain Ash
Education: Mountain Ash Grammar School
Higher education: Swansea University; Warwick University
Constituency: residential, large Asian community, north of Birmingham

Gerrard, Neil
Labour MP for Walthamstow since 1992

Majority: 15,181 (44.1%)
Turnout: 53.5%

	Votes	Share %	Change %
Neil Gerrard, Labour	21,402	62.2	−0.9
Nick Boys Smith, Conservative	6,221	18.1	−2.2
Peter Dunphy, Liberal Democrat	5,024	14.6	0.9
Simon Donovan, Soc Alt	806	2.3	n/a
William Phillips, British National party	389	1.1	n/a
Gerda Mayer, UK Independence party	298	0.9	n/a
Barbara Duffy, ProLife Alliance	289	0.8	n/a

Andrew Roth says: "quietly rebellious idealist"

Recent parliamentary career: information committee (2001–); environmental audit committee (2001–); PPS to Dawn Primarolo (1997–97)
Background: computing lecturer, Hackney College (1968–92); teacher; Waltham Forest councillor and leader
Born: July 3 1942 in Farnworth, Lancashire
Education: Manchester Grammar School
Higher education: Oxford, Wadham; Chelsea College, London; Polytechnic of South Bank
Constituency: north-east London suburb, working-class, ethnic minorities

Gibb, Nick
Conservative MP for Bognor Regis and Littlehampton since 1997

Majority: 5,643 (14.5%)
Turnout: 58.3%

	Votes	Share %	Change %
Nick Gibb, Conservative	17,602	45.2	1
George O'Neill, Labour	11,959	30.7	2.2
Pamela Peskett, Liberal Democrat	6,846	17.6	–6.4
George Stride, UK Independence party	1,779	4.6	n/a
Lilius Haggard-Cheyne, Green party	782	2	n/a

Andrew Roth says: "fulltime Commons defender of the 'sensible' Tory record on taxation and social security"

Recent parliamentary career: opposition spokesperson, DTLGR (2001–); opposition spokesperson, DTI (1999–2001); opposition spokesperson, Treasury (1998–99)
Background: chartered accountant; author of several pamphlets on taxation
Born: September 3 1960 in Amersham, Berkshire
Education: Maidstone Grammar School; Roundhay High School; Thornes House, Wakefield
Higher education: Durham University
Constituency: West Sussex seaside towns, white wealthy middle class pensioners

Gibson, Dr Ian
Labour MP for Norwich North since 1997

Majority: 5,863 (12.8%)
Turnout: 60.9%

	Votes	Share %	Change %
Ian Gibson, Labour	21,624	47.4	–2.3
Kay Mason, Conservative	15,761	34.6	2.1
Moira Toye, Liberal Democrat	6,750	14.8	2.2
Rob Tinch, Green party	797	1.8	n/a
Guy Cheyney, UK Independence party	471	1	n/a
Michael Betts, Independent	211	0.5	n/a

Andrew Roth says: "an important and active scientific voice in the Commons"

Recent parliamentary career: science and technology committee (1997–)
Background: scientist and dean of biology; vice chair, MSF parliamentary group
Born: September 26 1938 in Dumfries
Education: Dumfries Academy
Higher education: Edinburgh University
Constituency: Norwich's less grand suburbs, many council houses

Gidley, Sandra
Liberal Democrat MP for Romsey since 2000

Majority: 2,370 (4.9%)
Turnout: 68.7%

	Votes	Share %	Change %
Sandra Gidley, Liberal Democrat	22,756	47	–3.6
Paul Raynes, Conservative	20,386	42.1	0.1
Stephen Roberts, Labour	3,986	8.2	4.5
Anthony McCabe, UK Independence party	730	1.5	–0.8
Derrick Large, Legalise Cannabis party	601	1.2	n/a

Maiden speech: "there is a lot of inspiration and individuality in the way in which many members of parliament conduct themselves. Why do we not allow our teachers to show a little of the same?"

Recent parliamentary career: entered parliament at 2000 byelection, taking seat from Conservative; Lib Dem spokesperson, health (2001–); health committee (2001–)

Background: pharmacist; Romsey councillor and mayor; antenatal teacher for National Childbirth Trust
Born: March 26 1957 in North Wales
Education: Eggars Grammar School; Alton AFCENT International, Netherlands; Windsor Girls' School
Higher education: Bath University
Constituency: market town and rich villages on River Test

Gildernew, Michelle
Sinn Fein MP for Fermanagh and South Tyrone since 2001

Majority: 53 (0.1%)
Turnout: 78%

	Votes	Share %	Change %
Michelle Gildernew, Sinn Fein	17,739	34.1	11
James Cooper, Ulster Unionist party	17,686	34	−17.5
Tommy Gallagher, Social Democratic and Labour party	9,706	18.7	−4.2
Jim Dixon, Ind UU	6,843	13.2	n/a
Maurice Morrow, Democratic Unionist party	n/a		
Jim Dixon, Independent Unionist	n/a		

Rosie Cowan, Guardian Unlimited: "young, enthusiastic and female she has impeccable republican lineage but no IRA record"

Recent parliamentary career: entered parliament 2001, taking seat from UUP; has not taken her seat in Parliament
Background: campaigner from a Republican family; member of NIA and Sinn Fein National Executive; was member of first SF negotiating team to meet the prime minister
Born: 1970 in Caledon
Education: Caledon School; St Catherine's School, Armagh
Higher education: University of Ulster, Colraine campus
Constituency: farming seat on border with Irish Republic; main town is Enniskillen; once held by hunger striker Bobby Sands

Gillan, Cheryl
Conservative MP for Chesham and Amersham since 1992

Majority: 11,882 (26.2%)
Turnout: 64.7%

	Votes	Share %	Change %
Cheryl Gillan, Conservative	22,867	50.5	0.1
John Ford, Liberal Democrat	10,985	24.3	0.5
Ken Hulme, Labour	8,497	18.8	−0.8
Ian Harvey, UK Independence party	1,367	3	n/a
Nick Wilkins, Green party	1,114	2.5	n/a
G Duval, ProLife Alliance	453	1	n/a

Andrew Roth says: "alternates between thinking for herself and loyally responding to Tory whips' wishes"

Recent parliamentary career: opposition whip (2001–); opposition spokesperson, FCO and DFID (1998–2001); opposition spokesperson, DTI (1997–98)
Background: marketing director; member of Worshipful Company of Marketers
Born: April 21 1952 in Llandaff, Cardiff
Education: Cheltenham Ladies' College
Higher education: College of Law, London
Constituency: affluent stockbroker belt, leafy hills north-west of London

Gilroy, Linda
Labour MP for Plymouth Sutton since 1997

Majority: 7,517 (19.2%)
Turnout: 57.1%

	Votes	Share %	Change %
Linda Gilroy, Labour	19,827	50.7	0.6
Oliver Colvile, Conservative	12,310	31.5	1.2
Alan Connett, Liberal Democrat	5,605	14.3	0.4
Alan Whitton, UK Independence party	970	2.5	n/a
Henry Leary, Socialist Labour Party	361	0.9	n/a

Andrew Roth says: "loyalist prone to supportive questions, but able to join with sympathetic Lib Dems on common causes"

Recent parliamentary career: PPS to Nick Raynsford (2001–)
Background: deputy director, Age Concern; regional manager, Gas Consumers' Council
Born: June 19 1949 in Moffat, Scotland
Education: Stirling High School
Higher education: Edinburgh University; Strathclyde University
Constituency: mixed city suburbs on coast

Godsiff, Roger
Labour MP for Birmingham Sparkbrook and Small Heath since 1997; Birmingham Small Heath (1992–97)

Majority: 16,246 (44.3%)
Turnout: 49.3%

	Votes	Share %	Change %
Roger Godsiff, Labour	21,087	57.5	–6.8
Qassim Afzal, Liberal Democrat	4,841	13.2	3.9
Shafaq Hussain, PJP	4,770	13	n/a
Iftkhar Hussain, Conservative	3,948	10.8	–6.7
Gul Mohammed, Independent	662	1.8	0.6
Wayne Vincent, UK Independence party	634	1.7	n/a
Abdul Aziz, Muslim	401	1.1	n/a
Salman Mirza, Socialist Alliance	304	0.8	n/a

Andrew Roth says: "counterbalanced his modest Commons contributions by intensive weekend activity among his constituents"

Recent parliamentary career: introduced private member's bill on football grounds (2001)
Background: banker; senior research officer at GMP; Lewisham councillor
Born: June 28 1946 in Lewisham
Education: Catford Comprehensive School
Constituency: inner south-east city, underprivileged, some locals want Asian MP

Goggins, Paul
Labour MP for Wythenshawe and Sale East since 1997

Majority: 12,608 (36%)
Turnout: 48.6%

	Votes	Share %	Change %
Paul Goggins, Labour	21,032	60	1.9
Vanessa Tucker, Liberal Democrat	4,320	12.3	–0.1
Susan Fildes, Conservative	8,424	24	–1.1
Lance Crookes, Green party	869	2.5	n/a
Fred Shaw, Socialist Labour Party	410	1.2	–0.9

Andrew Roth says: "Blair loyalist concerned to improve the social security system"

Recent parliamentary career: PPS to David Blunkett (2001–); PPS to John Denham (1998–2001)
Background: director of national charities, including Church Action on Poverty

Born: October 16 1953 in Manchester
Education: St Bede's RC Grammar School, Manchester
Higher education: Manchester Polytechnic; Durham Theology College
Constituency: outer Greater Manchester suburbs, working-class, council-estate seat

Goodman, Paul
Conservative MP for Wycombe since 2001

Majority: 3,168 (7.1%)
Turnout: 60.3%

	Votes	Share %	Change %
Paul Goodman, Conservative	19,064	42.4	2.5
Chauhdry Shafique, Labour	15,896	35.3	−0.1
Dee Tomlin, Liberal Democrat	7,658	17	−1.5
Christopher Cooke, UK Independence party	1,059	2.4	n/a
John Laker, Green party	1,057	2.4	1
David Fitton, Independent	240	0.5	n/a

Maiden speech: "the challenge of reconciling individual freedom with social obligation is perhaps the greatest challenge of our times"

Recent parliamentary career: entered parliament 2001; work and pensions committee (2001–); deregulation committee (2001–)
Background: journalist on Catholic Herald and Daily Telegraph; speechwriter for William Hague; chair, Federation of Conservative Students; spent two years as a novice monk
Born: November 17 1959
Education: Cranleigh School
Higher education: York University
Constituency: urban High Wycombe town plus affluent villages in hilly Buckinghamshire

Gray, James
Conservative MP for North Wiltshire since 1997

Majority: 3,878 (7.3%)
Turnout: 66.6%

	Votes	Share %	Change %
James Gray, Conservative	24,090	45.5	1.7
Hugh Pym, Liberal Democrat	20,212	38.2	0.4
Jo Garton, Labour	7,556	14.3	0.1
Neil Dowdney, UK Independence party	1,090	2.1	n/a

Andrew Roth says: "Scottish Unionist and partisan loyalist... considered Tim-nice-but-dim by some former lobbying colleagues"

Recent parliamentary career: opposition spokesperson, MOD (2001–); broadcasting committee (2001)
Background: managing director; member of Territorial Army, armed forces parliamentary scheme and Honourable Artillery Company
Born: November 7 1954 in Glasgow
Education: Glasgow High School
Higher education: Glasgow University; Oxford, Christ Church
Constituency: mainly rural, managerial, includes Chippenham

Grayling, Chris
Conservative MP for Epsom and Ewell since 2001

Majority: 10,080 (21.6%)
Turnout: 62.8%

	Votes	Share %	Change %
Chris Grayling, Conservative	22,430	48.1	2.5
Charles Mansell, Labour	12,350	26.5	2.2
John Vincent, Liberal Democrat	10,316	22.1	−0.7
Graham Webster-Gardiner, UK Independence party	1,547	3.3	n/a

Maiden speech: "on [a tourist plaque in my constituency] was the inscription: 'On this site, in 1762, nothing happened.' At first, I thought it was a tribute to the first four years of Labour government"

Recent parliamentary career: entered parliament 2001; transport, local government, and the regions committee (2001–)
Background: international management consultant; television journalist and producer for BBC and Channel Four; Merton councillor; author
Born: April 1 1962
Education: Royal Grammar School, High Wycombe
Constituency: inner-Surrey commuter belt, managerial affluent area famous for racecourse

Green, Damian
Conservative MP for Ashford since 1997

Majority: 7,359 (15.3%)
Turnout: 62.5%

	Votes	Share %	Change %
Damian Green, Conservative	22,739	47.4	6
John Adams, Labour	15,380	32.1	0.4
Keith Fitchett, Liberal Democrat	7,236	15.1	−4.6
Richard Boden, Green party	1,353	2.8	1.6
David Waller, UK Independence party	1,229	2.6	n/a

Andrew Roth says: "a strong partisan Labour budget basher in competition with his predominantly right-wing colleagues"

Recent parliamentary career: shadow secretary of state, DFES (2001–); opposition spokesperson, DETR (1999–2001)
Background: journalist at BBC, Channel 4, *The Times*; special adviser to prime minister's policy unit (1992–94); public-affairs consultant
Born: January 17 1956 in Barry, South Glamorgan
Education: Reading School
Higher education: Oxford, Balliol
Constituency: fast-developing Channel Tunnel boom town

Green, Matthew
Liberal Democrat MP for Ludlow since 2001

Majority: 1,630 (3.8%)
Turnout: 68.4%

	Votes	Share %	Change %
Matthew Green, Liberal Democrat	18,620	43.2	13.5
Martin Taylor-Smith, Conservative	16,990	39.4	−3
Nigel Knowles, Labour	5,785	13.4	−12
Jim Gaffney, Green party	871	2	0.3
Phil Gutteridge, UK Independence party	858	2	n/a

Maiden speech: "[Ludlow's] electorate are relaxed, friendly and not easily stirred. Indeed, they probably have not been stirred for 115 years"

Recent parliamentary career: entered parliament 2001, taking seat from Conservative
Background: businessman and managing director; member of Lib Dems' West Midlands executive; keen rugby and cricket player
Born: April 12 1970
Education: Priory School, Shrewsbury

Higher education: Birmingham University
Constituency: big, rural, hills and small towns, increasingly middle class, shock Lib Dem gain 2001 on back of local concern over hospital closures

Greenway, John
Conservative MP for Ryedale since 1987

Majority: 4,875 (11.1%)
Turnout: 66%

	Votes	Share %	Change %
John Greenway, Conservative	20,711	47.2	3.4
Keith Orrell, Liberal Democrat	15,836	36.1	2.7
David Ellis, Labour	6,470	14.7	–3.3
Stephen Feaster, UK Independence party	882	2	n/a

Andrew Roth says: "transparently honest man but a diffuse speaker and indecisive thinker apart from his professional expertise"

Recent parliamentary career: opposition spokesperson, DCMS (2000–); opposition spokesperson for home affairs (1997–2000)
Background: police officer; insurance broker; financial journalist; North Yorkshire councillor
Born: February 15 1946 in Northwich, Cheshire
Education: Sir John Deane's Grammar School
Higher education: Hendon Police College
Constituency: huge, Yorkshire Moors, villages, and Castle Howard

Grieve, Dominic
Conservative MP for Beaconsfield since 1997

Majority: 13,065 (31.1%)
Turnout: 61.5%

	Votes	Share %	Change %
Dominic Grieve, Conservative	22,233	52.9	3.7
Stephen Lathrope, Labour	9,168	21.8	1.8
Stephen Lloyd, Liberal Democrat	9,017	21.5	0.1
Andrew Moffat, UK Independence party	1,626	3.9	n/a

Andrew Roth says: "assiduous churchy barrister, son of a former churchy barrister Tory MP"

Recent parliamentary career: opposition spokesperson, HO (2001–); opposition spokesperson, constitutional affairs (1999–2001); environmental audit committee (1997–2001); joint committee on statutory instruments (1997–2001)
Background: barrister; Hammersmith and Fulham councillor; soldier in Territorial Army; churchwarden
Born: May 24 1956
Education: Westminster School
Higher education: Central London Polytechnic; Oxford, Magdalen
Constituency: Tony Blair stood here in 1982 byelection; M40 Chilterns commuterland

Griffiths, Jane
Labour MP for Reading East since 2001

Majority: 5,588 (12.8%)
Turnout: 58.4%

	Votes	Share %	Change %
Jane Griffiths, Labour	19,531	44.8	2.1
Barry Tanswell, Conservative	13,943	32	–3.2
Tom Dobrashian, Liberal Democrat	8,078	18.5	0
Miriam Kennett, Green party	1,053	2.4	n/a
Amy Thornton, UK Independence party	525	1.2	n/a
Darren Williams, Socialist Alliance	394	0.9	n/a
Peter Hammerson, Independent	94	.2	n/a

Andrew Roth says: "pro-EU partisan loyalist with an international outlook"

Recent parliamentary career: public accounts committee (1997–99)
Background: foreign news editor, BBC World Service; multilingual; established all-party group on male cancers; Reading councillor
Born: April 17 1954
Education: Cedars Grammar School, Leighton Buzzard
Higher education: Durham University
Constituency: growing town on rail line to London,

Griffiths, Nigel
Labour MP for Edinburgh South since 1987

Majority: 5,499 (14.8%)
Turnout: 58.1%

	Votes	Share %	Change %
Nigel Griffiths, Labour	15,671	42.2	–4.6
Marilyne MacLaren, Liberal Democrat	10,172	27.4	9.8
Gordon Buchan, Conservative	6,172	16.6	–4.7
Heather Williams, Scottish National party	3,683	9.9	–3
Colin Fox, Scottish Socialist party	933	2.5	n/a
Ms Linda Hendry, LCA	535	1.4	n/a
Linda Hendry, Legalise Cannabis party			n/a

Andrew Roth says: "quick thinker with a flair for piggybacking on any consumer news story"

Recent parliamentary career: junior minister, DTI (2001–); public accounts committee (1999–2001); procedure committee (1999–2001); junior minister, DTI (1997–98)
Background: Edinburgh councillor; author; columnist; researcher for Gordon Brown; pressure group activist
Born: May 20 1955 in Glasgow
Education: Hawick Comprehensive School
Higher education: Edinburgh University
Constituency: elegant south side of Edinburgh, professional and managerial

Griffiths, Win
Labour MP for Bridgend since 1987

Majority: 10,045 (27.2%)
Turnout: 60.2%

	Votes	Share %	Change %
Win Griffiths, Labour	19,422	52.5	–5.6
Tania Brisby, Conservative	9,377	25.3	2.5
Jane Barraclough, Liberal Democrat	5,330	14.4	2.9
Monica Mahoney, Plaid Cymru	2,652	7.2	3.4
Sally Jeremy, ProLife Alliance	223	0.6	n/a

Andrew Roth says: "mild, moderate, religious minded internationalist idealist"

Recent parliamentary career: House of Commons representative in drawing up the Charter of Fundamental Rights (1999); junior minister, Welsh Office (1997–98)
Background: consultant to NUT; history teacher; Vale of Glamorgan councillor; MEP (1979–89)
Born: February 11 1943 in Grahamstown, South Africa
Education: Brecon Boys' Grammar School
Higher education: Cardiff University
Constituency: Mid Glamorgan, mainly urban, prosperous in parts

Grogan, John
Labour MP for Selby since 1997

Majority: 2,138 (4.3%)
Turnout: 64.5%

	Votes	Share %	Change %
John Grogan, Labour	22,652	45.1	–0.8
Michael Mitchell, Conservative	20,514	40.8	1.7
Jeremy Wilcock, Liberal Democrat	5,569	11.1	–0.9
Ms Helen Kenwright, Green party	902	1.8	n/a
Bob Lewis, UK Independence party	635	1.3	n/a

Andrew Roth says: "very witty political staffer rewarded for his patience by becoming the first ever Labour MP for this seat"

Recent parliamentary career: Northern Ireland affairs committee (1997–2001)
Background: self-employed conference organiser; Labour party press officer; personal assistant to MEP (1984) and leader of Wolverhampton council (1985–87)
Born: February 24 1961 in Halifax
Education: St Michael's College, Leeds
Higher education: Oxford, St John's
Constituency: some mining, flatlands south of York

Gummer, Rt Hon John
Conservative MP for Suffolk Coastal since 1983; Eye (1979–83); Lewisham West (1970–74)

Majority: 4,326 (8.5%)
Turnout: 66.4%

	Votes	Share %	Change %
John Gummer, Conservative	21,847	43.3	4.7
Nigel Gardner, Labour	17,521	34.8	2
Tony Schur, Liberal Democrat	9,192	18.2	–3.2
Michael Burn, UK Independence party	1,847	3.7	n/a

Andrew Roth says: "moral certainties but flexible loyalties, has unequalled talent for anointing any Tory decision with sanctimony"

Recent parliamentary career: secretary of state, environment (1993–97); minister of state, MAFF (1989–93)
Background: publisher, journalist, company chairman; author of The Permissive Society; gained infamy while MAFF minister for feeding his young daughter a hamburger during BSE crisis
Born: November 26 1939 in Stockport
Education: King's School, Rochester
Higher education: Cambridge, Selwyn
Constituency: Suffolk sea frontage, including Felixstowe, Woodbridge and Sizewell nuclear plant

H

Hague, Rt Hon William
Conservative MP for Richmond since 1989

Majority: 16,319 (37.0%)
Turnout: 67.4%

	Votes	Share %	Change %
William Hague, Conservative	25,951	58.9	10
Fay Tinnion, Labour	9,632	21.9	−5.9
Edward Forth, Liberal Democrat	7,890	17.9	−0.5
Boney Maronie, official Monster Raving Loony party	561	1.3	n/a
Aidan Rankin, UK Independence party			n/a

William Hague after resignation (2001): "I believe strongly, passionately for everything I've fought for but it's also vital for leaders to listen and parties to change"

Recent parliamentary career: leader of the Conservative party (1997–2001); secretary of state, Wales (1995–97); minister of state, social security (1994–95); junior minister, social security (1993–94)
Background: management consultant, McKinsey and Company; political adviser to Geoffrey Howe; president of Oxford Union (1981)
Born: March 26 1961 in Rotherham
Education: Wath-upon-Deane Comprehensive School
Higher education: Insead Business School, France; Oxford, Magdalen
Constituency: Yorkshire fells and farmland, Swaledale and Wensleydale

Hain, Rt Hon Peter
Labour MP for Neath since 1991

Majority: 14,816 (42.3%)
Turnout: 62.4%

	Votes	Share %	Change %
Peter Hain, Labour	21,253	60.7	−12.8
Alun Llywelyn, Plaid Cymru	6,437	18.4	10.3
David Davies, Liberal Democrat	3,335	9.5	3.2
David Devine, Conservative	3,310	9.5	0.8
Huw Pudner, Socialist Alliance	483	1.4	n/a
Gerardo Brienza, ProLife Alliance	202	0.6	n/a

Andrew Roth says: "controversial agitator transformed into loyal minister"

Recent parliamentary career: minister of state, FCO (2001–); minister of state, DTI (2001–01); minister of state, FCO (1999–2001); junior minister, Wales (1997–99)
Background: researcher, Union of Communication Workers (1976–87); author of books on democracy, apartheid and radicalism; anti-apartheid activist
Born: February 16 1950 in Nairobi
Education: Pretoria Boys' High School; Emanuel School, Battersea
Higher education: Sussex University; Queen Mary's College, London
Constituency: industrial south Wales valleys above Swansea

Hall, Mike
Labour MP for Weaver Vale since 1997; Warrington South (1992–97)

Majority: 9,637 (24.6%)
Turnout: 57.6%

	Votes	Share %	Change %
Mike Hall, Labour	20,611	52.5	−3.9
Carl Cross, Conservative	10,974	27.9	−0.7
Nigel Griffiths, Liberal Democrat	5,643	14.4	2.1
Michael Cooksley, Independent	1,484	3.8	n/a
Jim Bradshaw, UK Independence party	559	1.4	n/a

Andrew Roth says: "hard hitting but recently in the shadows"

Recent parliamentary career: PPS to Alan Milburn (2001–); government whip (1998–2001); PPS Ann Taylor (1997–98)

Background: trade unionist (ASTMS and NUS); Warrington councillor; taught history and PE for five years
Born: September 20 1952 in Ashton-under-Lyne
Education: St Damian's Secondary Modern School
Higher education: Victoria University, Manchester; Padgate College of Education; Bangor University; Stretford Technical College
Constituency: the western, salt-mining part of Cheshire centred on Northwich

Hall, Patrick
Labour MP for Bedford since 1997

Majority: 6,157 (15.1%)
Turnout: 59.9%

	Votes	Share %	Change %
Patrick Hall, Labour	19,454	47.9	–2.7
Nicky Attenborough, Conservative	13,297	32.8	–0.9
Michael Headley, Liberal Democrat	6,425	15.8	3.5
Dr Richard Rawlins, Independent	973	2.4	n/a
Jennifer Lo Bianco, UK Independence party	430	1.1	n/a

Andrew Roth says: "naïve-sounding, moderate Blairite"

Recent parliamentary career: environment, food, and rural affairs committee (2001–); joint committee on consolidation of bills (1997–); European scrutiny committee (1999–2001)
Background: local government planning officer; Bedfordshire councillor
Born: October 20 1951 in Birmingham
Education: Bedford Modern School
Higher education: Birmingham University
Constituency: developing county town north of London with long-standing industrial base

Hamilton, David
Labour MP for Midlothian since 2001

Majority: 9,014 (31.4%)
Turnout: 59.1%

	Votes	Share %	Change %
David Hamilton, Labour	15,145	52.7	–0.8
Ian Goldie, Scottish National party	6,131	21.3	–4.2
Jacqueline Bell, Liberal Democrat	3,686	12.8	3.6
Robin Traquair, Conservative	2,748	9.6	–1.3
Bob Goupillot, Scottish Socialist party	837	2.9	n/a
John Holden, ProLife Alliance	177	0.6	n/a

Maiden speech: "I hope that we will not forget the values for which many of us came into politics – free education, a free health service and support for the weak"

Recent parliamentary career: entered parliament 2001; broadcasting committee (2001–); procedure committee (2001–)
Background: became a miner at 16, dismissed 20 years later while coordinating 22 strike centres during 1984–95 miners' strike; local councillor; worked in voluntary sector
Born: October 24 1950
Education: Dalkeith High School
Constituency: ancient Scottish town south-east of Edinburgh in former coalfield

Hamilton, Fabian
Labour MP for Leeds North East since 1997

Majority: 7,089 (17.8%)
Turnout: 62%

	Votes	Share %	Change %
Fabian Hamilton, Labour	19,540	49.1	–0.1
Owain Rhys, Conservative	12,451	31.3	–2.6
Jonathan Brown, Liberal Democrat	6,325	15.9	2
Ms Celia Foote, Left All	770	1.9	n/a
Miles Jeffrey, UK Independence party	382	1	n/a
Colin Muir, Socialist Labour Party	173	0.4	–0.6
Mohammed Zaman, Independent	132	0.3	n/a
Celia Foote, Left Alliance			n/a

Andrew Roth says: "to some an affable loyalist, to others a ruthless opportunist in benign disguise"

Recent parliamentary career: foreign affairs committee (2001–); administration committee (1997–2001)
Background: computer systems consultant; Leeds councillor; selected for seat in 1997 after noted left-winger Liz Davies had been deselected
Born: April 12 1955 in London
Education: Brentwood School
Higher education: York University
Constituency: diverse Leeds seat including innercity, smart suburbs and farmland

Hammond, Philip
Conservative MP for Runnymede and Weybridge since 1997

Majority: 8,360 (19.7%)
Turnout: 56.1%

	Votes	Share %	Change %
Philip Hammond, Conservative	20,646	48.7	0.1
Jane Briginshaw, Labour	12,286	29	–0.4
Chris Bushill, Liberal Democrat	6,924	16.3	0
Christopher Browne, UK Independence party	1,332	3.1	n/a
Charles Gilman, Green party	1,238	2.9	n/a

Andrew Roth says: "intelligent picador, able to penetrate Labour defences with sharp questions"

Recent parliamentary career: opposition spokesperson, DTI (2001–); opposition spokesperson, DoH (1998–2001); unopposed bills panel (1997–2001)
Background: medical company director; consultant to Malawi government
Born: December 4 1955 in Epping
Education: Shenfield School, Brentwood
Higher education: Oxford, University College
Constituency: Surrey suburbs including Chertsey, Walton and plush Virginia Water

Hancock, Mike
Liberal Democrat MP for Portsmouth South since 1997; SDP MP for Portsmouth South (1984–87)

Majority: 6,094 (15.5%)
Turnout: 50.9%

	Votes	Share %	Change %
Mike Hancock, Liberal Democrat	17,490	44.6	5.1
Philip Warr, Conservative	11,396	29.1	–2
Graham Heaney, Labour	9,361	23.9	–1.4
John Molyneux, Socialist Alliance	647	1.7	n/a
Michael Tarrant, UK Independence party	321	0.8	n/a

Andrew Roth says: "deeply-rooted working-class type with union roots unusual for a Lib Dem"

Recent parliamentary career: defence committee (1999–); Lib Dem spokesperson, foreign affairs, Europe, and defence (1997–99)
Background: television director; district officer, Mencap; Hampshire councillor and leader; persistent in trying to regain his seat
Born: April 9 1946 in Portsmouth

Education: Copnor and Portsea School
Constituency: dense harbourside seat including city centre and ferryport

Hanson, David
Labour MP for Delyn since 1992

Majority: 8,605 (24.9%)
Turnout: 63.3%

	Votes	Share %	Change %
David Hanson, Labour	17,825	51.5	-5.7
Paul Brierley, Conservative	9,220	26.6	0.6
Tudor Jones, Liberal Democrat	5,329	15.4	5.2
Paul Rowlinson, Plaid Cymru	2,262	6.5	2.7

Andrew Roth says: "can seem 'silicon-chipped' when he asks over-loyal questions"

Recent parliamentary career: PPS to Tony Blair (2001–); junior minister, Wales Office (1999–2001); government whip (1998–99); PPS to Alistair Darling (1997–98)
Background: charity director, Mencap; Vale Royal councillor
Born: July 5 1957 in Liverpool
Education: Verdin Comprehensive School, Winsford, Cheshire
Higher education: Hull University
Constituency: coastal North Wales, used to be called Flintshire, mixed economy

Harman, Rt Hon Harriet
Labour MP for Camberwell and Peckham since 1997; Peckham (1982–97)
Majority: 14,123 (56.3%)
Turnout: 46.8%

	Votes	Share %	Change %
Harriet Harman, Labour	17,473	69.6	0.3
Donnachadh McCarthy, Liberal Democrat	3,350	13.3	2.1
Jonathan Morgan, Conservative	2,740	10.9	-1
Storm Poorun, Green party	805	3.2	n/a
John Mulrenan, Socialist Alliance	478	1.9	n/a
Robert Adams, Socialist Labour party	188	0.8	-1.6
Frank Sweeney, Workers' Revolutionary party	70	0.3	-0.1

Andrew Roth says: "the chilly beautiful face of New Labour"

Recent parliamentary career: solicitor general, law officers' department (2001–); secretary of state, DSS (1997–98)
Background: legal officer, National Council for Civil Liberties; civil rights and equality activist
Born: July 30 1950 in London
Education: St Paul's School, London
Higher education: York University
Constituency: southern innercity London, high unemployment, social and economic problems

Harris, Dr Evan
Liberal Democrat MP for Oxford West and Abingdon since 1997

Majority: 9,185 (17.8%)
Turnout: 64.5%

	Votes	Share %	Change %
Evan Harris, Liberal Democrat	24,670	47.8	4.9
Ed Matts, Conservative	15,485	30	-2.7
Gillian Kirk, Labour	9,114	17.7	-2.5
Mike Woodin, Green party	1,423	2.8	1.7
Marcus Watney, UK Independence party	451	0.9	n/a
Ms Sigrid Shreeve, Independent	332	0.6	n/a
Robert Twigger, Ext Club	93	0.2	n/a

Andrew Roth says: "Lib Dems' NHS 'Oliver', always demanding yet more funds"

Recent parliamentary career: Lib Dem spokesperson, health and women (2001–); spokesperson, education and employment and women (1999–2001); spokesperson, DoH (1997–99)
Background: NHS doctor; member of Liberty, Amnesty, Green Lib Dems, Lib Dems for Gay and Lesbian Rights, British Chess Federation
Born: October 21 1965 in Sheffield
Education: Blue Coat School, Liverpool
Higher education: Oxford, Wadham; Oxford University Medical School; Harvard High School
Constituency: Inspector Morse territory, students plus rich locals

Harris, Tom
Labour MP for Glasgow Cathcart since 2001

Majority: 10,816 (39.5%)
Turnout: 52.6%

	Votes	Share %	Change %
Tom Harris, Labour	14,902	54.4	–3
Josephine Docherty, Scottish National party	4,086	14.9	–3.6
Richard Cook, Conservative	3,662	13.4	0.7
Tom Henery, Liberal Democrat	3,006	11	4.1
Ronnie Stevenson, Scottish Socialist party	1,730	6.3	n/a

Maiden speech: "I believe that this sovereign parliament of the United Kingdom remains the best hope for radical change in the lives of the millions of people that we represent"

Recent parliamentary career: entered parliament 2001
Background: Labour's Scottish press officer; journalist
Born: January 1 1964 in Scotland
Education: Garnock Academy, Kilbirnie
Higher education: Napier College, Edinburgh
Constituency: runs from Glasgow city centre to the southern outskirts around Hampden Park

Harvey, Nick
Liberal Democrat MP for North Devon since 1992

Majority: 2,984 (6.0%)
Turnout: 68.3%

	Votes	Share %	Change %
Nick Harvey, Liberal Democrat	21,784	44.2	–6.6
Clive Allen, Conservative	18,800	38.2	–1.3
Viv Gale, Labour	4,995	10.1	0.3
Roger Knapman, UK Independence party	2,484	5	n/a
Joanne Bell, Green party	1,191	2.4	n/a

Andrew Roth says: "shrewdly sensible and independent minded, held back only by need of a hair transplant"

Recent parliamentary career: Lib Dem spokesperson, culture, media and sport (2001–); spokesperson, health (1999–2001); spokesperson, constitution (1997–99)
Background: communications and marketing consultant
Born: August 3 1961 in Chandler's Ford, Hampshire
Education: Sherborne House School, Chandler's Ford
Higher education: Middlesex Polytechnic; Queen's College, Taunton
Constituency: seaside and farms around Barnstaple, dependent on agriculture, tourism and industry

Haselhurst, Rt Hon Sir Alan
Conservative MP for Saffron Walden since 1977; Middleton and Prestwich (1970–74)

Majority: 12,004 (24.0%)
Turnout: 65.2%

	Votes	Share %	Change %
Alan Haselhurst, Conservative	24,485	48.9	3.6
Elfreda Tealby-Watson, Liberal Democrat	12,481	24.9	−1.9
Tania Rogers, Labour	11,305	22.6	1.1
Richard Glover, UK Independence party	1,769	3.5	n/a

Andrew Roth says: "firm but fair; remains a one nation pro-European"

Recent parliamentary career: ran for speakership (2000); deputy speaker and chairman; ways and means(1997–); standing orders committee (1998–); chair, unopposed bills panel (1997–); Court of Referees (1997–)
Background: secretary; treasurer; librarian; member of Essex County Cricket Club
Born: June 23 1937 in Yorkshire
Education: King Edward VI School, Birmingham; Cheltenham College
Higher education: Oxford, Oriel
Constituency: rural pleasant north-western Essex, small towns and villages, Stansted Airport

Havard, Dai
Labour MP for Merthyr Tydfil and Rhymney since 2001

Majority: 14,923 (47.1%)
Turnout: 57.2%

	Votes	Share %	Change %
Dai Havard, Labour	19,574	61.8	−14.9
Robert Hughes, Plaid Cymru	4,651	14.7	8.7
Keith Rogers, Liberal Democrat	2,385	7.5	0
Richard Cuming, Conservative	2,272	7.2	0.8
Jeff Edwards, Independent	1,936	6.1	n/a
Ken Evans, Socialist Labour Party	692	2.2	n/a
Anthony Lewis, ProLife Alliance	174	0.6	n/a

Maiden speech: "I recognise the power of the links between organised labour and the party that we have helped to form"

Recent parliamentary career: entered parliament 2001
Background: locally born; jobbing maintenance man; MSF Union's head in Wales
Born: Aug 7 1950 in Quaker's Yard, Merthyr Vale
Education: St Peters College, Birmingham
Higher education: Warwick University
Constituency: runs from Brecon Beacons National Park through the Valleys; Merthyr is the biggest town

Hawkins, Nick
Conservative MP for Surrey Heath since 1997; Blackpool South (1992–97)

Majority: 10,819 (24.0%)
Turnout: 59.5%

	Votes	Share %	Change %
Nick Hawkins, Conservative	22,401	49.7	−1.9
Mark Lelliott, Liberal Democrat	11,582	25.7	3.9
James Norman, Labour	9,640	21.4	0.4
Nigel Hunt, UK Independence party	1,479	3.3	n/a

Andrew Roth says: "overeager loyalism successfully conceals his intelligence"

Recent parliamentary career: opposition spokesperson, DFID (2001–); opposition spokesperson, LCD and home affairs (1999–2001)
Background: Royal Navy cadet; barrister, consultant; legal adviser specialising in commercial law
Born: March 27 1957 in St Albans, Hertfordshire
Education: Bedford Modern School
Higher education: Inns of Court School of Law; Middle Temple; Oxford, Lincoln College
Constituency: stockbroker belt Surrey seat around Camberley and Frimley

Hayes, John
Conservative MP for South Holland and The Deepings since 1997

Majority: 11,099 (24.0%)
Turnout: 62.5%

	Votes	Share %	Change %
John Hayes, Conservative	25,611	55.4	6.1
Graham Walker, Labour	14,512	31.4	–1.9
Grace Hill, Liberal Democrat	4,761	10.3	–5.3
Malcolm Charlesworth, UK Independence party	1,318	2.9	n/a

Andrew Roth says: "assiduous but patronising hardline Eurosceptic"

Recent parliamentary career: opposition whip (2001–); opposition spokesperson, DFEE (2000–); vice chairman, Conservative party (1998–2000)
Background: sales director; Nottinghamshire councillor
Born: June 23 1958 in Woolwich
Education: Colfe's Grammar School
Higher education: Nottingham University
Constituency: Britain's arable farming heartland, flat south-eastern Lincolnshire

Heal, Sylvia
Labour MP for Halesowen and Rowley Regis since 1997; Mid Staffordshire (1990–92)

Majority: 7,359 (18.8%)
Turnout: 59.8%

	Votes	Share %	Change %
Sylvia Heal, Labour	20,804	53	–1.1
Les Jones, Conservative	13,445	34.2	1.3
Patrick Harley, Liberal Democrat	4,089	10.4	1.9
Alan Sheath, UK Independence party	936	2.4	n/a

Andrew Roth says: "has the concerns of a social worker and the foreign and defence views of a former Welsh left-winger"

Recent parliamentary career: deputy speaker (2000–); unopposed bills panel (2000–); standing orders committee (2000–); court of referees (2000–); PPS to Geoff Hoon (1999–2000)
Background: social worker; JP; member of Action for South Africa, One World Action
Born: July 20 1942 in Flintshire
Education: Elfed Secondary Modern School, Buckley
Higher education: Swansea University; College Harlech
Constituency: twin West Midlands towns with mixed political heritage, prosperous, some industrial working-class areas

Heald, Oliver
Conservative MP for North East Hertfordshire since 1997; North Hertfordshire (1992–97)

Majority: 3,444 (7.7%)
Turnout: 64.9%

	Votes	Share %	Change %
Oliver Heald, Conservative	19,695	44.1	2.3
Ivan Gibbons, Labour	16,251	36.4	0.6
Alison Kingman, Liberal Democrat	7,686	17.2	−1.1
Malcolm Virgo, UK Independence party	1,013	2.3	n/a

Andrew Roth says: "loquacious barrister who believes compassion and efficiency must go hand in hand"

Recent parliamentary career: opposition spokesperson, DOH (2000–); whip (1997–2000)
Background: barrister, specialising in employment law
Born: December 15 1954 in Reading
Education: Reading School
University: Cambridge, Pembroke
Constituency: North Hertfordshire commuter towns of Baldock, Royston, and Letchworth

Healey, John
Labour MP for Wentworth since 1997

Majority: 16,449 (48.7%)
Turnout: 52.8%

	Votes	Share %	Change %
John Healey, Labour	22,798	67.5	−4.8
Mike Roberts, Conservative	6,349	18.8	3.8
David Wildgoose, Liberal Democrat	3,652	10.8	1.5
John Wilkinson, UK Independence party	979	2.9	n/a

Andrew Roth says: "centre-left moderniser with a reputation for preferring beer to wine"

Recent parliamentary career: junior minister, DFES (2001–); PPS to Gordon Brown (1999–2001)
Background: journalist; disability campaigner; head of communications, MSFU
Born: February 13 1960 in Wakefield
Education: St Peter's School, York; Lady Lumley's Comprehensive School, Pickering
Higher education: Cambridge, Christ's College
Constituency: Rother and Dearne valleys in South Yorkshire, ex-mining seat

Heath, David
Liberal Democrat MP for Somerton and Frome since 1997

Majority: 668 (1.2%)
Turnout: 70.3%

	Votes	Share %	Change %
David Heath, Liberal Democrat	22,983	43.6	4.1
Jonathan Marland, Conservative	22,315	42.4	3.1
Andrew Perkins, Labour	6,113	11.6	−4.7
Peter Bridgwood, UK Independence party	919	1.7	n/a
Ms Jean Pollock, Liberal	354	0.7	n/a

Andrew Roth says: "one of the West Country's most impressive former county leaders"

Recent parliamentary career: Lib Dem spokesperson, work and pensions (2001–); spokesperson, Europe (1997–99)
Background: optician; parliamentary consultant; Somerset council leader; pig breeder
Born: March 16 1954 in Westbury-sub-Mendip, Somerset
Education: Millfield School, Somerset
Higher education: St John's College, Oxford; City University
Constituency: agricultural seat in north of Somerset around the Mendip Hills

Heathcoat-Amory, Rt Hon David
Conservative MP for Wells since 1983

Majority: 2,845 (5.5%)
Turnout: 69.1%

	Votes	Share %	Change %
David Heathcoat-Amory, Conservative	22,462	43.8	4.4
Graham Oakes, Liberal Democrat	19,617	38.3	−0.2
Andy Merryfield, Labour	7,915	15.4	−2.7
Steve Reed, UK Independence party	1,104	2.2	n/a
C Wells, Wessex Regionalist	167	0.3	n/a

Andrew Roth says: "the kind of Englishman who travels abroad with a tin of Marmite sandwiches"

Recent parliamentary career: shadow secretary of state, DTI (2000–01); shadow chief secretary to the Treasury (1997–2000); junior minister, Treasury (1994–96)
Background: chartered accountant; finance director; farmer; Lloyds underwriter
Born: March 21 1949 in London
Education: Eton College
Higher education: Balliol College, Oxford
Constituency: northern Somerset seat centred on Glastonbury and Cheddar Gorge

Henderson, Doug
Labour MP for Newcastle upon Tyne North since 1987

Majority: 14,450 (39.8%)
Turnout: 57.5%

	Votes	Share %	Change %
Doug Henderson, Labour	21,874	60.2	−2
Phillip Smith, Conservative	7,424	20.4	1
Graham Soult, Liberal Democrat	7,070	19.4	4.9
Pete Burnett, Socialist Alliance	7,070	19.4	n/a

Andrew Roth says: "fairly able and articulate; a discursive rather than partisan debater"

Recent parliamentary career: minister of state, MoD (1998-99); minister of state, FCO (1997-98)
Background: research officer; Scottish organiser for GMB union; apprentice, Rolls-Royce; running enthusiast
Born: June 9 1949 in Edinburgh
Education: Waid Academy, Fife
Higher education: Strathclyde University, Glasgow
Constituency: northern urban Newcastle seat centred on Gosforth, includes airport

Henderson, Ivan
Labour MP for Harwich since 1997

Majority: 2,596 (5.4%)
Turnout: 62.1%

	Votes	Share %	Change %
Ivan Henderson, Labour	21,951	45.6	6.8
Ian Sproat, Conservative	19,355	40.2	3.7
Peter Wilcock, Liberal Democrat	4,099	8.5	−4.6
Tony Finnegan-Butler, UK Independence party	2,463	5.1	n/a
Clive Lawrance, Independent	247	0.5	n/a

Andrew Roth says: "one of the shrinking minority of working class MPs in a party increasingly dominated by professionals"

Recent parliamentary career: PPS to Keith Bradley (2001–); joint committee on statutory instruments (1999–)

Background: dockworker and shop steward; Harwich councillor; first Labour MP for Harwich
Born: June 7 1958 in Harwich
Education: Sir Anthony Dean Comprehensive School, Harwich
Constituency: east coast port town with rural hinterland around Walton-on-the-Naze and Clacton

Hendrick, Mark
Labour MP for Preston since 2000

Majority: 12,268 (34%)
Turnout: 50%

	Votes	Share %	Change %
Mark Hendrick, Labour	20,540	57	11.3
Graham O'Hare, Conservative	8,272	23	−2
Bill Chadwick, Liberal Democrat	4,746	13.2	−3
Bilal Patel, Independent	1,241	3.4	n/a
Richard Merrick, Green party	1,019	2.8	0.7
David Braid, Independent	223	0.6	n/a

Maiden speech: "people can still have a hotpot on a cold evening and fish and chips on a Friday, in spite of European integration"

Recent parliamentary career: European scrutiny committee (2001–); won Preston byelection in October 2000
Background: researcher on science and engineering research council; Salford councillor for eight years; MEP for Lancashire Central (1994–99)
Born: November 2 1958
Education: Salford Grammar School
Higher education: Liverpool Polytechnic; Manchester University
Constituency: substantial north-west town and industrial centre on M6

Hendry, Charles
Conservative MP for Wealden since 2001; High Peak (1992–97)

Majority: 13,772 (26.1%)
Turnout: 63.5%

	Votes	Share %	Change %
Charles Hendry, Conservative	26,279	49.8	0
Steve Murphy, Liberal Democrat	12,507	23.7	−2
Kathy Fordham, Labour	10,705	20.3	3.1
Keith Riddle, UK Independence party	1,539	2.9	n/a
Julian Salmon, Green party	1,273	2.4	n/a
Cyril Thornton, Pensioner	453	0.9	n/a

Maiden speech (as MP for Wealden): "If we do not stand up for farming, the whole fabric of our countryside will be in jeopardy and will be changed forever"

Recent parliamentary career: opposition whip (2001–); re-elected to parliament (2001); chief of staff to William Hague (1997–98)
Background: public-relations consultant; special adviser to social security secretary
Born: May 6 1959
Education: Rugby School
Higher education: Edinburgh University
Constituency: well-wooded ridges and valleys including Ashdown Forest and Sussex small towns

Hepburn, Stephen
Labour MP for Jarrow since 1997

Majority: 17,595 (51.1%)
Turnout: 54.6%

	Votes	Share %	Change %
Stephen Hepburn, Labour	22,777	66.1	1.2
James Selby, Liberal Democrat	5,182	15	3.9
Donald Wood, Conservative	5,056	14.7	–0.2
Alan Badger, UK Independence party	716	2.1	n/a
Alan Le Blond, Independent	391	1.1	n/a
John Bissett, Socialist party	357	1	n/a

Andrew Roth says: "loyal short-tempered local son"

Recent parliamentary career: defence committee (1999–2001); administration committee (1997–2001)
Background: South Tyneside councillor and deputy leader
Born: December 6 1959 in Jarrow
Education: Springfield Comprehensive School
Higher education: Newcastle University
Constituency: former shipbuilding town south of Newcastle famous for its march against unemployment in the 1930s

Heppell, John
Labour MP for Nottingham East since 1992

Majority: 10,320 (34.7%)
Turnout: 45.5%

	Votes	Share %	Change %
John Heppell, Labour	17,530	59	–3.3
Richard Allan, Conservative	7,210	24.3	0.8
Tim Ball, Liberal Democrat	3,874	13	2.9
Pete Radcliff, Socialist Alliance	1,117	3.8	n/a

Andrew Roth says: "strong and long-winded defender of railways"

Recent parliamentary career: government whip (2001–); committee of selection (2001–); PPS to John Prescott (1997–2001);
Background: fitter for British Rail and NCB; workshop supervisor; Nottinghamshire councillor; NUR and RMT rail union activist
Born: November 3 1948 in Newcastle upon Tyne
Education: Rutherford Grammar School
Higher education: Ashington Technical College
Constituency: long, thin seat on edge of Nottingham with mix of suburbs and council estates

Hermon, Sylvia
Ulster Unionist party MP for North Down since 2001

Majority: 7,324 (19.7%)
Turnout: 58.8%

	Votes	Share %	Change %
Sylvia Hermon, Ulster Unionist party	20,833	56	24.9
Robert McCartney, United Kingdom Unionist	13,509	36.3	1.2
Marrietta Farrell, Social Democratic and Labour party	1,275	3.4	–1
Julian Robertson, Conservative	815	2.2	–2.7
Chris Carter, Independent	444	1.2	n/a
Eamon McConvey, Sinn Fein	313	0.8	n/a

Maiden speech: "the people of North Down have returned someone who remains strongly pro-agreement, the Good Friday agreement must not be allowed to stumble and fall at this stage"

Recent parliamentary career: entered parliament 2001, taking seat from the United Kingdom Unionist

Background: law lecturer, Queen's University (1978–88); married to former RUC Chief Constable Sir John Hermon
Born: August 11 1955
Education: Dungannon High School for Girls
Higher education: Aberystwyth University
Constituency: smart north coast, many of the seat's well-paid voters work for the government, last two MPs were independent unionists

Hesford, Stephen
Labour MP for Wirral West since 1997

Majority: 4,035 (10.0%)
Turnout: 65%

	Votes	Share %	Change %
Stephen Hesford, Labour	19,105	47.2	2.3
Chris Lynch, Conservative	15,070	37.2	−1.8
Simon Holbrook, Liberal Democrat	6,300	15.6	2.9

Andrew Roth says: "caring, loyal, mildly-left barrister"

Recent parliamentary career: Northern Ireland affairs committee (1998–2001); health committee (1999–2001)
Background: barrister; parliamentary assistant to Joan Lestor MP; member of Greenpeace, Liberty, Amnesty
Born: May 27 1957 in Lowton, Lancashire
Education: Urmstron Grammar School, Bradford
Higher education: Bradford University; Westminster University; Inns of Court School of Law
Constituency: the most upmarket suburbs on the Wirral, packed with commuters

Hewitt, Rt Hon Patricia
Labour MP for Leicester West since 1997

Majority: 9,639 (29.0%)
Turnout: 50.9%

	Votes	Share %	Change %
Patricia Hewitt, Labour	18,014	54.2	−1
Chris Shaw, Conservative	8,375	25.2	1.5
Andrew Vincent, Liberal Democrat	5,085	15.3	1.1
Matthew Gough, Green party	1,074	3.2	n/a
Shaun Kirkpatrick, Socialist Labour party	350	1.1	0
Steve Score, Socialist Alliance	321	1	n/a

Andrew Roth says: "highly-talented and ambitious campaigner who hit the front bench punching"

Recent parliamentary career: secretary of state, DTI and minister for women (2001–); minister of state, DTI (1999–2001); junior minister, Treasury (1998–99)
Background: head of research, Anderson Consulting; deputy director, IPPR; author of civil rights books; press officer and policy coordinator for Neil Kinnock
Born: December 2 1948 in Canberra, Australia
Education: Church of England Grammar School, Canberra
Higher education: Australian National University; Cambridge, Newnham
Constituency: western edge of Leicester with many council houses

Heyes, David
Labour MP for Ashton under Lyne since 2001

Majority: 15,518 (43.4%)
Turnout: 49.1%

	Votes	Share %	Change %
David Heyes, Labour	22,340	62.5	−5
Tim Charlesworth, Conservative	6,822	19.1	0.2
Kate Fletcher, Liberal Democrat	4,237	11.9	2.2
Roger Woods, British National party	1,617	4.5	n/a
Nigel Rolland, Green party	748	2.1	n/a

Andrew Roth says: "docile low-profile new MP"

Recent parliamentary career: entered parliament 2001; public administration committee (2001–)
Background: NALGO organiser; Citizens' Advice Bureau manager; vice chair of Ashton Labour party; Oldham councillor
Born: April 2 1946
Education: Blackley Technical High School
Higher education: Open University
Constituency: traditional town on the edge of Manchester with many manual workers

Hill, Keith
Labour MP for Streatham since 1992

Majority: 14,270 (38.6%)
Turnout: 48.7%

	Votes	Share %	Change %
Keith Hill, Labour	21,041	56.9	−5.9
Roger O'Brien, Liberal Democrat	6,771	18.3	4.7
Stephen Hocking, Conservative	6,639	17.9	−3.8
Sajeed Muhamad, Green party	1,641	4.4	n/a
Greg Tucker, Socialist Alliance	906	2.5	n/a

Andrew Roth says: "bright and forward looking"

Recent parliamentary career: deputy chief whip (2001–); minister of state, DETR (1999–2001); junior minister, DETR (1999–99); government whip (1998–99); PPS to Hilary Armstrong (1997–98); accommodation and works committee (2001–); committee of selection (2001–)
Background: member of Labour party NEC (to 2001); political officer, RMT (formerly NUR); politics lecturer; research officer for Labour in 1970s
Born: July 28 1943 in Leicester
Education: Leicester Boys' Grammar School
Higher education: Aberystwyth University; Oxford, Corpus Christi
Constituency: runs from Lambeth Town Hall in Brixton to outer London, plenty of rented housing in a suburb that has gone down in the world

Hinchliffe, David
Labour MP for Wakefield since 1987

Majority: 7,954 (19.3%)
Turnout: 54.5%

	Votes	Share %	Change %
David Hinchliffe, Labour	20,592	49.9	−7.5
Thelma Karran, Conservative	12,638	30.6	2.1
Douglas Dale, Liberal Democrat	5,097	12.4	1.2
Sarah Greenwood, Green party	1,075	2.6	n/a
Janice Cannon, UK Independence party	677	1.6	n/a
Abdul Aziz, Socialist Labour Party	634	1.5	n/a
Mick Griffiths, Socialist Alliance	541	1.3	n/a

Andrew Roth says: "dedicated, assiduous, caring, locally-born former social worker"

Recent parliamentary career: chair, health committee (1997–); resigned from Labour frontbench (1995) in protest at party's modernisation

Background: social worker; special interest in health and social services
Born: October 14 1948 in Wakefield
Education: Cathedral Church of England Secondary Modern School, Wakefield
Higher education: Bradford University; Leeds Polytechnic; Wakefield Technical College
Constituency: market and county town south of Leeds in industrial, ex-mining South Yorkshire

Hoban, Mark
Conservative MP for Fareham since 2001

Majority: 7,009 (15.5%)
Turnout: 62.5%

	Votes	Share %	Change %
Mark Hoban, Conservative	21,389	47.1	0.3
James Carr, Labour	14,380	31.6	4.6
Hugh Pritchard, Liberal Democrat	8,503	18.7	−0.9
William O'Brien, UK Independence party	1,175	2.6	n/a

Maiden speech: "my constituents do not see Britain's role as simply being part of an increasingly introspective and insular EU, but they see Britain as part of a network of nations"

Recent parliamentary career: entered parliament 2001
Background: chartered accountant, Price Waterhouse Coopers; adviser to banks and businesses
Born: March 31 1964 in north-east England
Education: St Leonard's Roman Catholic Comprehensive School
Higher education: London School of Economics
Constituency: prosperous urban area between Southampton and Portsmouth

Hodge, Margaret
Labour MP for Barking since 1994

Majority: 9,534 (37.9%)
Turnout: 45.5%

	Votes	Share %	Change %
Margaret Hodge, Labour	15,302	60.9	−4.9
Mark Page, Conservative	5,768	23	5.4
Anura Keppetipola, Liberal Democrat	2,450	9.8	0.3
Mark Tolman, British National party	1,606	6.4	3.7
John Dumbleton, UK Independence party	n/a		

Andrew Roth says: "late arriving minister… wealthy ex-left-wing, Islington based"

Recent parliamentary career: minister of state, DFES (2001–); junior minister, DFEE (1998–2001); won 1994 byelection
Background: senior consultant, Price Waterhouse; leader of Islington Council for ten years
Born: September 8 1944 in Egypt
Education: Bromley High School; Oxford High School
Higher education: London School of Economics
Constituency: outer edge of east London with much industry

Hoey, Kate
Labour MP for Vauxhall since 1989

Majority: 13,018 (39.0%)
Turnout: 44.8%

	Votes	Share %	Change %
Kate Hoey, Labour	19,738	59.1	−4.7
Anthony Bottrall, Liberal Democrat	6,720	20.1	4.1
Gareth Compton, Conservative	4,489	13.4	−1.8
Shane Collins, Green party	1,485	4.5	2.3
Theresa Bennett, Socialist Alliance	853	2.6	n/a
Martin Boyd, Independent	107	0.3	n/a

Andrew Roth says: "rare Labour unionist from Ulster Protestant stock"

Recent parliamentary career: junior minister, DCMS (1999–2001); junior minister, HO (1998–99)
Background: politics lecturer, Kingsway College; educational adviser, Arsenal Football Club (1982–89); Hackney and Southwark councillor; student activist for civil rights; backs foxhunting; sacked as sports minister (2001)
Born: June 21 1946 in Ulster
Education: Belfast Royal Academy
Higher education: Ulster College of Physical Education; City of London College
Constituency: inner south London from Waterloo to Clapham Common

Hogg, Rt Hon Douglas QC
Conservative MP for Sleaford and North Hykeham since 1997; Grantham (1979–97)

Majority: 8,622 (17.7%)
Turnout: 65.3%

	Votes	Share %	Change %
Douglas Hogg, Conservative	24,190	49.7	5.8
Elizabeth Donnelly, Labour	15,568	32	−2.3
Robert Arbon, Liberal Democrat	7,894	16.2	1
Michael Ward-Barrow, UK Independence party	1,067	2.2	n/a

Simon Hoggart, the *Guardian*: "one of the rudest men in British politics, if not the entire world"

Recent parliamentary career: home affairs committee (1997–2001); minister, MAFF (1995–97), where he had to cope with the BSE crisis
Background: president of the Oxford Union; barrister; made his name as an abrasive liberal Tory MP
Born: February 5 1945
Education: Eton College
Higher education: Oxford, Christ Church
Constituency: big rural seat that runs from Grantham to the edge of Lincoln

Holmes, Paul
Liberal Democrat MP for Chesterfield since 2001

Majority: 2,586 (5.8%)
Turnout: 60.7%

	Votes	Share %	Change %
Paul Holmes, Liberal Democrat	21,249	47.8	8.2
Reg Race, Labour	18,663	42	−8.8
Simon Hitchcock, Conservative	3,613	8.1	−1.1
Jeannie Robinson, Socialist Alliance	437	1	n/a
Bill Harrison, Socialist Labour Party	295	0.7	n/a
Christopher Rawson, Independent	184	0.4	n/a

Maiden speech: "governments of all parties would do better if they carried their work force with them after consultation rather than regarding staff as an enemy within who inflict scars upon one's back"

Recent parliamentary career: entered parliament 2001, taking seat from Labour; education and skills committee (2001–)
Background: headteacher of sixth form college, resigned to fight Chesterfield; Chesterfield councillor for 10 years

Born: January 16 1957 in Sheffield
Education: Firth Park School
Higher education: Sheffield University; York University
Constituency: self-contained town on the M1 just east of the Peak District that has developed since end of coal mining

Hood, Jimmy
Labour MP for Clydesdale since 1987

Majority: 7,794 (20.4%)
Turnout: 59.3%

	Votes	Share %	Change %
Jimmy Hood, Labour	17,822	46.6	−5.9
Jim Wright, Scottish National party	10,028	26.2	4.1
Kevin Newton, Conservative	5,034	13.2	−3.1
Ms Moira Craig, Liberal Democrat	4,111	10.8	2.4
Paul Cockshott, Scottish Socialist party	974	2.6	n/a
Donald McKay, UK Independence party	253	0.7	n/a

Andrew Roth says: "pro-European Campaign Groupie and a skilled and pragmatic committee chairman"

Recent parliamentary career: chair, European scrutiny committee (1998–); defence committee (1997–2001); administration committee (1997–2001)
Background: mining engineer; trade union activist (NUM); Newark and Sherwood councillor
Born: May 16 1948 in Lesmahagow
Education: Lesmahagow Higher Grade School
Higher education: Nottingham University
Constituency: ex-mining seat on M74 south of Glasgow, Lanark is largest town

Hoon, Rt Hon Geoff
Labour MP for Ashfield since 1992

Majority: 13,268 (33.7%)
Turnout: 53.6%

	Votes	Share %	Change %
Geoff Hoon, Labour	22,875	58.1	−7.1
Julian Leigh, Conservative	9,607	24.4	4.1
Bill Smith, Liberal Democrat	4,428	11.3	1.7
Melvin Harby, Independent	1,471	3.7	n/a
George Watson, Socialist Alliance	589	1.5	n/a
Katrina Howse, Socialist Labour party	380	1	n/a

Andrew Roth says: "pleasant moderate who wears his brains lightly"

Recent parliamentary career: secretary of state, MoD (1999–); minister of state, FCO (1998–99); junior minister, LCD (1997–98)
Background: barrister; law lecturer, Leeds University; MEP (1984–94)
Born: December 6 1953 in Derby
Education: Nottingham High School
Higher education: Cambridge, Jesus
Constituency: west Nottinghamshire, around the former mining town of Eastwood

Hope, Phil
Labour MP for Corby since 1997

Majority: 5,700 (12.1%)
Turnout: 65.3%

	Votes	Share %	Change %
Phil Hope, Labour	23,283	49.3	−6.1
Andrew Griffith, Conservative	17,583	37.2	3.8
Kevin Scudder, Liberal Democrat	4,751	10.1	2.6
Ian Gillman, UK Independence party	855	1.8	n/a
Andy Dickson, Socialist Labour Party	750	1.6	n/a

Andrew Roth says: "reforming do-gooder and overeager party loyalist"

Recent parliamentary career: PPS to John Prescott (2001–); committee of selection (1999–); PPS to Nick Raynsford, (1999–2001)
Background: management and community work consultant (1985–97); director of printing cooperative; schoolteacher; Kettering and Northamptonshire councillor
Born: April 19 1955 in London
Education: Wandsworth Comprehensive School, Northamptonshire
Higher education: Exeter University
Constituency: former steel town in Northamptonshire that now has new industry, seat includes some rural areas too

Hopkins, Kelvin
Labour MP for Luton North since 1997

Majority: 9,977 (25.5%)
Turnout: 59.3%

	Votes	Share %	Change %
Kelvin Hopkins, Labour	22,187	56.7	2.1
Amanda Sater, Conservative	12,210	31.2	−3.1
Bob Hoyle, Liberal Democrat	3,795	9.7	0.6
Colin Brown, UK Independence party	934	2.4	n/a

Andrew Roth says: "rebellion-prone left-wing economist"

Recent parliamentary career: broadcasting committee (1999–2001); took part in all eight major rebellions against government whip in 1997 parliament
Background: economist and political researcher for TUC and Unison; Luton councillor; author of various NALGO publications
Born: August 22 1941 in Leicester
Education: Queen Elizabeth's Grammar School, High Barnet
Higher education: Nottingham University
Constituency: northern part of tough town on M1, north of London

Horam, John
Conservative MP for Orpington since 1992; SDP MP for Gateshead West (1981–83); Labour MP for Gateshead West (1970–81)

Majority: 269 (0.6%)
Turnout: 68.4%

	Votes	Share %	Change %
John Horam, Conservative	22,334	43.9	3.3
Chris Maines, Liberal Democrat	22,065	43.3	7.6
Chris Purnell, Labour	5,517	10.8	−7.1
John Youles, UK Independence party	996	2	n/a

Andrew Roth says: "the only known double turncoat to have represented three parties in the Commons"

Recent parliamentary career: chair, environmental audit committee (1997–)
Background: market-research officer; feature writer; managing director; joined SDP from Labour 1981; joined Conservatives 1990

Born: March 7 1939 in Preston
Education: Silcoates School, Wakefield
Higher education: Cambridge, St Catherine's
Constituency: Kentish green belt suburbia on London borders and with many commuters

Howard, Rt Hon Michael
Conservative MP for Folkestone and Hythe since 1983

Majority: 5,907 (12.9%)
Turnout: 64.1%

	Votes	Share %	Change %
Michael Howard, Conservative	20,645	45	6
Peter Carroll, Liberal Democrat	14,738	32.1	5.2
Albert Catterall, Labour	9,260	20.2	–4.7
John Baker, UK Independence party	1,212	2.6	n/a

Andrew Roth says: "his political opportunism has warred with his classic right-wing views and first-class legal mind"

Recent parliamentary career: shadow chancellor (2001–); shadow secretary of state, FCO (1997–99); home secretary (1993–97); secretary of state, employment (1990–93)
Background: barrister; QC; junior counsel to the crown; president of Cambridge University Union
Born: July 7 1941 in Gorseinon, Wales
Education: Llanelli Grammar School
Higher education: Cambridge, Peterhouse
Constituency: Channel Tunnel port town and nearby Romney Marsh

Howarth, Rt Hon Alan
Labour MP for Newport East since 1997; Stratford-on-Avon (1995–97); Conservative MP for Stratford-on-Avon (1983–95)

Majority: 9,874 (31.5%)
Turnout: 55.7%

	Votes	Share %	Change %
Alan Howarth, Labour	17,120	54.7	–3
Ian Oakley, Conservative	7,246	23.2	1.8
Alistair Cameron, Liberal Democrat	4,394	14.1	3.7
Madoc Batcup, Plaid Cymru	1,519	4.9	3
Liz Screen, Socialist Labour Party	420	1.3	–3.9
Neal Reynolds, UK Independence party	410	1.3	n/a

Andrew Roth says: "he seems infinitely calm, emollient and persuasive, but lonely, with a tortured conscience"

Recent parliamentary career: intelligence and security committee (2001–); junior minister, DCMS (1998–2001); junior minister, DFEE (1997–98); junior minister, DFEE (1989–92)
Background: joined Labour party (October 1995); director, Conservative Research Department (1979–81); teacher at Westminster School; senior research assistant to field marshal Montgomery on A History of Warfare (1965–67)
Born: June 11 1944 in London
Education: Rugby School
Higher education: Cambridge, King's
Constituency: eastern part of South Wales town of Newport, contains closing Llanwern steelworks

Howarth, George
Labour MP for Knowsley North and Sefton East since 1986

Majority: 18,927 (50.4%)
Turnout: 53%

	Votes	Share %	Change %
George Howarth, Labour	25,035	66.7	-3.2
Keith Chapman, Conservative	6,108	16.3	-1
Richard Roberts, Liberal Democrat	5,173	13.8	2.7
Ron Waugh, Socialist Labour Party	574	1.5	-0.2
Thomas Rossiter, Ind R	356	1	n/a
David Jones, Ind J	271	0.7	n/a

Andrew Roth says: "efficient and fair-minded anti-militant"

Recent parliamentary career: minister of state, NIO (1999–2001); junior minister, HO (1997–99)
Background: chief executive, Walm Cooperative centre; industrial engineer and fitter; further education teacher; Huyton councillor
Born: June 29 1949 in Knowsley
Education: Knowsley Secondary School
Higher education: Liverpool Polytechnic
Constituency: typical Mersyside Labour seat, contains Aintree racecourse

Howarth, Gerald
Conservative MP for Aldershot since 1997; Cannock and Burntwood (1983–92)

Majority: 6,564 (14.5%)
Turnout: 57.9%

	Votes	Share %	Change %
Gerald Howarth, Conservative	19,106	42.2	-0.5
Adrian Collett, Liberal Democrat	12,542	27.7	-2.8
Luke Akehurst, Labour	11,391	25.1	1
Derek Rumsey, UK Independence party	797	1.8	n/a
Adam Stacey, Green party	630	1.4	n/a
Arthur Pendragon, Independent	459	1	0.3
Alan Hope, Official Monster Raving Loony party	390	0.9	n/a

Andrew Roth says: "a hard-right radical"

Recent parliamentary career: defence committee (2001–); home affairs committee (1997–2001); PPS to Margaret Thatcher (1991–92)
Background: banker specialising in loans; adviser and director of several companies specialising in fireworks, armaments, aerospace design and insurance brokering; backs causes including capital punishment; demonstrated in favour of US forced in Vietnam; on immigration committee of pro-repatriation Monday Club (1971)
Born: September 12 1947 in Guildford
Education: Bloxham School, Banbury
Higher education: Southampton University
Constituency: Hampshire town with a strong military tradition

Howells, Dr Kim
Labour MP for Pontypridd since 1989

Majority: 17,684 (46.1%)
Turnout: 58%

	Votes	Share %	Change %
Kim Howells, Labour	22,963	59.9	-4
Bleddyn Hancock, Plaid Cymru	5,279	13.8	7.3
Prudence Dailey, Conservative	5,096	13.3	0.4
Eric Brooke, Liberal Democrat	4,152	10.8	-2.6
Sue Warry, UK Independence party	603	1.6	n/a
John Biddulph, ProLife Alliance	216	0.6	n/a

Andrew Roth says: "recently-braked loose cannon of left-wing politics"
Recent parliamentary career: junior minister, DCMS (2001–); junior minister, DTI (1998–2001); junior minister, DFEE (1997–98)
Background: research officer, NUM; freelance writer and broadcast journalist
Born: November 27 1946 in Pontypridd
Education: Mountain Ash Grammar School
Higher education: Warwick University; Hornsey College of Art; Cambridge College of Art and Technology
Constituency: Taff and Ely valleys north-west of Cardiff

Hoyle, Lindsay
Labour MP for Chorley since 1997

Majority: 8,444 (17.6%)
Turnout: 62.3%

	Votes	Share %	Change %
Lindsay Hoyle, Labour	25,088	52.3	–0.7
Peter Booth, Conservative	16,644	34.7	–1.2
Stephen Fenn, Liberal Democrat	5,372	11.2	2.7
Graham Frost, UK Independence party	848	1.8	n/a

Andrew Roth says: "loyal Blairite who learned that 'blind loyalty by the robot tendency is not necessarily rewarded by government ministers'"

Recent parliamentary career: trade and industry committee (1998–); catering committee (1997–)
Background: company director; Chorley leader and mayor; Adlington councillor; called for Heathrow to be named after Princess Diana (1997); son of ex-MP Doug Hoyle
Born: June 10 1958 in Chorley
Education: Anderton County Primary School; Lords College, Bolton; Horwich College of Further Education
Higher education: Bolton TIC
Constituency: bellwether seat, Lancashire town with Royal Ordnance factory

Hughes, Beverley
Labour MP for Stretford and Urmston since 1997

Majority: 13,239 (34.0%)
Turnout: 55%

	Votes	Share %	Change %
Beverley Hughes, Labour	23,804	61.1	2.6
Jonathan Mackie, Conservative	10,565	27.1	–3.4
John Bridges, Liberal Democrat	3,891	10	1.8
Katie Price, Independent	713	1.8	n/a

Andrew Roth says: "another of Labour's locally-rooted lecturers and municipal politicians"

Recent parliamentary career: junior minister, HO (2001–); junior minister, DETR (1999–2001); PPS to Hilary Armstrong (1998–99)
Background: probation officer; social policy lecturer, Manchester University; Trafford councillor
Born: March 30 1950 in Venezuela
Education: Ellesmere Port Grammar School
Higher education: Liverpool University; Manchester University
Constituency: south-west of central Manchester, includes Old Trafford and hard-hit Moss Side

Hughes, Kevin
Labour MP for Doncaster North since 1992

Majority: 15,187 (48.4%)
Turnout: 50.5%

	Votes	Share %	Change %
Kevin Hughes, Labour	19,788	63.1	−6.7
Anita Kapoor, Conservative	4,601	14.7	−0.1
Colin Ross, Liberal Democrat	3,323	10.6	2.2
Martin Williams, Independent	2,926	9.3	n/a
John Wallis, UK Independence party	725	2.3	n/a

Andrew Roth says: "youngish Yorkshire ex-miner 'not noted for his gentle touch'"

Recent parliamentary career: government whip (1997–2001)
Background: miner for 20 years; Doncaster councillor; former Communist party member
Born: December 15 1952 in Doncaster
Education: Owston Park Secondary School
Higher education: Sheffield University
Constituency: part of Doncaster plus farming land to north and north-east of town

Hughes, Simon
Liberal Democrat MP for North Southwark and Bermondsey since 1997; Southwark and Bermondsey (1983–97)

Majority: 9,632 (26.1%)
Turnout: 50.1%

	Votes	Share %	Change %
Simon Hughes, Liberal Democrat	20,991	56.9	8.3
Kingsley Abrams, Labour	11,359	30.8	−9.5
Ewan Wallace, Conservative	2,800	7.6	0.7
Ruth Jenkins, Green party	752	2	n/a
Ms Lianne Shore, National Front	612	1.7	n/a
Rob McWhirter, UK Independence party	271	0.7	n/a
John Davies, Independent	77	0.2	n/a

Andrew Roth says: "'Mr Muscular Christian' – the clean-cut, jut-jawed, bright-eyed, green-tinted radical community politician"

Recent parliamentary career: Lib Dem spokesperson, home affairs (1997–2001); ran for Lib Dem party leadership (1999)
Background: barrister; trained at European Commission; briefly member of general synod; very hard-working; attention-seeking winner of byelection (1983) who holds only inner city Lib Dem seat
Born: May 17 1951 in Bramhall, Cheshire
Education: Llandaff Cathedral School; Christ College School, Brecon
Higher education: Inns of Court School of Law; College of Europe; Cambridge, Selwyn
Constituency: Tate Modern and Thames shore running through Bermondsey to Rotherhide

Humble, Joan
Labour MP for Blackpool North and Fleetwood since 1997

Majority: 5,721 (13.5%)
Turnout: 57.2%

	Votes	Share %	Change %
Joan Humble, Labour	21,610	50.8	−1.4
Alan Vincent, Conservative	15,889	37.3	1.8
Steven Bate, Liberal Democrat	4,132	9.7	1.1
Colin Porter, UK Independence party	950	2.2	n/a

Andrew Roth says: "locally-focussed Christian socialist"

Recent parliamentary career: work and pensions committee (2001–); social security committee (1998–2001)
Background: DoH civil servant; Lancashire councillor
Born: March 3 1951 in Skipton, North Yorkshire

Education: Greenhead Grammar School
Higher education: Lancaster University
Constituency: northern, less busy part of Britain's biggest seaside resort, includes Thornton, Cleveleys and Fleetwood

Hume, John

Social Democratic and Labour party MP for Foyle since 1983

Majority: 11,550 (23.6%)
Turnout: 68.9%

	Votes	Share %	Change %
John Hume, Social Democratic and Labour party	24,538	50.2	−2.3
Mitchel McLaughlin, Sinn Fein	12,988	26.6	2.7
William Hay, Democratic Unionist party	7,414	15.2	−6.3
Andrew Davidson, Ulster Unionist party	3,360	6.9	n/a
Colm Cavanagh, Alliance party of Northern Ireland	579	1.2	−0.5

Andrew Roth says: "leading non-violent voice of Ulster's Catholics; rich in morose self-pity and thin-skinned egotism"

Recent parliamentary career: leader, SDLP (1979–2001); resigned (September 2001) on health grounds
Background: lecturer in international affairs; French and history teacher; received many awards for peace work in Northern Ireland, including Nobel Peace Prize (1998); trained for priesthood
Born: January 18 1937 in Derry
Education: St Columb's College, Derry
Higher education: St Patrick's College, Maynooth; Harvard; Trinity College, Dublin; Dublin City University
Constituency: urban constituency covering Northern Ireland's second city, Derry to nationalists; Londonderry to others

Hunter, Andrew

Conservative MP for Basingstoke since 1983

Majority: 880 (1.8%)
Turnout: 60.7%

	Votes	Share %	Change %
Andrew Hunter, Conservative	20,490	42.7	−0.6
Jon Hartley, Labour	19,610	40.9	1.8
Steve Sollitt, Liberal Democrat	6,693	14	−3
Kim Graham, UK Independence party	1,202	2.5	n/a

Andrew Roth says: "assiduous, peace-through-strength hard-rightist"

Recent parliamentary career: environment, food, and rural affairs committee (2001–); Northern Ireland affairs committee (1994–2001)
Background: assistant master, Harrow school; vice president, National Prayer Book society; member of Society of the Sealed Knot; only British MP in Orange Order; once vice chair of Monday Club
Born: January 8 1943 in Harpenden, Hertfordshire
Education: St George's, Harpenden
Higher education: Durham University; Cambridge, Jesus; Cambridge, Westcott House
Constituency: country market town that has outgrown its roots with new industry including electronics, finance, and computers

Hurst, Alan

Labour MP for Braintree since 1997

Majority: 358 (0.7%)
Turnout: 63.6%

	Votes	Share %	Change %
Alan Hurst, Labour	21,123	42	−0.7
Brooks Newmark, Conservative	20,765	41.3	1.2
Peter Turner, Liberal Democrat	5,664	11.3	−0.2
James Abbott, Green party	1,241	2.5	1.2
Michael Nolan, LCA	774	1.5	n/a
Charlie Cole, UK Independence party	748	1.5	n/a

Andrew Roth says: "low-profiled, gentlemanly and not overly partisan"

Recent parliamentary career: agriculture committee (1997–2001)
Background: solicitor and partner in law firm; Southend councillor and deputy leader
Born: September 2 1945 in Southend-on-Sea
Education: Westcliff High School, Southend
Higher education: Liverpool University
Constituency: big seat in central Essex, mixed urban working-class and wealthy villages

Hutton, Rt Hon John
Labour MP for Barrow and Furness since 1992

Majority: 9,889 (25.4%)
Turnout: 60.3%

	Votes	Share %	Change %
John Hutton, Labour	21,724	55.7	−1.6
James Airey, Conservative	11,835	30.3	3.1
Barry Rabone, Liberal Democrat	4,750	12.2	3.4
John Smith, UK Independence party	711	1.8	n/a

Andrew Roth says: "pragmatic, pro-European defence specialist"

Recent parliamentary career: minister of state, DoH (2001–); minister of state, DoH (1999–2001); junior minister, DoH (1998–99)
Background: senior law lecturer at Newcastle University (1981–92)
Born: May 6 1955
Education: Westcliff High School, Southend
Higher education: Oxford, Magdalen
Constituency: remote west Cumbria beyond Lake District, Trident yard creates jobs

I

Iddon, Dr Brian
Labour MP for Bolton South East since 1997

Majority: 12,871 (37.7%)
Turnout: 50.1%

	Votes	Share %	Change %
Brian Iddon, Labour	21,129	61.9	−7
Haroon Rashid, Conservative	8,258	24.2	4.5
Frank Harasiwka, Liberal Democrat	3,941	11.5	2.7
William Kelly, Socialist Labour Party	826	2.4	n/a

Andrew Roth says: "crusader for a royal commission on drugs and local left-wing old Labour Eurosceptic"

Recent parliamentary career: science and technology committee (2000–); environmental audit committee (2001–)
Background: has a PhD in organic chemistry; chartered chemist; chemistry lecturer at Salford University; Bolton councillor

Born: July 5 1940 in Tarleton, Lancashire
Education: Christ Church Boy's School, Southport
Higher education: Hull University; Southport Technical College
Constituency: central Bolton and industrial surrounds of hard-hit north-west town

Illsley, Eric
Labour MP for Barnsley Central since 1987

Majority: 15,130 (54.9%)
Turnout: 45.8%

	Votes	Share %	Change %
Eric Illsley, Labour	19,181	69.6	–7.4
Alan Hartley, Liberal Democrat	4,051	14.7	5.2
Ian McCord, Conservative	3,608	13.1	3.3
Henry Rajch, Socialist Alliance	703	2.6	n/a

Andrew Roth says: "active, articulate and well informed"

Recent parliamentary career: foreign affairs committee (1997–); procedure committee (1997–)
Background: head of general department and chief administration officer, NUM
Born: April 9 1955 in Barnsley
Education: Barnsley Holgate Grammar School
Higher education: Leeds University; Barnsley Technical College
Constituency: the central part of Britain's former coal-mining stronghold

Ingram, Rt Hon Adam
Labour MP for East Kilbride since 1987

Majority: 12,755 (30.6%)
Turnout: 62.6%

	Votes	Share %	Change %
Adam Ingram, Labour	22,205	53.3	–3.2
Archie Buchanan, Scottish National party	9,450	22.7	1.8
Ewan Hawthorn, Liberal Democrat	4,278	10.3	3.1
Margaret McCulloch, Conservative	4,238	10.2	–1.8
David Stevenson, Scottish Socialist party	1,519	3.6	n/a

Andrew Roth says: "long operated as a behind-the-scenes fixer"

Recent parliamentary career: minister of state, NIO (1997–)
Background: computer programmer; NALGO organiser (1977–87); East Kilbride councillor and leader
Born: February 1 1947 in Glasgow
Education: Cranhill Secondary School
Higher education: Open University
Constituency: large, successful Scottish new town with skilled industrial workers

J

Jack, Rt Hon Michael
Conservative MP for Fylde since 1987

Majority: 9,610 (21.5%)
Turnout: 62%

	Votes	Share %	Change %
Michael Jack, Conservative	23,383	52.3	3.4
John Stockton, Labour	13,773	30.8	–0.9
John Begg, Liberal Democrat	6,599	14.8	0.2
Mrs Lesley Brown, UK Independence party	982	2.2	n/a

Andrew Roth says: "moderate Tory, strong on caring and the needs of the north"

Recent parliamentary career: environment, food and rural affairs committee (2001–); opposition spokesperson, MAFF (1997–98); opposition spokesperson, DoH (1997–97); financial secretary to the Treasury (1995–97)
Background: sales director, Proctor and Gamble; personal assistant to director, Proctor and Gamble; Marks and Spencer; pro-European, did not thrive under William Hague
Born: September 17 1946 in Folkestone
Education: Bradford Grammar School
Higher education: Leicester University; Bradford Technical College
Constituency: coastal seat between Blackpool and Preston, many prosperous pensioners

Jackson, Glenda
Labour MP for Hampstead and Highgate since 1992

Majority: 7,876 (22.3%)
Turnout: 54.2%

	Votes	Share %	Change %
Glenda Jackson, Labour	16,601	46.9	–10.5
Andrew Mennear, Conservative	8,725	24.6	–2.6
Jonathan Simpson, Liberal Democrat	7,273	20.5	8.1
Andrew Cornwell, Green party	1,654	4.7	n/a
Maddy Cooper, Socialist Alliance	559	1.6	n/a
Brian McDermott, UK Independence party	316	0.9	n/a
Ms Sister XNunoftheabove, Ind X	144	0.4	n/a
Mary Teale, ProLife Alliance	92	0.3	n/a
Amos Klein, Independent	43	0.1	n/a

Andrew Roth says: "formidable loyal Blairite reformer who treats politics as another serious job"

Recent parliamentary career: junior minister, DETR (1997–99) resigned in reshuffle; tried to become Labour's candidate for London mayor (1999), losing to Frank Dobson
Background: actress and Oscar-winning film star (Women in Love, Mary, Queen of Scots); member of Amnesty; campaigner for Oxfam, Shelter, Friends of the Earth
Born: May 9 1936 in Birkenhead
Education: West Kirkby County Grammar School
Higher education: RADA
Constituency: upmarket north London villages of Hampstead and Highgate plus multicultural Kilburn

Jackson, Helen
Labour MP for Sheffield Hillsborough since 1992

Majority: 14,569 (34.2%)
Turnout: 56.6%

	Votes	Share %	Change %
Helen Jackson, Labour	24,170	56.8	–0.1
John Commons, Liberal Democrat	9,601	22.6	–3.2
Graham King, Conservative	7,801	18.3	3.8
Peter Webb, UK Independence party	964	2.3	n/a

Andrew Roth says: "egalitarian campaigner who is very seriously interested in transferring life's benefits to her poorest constituents"

Recent parliamentary career: PPS to John Reid (2001–); transport, local government, and the regions committee (2001–); modernisation of the House of Commons committee (1997–); PPS to Peter Mandelson (1999–2001); PPS to Mo Mowlam (1997–99)
Background: special-needs teacher; full-time Sheffield councillor involved in local economic development
Born: May 19 1939 in Leeds
Education: Berkhamsted Girls School
Higher education: Oxford, St Hilda's; CF Mott College of Education, Prescott
Constituency: north-western part of South Yorkshire city, mixed housing; semi-rural

Jackson, Robert
Conservative MP for Wantage since 1983

Majority: 5,600 (11.4%)
Turnout: 64.5%

	Votes	Share %	Change %
Robert Jackson, Conservative	19,475	39.6	–0.2
Stephen Beer, Labour	13,875	28.2	–0.7
Neil Fawcett, Liberal Democrat	13,776	28	1.5
David Brooks-Saxl, Green party	1,062	2.2	1.1
Nikolai Tolstoy, UK Independence party	941	1.9	n/a

Andrew Roth says: "dissident Europhile intellectual with a talent for treading on colleagues' long toes"

Recent parliamentary career: science and technology committee (1999–); junior minister, civil service (1992–93)
Background: academic; consultant; author of books on Europe, international politics; special adviser to governor of Rhodesia (1980)
Born: September 24 1946 in Bulawayo, Rhodesia
Education: Falcon College, Rhodesia
Higher education: Oxford, St Edmund Hall; Oxford, All Souls
Constituency: small towns south-west of Oxford, including Didcot, Wantage and Wallingford

Jamieson, David
Labour MP for Plymouth Devonport since 1992

Majority: 13,033 (31.2%)
Turnout: 56.6%

	Votes	Share %	Change %
David Jamieson, Labour	4,322	58.3	–2.6
John Glen, Conservative	1,289	27.1	2.9
Keith Baldry, Liberal Democrat	4,513	10.8	0.1
Michael Parker, UK Independence party	958	2.3	n/a
Tony Staunton, Socialist Alliance	334	0.8	n/a
Rob Hawkins, Socialist Labour party	303	0.7	n/a

Andrew Roth says: "strongly opinionated, hard-hitting and sardonic speaker"

Recent parliamentary career: junior minister, DTLGR (2001–); government whip (1997–2001); accommodation and works committee (1998–2001)
Background: mathematics teacher and community college vice principal; Solihull councillor
Born: May 18 1947 in Solihull
Education: Tudor Grange Grammar School
Higher education: Open University; Solihull Technical College; St Peter's College, Saltley
Constituency: north part of ancient Devon city, includes dockyard, naval base and much council housing

Jenkin, Hon Bernard
Conservative MP for North Essex since 1992; North Colchester (1992–97)

Majority: 7,186 (16.0%)
Turnout: 62.7%

	Votes	Share %	Change %
Bernard Jenkin, Conservative	21,325	47.5	3.6
Philip Hawkins, Labour	14,139	31.5	–1.7
Trevor Ellis, Liberal Democrat	7,867	17.5	–2.1
George Curtis, UK Independence party	1,613	3.6	n/a

Andrew Roth says: "ambitious, flexibly right-wing MP whose icon is Baroness Thatcher"

Recent parliamentary career: shadow defence secretary (2001–); ran Iain Duncan Smith's leadership campaign (2001); opposition spokesperson, DETR (1998–2001)
Background: manager and adviser, Legal and General Group; sales executive; son of former MP Patrick (now Lord) Jenkin; adviser to Leon Brittan MP (1986–88)
Born: April 9 1959 in London
Education: Highgate School; William Ellis School, London
Higher education: Cambridge, Corpus Christi
Constituency: rural Essex around Colchester

Jenkins, Brian
Labour MP for Tamworth since 1997; South East Staffordshire (1996–97)

Majority: 4,598 (11.4%)
Turnout: 57.8%

	Votes	Share %	Change %
Brian Jenkins, Labour	19,722	49	–2.8
Luis Gunter, Conservative	15,124	37.6	0.9
Jennifer Pinkett, Liberal Democrat	4,721	11.7	3.6
Paul Sootheran, UK Independence party	683	1.7	n/a

Andrew Roth says: "claims that, as a council leader, he was Blairite before Tony Blair"

Recent parliamentary career: broadcasting committee (2001–); public accounts committee (2001–); PPS to Joyce Quin (1999–2001); PPS to minister of state, FCO (1998–99)
Background: communications and media studies lecturer; industrial engineer, Percy Lane and Jaguar cars; instrument mechanic, CEGB; Tamworth councillor
Born: September 19 1942 in Tamworth
Education: Kingsbury High School
Higher education: London School of Economics; Wolverhampton Polytechnic
Constituency: Staffordshire town north-east of Birmingham with many commuters

Johnson, Alan
Labour MP for Hull West and Hessle since 1997

Majority: 10,951 (37.9%)
Turnout: 45.8%

	Votes	Share %	Change %
Alan Johnson, Labour	16,880	58.4	–0.3
John Sharp, Conservative	5,929	20.5	2.4
Angela Wastling, Liberal Democrat	4,364	15.1	–3.1
John Cornforth, UK Independence party	878	3	n/a
David Harris, Independent	512	1.8	n/a
David Skinner, Socialist Labour Party	353	1.2	n/a

Andrew Roth says: "articulate and 'immensely able' spokesman"

Recent parliamentary career: minister of state, DTI (2001–); junior minister, DTI (1999–2001)

Background: postman; general secretary, UCW; director, Unity Bank Trust
Born: May 17 1950 in London
Education: Sloane Grammar School, Chelsea
Constituency: city centre and fishing port of isolated east coast town

Johnson, Boris
Conservative MP for Henley since 2001

Majority: 8,458 (19.1%)
Turnout: 64.3%

	Votes	Share %	Change %
Boris Johnson, Conservative	20,466	46.1	−0.3
Catherine Bearder, Liberal Democrat	12,008	27	2.3
Janet Matthews, Labour	9,367	21.1	−1.6
Philip Collins, UK Independence party	1,413	3.2	n/a
Oliver Tickell, Green party	1,147	2.6	n/a

Maiden speech: "Michael Heseltine is a hard act to follow, so I approach this moment with much the same sense of self-doubt as Simba in The Lion King"

Recent parliamentary career: entered parliament 2001; notably endorsed Kenneth Clarke's leadership bid (2001)
Background: editor of the *Spectator*; *Daily Telegraph* columnist and Brussels correspondent
Born: June 19 1964 in New York
Education: Eton College
Higher education: Balliol College, Oxford
Constituency: opulent Thames side town and surrounding countryside towards Oxford

Johnson, Melanie
Labour MP for Welwyn-Hatfield since 1997

Majority: 1,196 (2.8%)
Turnout: 63.9%

	Votes	Share %	Change %
Melanie Johnson, Labour	18,484	43.2	−3.9
Grant Shapps, Conservative	17,288	40.4	3.9
Daniel Cooke, Liberal Democrat	6,021	14.1	0.6
Malcolm Biggs, UK Independence party	798	1.9	n/a
Fiona Pinto, ProLife Alliance	230	0.5	0

Andrew Roth says: "loyalist reformer who believes more women MPs will make for 'a different style of working'"

Recent parliamentary career: junior minister, DTI (2001–); junior minister, Treasury (1999–2001)
Background: school inspector; general manager, Cambridge FHSA; Cambridgeshire councillor
Born: February 5 1955 in Ipswich
Education: Clifton High School, Bristol
Higher education: University College, London; Cambridge, King's
Constituency: twin Hertfordshire new towns with much light industry

Jones, Helen
Labour MP for Warrington North since 1997

Majority: 15,156 (39.0%)
Turnout: 53.7%

	Votes	Share %	Change %
Helen Jones, Labour	24,026	61.8	−0.3
James Usher, Conservative	8,870	22.8	−1.2
Roy Smith, Liberal Democrat	5,232	13.5	3.1
Jack Kirkham, UK Independence party	782	2	n/a

Andrew Roth says: "intelligent, battle-hardened left-wing solicitor built into the Labour machine"

Recent parliamentary career: unopposed bills panel (1999–); education and employment committee (1999–2001); education subcommittee (1999–2001)
Background: solicitor; English teacher; development officer, Mind; justice and peace officer; Labour party liaison officer, MSF union
Born: December 24 1954 in Chester
Education: Ursuline Convent, Chester
Higher education: Liverpool University; University College, London
Constituency: innercity core of industrial town just north of Mersey

Jones, Jon Owen
Labour MP for Cardiff Central since 1992

Majority: 659 (1.9%)
Turnout: 58.3%

	Votes	Share %	Change %
Jon Owen Jones, Labour	13,451	38.6	–5.1
Jenny Willott, Liberal Democrat	12,792	36.7	11.8
Gregory Walker, Conservative	5,537	15.9	–4.1
Richard Grigg, Plaid Cymru	1,680	4.8	1.2
Stephen Bartley, Green party	661	1.9	n/a
Julian Goss, Socialist Alliance	283	0.8	n/a
Frank Hughes, UK Independence party	221	0.6	n/a
Madeleine Jeremy, ProLife Alliance	217	0.6	n/a

Andrew Roth says: "environmentalist, Welsh speaking...former semi hard-left teacher"

Recent parliamentary career: introduced private member's bill to legalise cannabis (2001); environmental audit committee (1999–); junior minister, WO (1998–99)
Background: science teacher; Cardiff councillor
Born: April 19 1954 in Rhondda
Education: Ysgol Gyfun Rhydyfelin
Higher education: Cardiff University; University of East Anglia
Constituency: socially diverse centre of Cardiff with mixed housing and many students; notable Lib Dem–Lab marginal

Jones, Kevan
Labour MP for Durham North since 2001

Majority: 18,683 (48.4%)
Turnout: 57%

	Votes	Share %	Change %
Kevan Jones, Labour	25,920	67.2	–3.1
Matthew Palmer, Conservative	7,237	18.8	4.3
Carole Field, Liberal Democrat	5,411	14	2.9

Maiden speech: "my constituency must be unique in having a place – a village, in fact – called No Place"

Recent parliamentary career: entered parliament 2001; defence committee (2001–)
Background: GMB union official; Newcastle councillor, chief whip of Labour group on Newcastle City Council; campaigner for "asbestos awareness"; assistant to Nicholas Brown MP (1985–89)
Born: April 25 1964
Education: Portland Comprehensive School
Higher education: Newcastle upon Tyne Polytechnic
Constituency: covers Chester-le-Street, Washington New Town and land between

Jones, Dr Lynne
Labour MP for Birmingham Selly Oak since 1992

Majority: 10,339 (25.8%)
Turnout: 56.3%

	Votes	Share %	Change %
Lynne Jones, Labour	21,015	52.4	–3.2
Ken Hardeman, Conservative	10,676	26.6	–1.2
David Osbourne, Liberal Democrat	6,532	16.3	4.2
Barney Smith, Green party	1,309	3.3	n/a
Beryl Williams, UK Independence party	568	1.4	n/a

Andrew Roth says: "rebellious utopian radical reformer and housing specialist"

Recent parliamentary career: science and technology committee (1997–)
Background: research fellow, Birmingham University; housing association manager; member of Liberty, Greenpeace, CND
Born: April 26 1951 in Birmingham
Education: Bartley Green Girls' Grammar School
Higher education: Birmingham University; Birmingham Polytechnic
Constituency: urban southern Birmingham around Bournville; once prosperous, now slightly less so

Jones, Martyn
Labour MP for Clwyd South since 1997; Clwyd South West (1987–97)

Majority: 8,898 (26.6%)
Turnout: 62.4%

	Votes	Share %	Change %
Martyn Jones, Labour	17,217	51.4	–6.7
Tom Biggins, Conservative	8,319	24.8	1.7
Dyfed Edwards, Plaid Cymru	3,982	11.9	5.6
David Griffiths, Liberal Democrat	3,426	10.2	0.8
Edwina Theunissen, UK Independence party	552	1.7	n/a

Andrew Roth says: "independent-minded left-winger who is hostile to gun control"

Recent parliamentary career: chair, Welsh affairs committee (1997–); vice chair, TGWU parliamentary group (2000–2001)
Background: microbiologist for Wrexham Brewery; Clwyd councillor; Christian socialist
Born: March 1 1947 in Crewe
Education: Grove Park Grammar School
Higher education: Liverpool College of Commerce; Liverpool Polytechnic; Trent Polytechnic
Constituency: scenic, rugged, Welsh-speaking North Wales

Jones, Nigel
Liberal Democrat MP for Cheltenham since 1992

Majority: 5,255 (12.5%)
Turnout: 61.9%

	Votes	Share %	Change %
Nigel Jones, Liberal Democrat	19,970	47.7	–1.8
Rob Garnham, Conservative	14,715	35.2	–1
Andy Erlam, Labour	5,041	12.1	2
Keith Bessant, Green party	735	1.8	n/a
Dancing Ken Hanks, Official Monster Raving Loony party	513	1.2	0.5
Jim Carver, UK Independence party	482	1.2	n/a
Tony Gates, ProLife Alliance	272	0.7	0.2
Roger Everest, Independent	107	0.3	n/a

Andrew Roth says: "clear minded, practical and egalitarian"

Recent parliamentary career: international development committee (1999–); Lib Dem spokesperson, DFID (1999–99); spokesperson, DCMS (1997–99); spokesperson, DTI (1997–99)
Background: locally born ICL computer consultant; Gloucestershire councillor; injured in 1998 sword attack by a constituent
Born: March 30 1948 in Cheltenham
Education: Prince Henry's Grammar School
Constituency: grand spa town in Gloucestershire Cotswolds, education and business centre

Jowell, Rt Hon Tessa
Labour MP for Dulwich and West Norwood since 1997; Dulwich (1992–97)

Majority: 12,310 (32.2%)
Turnout: 54.3%

	Votes	Share %	Change %
Tessa Jowell, Labour	20,999	54.9	–6.1
Nick Vineall, Conservative	8,689	22.7	–1.5
Caroline Pidgeon, Liberal Democrat	5,806	15.2	4.4
Jenny Jones, Green party	1,914	5	n/a
Brian Kelly, Socialist Alliance	839	2.2	n/a

Andrew Roth says: "high-flying Blairite moderniser whose style is 'direct, thoughtful, but never patronising'"

Recent parliamentary career: secretary of state, DCMS (2001–); minister of state, DFEE (1999–2001); minister of state, DoH (1997–99)
Background: social worker; assistant director, Mind; Research Fellow at IPPR, Kings Fund
Born: September 17 1947 in London
Education: St Margaret's School, Aberdeen
Higher education: Edinburgh University; Aberdeen University; Goldsmith's College, London
Constituency: south London suburbia, affluent middle class residential areas

Joyce, Eric
Labour MP for Falkirk West since 2000

Majority: 8,532 (27.6%)
Turnout: 57.7%

	Votes	Share %	Change %
Eric Joyce, Labour	16,022	51.9	8.4
David Kerr, Scottish National party	7,490	24.3	–15.6
Simon Murray, Conservative	2,321	7.5	–0.8
Hugh O'Donnell, Liberal Democrat	2,203	7.1	3.9
William Buchanan, Ind B	1,464	4.7	n/a
Mhairi McAlpine, Scottish Socialist party	707	2.3	n/a
Hugh Lynch, Independent	490	1.6	n/a
Ronnie Forbes, Socialist Labour party	194	0.6	n/a

Maiden speech: "Unemployment in my constituency is a considerable enemy today. However, it has fallen sharply in the past few years, and continues to do so."

Recent parliamentary career: entered parliament 2000; Scottish affairs committee (2001–); procedure committee (2001–)
Background: commission for racial equality (1999–2000); army major (1992–99)
Born: October 13 1960
Education: Perth High School
Higher education: Stirling University; Bath University; Keele University
Constituency: contains all of the industrial Central Belt town of Falkirk

K

Kaufman, Rt Hon Gerald
Labour MP for Manchester Gorton since 1983; Ardwick (1970–83)

Majority: 11,304 (41.5%)
Turnout: 42.7%

	Votes	Share %	Change %
Gerald Kaufman, Labour	17,099	62.8	–2.5
Jackie Pearcey, Liberal Democrat	5,795	21.3	3.8
Christopher Causer, Conservative	2,705	9.9	–1.8
Bruce Bingham, Green party	835	3.1	1.2
Rashid Bhatti, UK Independence party	462	1.7	n/a
Kirsty Muir, Socialist Labour party	333	1.2	–0.2

Andrew Roth says: "slashing Tory basher whose lacerating language conceals a loyalist"

Recent parliamentary career: chair, culture, media and sport committee (1997–), where he has won attention for his sharp questioning and strong views; member, Royal Commission on the Reform of the House of Lords; Labour's high-profile shadow foreign secretary (1987–92)
Background: Booker Prize judge (1999); writes on cinema; journalist for five decades; industry minister (1975–79); Harold Wilson's press aide
Born: June 21 1930 in Leeds
Education: Leeds Grammar School
Higher education: Oxford, Queen's
Constituency: south-east Manchester, declining innercity and residential, high unemployment

Keeble, Sally
Labour MP for Northampton North since 1997

Majority: 7,893 (19.0%)
Turnout: 56%

	Votes	Share %	Change %
Sally Keeble, Labour	20,507	49.4	–3.3
John Whelan, Conservative	12,614	30.4	–3
Richard Church, Liberal Democrat	7,363	17.7	5
Torbica Dusan, UK Independence party	596	1.4	n/a
Gordon White, Socialist Alliance	414	1	n/a

Andrew Roth says: "intelligent and confident; one of the 'new realism' apparatchiks"

Recent parliamentary career: junior minister, DTLGR (2001–); PPS to Hilary Armstrong (1999–2001)
Background: journalist in South Africa and Birmingham; public affairs consultant; leader of Southwark Council; Labour press officer; head of communications, GMB
Born: October 13 1951
Education: Cheltenham Ladies' College
Higher education: Oxford, St Hugh's; University of South Africa
Constituency: designated new town, growing population and local-authority housing

Keen, Alan
Labour MP for Feltham and Heston since 1992

Majority: 12,657 (35.0%)
Turnout: 49.4%

	Votes	Share %	Change %
Alan Keen, Labour	21,406	59.2	–0.5
Liz Mammatt, Conservative	8,749	24.2	–2.7
Andy Darley, Liberal Democrat	4,998	13.8	4.7
Surinder Cheema, Socialist Labour party	651	1.8	n/a
Warwick Prachar, Ind Prachar	204	0.6	n/a
Asa Khaira, Ind K	169	0.5	n/a

Andrew Roth says: "locally-centred, mainstream multi-cause groupie"

Recent parliamentary career: Culture, media and sport committee (1997–)
Background: fire protection consultant; systems analyst; accountant; manager; married to Ann Keen MP
Born: November 25 1937 in Lewisham
Education: St William Turner School, Cleveland
Constituency: next to Heathrow, outer suburbs, whitecollar

Keen, Ann
Labour MP for Brentford and Isleworth since 1997

Majority: 10,318 (23.2%)
Turnout: 53%

	Votes	Share %	Change %
Ann Keen, Labour	23,275	52.3	–5.1
Tim Mack, Conservative	12,957	29.1	–2.7
Gareth Hartwell, Liberal Democrat	5,994	13.5	5.3
Nic Ferriday, Green party	1,324	3	1.8
Gerald Ingram, UK Independence party	412	0.9	n/a
Danny Faith, Socialist Alliance	408	0.9	n/a
Asa Khaira, Independent	144	0.3	n/a

Andrew Roth says: "a union and party loyalist who is the third member of her family in the Commons"

Recent parliamentary career: PPS to Gordon Brown (2001–); PPS to Frank Dobson (1999–99)
Background: nurse; professor of nursing, Thames Valley University; married to Alan Keen MP
Born: November 26 1948
Education: Elfed Secondary Modern School, Clwyd
Higher education: Surrey University
Constituency: on Thames north bank, mixed housing, large Asian community

Keetch, Paul
Liberal Democrat MP for Hereford since 1997

Majority: 968 (2.2%)
Turnout: 63.5%

	Votes	Share %	Change %
Paul Keetch, Liberal Democrat	18,244	40.9	–7
Virginia Taylor, Conservative	17,276	38.7	3.4
David Hallam, Labour	6,739	15.1	2.5
Clive Easton, UK Independence party	1,184	2.7	n/a
David Gillett, Green party	1,181	2.7	n/a

Andrew Roth says: "locally-born, locally-educated and locally-active campaigner"

Recent parliamentary career: Lib Dem spokesperson, defence (2001–); foreign affairs and defence committee (1999–2001)
Background: banker; owner of water hygiene business
Born: May 21 1961 in Hereford
Education: Hereford Sixth Form College; Hereford High School for Boys
Constituency: robust, remote English city, still without a bypass, surrounded by attractive leafy countryside

Kelly, Ruth
Labour MP for Bolton West since 1997

Majority: 5,518 (13.4%)
Turnout: 62.4%

	Votes	Share %	Change %
Ruth Kelly, Labour	19,381	47	−2.5
James Stevens, Conservative	13,863	33.6	−1.5
Barbara Ronson, Liberal Democrat	7,573	18.4	7.6
David Toomer, Socialist Alliance	397	1	n/a

Andrew Roth says: "thoughtful, ultraloyal Blairite moderniser and social democratic economist"

Recent parliamentary career: economic secretary, Treasury (2001–); PPS to Nick Brown (1998–2001); Treasury committee (1998–98)
Background: economist; journalist, the *Guardian* (1990–94); deputy head, inflation report division, Bank of England (1994–97)
Born: May 9 1968 in Limavady, Northern Ireland
Education: Sutton High School; Westminster College
Higher education: London School of Economics; Oxford, Queens
Constituency: smart residential part of an old north-west mill town

Kemp, Fraser
Labour MP for Houghton and Washington East since 1997

Majority: 19,818 (58.9%)
Turnout: 49.5%

	Votes	Share %	Change %
Fraser Kemp, Labour	24,628	73.2	−3.2
Tony Devenish, Conservative	4,810	14.3	1.4
Richard Ormerod, Liberal Democrat	4,203	12.5	4.8

Andrew Roth says: "Labour's sinister 'Mr Big' and an apparatchik of outstanding ability and street cred"

Recent parliamentary career: assistant whip (2001–); outspoken opponent of electoral reform
Background: civil servant; Labour party organiser and election coordinator (1981–96)
Born: September 1 1958 in Washington, Tyne and Wear
Education: Washington Comprehensive School, Tyne and Wear
Constituency: new town plus older ex-mining centres

Kennedy, Rt Hon Charles
Liberal Democrat MP for Ross, Skye and Inverness West since 1997; Ross, Cromarty and Skye (1983–97)

Majority: 12,952 (37.2%)
Turnout: 61.6%

	Votes	Share %	Change %
Charles Kennedy, Liberal Democrat	18,832	54.1	15.4
Donald Crichton, Labour	5,880	16.9	−11.8
Jean Urquhart, Scottish National party	4,901	14.1	−5.5
Angus Laing, Conservative	3,096	8.9	−2
Eleanor Scott, Green party	699	2	1.2
Stuart Topp, Scottish Socialist party	683	2	n/a
Philip Anderson, UK Independence party	456	1.3	n/a
James Crawford, Country	265	0.8	n/a

Andrew Roth says: "shrewd, bantering middleweight political boxer who takes politics seriously but not himself"

Recent parliamentary career: leader of the Lib Dems (1999–); spokesperson, agriculture, fisheries, food, and rural affairs (1997–99); spokesperson, Europe (1992–97); Lib Dem party president (1990–94)
Background: elected unexpectedly aged 24 in 1983; high-profile Alliance and Lib Dem MP; former journalist with BBC Highland; broadcaster; student politician
Born: November 25 1959 in Inverness
Education: Lochaber High School, Fort William
Higher education: Glasgow University; Indiana University, USA
Constituency: possibly the most beautiful constituency in Britain, vast, includes Isle of Skye

Kennedy, Jane

Labour MP for Liverpool Wavertree since 1997; Liverpool Broadgreen (1992–97)

Majority: 12,319 (38.3%)
Turnout: 44.3%

	Votes	Share %	Change %
Jane Kennedy, Labour	20,155	62.7	–1.7
Christopher Newby, Liberal Democrat	7,836	24.4	2.9
Geoffrey Allen, Conservative	3,091	9.6	–1.2
Michael Lane, Socialist Labour Party	359	1.1	n/a
Mark O'Brien, Socialist Alliance	349	1.1	n/a
Neil Miney, UK Independence party	348	1.1	n/a

Andrew Roth says: "low profiled Christian socialist apparatchik"

Recent parliamentary career: minister of state, NIO (2001–); junior minister, LCD (1999–2001)
Background: child-care officer and care assistant, Liverpool City Council
Born: May 4 1958 in Cumbria
Education: Haughton School, Darlington; Queen Elizabeth Sixth Form College, Darlington
Higher education: Liverpool University
Constituency: suburban middle class Liverpool

Key, Robert

Conservative MP for Salisbury since 1983

Majority: 8,703 (16.5%)
Turnout: 65.3%

	Votes	Share %	Change %
Robert Key, Conservative	24,527	46.6	3.7
Yvonne Emmerson-Peirce, Liberal Democrat	15,824	30.1	–2.1
Sue Mallory, Labour	9,199	17.5	–0.1
Malcolm Wood, UK Independence party	1,958	3.7	n/a
Hamish Soutar, Green party	1,095	2.1	1

Andrew Roth says: "bright and bouncy over-enthusiast for any job on hand"

Recent parliamentary career: opposition spokesperson, DTI (2001–); opposition spokesperson, defence (1997–2001)
Background: Harrow School economics master (1969–83)
Born: April 22 1945 in Plymouth
Education: Salisbury Cathedral School; Sherborne School
Higher education: Cambridge, Clare
Constituency: smart South Wiltshire county town and rural surrounds, includes Stonehenge

Khabra, Piara

Labour MP for Ealing Southall since 1992

Majority: 13,683 (29.2%)
Turnout: 56.9%

	Votes	Share %	Change %
Piara Khabra, Labour	22,239	47.5	−12.5
Daniel Kawczynski, Conservative	8,556	18.3	−2.5
Avtar Lit, Sunrise	5,764	12.3	n/a
Baldev Sharma, Liberal Democrat	4,680	10	−0.4
Margaret Cook, Green party	2,119	4.5	n/a
Salvinder Dhillon, Community	1,214	2.6	n/a
Mushtaq Choudhry, Independent	1,166	2.5	n/a
Harpal Brar, Socialist Labour party	921	2	−1.9
Mohammed Bhutta, Qari	169	0.4	n/a

Andrew Roth says: "hot-tempered MP whose parliamentary excitements centre largely on his support for euthanasia"

Recent parliamentary career: international development committee (1997–)
Background: community worker; primary school teacher; JP; served in Indian Army (1942–46); the oldest MP in the Commons
Born: November 20 1924 in Punjab, India
Higher education: Punjab University; Whitelands College
Constituency: west London, strongly Asian, near Heathrow

Kidney, David
Labour MP for Stafford since 1997

Majority: 5,032 (11.4%)
Turnout: 65.3%

	Votes	Share %	Change %
David Kidney, Labour	21,285	48	0.5
Philip Cochrane, Conservative	16,253	36.6	−2.6
Jeanne Pinkerton, Liberal Democrat	4,205	9.5	−1.1
Richard Bradford, UK Independence party	2,315	5.2	n/a
Michael Hames, R & R Loony	308	0.7	n/a

Andrew Roth says: "fair minded and not overly partisan"

Recent parliamentary career: Treasury committee (1998–2001); Treasury subcommittee (1998–2001)
Background: solicitor; Stafford councillor
Born: March 21 1955 in Stoke-on-Trent
Education: Longdon High School; Stoke-on-Trent Sixth Form College
Higher education: Bristol University
Constituency: Midlands town plus semi-rural surrounds

Kilfoyle, Peter
Labour MP for Liverpool Walton since 1991

Majority: 17,996 (63.2%)
Turnout: 43%

	Votes	Share %	Change %
Peter Kilfoyle, Labour	22,143	77.8	−0.6
Kiron Reid, Liberal Democrat	4,147	14.6	3.5
Stephen Horgan, Conservative	1,726	6.1	−0.2
Paul Forrest, UK Independence party	442	1.6	n/a

Andrew Roth says: "a street fighter with an authoritarian streak who has worked behind the scenes to improve delivery to the public"

Recent parliamentary career: junior minister, MoD (1999–2000), resigned to allow scope for public airing of his doubts about New Labour; junior minister, Office of Public Service (1997–99)

Background: labourer; dockman; PE teacher; Labour party regional organiser (1986–91)
Born: June 9 1946 in Liverpool
Education: St Edward's College, Liverpool
Higher education: Christ's College, Liverpool; Durham University
Constituency: Labour's highest share of the vote in Britain, inner city

King, Andy
Labour MP for Rugby and Kenilworth since 1997

Majority: 2,877 (5.3%)
Turnout: 67.4%

	Votes	Share %	Change %
Andy King, Labour	24,221	45	1.9
David Martin, Conservative	21,344	39.7	−2.6
Gwen Fairweather, Liberal Democrat	7,444	13.8	−0.5
Paul Garrett, UK Independence party	787	1.5	n/a

Andrew Roth says: "not overly partisan, unless provoked by the 'organised hypocrisy' of Conservatives"

Recent parliamentary career: deregulation committee (1999–); social security committee (1999–2001)
Background: postal officer; social worker; Northamptonshire councillor
Born: September 14 1948 in Bellshill
Education: St John the Baptist School, Uddingston; Missionary Institute, London
Higher education: Hatfield Polytechnic; Nene College, Northampton; Coatbridge Technical College
Constituency: mixed seat on edge of West Midlands conurbation

King, Oona
Labour MP for Bethnal Green and Bow since 1997

Majority: 10,057 (26.2%)
Turnout: 48.6%

	Votes	Share %	Change %
Oona King, Labour	19,380	50.4	4.1
Shahagir Faruk, Conservative	9,323	24.2	3.1
Janet Ludlow, Liberal Democrat	5,946	15.5	3.5
Anna Bragga, Green party	1,666	4.3	2.5
Michael Davidson, British National party	1,267	3.3	−4.2
Dennis Delderfield, NBP	888	2.3	n/a

Andrew Roth says: "well-read multiculturalist with a good sense of humour and sharp elbows"

Recent parliamentary career: transport, local government, and the regions committee (2001–); international development committee (1997–2001)
Background: political researcher; trade union regional organiser (GMB); political assistant to Glenys Kinnock MEP; member of Oxfam, Amnesty; daughter of Preston King, US civil rights activist and academic
Born: October 22 1967 in Sheffield
Education: Haverstock Comprehensive School
Higher education: York University; University of California, Berkeley
Constituency: poor, plus Yuppies, Bangladeshi voters, city overspill

Kirkbride, Julie
Conservative MP for Bromsgrove since 1997

Majority: 8,138 (17.9%)
Turnout: 67.1%

	Votes	Share %	Change %
Julie Kirkbride, Conservative	23,640	51.8	4.6
Peter McDonald, Labour	15,502	33.9	–3.9
Margaret Rowley, Liberal Democrat	5,430	11.9	0
Ian Gregory, UK Independence party	1,112	2.4	n/a

Andrew Roth says: "northern daughter of the working class who rejected her background"

Recent parliamentary career: culture, media and sport committee (1999–); catering committee (1998–)
Background: journalist, BBC and *Daily Telegraph*; married (1997) to Andrew Mackay MP
Born: June 5 1960 in Halifax
Education: Highlands Grammar School
Higher education: Graduate School of Journalism, University of California, Berkeley; Cambridge, Girton
Constituency: north-eastern end of Worcestershire, mostly middle class, many residents work in Birmingham

Kirkwood, Archie
Liberal Democrat MP for Roxburgh and Berwickshire since 1983

Majority: 7,511 (26.1%)
Turnout: 61.2%

	Votes	Share %	Change %
Archie Kirkwood, Liberal Democrat	14,044	48.8	2.3
George Turnbull, Conservative	6,533	22.7	–1.2
Catherine Maxwell-Stuart, Labour	4,498	15.6	0.6
Roderick Campbell, Scottish National party	2,806	9.7	–1.6
Amanda Millar, Scottish Socialist party	463	1.6	n/a
Peter Neilson, UK Independence party	453	1.6	n/a

Andrew Roth says: "caring, chirpy, widely popular key Lib Dem stalwart; unpretentious and constructive parliamentary figure"

Recent parliamentary career: chair, work and pensions committee (2001–); Lib Dem spokesperson, social security (1997–2000); Lib Dem leader of the House (1994–97); Lib Dem chief whip (1992–97) where he helped secure passage of Maastricht legislation
Background: solicitor; notary; trustee on Joseph Rowntree Reform Trust
Born: April 22 1946 in Glasgow
Education: Cranhill Secondary School
Higher education: Heriot-Watt University
Constituency: border country with small towns in east Scotland

Knight, Rt Hon Greg
Conservative MP for Yorkshire East since 2001; Derby North (1983–97)

Majority: 4,682 (10.9%)
Turnout: 59.9%

	Votes	Share %	Change %
Greg Knight, Conservative	19,861	45.9	3.2
Tracey Simpson-Laing, Labour	15,179	35	–0.9
Mary-Rose Hardy, Liberal Democrat	6,300	14.5	–4
Trevor Pearson, UK Independence party	1,661	3.8	n/a
Paul Dessoy, Independent	313	0.7	n/a

Andrew Roth says: "many sided ex-solicitor who wrote the 1983 Conservative campaign song 'Maggie Will Always Be Around'"

Recent parliamentary career: re-elected to parliament 2001; deputy chief whip (1993–96), where he helped John Major's government survive its lack of a majority

Background: solicitor; business consultant; author of books on parliamentary anecdotes
Born: April 4 1949
Education: Alderman Newton's Grammar School
Higher education: Guildford College of Law
Constituency: coastal Yorkshire plus rural inland Wolds, seaside resorts and market towns

Knight, Jim
Labour MP for Dorset South since 2001

Majority: 153 (0.3%)
Turnout: 65.5%

	Votes	Share %	Change %
Jim Knight, Labour	19,027	42	6
Ian Bruce, Conservative	18,874	41.6	5.5
Andy Canning, Liberal Democrat	6,531	14.4	–5.8
Laurie Moss, UK Independence party	913	2	0.3

Maiden speech: "It is crucial for the south Dorset economy that we retain strong international links, the presence of the armed forces and a vibrant defence industry"

Recent parliamentary career: entered parliament 2001, taking seat from Conservative; defence committee (2001–)
Background: publisher, manager and director of arts and publishing firms; Mendip councillor
Born: March 6 1965
Education: Eltham College, London
Higher education: Fitzwilliam College, Cambridge
Constituency: Weymouth seaside resort, Portland naval base and rural surrounds

Kumar, Dr Ashok
Labour MP for Middlesbrough South and East Cleveland since 1997; Langbaurgh (1991–92)

Majority: 9,351 (21.3%)
Turnout: 61.5%

	Votes	Share %	Change %
Ashok Kumar, Labour	24,321	55.3	0.6
Barbara Harpham, Conservative	14,970	34	–0.9
Linda Parrish, Liberal Democrat	4,700	10.7	3.2

Andrew Roth says: "regionally preoccupied MP who has built his reputation mainly on work as a local councillor"

Recent parliamentary career: trade and industry committee (2001–); deregulation committee (1999–); science and technology committee (1997–)
Background: research scientist and Fellow of Imperial College; Middlesbrough councillor; MP for Langbaugh (the former name of his current seat) after narrowly winning 1991 byelection
Born: May 28 1956 in Hardwar, India
Education: Rykneld School for Boys
Higher education: Aston University; Derby and District College of Art and Technology
Constituency: includes coastal Saltburn, some farming, and Middlesbrough suburbs

L

Ladyman, Dr Stephen
Labour MP for South Thanet since 1997

Majority: 1,792 (4.6%)
Turnout: 64.2%

	Votes	Share %	Change %
Stephen Ladyman, Labour	18,002	45.7	−0.5
Mark Macgregor, Conservative	16,210	41.1	1.3
Guy Voizey, Liberal Democrat	3,706	9.4	−2.3
William Baldwin, Independent	770	2	n/a
Terry Eccott, UK Independence party	501	1.3	n/a
Bernard Franklin, National Front	242	0.6	n/a

Andrew Roth says: "late-emerging IT specialist"

Recent parliamentary career: PPS to Adam Ingram (2001–); transport subcommittee (2000–2001); environment, transport and regional affairs committee (1999–2001)
Background: computer manager in pharmaceutical industry; Thanet councillor; manages under 15s Ramsgate football club
Born: November 6 1952 in Ormskirk
Education: Birkenhead Institute
Higher education: Strathclyde University; Liverpool Polytechnic
Constituency: Kent coast towns of Ramsgate, Sandwich and Broadstairs

Laing, Eleanor
Conservative MP for Epping Forest since 1997

Majority: 8,426 (19.8%)
Turnout: 58.4%

	Votes	Share %	Change %
Eleanor Laing, Conservative	20,833	49.1	3.6
Christopher Naylor, Labour	12,407	29.3	−6.3
Michael Heavens, Liberal Democrat	7,884	18.6	5.3
Andrew Smith, UK Independence party	1,290	3	n/a

Andrew Roth says: "very ideological, highly partisan Scots unionist"

Recent parliamentary career: opposition spokesperson, DFES (2001–); opposition spokesperson, constitutional affairs (2000–01); opposition whip (1999–2000)
Background: special adviser to John MacGregor; solicitor; executive officer, Conservative central office; public relations consultant
Born: February 1 1958 in Paisley
Education: St Columba's School, Kilmacolm
Higher education: Edinburgh University
Constituency: smart Essex suburbs around Loughton, Theydon Bois and Chigwell

Lait, Jacqui
Conservative MP for Beckenham since 1997; Hastings and Rye (1992–97)

Majority: 4,959 (10.9%)
Turnout: 63.1%

	Votes	Share %	Change %
Jacqui Lait, Conservative	20,618	45.3	4.1
Richard Watts, Labour	15,659	34.4	−3
Alex Feakes, Liberal Democrat	7,308	16	−2.4
Karen Moran, Green party	961	2.1	n/a
Christopher Pratt, UK Independence party	782	1.7	n/a
Rif Winfield, Liberal	234	0.5	−0.5

Andrew Roth says: "rooted, realistic and commonsensical"

Recent parliamentary career: shadow secretary of state, SO (2001–); catering committee (2001); opposition spokesperson, social security (2000–01); deregulation committee (1997–2001); re-elected in 1997 byelection; opposition whip (1996–99); first woman in Conservative whips' office (1996–97)

Background: public-relations consultant; parliamentary adviser and consultant;office; trustee of National Missing Persons' Helpline
Born: December 10 1947 in Glasgow
Education: Paisley Grammar School
Higher education: Strathclyde University
Constituency: upmarket Bromley dormitory suburb between Crystal Palace and Kent

Lamb, Norman
Lib Dem MP for Norfolk North since 2001

Majority: 483 (0.9%)
Turnout: 70.2%

	Votes	Share %	Change %
Norman Lamb, Liberal Democrat	23,978	42.7	8.4
David Prior, Conservative	23,495	41.8	5.3
Mike Gates, Labour	7,490	13.3	−11.7
Mike Sheridan, Green party	649	1.2	n/a
Paul Simison, UK Independence party	608	1.1	n/a

Maiden speech: "We have a duty to make politics much more relevant and to behave in a way that will rebuild people's trust in the political process"

Recent parliamentary career: entered parliament 2001, taking seat from Conservative
Background: employment lawyer; Norwich councillor and Lib Dem group leader
Born: September 16 1957
Education: Wymondham College, Norfolk
Higher education: Leicester University; City of London Polytechnic
Constituency: north Norfolk coast around Sheringham and Cromer plus most of the Norfolk Broads

Lammy, David
Labour MP for Tottenham since 2000

Majority: 16,916 (53.6%)
Turnout: 48.2%

	Votes	Share %	Change %
David Lammy, Labour	21,317	67.5	14
Uma Fernandes, Conservative	4,401	13.9	−2.1
Meher Khan, Liberal Democrat	3,008	9.5	−9.6
Peter Budge, Green party	1,443	4.6	0.9
Weyman Bennett, Socialist Alliance	1,162	3.7	n/a
Unver Shefki, Reform 2000	270	0.9	−0.2

Maiden speech: "I am not just a black politician for black people; I am a politician for all people"

Recent parliamentary career: PPS to Estelle Morris (2001–); public administration committee (2000–2001); procedure committee (2000–2001); elected in byelection (2000)
Background: barrister and attorney; worked for Amnesty and Prisoners Abroad; member of all-party group on Rwanda, Aids, British-Caribbean
Born: June 19 1972 in Tottenham
Education: King's School, Peterborough
Higher education: School of Oriental and African Studies, London University; Harvard Law School
Constituency: third most multiracial in Britain; runs from London's Cypriot heartland of Green Lanes to River Lea

Lansley, Andrew
Conservative MP for South Cambridgeshire since 1997

Majority: 8,403 (17.3%)
Turnout: 67.1%

	Votes	Share %	Change %
Andrew Lansley, Conservative	21,387	44.2	2.2
Amanda Taylor, Liberal Democrat	12,984	26.9	1.1
Joan Herbert, Labour	11,737	24.3	−0.8
Simon Saggers, Green party	1,182	2.5	n/a
Helene Davies, UK Independence party	875	1.8	n/a
Beata Klepacka, ProLife Alliance	176	0.4	n/a

Andrew Roth says: "highly intelligent, well-informed and conspicuously active"

Recent parliamentary career: opposition spokesperson, CO (1999–2001); vice chairman, Conservative party (1998–99)
Background: civil servant; director, Conservative Research Department; director, British Chambers of Commerce; vice president, Local Government Association; author
Born: December 11 1956 in Hornchurch
Education: Brentwood School
Higher education: Exeter University
Constituency: edge of Cambridge and rural land to south of city

Lawrence, Jackie
Labour MP for Preseli Pembrokeshire since 1997

Majority: 2,946 (8.1%)
Turnout: 67.8%

	Votes	Share %	Change %
Jackie Lawrence, Labour	15,206	41.4	−6.9
Stephen Crabb, Conservative	12,260	33.3	5.6
Rhys Sinnet, Plaid Cymru	4,658	12.7	6.4
Alexander Dauncey, Liberal Democrat	3,882	10.6	−2.4
Trish Bowen, Socialist Labour party	452	1.2	n/a
Hugh Jones, UK Independence party	319	0.9	n/a

Andrew Roth says: "locally-based thoughtful mainstreamer"

Recent parliamentary career: trade and industry committee (2001–)
Background: parliamentary assistant to Nick Ainger MP; bank worker; Dyfed councillor
Born: August 9 1948 in Birmingham
Education: Upperthorpe School, Darlington
Higher education: Open University
Constituency: remote Pembrokeshire, oil, docks and St David's

Laws, David
Liberal Democrat MP for Yeovil since 2001

Majority: 3,928 (8.2%)
Turnout: 63.4%

	Votes	Share %	Change %
David Laws, Liberal Democrat	21,266	44.2	−4.5
Marco Forgione, Conservative	17,338	36	8.3
Joe Conway, Labour	7,077	14.7	−0.2
Neil Boxall, UK Independence party	1,131	2.4	n/a
Alex Begg, Green party	786	1.6	0.3
Tony Prior, Liberal	534	1.1	n/a

Michael White, the *Guardian*: "heavyweight policy analyst"

Recent parliamentary career: entered parliament 2001; Treasury committee (2001–); tipped as Lib Dem high-flyer and potential future leader
Background: investment banker and self-made millionaire; vice president, JP Morgan and Co;

managing director, Barclays de Zoete Wedd; parliamentary economic adviser to Lib Dems (1994–97); director, policy and research (1997–99)
Born: November 30 1965
Education: St George's College, Weybridge
Higher education: Cambridge, Kings College
Constituency: Yeovil town and surrounds, more urban than rural

Laxton, Bob
Labour MP for Derby North since 1997

Majority: 6,982 (15.9%)
Turnout: 57.6%

	Votes	Share %	Change %
Bob Laxton, Labour	22,415	50.9	–2.3
Barry Holden, Conservative	15,433	35	0.7
Bob Charlesworth, Liberal Democrat	6,206	14.1	5.1

Andrew Roth says: "one of Labour's rare proles"

Recent parliamentary career: PPS to Alan Johnson (2001–); trade and industry committee (1997–2001)
Background: trade unionist (CWU); telecoms engineer; Derby councillor
Born: September 7 1944 in Derby
Education: Woodlands Secondary School
Higher education: Derby College of Art & Technology
Constituency: suburbs to north of Derby city centre with rail and aero-engine factories

Lazarowicz, Mark
Labour MP for Edinburgh North and Leith since 2001

Majority: 8,817 (26.6%)
Turnout: 53.2%

	Votes	Share %	Change %
Mark Lazarowicz, Labour	15,271	46	–0.9
Sebastian Tombs, Liberal Democrat	6,454	19.4	6.4
Kaukab Stewart, Scottish National party	5,290	15.9	–4.2
Iain Mitchell, Conservative	4,626	13.9	–4
Catriona Grant, Scottish Socialist party	1,334	4	n/a
David Jacobsen, Socialist Labour party	259	0.8	n/a

Maiden speech: "I am proud to be the first [local] MP to carry the Co-operative as well as the Labour banner"

Recent parliamentary career: entered parliament 2001; Scottish affairs committee (2001–); introduced private member's bill on employee shares (2001)
Background: Edinburgh councillor; advocate; author
Born: August 8 1953
Education: St Benedict's School, London
Higher education: St Andrews University; Edinburgh University
Constituency: pairing of smart Edinburgh New Town and developing port district of Leith

Leigh, Edward
Conservative MP for Gainsborough since 1997; Gainsborough and Horncastle (1983–97)

Majority: 8,071 (19.1%)
Turnout: 64.3%

	Votes	Share %	Change %
Edward Leigh, Conservative	19,555	46.2	3.1
Alan Rhodes, Labour	11,484	27.1	−1.7
Steve Taylor, Liberal Democrat	11,280	26.7	−1.4

Andrew Roth says: "intelligent but prankish and unpredictable radical right-wing intellectual"

Recent parliamentary career: chair, public accounts committee (2001–); international development committee (2001); public accounts committee (2000–01); social security committee (1997–2001)
Background: barrister, arbitrator; Conservative Research Department; private office of Margaret Thatcher (1976–77)
Born: July 20 1950 in London
Education: Lycée Français de Londres; Oratory School, Berkshire
Higher education: Durham University
Constituency: flat farming land north of Lincoln, plus the Lincolnshire Wolds

Lepper, David
Labour MP for Brighton Pavilion since 1997

Majority: 9,643 (23.6%)
Turnout: 58.9%

	Votes	Share %	Change %
David Lepper, Labour	19,846	48.7	−5.9
David Gold, Conservative	10,203	25.1	−2.6
Ruth Berry, Liberal Democrat	5,348	13.1	3.6
Keith Taylor, Green party	3,806	9.4	6.8
Ian Fyvie, Socialist Labour party	573	1.4	n/a
Bob Dobbs, Free	409	1	n/a
Stuart Hutchin, UK Independence party	361	0.9	n/a
Marie Paragallo, ProLife Alliance	177	0.4	n/a

Andrew Roth says: "balding, broad forehead, beaky ... Blairite former teacher-councillor"

Recent parliamentary career: environment, food, and rural affairs committee (2001–); broadcasting committee (1997–); public administration committee (1999–2001)
Background: secondary school teacher; leader and mayor of Brighton Council; author of publications on cinema
Born: September 15 1945 in Richmond, Surrey
Education: Wimbledon County Secondary School
Higher education: Sussex University; Kent University; Central London Polytechnic
Constituency: the busy centre of Brighton, including main hotels, night life and the piers

Leslie, Christopher
Labour MP for Shipley since 1997

Majority: 1,428 (3.1%)
Turnout: 66.1%

	Votes	Share %	Change %
Christopher Leslie, Labour	20,243	44	0.6
David Senior, Conservative	18,815	40.9	3.1
Helen Wright, Liberal Democrat	4,996	10.9	−4.2
Martin Love, Green party	1,386	3	n/a
Walter Whittaker, UK Independence party	580	1.3	n/a

Andrew Roth says: "one of Labour's most able young super loyal debaters"

Recent parliamentary career: junior minister, CO (2001–), the youngest member in the government; PPS to Lord Falconer, minister, CO (1998–2001)
Background: political research assistant; office administrator; Bradford councillor

Born: June 28 1972 in Keighley
Education: Bingley Grammar School
Higher education: Leeds University
Constituency: Bradford commuter town on southern edge of Yorkshire Dales, includes Saltaire

Letwin, Oliver
Conservative MP for West Dorset since 1997

Majority: 1,414 (2.8%)
Turnout: 67%

	Votes	Share %	Change %
Oliver Letwin, Conservative	22,126	44.6	3.5
Simon Green, Liberal Democrat	20,712	41.8	4.1
Richard Hyde, Labour	6,733	13.6	–4.1

Andrew Roth says: "an intellectual ballet dancer who usually dances over the heads of fellow MPs"

Recent parliamentary career: shadow home secretary (2001–); opposition spokesperson, Treasury (1999–01); opposition spokesperson, constitutional affairs (1998–99)
Background: research fellow; special adviser, prime minister's policy unit (1983–86) where he helped to create poll tax; special adviser to Sir Keith Joseph; merchant banker, NM Rothschild; author
Born: May 19 1956 in London
Education: Eton College
Higher education: London Business School; Cambridge, Trinity
Constituency: rural north of Dorset including Dorchester and Tolpuddle

Levitt, Tom
Labour MP for High Peak since 1997

Majority: 4,489 (9.3%)
Turnout: 65.2%

	Votes	Share %	Change %
Tom Levitt, Labour	22,430	46.6	–4.2
Simon Chapman, Conservative	17,941	37.3	1.8
Peter Ashenden, Liberal Democrat	7,743	16.1	4.9
Hugh Price, UK Independence party	n/a		

Andrew Roth says: "genial super-loyalist reformer"

Recent parliamentary career: PPS to Barbara Roche (1999–); standards and privileges committee (1997–)
Background: sensory awareness consultant and trainer; biology and science teacher (1976–95); Derbyshire councillor
Born: April 10 1954 in Crewe
Education: Westwood High School, Leek
Higher education: Oxford University; Lancaster University
Constituency: Kinder Scout and Dark Peak hills, small towns

Lewis, Ivan
Labour MP for Bury South since 1997

Majority: 12,772 (32.3%)
Turnout: 58.8%

	Votes	Share %	Change %
Ivan Lewis, Labour	23,406	59.2	2.3
Nicola Le Page, Conservative	10,634	26.9	–5.4
Tim Pickstone, Liberal Democrat	5,499	13.9	5.5

Andrew Roth says: "youthful Blairite showing 'glutinous fealty' as displayed by 'robotic' loyalist interjections"

Recent parliamentary career: junior minister, DFES (2001–); PPS to Stephen Byers (1999–2001)
Background: charity executive; community care manager; chief executive, Manchester Jewish Federation; Bury councillor
Born: March 4 1967 in Prestwich
Education: William Hulme's Grammar School; Stand College; Bury Further Education College
Constituency: borders Salford, covers residential Prestwich and Whitefield, large orthodox Jewish community

Lewis, Dr Julian
Conservative MP for New Forest East since 1997

Majority: 3,829 (9.0%)
Turnout: 63.2%

	Votes	Share %	Change %
Julian Lewis, Conservative	17,902	42.4	–0.5
Brian Dash, Liberal Democrat	14,073	33.4	1.1
Alan Goodfellow, Labour	9,141	21.7	–3.1
William Howe, UK Independence party	1,062	2.5	n/a

Andrew Roth says: "formerly central office's most assiduous political dirt digger"

Recent parliamentary career: opposition whip (2001–); defence committee (2000–01); Welsh affairs committee (1998–2001)
Background: HM Royal Naval Reserve; historian; political researcher; defence consultant; deputy director, Conservative Research Department (1990–96); author
Born: September 26 1951 in Swansea
Education: Dynevor Grammar School, Swansea
Higher education: Oxford, Balliol and St Antony's
Constituency: woods plus growing shoreline suburbs east of Bournemouth

Lewis, Terry
Labour MP for Worsley since 1983

Majority: 11,787 (33.3%)
Turnout: 51%

	Votes	Share %	Change %
Terry Lewis, Labour	20,193	57.1	–5.1
Tobias Ellwood, Conservative	8,406	23.8	–0.4
Robert Bleakley, Liberal Democrat	6,188	17.5	3.9
Dorothy Entwhistle, Socialist Labour party	576	1.6	n/a

Andrew Roth says: "recently quiet but still rebellious former extrovert"

Recent parliamentary career: standards and privileges committee (1997–2001)
Background: local government officer; deputy leader, Bolton council; Eurosceptic
Born: December 29 1935 in Salford
Education: Our Lady of Mount Carmel Secondary Modern School, Salford
Constituency: smarter edge of Salford, north of central Manchester

Liddell, Rt Hon Helen
Labour MP for Airdrie and Shotts since 1994; Monklands East (1994–97)

Majority: 12,340 (38.9%)
Turnout: 54.4%

	Votes	Share %	Change %
Helen Liddell, Labour	18,478	58.2	–3.6
Alison Lindsay, Scottish National party	6,138	19.3	–5.1
John Love, Liberal Democrat	2,376	7.5	3.3
Gordon McIntosh, Conservative	1,960	6.2	–2.7
Ms Mary Dempsey, Scottish Unionist	1,439	4.5	n/a
Kenny McGuigan, Scottish Socialist party	1,171	3.7	n/a
Chris Herriot, Socialist Labour Party	174	0.6	n/a

Andrew Roth says: "Scottish Labour version of Margaret Thatcher: able and pugnacious underneath an Iron Lady hairdo"

Recent parliamentary career: secretary of state, SO (2001–); minister of state, DTI (1999–2001); minister of state, DETR (1999–99); minister of state, SO (1998–99)
Background: member of Labour party NEC (2001–); journalist, BBC Scottish economics correspondent; general secretary of Labour party in Scotland (1977–88)
Born: December 6 1950 in Monklands
Education: St Patrick's High School, Coatbridge
Higher education: Strathclyde University
Constituency: John Smith's old seat centred on Airdrie new town, south of Glasgow

Liddell-Grainger, Ian
Conservative MP for Bridgwater since 2001

Majority: 4,987 (10.5%)
Turnout: 64.6%

	Votes	Share %	Change %
Ian Liddell-Grainger, Conservative	19,354	40.5	3.6
Ian Thorn, Liberal Democrat	14,367	30	–3.6
William Monteith, Labour	12,803	26.8	2
Vicky Gardner, UK Independence party	1,323	2.8	n/a

Maiden speech: "[Bridgwater] is a very diverse constituency, running from Exmoor down to the Levels. It is very large, and resembles, if anything, a banana."

Recent parliamentary career: entered parliament 2001; public administration committee (2001–); introduced private member's bill on patents (2001)
Background: farmer; company director; consultant to the army land command HQ and MoD; chair of Countryside Alliance, Devon; major in Territorial Army; chair, Action Research charity; about 283rd in line for the throne
Born: February 23 1959
Education: Millfield School
Higher education: South Scotland Agricultural College, Edinburgh
Constituency: runs from Quantock Hills to Minehead on Somerset coast

Lidington, David
Conservative MP for Aylesbury since 1992

Majority: 10,009 (20.4%)
Turnout: 61.4%

	Votes	Share %	Change %
David Lidington, Conservative	23,230	47.3	3.1
Peter Jones, Liberal Democrat	13,221	26.9	–2.6
Keith White, Labour	11,388	23.2	1
Justin Harper, UK Independence party	1,248	2.5	n/a

Andrew Roth says: "highly intelligent, civilised and articulate young politician"

Recent parliamentary career: opposition spokesperson, Treasury (2001–); opposition spokesperson, home affairs (1999–2001); PPS to William Hague (1997–99)

Background: worked for BP, Rio Tinto Zinc; senior consultant, Public Policy Unit (1991–92); special adviser to Douglas Hurd (1987–90)
Born: June 30 1956 in Lambeth
Education: Haberdashers' Aske's School
Higher education: Cambridge, Sidney Sussex
Constituency: leafy Buckinghamshire, attractive old town and surrounding prosperous area

Lilley, Rt Hon Peter
Conservative MP for Hitchin and Harpenden since 1997; St Albans (1983–97)

Majority: 6,663 (14.9%)
Turnout: 66.9%

	Votes	Share %	Change %
Peter Lilley, Conservative	21,271	47.4	1.5
Alan Amos, Labour	14,608	32.5	−0.6
John Murphy, Liberal Democrat	8,076	18	−2.1
John Saunders, UK Independence party	606	1.4	n/a
Peter Rigby, Independent	363	0.8	n/a

Andrew Roth says: "now-vanished former leading frontbencher; once tagged a 'bastard' by John Major"

Recent parliamentary career: called for legalisation of cannabis (2001); deputy leader, Conservative party (1998–99); used a speech (1999) to question further privatisation, shocking his party and leading to his dismissal; shadow chancellor (1997–98); secretary of state, DSS (1992–97); secretary of state, DTI (1990–92)
Background: company director; investment adviser on North Sea oil; economic adviser
Born: August 23 1943 in Hayes, Kent
Education: Dulwich College
Higher education: Cambridge, Clare
Constituency: prosperous London commuters on fast rail link to King's Cross

Linton, Martin
Labour MP for Battersea since 1997

Majority: 5,053 (13.8%)
Turnout: 54.5%

	Votes	Share %	Change %
Martin Linton, Labour	18,498	50.3	−0.4
Lucy Shersby, Conservative	13,445	36.5	−2.9
Siobhan Vitelli, Liberal Democrat	4,450	12.1	4.8
Thomas Barber, Independent	411	1.1	n/a

Andrew Roth says: "would-be electoral reformer, he shows an angular awkwardness which irritates Tory opponents"

Recent parliamentary career: PPS to Baroness Blackstone (2001–); administration committee (2001–); home affairs committee (1997–2001)
Background: journalist on *Daily Mail*, *FT*, *Daily Star*, *Guardian*; Wandsworth councillor; noted Labour progressive
Born: August 11 1944 in Stockholm, Sweden
Education: Christ's Hospital, Sussex
Higher education: Oxford, Pembroke; Lyons University, France
Constituency: once poor, now posh inner London suburb south of Thames

Lloyd, Tony
Labour MP for Manchester Central since 1997; Stretford (1983–97)

Majority: 13,742 (53.0%)
Turnout: 39.1%

	Votes	Share %	Change %
Tony Lloyd, Labour	17,812	68.7	−2.3
Philip Hobson, Liberal Democrat	4,070	15.7	3.4
Aaron Powell, Conservative	2,328	9	−2.8
Vanessa Hall, Green party	1,018	3.9	n/a
Ron Sinclair, Socialist Labour party	484	1.9	−0.5
Terrenia Brosnan, ProLife Alliance	216	0.8	n/a

Andrew Roth says: "well-informed, thoughtful and realistic regionalist and internationalist"

Recent parliamentary career: minister of state, FCO (1997–99)
Background: Salford University lecturer; wrote for *Chemical Engineer*; Trafford councillor
Born: February 25 1950 in Trafford
Education: Stretford Grammar School
Higher education: Nottingham University; Manchester Business School
Constituency: Manchester city centre together with hard-hit surrounding areas such as Miles Platting, Newton Heath, and Ancoats

Llwyd, Elfyn
Plaid Cymru MP for Meirionnydd Nant Conwy since 1992

Majority: 5,684 (26.9%)
Turnout: 63.5%

	Votes	Share %	Change %
Elfyn Llwyd, Plaid Cymru	10,459	49.6	−1.1
Denise Jones, Labour	4,775	22.7	−0.3
Lisa Francis, Conservative	3,962	18.8	2.8
Dafydd Raw-Rees, Liberal Democrat	1,872	8.9	1.9

Andrew Roth says: "assiduous, highly intelligent, constructive Welsh nationalist"

Recent parliamentary career: Plaid Cymru parliamentary leader (1999–); PC spokesperson, social security, treasury, and disability (1997–); PC whip (1995–); Welsh affairs committee (1998–2001)
Background: solicitor (at firm Lloyd George and George); barrister; keen sportsman: president of angling, football, and rugby clubs; changed his surname from Hughes in 1970
Born: September 26 1951 in Betws-y-Coed
Education: Llanrwst Grammar School
Higher education: University College, Aberystwyth; College of Law, Chester
Constituency: small, Welsh-speaking, covers Snowdonia, Harlech, Barmouth and Blaenau Ffestiniog

Lord, Michael
Conservative MP for Central Suffolk and North Ipswich since 1997; Central Suffolk (1983–97)

Majority: 3,469 (7.3%)
Turnout: 63.5%

	Votes	Share %	Change %
Michael Lord, Conservative	20,924	44.4	1.8
Carole Jones, Labour	17,455	37.1	1.2
Ann Elvin, Liberal Democrat	7,593	16.1	−4.5
Jonathan Wright, UK Independence party	1,132	2.4	n/a

Andrew Roth says: "normally a pleasant locally-rooted constituency man and a sensitive and knowledgeable agricultural expert"

Recent parliamentary career: unopposed bills panel (2000–); standing orders committee (1998–); deputy speaker (1997–); Court of Referees (1997–); Eurosceptic rebel before becoming deputy speaker
Background: arboricultural consultant; farmer; North Bedfordshire councillor
Born: October 17 1938 in Denton, Manchester
Education: William Hulme's Grammar School

Higher education: Cambridge, Christ's
Constituency: runs from Ipswich inland towards Framlingham and Wickham Market

Loughton, Tim
Conservative MP for East Worthing and Shoreham since 1997

Majority: 6,139 (14.2%)
Turnout: 59.9%

	Votes	Share %	Change %
Tim Loughton, Conservative	18,608	43.2	2.7
Daniel Yates, Labour	12,469	29	5.1
Paul Elgood, Liberal Democrat	9,876	22.9	–7.7
Jim McCulloch, UK Independence party	1,195	2.8	n/a
Christopher Baldwin, LCA	920	2.1	n/a

Andrew Roth says: "assiduous debater, although specialist opponents can consider his viewpoints 'complete and utter rubbish'"

Recent parliamentary career: opposition spokesperson, DOH (2001–); spokesperson on environment, regions, urban regeneration, housing, and poverty (2000–01); environmental audit committee (1997–2001)
Background: fund manager, company director; Conservative activist in Wandsworth
Born: May 30 1962 in Eastbourne
Education: The Priory School, Lewes
Higher education: Warwick University; Cambridge, Clare
Constituency: eastern half of Worthing plus Adur council covering Shoreham and Lancing

Love, Andrew
Labour MP for Edmonton since 1997

Majority: 9,772 (28.1%)
Turnout: 55.8%

	Votes	Share %	Change %
Andrew Love, Labour	20,481	58.9	–1.4
David Burrowes, Conservative	10,709	30.8	0.6
Douglas Taylor, Liberal Democrat	2,438	7	0.7
Gwyneth Rolph, UK Independence party	406	1.2	n/a
Erol Basarik, Reform 2000	344	1	n/a
Howard Medwell, Socialist Alliance	296	0.9	n/a
Dr Ram Saxena, Independent	100	0.3	n/a

Andrew Roth says: "amiable, engaging, Scots burr, loyal, veteran of local government and the Co-operative party"

Recent parliamentary career: PPS to Jacqui Smith (2001–); deregulation committee (1999–); public accounts committee (1997–2001)
Background: chartered secretary; parliamentary officer, Co-operative party; charity fundraiser
Born: March 21 1949 in Greenock
Education: Greenock High School
Higher education: Strathclyde University
Constituency: outer London seat with some innercity characteristics, bordering River Lea

Lucas, Ian
Labour MP for Wrexham since 2001

Majority: 9,188 (30.5%)
Turnout: 59.5%

	Votes	Share %	Change %
Ian Lucas, Labour	15,934	53	–3.1
Felicity Elphick, Conservative	6,746	22.5	–1.4
Ron Davies, Liberal Democrat	5,153	17.2	3.9
Malcolm Evans, Plaid Cymru	1,783	5.9	2.7
Jane Brookes, UK Independence party	432	1.4	n/a

Maiden speech: "Wrexham people are ready to seize new opportunities and compete in a changing world"

Recent parliamentary career: entered parliament 2001; procedure committee (2001–); environmental audit committee (2001–)
Background: solicitor; based in Oswestry; chair, Society of Labour Lawyers (1996–)
Born: September 18 1960
Education: Newcastle Royal Grammar School
Higher education: New College, Oxford
Constituency: former mining town in north-east Wales near Shropshire border

Luff, Peter
Conservative MP for Mid Worcestershire since 1997; Worcester (1992–97)

Majority: 10,627 (23.7%)
Turnout: 62.4%

	Votes	Share %	Change %
Peter Luff, Conservative	22,937	51.1	3.7
David Bannister, Labour	12,310	27.4	–1.5
Robert Woodthrope-Browne, Liberal Democrat	8,420	18.8	0.2
Tony Eaves, UK Independence party	1,230	2.7	n/a

Andrew Roth says: "a shrewder lobbyist than his jovial loyalism conceals"

Recent parliamentary career: opposition whip (2001–); information committee (2001); opposition whip (2000–01); PPS to Ann Widdecombe (1996–97)
Background: public-relations consultant; research assistant; family printing business; Tory Reform Group Europhile
Born: February 18 1955 in Windsor
Education: Windsor Grammar School
Higher education: Cambridge, Corpus Christi
Constituency: rural Worcestershire from Droitwich to Evesham on the edge of the Cotswolds

Luke, Iain
Labour MP for Dundee East since 2001

Majority: 4,475 (13.8%)
Turnout: 57.2%

	Votes	Share %	Change %
Iain Luke, Labour	14,635	45.2	–5.9
Stewart Hosie, Scottish National party	10,160	31.4	4.9
Alan Donnelly, Conservative	3,900	12.1	–3.7
Raymond Lawrie, Liberal Democrat	2,784	8.6	4.5
Harvey Duke, Scottish Socialist party	879	2.7	n/a

Maiden speech: "gone are the days when Dundee was known as the city of jute, jam and journalism. Now, we boast many leading-edge companies"

Recent parliamentary career: entered parliament 2001; broadcasting committee (2001–)
Background: civil servant; lecturer in public administration, housing, and European studies for 18 years
Born: October 8 1951
Education: Stobswell Secondary School

Higher education: Dundee University; Edinburgh University
Constituency: Central Belt Scottish city, an SNP target

Lyons, John
Labour MP for Strathkelvin and Bearsden since 2001

Majority: 11,717 (28.2%)
Turnout: 66.1%

	Votes	Share %	Change %
John Lyons, Labour	19,250	46.4	−6.5
Gordon MacDonald, Liberal Democrat	7,533	18.2	8.5
Calum Smith, Scottish National party	6,675	16.1	−0.2
Murray Roxburgh, Conservative	6,635	16	−4.1
Willie Telfer, Scottish Socialist party	1,393	3.4	n/a

Maiden speech: "we want everyone in our constituency to share in any improvement that might come along, and we want social inclusion to be a reality for all constituents"

Recent parliamentary career: entered parliament 2001; Scottish affairs committee (2001–); broadcasting committee (2001–); procedure committee (2001–); public administration committee (2001–)
Background: mechanical engineer; Unison officer
Born: July 11 1949 in Scotland
Education: Woodside Secondary School, Glasgow
Higher education: Stirling University
Constituency: middle class dormitory town north of Glasgow

M

McAvoy, Thomas
Labour MP for Glasgow Rutherglen since 1987

Majority: 12,625 (43.2%)
Turnout: 56.3%

	Votes	Share %	Change %
Thomas McAvoy, Labour	16,760	57.4	−0.1
Anne McLaughlin, Scottish National party	4,135	14.2	−1.1
David Jackson, Liberal Democrat	3,689	12.6	−1.9
Malcolm Macaskill, Conservative	3,301	11.3	2
Bill Bonnar, Scottish Socialist party	1,328	4.6	n/a

Andrew Roth says: "personal crusades have been for peace in Northern Ireland and against abortion"

Recent parliamentary career: government whip (1997–); finance and services committee (1997–)
Background: engineering shop steward; Strathclyde councillor
Born: December 14 1943 in Rutherglen
Education: St Columbkilles Primary and Junior School
Constituency: previously independent borough to south-east of Glasgow

McCabe, Stephen
Labour MP for Birmingham Hall Green since 1997

Majority: 6,648 (20.1%)
Turnout: 57.5%

	Votes	Share %	Change %
Stephen McCabe, Labour	18,049	54.6	1.1
Chris White, Conservative	11,401	34.5	1.1
Punjab Singh, Liberal Democrat	2,926	8.8	−0.8
Peter Johnson, UK Independence party	708	2.1	n/a

Andrew Roth says: "thoughtful, low-profile, first ever Labour incumbent"

Recent parliamentary career: Northern Ireland affairs committee (1998–)
Background: social worker; education adviser; MSF union shop steward; Birmingham councillor
Born: August 4 1955 in Johnstone
Education: Port Glasgow Senior Secondary School, Bradford
Higher education: Moray House Teacher Training College
Constituency: outer Birmingham suburbs to south and south-east of city

McCafferty, Chris
Labour MP for Calder Valley since 1997

Majority: 3,094 (6.5%)
Turnout: 63%

	Votes	Share %	Change %
Chris McCafferty, Labour	20,244	42.7	−3.4
Sue Robson-Catling, Conservative	17,150	36.2	1.1
Michael Taylor, Liberal Democrat	7,596	16	1.3
Steve Hutton, Green party	1,034	2.2	n/a
John Nunn, UK Independence party	729	1.5	n/a
Philip Lockwood, LCA	672	1.4	n/a

Andrew Roth says: "low-profiled local councillor who concentrates on women's health issues at home and abroad"

Recent parliamentary career: international development committee (2001–)
Background: women's health adviser; disabled welfare worker; marriage registrar; Calderdale councillor
Born: October 14 1945 in Australia
Education: Footscray High School, Australia; Whalley Range Grammar Girls'
Constituency: runs south of Halifax from Hebden Bridge to Todmorden and Brighouse

McCartney, Ian
Labour MP for Makerfield since 1992

Majority: 17,750 (50.9%)
Turnout: 50.9%

	Votes	Share %	Change %
Ian McCartney, Labour	23,879	68.5	−5.1
Mrs Jane Brooks, Conservative	6,129	17.6	2.2
David Crowther, Liberal Democrat	3,990	11.5	3.2
Malcolm Jones, Socialist Alliance	858	2.5	n/a

Andrew Roth says: "undersized, underestimated hyperactive minister"

Recent parliamentary career: minister of state, DWP (2001–); minister of state, CO (1999–2001); minister of state, DTI (1997–99)
Background: trade unionist (TGWU); MP's secretary; Wigan councillor
Born: April 25 1951 in Lennoxtown, Stirlingshire
Education: Lenzie Academy; Langside College, Glasgow
Constituency: small Lancashire towns in former coalfield, very white and very Labour

McDonagh, Siobhain
Labour MP for Mitcham and Morden since 1997

Majority: 13,785 (36.3%)
Turnout: 57.8%

	Votes	Share %	Change %
Siobhain McDonagh, Labour	22,936	60.4	2
Harry Stokes, Conservative	9,151	24.1	−5.6
Nicholas Harris, Liberal Democrat	3,820	10.1	2.5
Tom Walsh, Green party	926	2.4	1.5
John Tyndall, British National party	642	1.7	0.6
Adrian Roberts, UK Independence party	486	1.3	n/a

Andrew Roth says: "low-profiled Blairite superloyalist...persuasive, articulate, prefers Cosmopolitan to New Statesman"

Recent parliamentary career: health committee (2000–)
Background: housing adviser; receptionist, London Homeless Persons' Unit; Merton councillor for 15 years; sister was general secretary of the Labour party (1998–2001)
Born: February 20 1960 in London
Education: Holy Cross Convent, New Malden
Higher education: Essex University
Constituency: southern half of London Borough of Merton, from Collier's Wood to St Hellier estates

MacDonald, Calum
Labour MP for Western Isles since 1987

Majority: 1,074 (8.1%)
Turnout: 60.3%

	Votes	Share %	Change %
Calum MacDonald, Labour	5,924	45	−10.6
Alasdair Nicholson, Scottish National party	4,850	36.9	3.5
Douglas Taylor, Conservative	1,250	9.5	2.9
John Horne, Liberal Democrat	849	6.5	3.4
Joanne Telfer, Scottish Socialist party	286	2.2	n/a

Andrew Roth says: "very bright, articulate, academic turned crofter"

Recent parliamentary career: minister, SO (1997–99); PPS to Donald Dewar (1997–97)
Background: crofter; chair, Future of Europe Trust (1990–97); political philosophy lecturer, University of California
Born: May 7 1956 in Stornoway
Education: Bayble School
Higher education: Edinburgh University; Nicolson Institute, Edinburgh; University of California
Constituency: much the smallest electorate in the UK but one of the biggest in area, 130 miles long; majority of Gaelic speakers

McDonnell, John
Labour MP for Hayes and Harlington since 1997

Majority: 13,466 (41.6%)
Turnout: 56.3%

	Votes	Share %	Change %
John McDonnell, Labour	21,279	65.7	3.7
Robert McLean, Conservative	7,813	24.1	−3.1
Nahid Boethe, Liberal Democrat	1,958	6	−1.4
Gary Birch, British National party	705	2.2	n/a
Wally Kennedy, Soc Alt	648	2	n/a

Andrew Roth says: "a hard campaigner but until recently still of the over-the-top tendency"

Recent parliamentary career: unopposed bills panel (1999–); deregulation committee (1999–); persistent rebel against government whip and left-wing critic of New Labour
Background: trade unionist (Unison); head of policy unit, Camden Council; GLC councillor; chief executive, Association of London Authorities (1987–95); Association of London government (1995–97)
Born: September 8 1951 in Liverpool
Education: Great Yarmouth Grammar School
Higher education: Brunel University; Birkbeck; London; Burnley Technical College
Constituency: Heathrow Airport and surrounding suburbs in outer west London

MacDougall, John
Labour MP for Central Fife since 2001

Majority: 10,075 (31.0%)
Turnout: 54.6%

	Votes	Share %	Change %
John MacDougall, Labour	18,310	56.3	–2.4
David Alexander, Scottish National party	8,235	25.3	0.3
Elizabeth Riches, Liberal Democrat	2,775	8.5	2.1
Jeremy Balfour, Conservative	2,351	7.2	–1.8
Morag Balfour, Scottish Socialist party	841	2.6	n/a

John MacDougall says: "it is extremely important that housing development in Fife is of a good mix and takes account of the needs of people, especially the young, in their search for affordable housing"

Recent parliamentary career: entered parliament 2001
Background: boilermaker; shop steward, oil-rig yard; convenor, Fife councillor; community activist for 20 years; on several organisations; JP
Born: December 8 1947 in Fife
Education: Templehall Secondary Modern School, Kirkcaldy; Royal Dockyard College, Rosyth; Fife College; Glenrothes College
Constituency: based around Glenrothes new town, north of Forth Bridges

McFall, John
Labour MP for Dumbarton since 1987

Majority: 9,575 (28.2%)
Turnout: 60.4%

	Votes	Share %	Change %
John McFall, Labour	16,151	47.5	–2.1
Iain Robertson, Scottish National party	6,576	19.3	–3.9
Eric Thomson, Liberal Democrat	5,265	15.5	7.9
Peter Ramsay, Conservative	4,648	13.7	–3.9
Les Robertson, Scottish Socialist party	1,354	4	n/a

Andrew Roth says: "highly regarded Scots MP...outspoken radical on social issues"

Recent parliamentary career: chair, Treasury committee (2001–); public administration committee (2000–01); minister of state, NIO (1998–99); government whip (1997–98); sponsored bill to ban fox hunting (1995)
Background: chemistry teacher and deputy head teacher (1974–87); director, Dumbarton Co-operative party
Born: October 4 1944 in Glasgow
Education: Dumbarton
Higher education: Strathclyde University; Open University
Constituency: attractive hill country west of Glasgow plus smart seaside Helensburgh and some industry

McGrady, Eddie
Social Democratic and Labour party MP for South Down since 1987

Majority: 13,858 (26.7%)
Turnout: 70.8%

	Votes	Share %	Change %
Eddie McGrady, Social Democratic and Labour party	24,136	46.4	–6.5
Mick Murphy, Sinn Fein	10,278	19.7	9.3
Dermot Nesbitt, Ulster Unionist party	9,173	17.6	–15.2
Jim Wells, Democratic Unionist party	7,802	15	n/a
Betty Campbell, Alliance party of Northern Ireland	685	1.3	–2.2

Andrew Roth says: "low-profiled SDLP pillar who is outshone by contemporaries"

Recent parliamentary career: Northern Ireland affairs committee (2001–); SDLP chief whip (1987–); defeated Enoch Powell (1987)
Background: accountant; Down councillor; member of NIA (1982–86 and 1998–)
Born: June 3 1935 in Downpatrick
Education: St Patrick's High School
Higher education: Belfast College of Technology
Constituency: beautiful Mountains of Mourne plus fishing and ferry ports

McGuinness, Martin
Sinn Fein MP for Mid Ulster since 1997

Majority: 9,953 (20.0%)
Turnout: 81.3%

	Votes	Share %	Change %
Martin McGuinness, Sinn Fein	25,502	51.1	11
Ian McCrea, Democratic Unionist party	15,549	31.1	–5.2
Elish Haughy, Social Democratic and Labour party	8,376	16.8	–5.3
Francie Donnelly, Workers' party	509	1	0.5

Andrew Roth says: "born-again Sinn Fein campaigner, 'formidable negotiator with considerable media skills'"

Recent parliamentary career: has not taken seat in parliament
Background: butcher's assistant; Sinn Fein chief negotiator; minister for education, NIA (1999–)
Born: May 23 1950 in Derry
Education: Christian Brothers' Technical College
Constituency: seat with the UK's highest turnout; rural west of Northern Ireland

McGuire, Anne
Labour MP for Stirling since 1997

Majority: 6,274 (17.4%)
Turnout: 67.7%

	Votes	Share %	Change %
Anne McGuire, Labour	15,175	42.2	–5.2
Geoff Mawdsley, Conservative	8,901	24.8	–7.7
Fiona Macaulay, Scottish National party	5,877	16.4	3
Clive Freeman, Liberal Democrat	4,208	11.7	5.5
Clark Mullen, Scottish Socialist party	1,012	2.8	n/a
Mark Ruskell, Green party	757	2.1	n/a

Andrew Roth says: "moderate, loyal, pro-European Scottish apparatchik"

Recent parliamentary career: government whip (1998–)
Background: deputy director, Scottish Council for Voluntary Organisations; Scottish National officer, Community Services Volunteers; teacher; Strathclyde councillor; GMB union organiser

Born: May 26 1949 in Glasgow
Education: Our Lady of St Francis Secondary School, Glasgow
Higher education: Glasgow University
Constituency: ancient Scottish town between Edinburgh and Glasgow, dominated by its castle

McIntosh, Anne

Conservative MP for Vale of York since 1997

Majority: 12,517 (25.8%)
Turnout: 66.1%

	Votes	Share %	Change %
Anne McIntosh, Conservative	25,033	51.6	6.9
Christopher Jukes, Labour	12,516	25.8	−0.7
Greg Stone, Liberal Democrat	9,799	20.2	−3.6
Peter Thornber, UK Independence party	1,142	2.4	n/a

Andrew Roth says: "widely educated, broadly experienced assiduous advocate of the scattergun approach to opposition"

Recent parliamentary career: opposition spokesperson, DCMS (2001–); transport, local government and the regions committee (2001); European scrutiny committee (2000–01); transport subcommittee (1999–2001); environment, transport and regional affairs committee (1999–2001)
Background: part-Danish; advocate; EU administrator (1989–99)
Born: September 20 1954 in Edinburgh
Education: Harrogate College
Higher education: Edinburgh University; Aarhus University, Denmark
Constituency: flatlands between Yorkshire Moors and the Dales

McIsaac, Shona

Labour MP for Cleethorpes since 1997

Majority: 5,620 (13.3%)
Turnout: 62%

	Votes	Share %	Change %
Shona McIsaac, Labour	21,032	49.6	−2
Stephen Howd, Conservative	15,412	36.3	2.9
Gordon Smith, Liberal Democrat	5,080	12	0.6
Janet Hatton, UK Independence party	894	2.1	n/a

Andrew Roth says: "assiduous press-the-flesher; counterbalances stoogey Westminster displays with locally appreciated successes"

Recent parliamentary career: PPS to Jane Kennedy (2001–); PPS to Adam Ingram (2000–01); standards and privileges committee (1997–2001)
Background: journalist; sub-editor on several women's magazines; food writer; pool lifeguard in Tooting
Born: April 3 1960 in Dunfermline
Education: Shape School, Brussels; Barne Barton Secondary Modern School, Plymouth; Stoke Damerel High School
Higher education: Durham University
Constituency: villages outside Grimsby plus market town of Brigg and seaside Cleethorpes

Mackay, Rt Hon Andrew

Conservative MP for Bracknell since 1997; East Berkshire (1983–97); Birmingham Stechford (1977–79)

Majority: 6,713 (13.7%)
Turnout: 60.7%

	Votes	Share %	Change %
Andrew Mackay, Conservative	22,962	46.7	−0.7
Janet Keene, Labour	16,249	33	3.2
Ray Earwicker, Liberal Democrat	8,424	17.1	1.7
Lawrence Boxall, UK Independence party	1,266	2.6	n/a

Andrew Roth says: "veteran mainstream right-wing libertarian who believes 'people are best able to decide how to run their own lives'"

Recent parliamentary career: opposition spokesperson, NI (1997–2001); deputy chief whip (1996–97)
Background: consultant to public companies; married Conservative MP Julie Kirkbride (1997)
Born: August 27 1949 in Birmingham
Education: Solihull School
Constituency: Bracknell new town in M4 corridor plus Sandhurst

McKechin, Ann
Labour MP for Glasgow Maryhill since 2001

Majority: 9,888 (44.5%)
Turnout: 40.1%

	Votes	Share %	Change %
Anne McKechin, Labour	13,420	60.4	−4.5
Alex Dingwall, Scottish National party	3,532	15.9	−1
Stuart Callison, Liberal Democrat	2,372	10.7	3.6
Gordon Scott, Scottish Socialist party	1,745	7.9	n/a
Gawain Towler, Conservative	1,162	5.2	−0.7

Maiden speech: "we must move away from the pre-eminence of individualism in our society, to create a society where the principle of caring for, and working with, our fellow citizens has priority"

Recent parliamentary career: entered parliament 2001; information committee (2001–); Scottish affairs committee (2001–)
Background: solicitor (1983–2001); campaigner for aid and international debt relief, women's officer of Glasgow Kelvin Labour party
Born: April 22 1961 in Scotland
Education: Paisley Grammar School
Higher education: Strathclyde University
Constituency: working-class seat in north Glasgow including north Kelvinside, Woodside, and Milton

McKenna, Rosemary
Labour MP for Cumbernauld and Kilsyth since 1997

Majority: 7,520 (25.4%)
Turnout: 59.7%

	Votes	Share %	Change %
Rosemary McKenna, Labour	16,144	54.4	−4.3
David McGlashan, Scottish National party	8,624	29	1.2
John O'Donnell, Liberal Democrat	1,934	6.5	2.7
Ms Alison Ross, Conservative	1,460	4.9	−1.9
Kenny McEwan, Scottish Socialist party	1,287	4.3	n/a
Thomas Taylor, Scot Ref			

Andrew Roth says: "strongly pro-devolution, pro-EU respected Blairite moderniser"

Recent parliamentary career: culture, media and sport committee (2001–); procedure committee (2001–); joint PPS to junior ministers (1999–2001)
Background: primary school teacher; Cumbernauld councillor and president of Convention of Scottish Local Authorities
Born: May 8 1941 in Renfrewshire

Education: St Augustine's Comprehensive School, Glasgow
Higher education: Notre Dame College of Education, Glasgow
Constituency: new town north-east of Glasgow around River Kelvin

MacKinlay, Andrew
Labour MP for Thurrock since 1992

Majority: 9,997 (26.7%)
Turnout: 48.8%

	Votes	Share %	Change %
Andrew MacKinlay, Labour	21,121	56.5	−6.8
Mike Penning, Conservative	11,124	29.8	3
John Lathan, Liberal Democrat	3,846	10.3	2.2
Christopher Sheppard, UK Independence party	1,271	3.4	n/a

Andrew Roth says: "normal traditional trade union MP flowering as a heroic independent when surrounded by Blairite sycophants"

Recent parliamentary career: foreign affairs committee (1997–); unopposed bills panel (1997–); challenged prime minister on over-loyal questions in the Commons (1998)
Background: trade unionist (officer, NALGO); local government clerk; Kingston upon Thames councillor
Born: April 24 1949 in Wembley
Education: St Joseph's Roman Catholic Primary School, Tolworth; Salesian College, Chertsey
Constituency: urban Essex, Lakeside shopping centre, Thames shore

Maclean, Rt Hon David
Conservative MP for Penrith and the Borders since 1983

Majority: 14,677 (33.1%)
Turnout: 65.3%

	Votes	Share %	Change %
David Maclean, Conservative	24,302	54.9	7.3
Geyve Walker, Liberal Democrat	9,625	21.8	−4.9
Michael Boaden, Labour	8,177	18.5	−3.1
Effie Crocker, UK Independence party	938	2.1	n/a
Mark Gibson, LCA	870	2	n/a
John Moffat, Independent	337	0.8	n/a

Andrew Roth says: "reverted [to] type in opposition as a hawkish 'Tebbitesque' Thatcherite"

Recent parliamentary career: minister of state, HO (1993–97); refused John Major's offer of promotion to Cabinet (1995)
Background: lawyer; consultant, Securicor
Born: May 16 1953 on Black Isle, Cromarty
Education: Fortrose Academy
Higher education: Aberdeen University
Constituency: England's largest seat, splendid Borders countryside, foot and mouth an issue

McLoughlin, Patrick
Conservative MP for West Derbyshire since 1986

Majority: 7,370 (14.6%)
Turnout: 67.4%

	Votes	Share %	Change %
Patrick McLoughlin, Conservative	24,280	48	5.9
Stephen Clamp, Labour	16,910	33.4	-0.1
Jeremy Beckett, Liberal Democrat	7,922	15.7	-1.8
Stuart Bavester, UK Independence party	672	1.3	n/a
Nick Delves, Official Monster Raving Loony party	472	0.9	0.4
Robert Goodall, Independent	333	0.7	n/a

Andrew Roth says: "ultimate token working class Tory loyalist"

Recent parliamentary career: accommodation and works committee (2001–); shadow minister, MAFF (1999–); opposition deputy chief whip (1997); shadow minister, NI (1997–99)
Background: agricultural worker; coal miner and NUM official who worked during miners' strike; was shipping and aviation minister (1989–92) although alarmed by flying and representing a landlocked constituency
Born: November 30 1957 in Cannock
Education: Cardinal Griffin Comprehensive School, Cannock
Higher education: Staffordshire College of Agriculture
Constituency: Peak District National Park, rural, small towns, Bakewell and Chatsworth

McNamara, Kevin
Labour MP for Hull North since 1983; Kingston-upon-Hull Central (1974–83); Kingston-upon-Hull North (1966–74)

Majority: 10,721 (37.5%)
Turnout: 45.4%

	Votes	Share %	Change %
Kevin McNamara, Labour	16,364	57.2	-8.6
Simone Butterworth, Liberal Democrat	5,643	19.7	5.1
Paul Charlson, Conservative	4,902	17.1	2.1
Tineka Robinson, UK Independence party	655	2.3	n/a
Roger Smith, Socialist Alliance	490	1.7	n/a
Carl Wagner, LCA	478	1.7	n/a
Christopher Veasey, Independent	101	0.4	n/a

Andrew Roth says: "recently muted, breezy-serious Catholic radical and anti-unionist"

Recent parliamentary career: standards and privileges committees (2001–); vice chairman, British-Irish parliamentary body; long-serving Labour opposition spokesperson, notably Northern Ireland (1987–94), where he called for dual sovereignty, upsetting Unionists
Background: lecturer in comtemporary British politics and law; history and politics teacher; columnist in Catholic Herald
Born: September 5 1934 in Liverpool
Education: St Mary's College, Crosby
Higher education: Hull University
Constituency: working-class north Hull, contains university and much council housing

McNulty, Tony
Labour MP for Harrow East since 1997

Majority: 11,124 (23.1%)
Turnout: 58.9%

	Votes	Share %	Change %
Tony McNulty, Labour	26,590	55.3	2.8
Peter Wilding, Conservative	15,466	32.2	-3.2
George Kershaw, Liberal Democrat	6,021	12.5	4.3

Andrew Roth says: "among the brightest of Blairite loyalists"

Recent parliamentary career: government whip (1999–); PPS to David Blunkett (1997–99)

Background: business lecturer at Polytechnic of North London; Harrow councillor; deputy leader, Labour group
Born: November 3 1958 in London
Education: Salvatorian College, Harrow; Stanmore Sixth Form College
Higher education: Liverpool University; Virginia Polytechnic Institute and State University
Constituency: mixed north-west London seat with many Asian voters, contains Kenton, Wealdstone, and Stanmore

MacShane, Denis
Labour MP for Rotherham since 1994

Majority: 13,077 (44.5%)
Turnout: 50.7%

	Votes	Share %	Change %
Denis MacShane, Labour	18,759	63.9	–7.4
Richard Powell, Conservative	5,682	19.4	5.1
Charles Hall, Liberal Democrat	3,117	10.6	0.2
Peter Griffith, UK Independence party	730	2.5	n/a
Dick Penycate, Green party	577	2	n/a
Freda Smith, Socialist Alliance	352	1.2	n/a
Geoffrey Bartholomew, JLDP	137	0.5	n/a

Simon Hoggart, the _Guardian_: "the thinking man's Michael Fabricant"

Recent parliamentary career: junior minister, FCO (2001–); PPS to ministers of state, FCO (1997–2001)
Background: BBC journalist (1970s); youngest-ever president of National Union of Journalists (1978); policy director, International Metalworkers' Federation in Geneva (1980–92); founder and director, European Policy Institute; one of Labour's most ardent pro-Europeans; multilingual
Born: May 21 1948 in Glasgow
Education: RC Secondary School
Higher education: Birkbeck College, London University; Oxford, Merton
Constituency: industrial pro-Labour town in South Yorkshire that has lost its steel and mining industries

Mactaggart, Fiona
Labour MP for Slough since 1997

Majority: 12,508 (32.1%)
Turnout: 53.8%

	Votes	Share %	Change %
Fiona Mactaggart, Labour	22,718	58.3	1.7
Diana Coad, Conservative	10,210	26.2	–3
Keith Kerr, Liberal Democrat	4,109	10.5	3.1
Michael Haines, Ind Haines	859	2.2	n/a
John Lane, UK Independence party	738	1.9	n/a
Choudry Nazir, Independent	364	0.9	n/a

Andrew Roth says: "intelligent, well-researched questioner and debater"

Recent parliamentary career: PPS to Chris Smith (1997–2001)
Background: primary-school teacher; lecturer in primary education; general secretary, Joint Council for the Welfare of Immigrants; associate editor, Renewal; chairman of executive, Liberty (1992–96); Wandsworth councillor
Born: September 12 1953
Education: Cheltenham Ladies' College
Higher education: King's College, London; Goldsmiths' College, London; London Institute of Education
Constituency: industrial town just west of London, dense suburbs and big Asian community

McWalter, Tony
Labour MP for Hemel Hempstead since 1997

Majority: 3,742 (8.2%)
Turnout: 63.6%

	Votes	Share %	Change %
Tony McWalter, Labour	21,389	46.7	1
Paul Ivey, Conservative	17,647	38.5	–0.6
Neil Stuart, Liberal Democrat	5,877	12.8	0.5
Barry Newton, UK Independence party	920	2	n/a

Andrew Roth says: "possibly the first Kantian philosopher in the Commons"

Recent parliamentary career: Northern Ireland affairs committee (1997–2001)
Background: philosophy lecturer at Thames Polytechnic; long-distance lorry driver; North Hertfordshire councillor
Born: March 20 1945 in Worksop, Nottinghamshire
Education: St Benedict's School, Ealing
Higher education: Aberystwyth University; McMaster University, Canada; Oxford, University College
Constituency: successful Hertfordshire new town with many IT companies

McWilliam, John
Labour MP for Blaydon since 1979

Majority: 7,809 (21.1%)
Turnout: 57.4%

	Votes	Share %	Change %
John McWilliam, Labour	20,340	54.9	–5.1
Peter Maughan, Liberal Democrat	12,531	33.8	10
Mark Watson, Conservative	4,215	11.4	–1.8

Andrew Roth says: "leading stalwart of the 'lost generation' of Labour MPs"

Recent parliamentary career: chair, committee of selection (1997–), where he had to deal with dispute over committee chairs (2001); deputy speaker, Westminster Hall (1999–)
Background: telecommunications engineer; Edinburgh councillor
Born: May 16 1941 in Grangemouth
Education: Leith Academy
Higher education: Heriot-Watt University; Napier College, Edinburgh
Constituency: Tyneside seat running south from Newcastle

Mahmood, Khalid
Labour MP for Birmingham Perry Barr since 2001

Majority: 8,753 (23.3%)
Turnout: 52.6%

	Votes	Share %	Change %
Khalid Mahmood, Labour	17,415	46.5	–16.5
David Binns, Conservative	8,662	23.2	1.5
Jon Hunt, Liberal Democrat	8,566	22.9	13
Avtar Northfield, Socialist Labour Democrat	1,544	4.1	n/a
Caroline Johnson, Socialist Alliance	465	1.2	n/a
Natalya Nattrass, UK Independence party	352	0.9	n/a
Michael Roche, Marxist	221	0.6	n/a
Robert Davidson, Muslim	192	0.5	n/a

Maiden speech: "Some may say that life begins at 40. Well, certainly my parliamentary life does"

Recent parliamentary career: entered parliament 2001; broadcasting committee (2001–)

Background: Kashmiri Muslim community worker; Birmingham City councillor; Britain's second Muslim MP; won hard-fought selection battle
Born: 1962 in Kashmir
Higher education: MBA in Management Studies
Constituency: secure Labour seat, urban, outer-ring council estates

Mahon, Alice
Labour MP for Halifax since 1987

Majority: 6,129 (15.1%)
Turnout: 57.8%

	Votes	Share %	Change %
Alice Mahon, Labour	19,800	49	−5.3
James Walsh, Conservative	13,671	33.9	1.8
John Durkin, Liberal Democrat	5,878	14.6	2.6
Helen Martinek, UK Independence party	1,041	2.6	n/a

Andrew Roth says: "aggressively sectarian, hard-left class warrior"

Recent parliamentary career: PPS to Chris Smith (1997–97); health committee (1991–97)
Background: nurse; lecturer in trade union studies; trade unionist (NUPE, then Unison); Labour MPs' delegate to national policy forum (1998–); opposed Kosovo War (1998)
Born: September 28 1937 in Halifax
Education: Halifax Grammar School
Higher education: Bradford University
Constituency: industrial and commercial town in Calder Valley west of Bradford

Malins, Humfrey
Conservative MP for Woking since MP since 1997; Croydon North West (1983–92)

Majority: 6,759 (15.7%)
Turnout: 60.3%

	Votes	Share %	Change %
Humfrey Malins, Conservative	19,747	46	7.6
Alan Hilliar, Liberal Democrat	12,988	30.3	3
Sabir Hussain, Labour	8,714	20.3	−0.7
Michael Harvey, UK Independence party	1,461	3.4	n/a

Andrew Roth says: "socially conscious but churchy puritanical libertarian"

Recent parliamentary career: opposition spokesperson, HO (2001–); home affairs committee (1997–2001)
Background: solicitor; Metropolitan stipendiary magistrate; recorder of the crown court; Mole Valley councillor; interest in drugs and immigration issues
Born: July 31 1945 in Nuneaton
Education: St John's, Leatherhead
Higher education: College of Law, Guildford; Oxford, Brasenose
Constituency: largest town in Surrey, affluent stockbroker belt

Mallaber, Judy
Labour MP for Amber Valley since 1997

Majority: 7,227 (16.2%)
Turnout: 60.3%

	Votes	Share %	Change %
Judy Mallaber, Labour	23,101	51.9	−2.8
Gillian Shaw, Conservative	15,874	35.7	2.2
Kate Smith, Liberal Democrat	5,538	12.4	4.7

Andrew Roth says: "highly intelligent, fluent and witty speaker with an elitist education"

Recent parliamentary career: education and employment committee (1997–2001); employment subcommittee (1997–2001)
Background: research officer, NUPE (1975–85); director, Local Government Information Unit; chair, Labour Research Department (1991–94); member of Liberty, Amnesty, Friends of the Earth; once member of Communist party
Born: July 10 1951 in London
Education: North London Collegiate School
Higher education: Oxford, St Anne's
Constituency: mixed Derbyshire seat between M1 and Peak District centred on Alfreton

Mallon, Seamus
Social Democratic and Labour party MP for Newry and Armagh since 1986

Majority: 3,575 (6.5%)
Turnout: 76.8%

	Votes	Share %	Change %
Seamus Mallon, Social Democratic and Labour party	20,784	37.4	–5.6
Conor Murphy, Sinn Fein	17,209	30.9	9.8
Paul Berry, Democratic Unionist party	10,795	19.4	n/a
Mrs Sylvia McRoberts, Ulster Unionist party	6,833	12.3	–21.5

Andrew Roth says: "the power behind John Hume's throne, 'Mr Mallon fills in the details'"

Recent parliamentary career: member, NIA (1973–74 and 1998–); deputy first minister, Northern Ireland Executive (1998–99); deputy leader, SDLP (1978–); SDLP spokesperson, constitutional affairs (1986–); SDLP spokesperson, justice (1986–); Irish Senate (1982)
Background: headmaster; civil rights activist; cofounder of SDLP
Born: August 17 1936 in Markethill, Armagh
Education: Christian Brothers' Abbey Grammar School, Newry
Higher education: St Joseph's College of Education, Belfast
Constituency: once the IRA's "bandit" country; rolling border country around Crossmaglen and Newry

Mandelson, Rt Hon Peter
Labour MP for Hartlepool since 1992

Majority: 14,571 (38.3%)
Turnout: 56.3%

	Votes	Share %	Change %
Peter Mandelson, Labour	22,506	59.2	–1.5
Gus Robinson, Conservative	7,935	20.9	–0.4
Nigel Boddy, Liberal Democrat	5,717	15	0.9
Arthur Scargill, Socialist Labour party	912	2.4	n/a
Ian Cameron, Ind Cam	557	1.5	n/a
John Booth, Ind Booth	424	1.1	n/a

Andrew Roth says: "alternately the most skilled packager of New Labour's moderate doctrines or the evil genius behind the abandonment of its traditional socialist values"

Recent parliamentary career: secretary of state, NI (1999–2001), resigning over Hinduja passport affair; secretary of state, DTI (1998), resigning over loan affair; minister without portfolio (1997–98)
Background: student activist; trade union researcher; television producer, LWT Weekend World (1982–85); Labour communications director (1985–92); chair of planning, PLP general election campaign (1999–2001)
Born: October 21 1953 in London
Education: Hendon Senior High School
Higher education: Oxford, St Catherine's
Constituency: traditional industrial seaside town on north-east coast

Mann, John
Labour MP for Bassetlaw since 2001

Majority: 9,748 (25.1%)
Turnout: 57%

	Votes	Share %	Change %
John Mann, Labour	21,506	55.3	−5.8
Alison Holley, Conservative	11,758	30.2	5.5
Neil Taylor, Liberal Democrat	4,942	12.7	2.4
Kevin Maloy, Socialist Labour party	689		

Maiden speech: "My village has what every village needs – a school, a pub and a post office. I shall be looking to this parliament for policies that sustain that basic social infrastructure of rural life."

Recent parliamentary career: entered parliament 2001
Background: head of research, AEEU (1988–90); National Training Officer, TUC (1990–95); Labour party trade union liaison officer; self-employed businessman
Born: October 1 1960 in Bradford
Education: Bradford Grammar School
Higher education: Manchester University
Constituency: Nottinghamshire seat around ex-mining town of Worksop

Maples, John
Conservative MP for Stratford-on-Avon since 1997; Lewisham West (1983–97)

Majority: 11,802 (21.5%)
Turnout: 64.4%

	Votes	Share %	Change %
John Maples, Conservative	27,606	50.3	2
Susan Juned, Liberal Democrat	15,804	28.8	3.3
Mushtaq Hussain, Labour	9,164	16.7	−3.8
Ronald Mole, UK Independence party	1,184	2.2	n/a
Mick Davies, Green party	1,156	2.1	n/a

Andrew Roth says: "highly intelligent, privately objective"

Recent parliamentary career: foreign affairs committee (2001–); shadow secretary of state, FCO (1999–2000); opposition spokesperson, MoD (1998–99); shadow secretary of state, DoH (1997–98)
Background: barrister; businessman; chief executive, Saatchi & Saatchi Government Relations; Conservative party deputy chairman (1994–5), where he wrote a memo, later leaked, which said Major government was weak and divided
Born: April 22 1943 in Hampshire
Education: Marlborough
Higher education: Harvard University; Cambridge, Downing
Constituency: William Shakespeare country in south Warwickshire

Marris, Robert
Labour MP for Wolverhampton South West since 2001

Majority: 3,487 (8.6%)
Turnout: 60.9%

	Votes	Share %	Change %
Robert Marris, Labour	19,735	48.3	−2.1
David Chambers, Conservative	16,248	39.7	−0.2
Mike Dixon, Liberal Democrat	3,425	8.4	0.2
Wendy Walker, Green party	805	2	n/a
Doug Hope, UK Independence party	684	1.7	n/a

Maiden speech: "Wolverhampton was proud to become a city last year. It took us only slightly more than 1,000 years to get there after our founding by Lady Wulfruna."

Recent parliamentary career: entered parliament 2001; work and pensions committee (2001–)
Background: solicitor, worked as a bus driver and trucker as a student in Canada
Born: April 8 1955
Education: St Edward's School, Oxford
Higher education: University of British Columbia; Birmingham Polytechnic
Constituency: Wolverhampton town centre running south towards Tettenhall and Merry Hill

Marsden, Gordon
Labour MP for Blackpool South since 1997

Majority: 8,262 (21.3%)
Turnout: 52.2%

	Votes	Share %	Change %
Gordon Marsden, Labour	21,060	54.3	–2.7
David Morris, Conservative	12,798	33	–1.4
Doreen Holt, Liberal Democrat	4,115	10.6	2
Val Cowell, UK Independence party	819	2.1	n/a

Andrew Roth says: "a loyalist who groans privately but backs the government publicly"

Recent parliamentary career: education and employment committee (1998–2001); education subcommittee (1998–)
Background: professional historian; editor *History Today*; Open University tutor; PR consultant to English Heritage
Born: November 28 1953 in Manchester
Education: Stockport Grammar School
Higher education: London University; Harvard University; Oxford, New College
Constituency: the bustling centre of Blackpool including Tower, Pleasure Beach and piers

Marsden, Paul
Labour MP for Shrewsbury and Atcham since 1997

Majority: 3,579 (7.2%)
Turnout: 66.6%

	Votes	Share %	Change %
Paul Marsden, Labour	22,253	44.6	7.6
Anthea McIntyre, Conservative	18,674	37.4	3.4
Jonathan Rule, Liberal Democrat	6,173	12.4	–12.6
Henry Curteis, UK Independence party	1,620	3.3	n/a
Ms Emma Bullard, Green party	931	1.9	n/a
James Gollins, Independent	258	0.5	n/a

Andrew Roth says: "claims to be more afraid of his wife than of the whips"

Recent parliamentary career: agriculture committee (1997–2001)
Background: quality manager, Taylor Woodrow and NatWest; member of English Heritage; National Trust
Born: March 18 1968 in Frodsham, Cheshire
Education: Helsby Grammar School
Higher education: Open University; Teesside Polytechnic; Mid Cheshire College
Constituency: elegant Shropshire county town by River Severn

Marshall, David
Labour MP for Glasgow Shettleston since 1979

Majority: 9,818 (48.0%)
Turnout: 39.7%

	Votes	Share %	Change %
David Marshall, Labour	13,235	64.7	−8.5
Jim Byrne, Scottish National party	3,417	16.7	2.7
Rosie Kane, Scottish Socialist party	1,396	6.8	n/a
Lewis Hutton, Liberal Democrat	1,105	5.4	1.4
Campbell Murdoch, Conservative	1,082	5.3	−0.2
Murdo Ritchie, Socialist Labour party	230	1.1	n/a

Andrew Roth says: "a quiet hard-left Glaswegian transport specialist"

Recent parliamentary career: unopposed bills panel (1997–); chair, Scottish affairs committee (1997–)
Background: tram and bus conductor; Glasgow councillor
Born: May 7 1941 in Glasgow
Education: Larbert High School; Woodside Senior School, Glasgow
Constituency: east and south inner Glasgow including newly refurbished Gorbals

Marshall, James
Labour MP for Leicester South since 1987; Leicester South (1974–83)

Majority: 13,243 (31.4%)
Turnout: 58%

	Votes	Share %	Change %
James Marshall, Labour	22,958	54.5	−3.5
Richard Hoile, Conservative	9,715	23.1	−0.6
Parmjit Singh Gill, Liberal Democrat	7,243	17.2	3.4
Margaret Layton, Green party	1,217	2.9	n/a
Arnie Gardner, Socialist Labour party	676	1.6	0.3
Kirti Ladwa, UK Independence party	333	0.8	n/a

Andrew Roth says: "quiet, sensible, unspectacular Eurosceptic"

Recent parliamentary career: Scottish affairs committee (2001–); European scrutiny committee (1998–); junior spokesperson, NI (1987–92)
Background: research scientist in wool industries; Leicester Polytechnic lecturer; parliamentary adviser, National Federation of Market Traders; Leeds councillor
Born: March 13 1941 in Sheffield
Education: Sheffield City Grammar School
Higher education: Leeds University
Constituency: mixed residential area in south Leicester, strongly Asian

Marshall-Andrews QC, Robert
Labour MP for Medway since 1997

Majority: 3,780 (9.8%)
Turnout: 59.5%

	Votes	Share %	Change %
Robert Marshall-Andrews, Labour	18,914	49	0.1
Mark Reckless, Conservative	15,134	39.2	2.3
Geoffrey Juby, Liberal Democrat	3,604	9.3	−0.9
Ms Nikki Sinclaire, UK Independence party	958	2.5	n/a

Andrew Roth says: "over-aged *enfant terrible* of minority of rebellious '97 newcomers"

Recent parliamentary career: joint committee on consolidation of bills (1997–)
Background: wealthy barrister and QC; witty Commons speaker and republican; rebels against conformity of New Labour and especially Kosovo War
Born: April 10 1944 in London

Education: Mill Hill School
Higher education: Bristol University
Constituency: industrial Kent seat including Isle of Grain, with port, and cathedral town of Rochester

Martin, Michael
Labour MP for Glasgow Springburn since 1979

Majority: 11,378 (47.2%)
Turnout: 43.7%

	Votes	Share %	Change %
Michael Martin, the speaker	16,053	66.6	n/a
Sandy Bain, Scottish National party	4,675	19.4	2.9
Carolyn Leckie, Scottish Socialist party	1,879	7.8	n/a
Daniel Houston, Scottish Unionist	1,289	5.4	n/a
Richard Silvester, Independent	208	0.9	n/a

Andrew Roth says: "a plain-spoken, warm-hearted, locally-rooted mainstream moderate Glasgow trade unionist"

Recent parliamentary career: speaker, House of Commons (2000–), the first Catholic speaker since the Reformation, crticised by some for accent and ability; deputy speaker, first deputy chairman of Ways and Means (1997–2000)
Background: trade union organiser; metalworker; Rolls-Royce engineer
Born: July 3 1945
Education: St Patrick's RC Boys' School, Glasgow
Constituency: north-east of Glasgow city centre including huge council tower blocks and much deprivation

Martlew, Eric
Labour MP for Carlisle since 1987

Majority: 5,702 (16.4%)
Turnout: 59.4%

	Votes	Share %	Change %
Eric Martlew, Labour	17,856	51.2	–6.2
Mike Mitchelson, Conservative	12,154	34.8	5.8
John Guest, Liberal Democrat	4,076	11.7	1.2
Colin Paisley, LCA	554	1.6	n/a
Paul Wilcox, Socialist Alliance	269	0.8	n/a

Andrew Roth says: "man of combative ability shelved by Blair, possibly because too old Labour"

Recent parliamentary career: environment, food and rural affairs committee (2001–); PPS to Baroness Jay of Paddington (1998–2001); PPS to Rt Hon David Clark, (1997–98)
Background: worked for Nestlé for 21 years as laboratory technician and personnel manager
Born: January 3 1949 in Ince, Makerfield
Education: Harraby Secondary School
Higher education: Carlisle College
Constituency: remote Borders city, foot and mouth an issue here

Mates, Michael
Conservative MP for East Hampshire since 1983; Petersfield (1974–83)

Majority: 8,890 (17.6%)
Turnout: 63.8%

	Votes	Share %	Change %
Michael Mates, Conservative	23,950	47.6	–0.4
Robert Booker, Liberal Democrat	15,060	30	1.9
Barbara Burfoot, Labour	9,866	19.6	2.5
Stephen Coles, UK Independence party	1,413	2.8	n/a

Andrew Roth says: "bright, genial, flexible One Nation pro-European ex-regular"

Recent parliamentary career: chair, Northern Ireland affairs committee (2001–); intelligence and security committee (2001–); minister of state, NIO (1992–93), resigned over links with disgraced businessman Azil Nadir; close ally of former MP Michael Heseltine
Background: army major and lieutenant-colonel, resigned commission (1975)
Born: June 9 1934 in London
Education: Blundell's School
Higher education: Cambridge, King's
Constituency: upmarket rural seat centred on Alton in Hampshire

Maude, Rt Hon Francis
Conservative MP for Horsham since 1997; North Warwickshire (1983–92)

Majority: 13,666 (26.9%)
Turnout: 63.8%

	Votes	Share %	Change %
Francis Maude, Conservative	26,134	51.5	0.7
Hubert Carr, Liberal Democrat	12,468	24.6	–0.2
Janet Sully, Labour	10,267	20.2	1.5
Hugo Miller, UK Independence party	1,472	2.9	n/a
Jim Duggan, Independent	429	0.8	n/a

Andrew Roth says: "Francis Maude is not a happy warrior. Mournful earnestness is more his style. This figures."

Recent parliamentary career: campaign manager for Michael Portillo (2001), the unsuccessful Conservative leadership candidate; shadow foreign secretary (2000–01); shadow chancellor (1998–2000); shadow culture secretary (1997–98); financial secretary to the Treasury (1990–92)
Background: banker; barrister; director, ASDA Group
Born: July 4 1953 in Oxford
Education: Abingdon School
Higher education: Inner Temple; College of Law; Cambridge, Corpus Christi
Constituency: prosperous, very safe, smart southern towns around Gatwick

Mawhinney, Rt Hon Sir Brian
Conservative MP for North West Cambridgeshire since 1997; Peterborough (1979–97)

Majority: 8,101 (18.4%)
Turnout: 62.3%

	Votes	Share %	Change %
Brian Mawhinney, Conservative	21,895	49.8	1.7
Anthea Cox, Labour	13,794	31.4	–0.8
Alastair Taylor, Liberal Democrat	6,957	15.8	0.7
Barry Hudson, UK Independence party	881	2	n/a
David Hall, Independent	429	1	n/a

Andrew Roth says: "a pragmatic, mainstream Ulster-born liberal Protestant and former medical lecturer … mirthless, publicly-genial, privately hard"

Recent parliamentary career: shadow home secretary (1997–98); minister without portfolio, Conservative party chairman (1995–97); transport secretary (1994–95), where he oversaw plans to sell off British Rail
Background: senior lecturer in medicine, London University; author of books on Northern Ireland

Born: July 26 1940 in Belfast
Education: Royal Belfast Academical Institute
Higher education: London University; Michigan University, USA; Queen's College, Belfast
Constituency: private housing estates and farms outside Peterborough

May, Theresa
Conservative MP for Maidenhead since 1997

Majority: 3,284 (7.5%)
Turnout: 63.6%

	Votes	Share %	Change %
Theresa May, Conservative	19,506	45	–4.8
Kathryn Newbound, Liberal Democrat	16,222	37.5	11.2
John O'Farrell, Labour	6,577	15.2	–2.9
Dr Denis Cooper, UK Independence party	741	1.7	n/a
Lloyd Clarke, Official Monster Raving Loony party	272	0.6	n/a

Andrew Roth says: "very bright, hyperactive, articulate and witty; has become increasingly Eurosceptic and sharply partisan"

Recent parliamentary career: shadow secretary of state, DTLGR (2001–); shadow education secretary (1999–2001); opposition spokesperson, education (1998–99)
Background: senior adviser and head of European Affairs Unit (1985–96); Merton borough councillor
Born: October 1 1956 in Eastbourne
Education: Wheatley Park Comprehensive School
Higher education: Oxford, St Hugh's
Constituency: Thamesside towns including Maidenhead, Cookham, Sonning, and Twyford

Meacher, Rt Hon Michael
Labour MP for Oldham West and Royton since 1997; Oldham West (1970–97)

Majority: 13,365 (33.5%)
Turnout: 57.6%

	Votes	Share %	Change %
Michael Meacher, Labour	20,441	51.2	–7.6
Duncan Reed, Conservative	7,076	17.7	–5.7
Nick Griffin, British National party	6,552	16.4	n/a
Marc Ramsbottom, Liberal Democrat	4,975	12.5	0.6
David Roney, Green party	918	2.3	n/a

Andrew Roth says: "the highly-competent veteran minister, the pioneer of many of Labour's advanced ideas"

Recent parliamentary career: minister of state, DEFRA (2001); minister of state, DETR (1997–2001); environmental audit committee (1997–)
Background: mocked in 1997 parliament for having several homes; as environment minister handled foot and mouth and global warming talks; sociology lecturer; author; journalist
Born: November 4 1939 in Hemel Hempstead
Education: Berkhamsted School
Higher education: London School of Economics; Oxford, New College
Constituency: hard-bitten north-west town; local politics currently dominated by BNP's unexpected success in 2001

Meale, Alan
Labour MP for Mansfield since 1987

Majority: 11,038 (29.9%)
Turnout: 55.2%

	Votes	Share %	Change %
Alan Meale, Labour	21,050	57.1	−7.3
William Wellesley, Conservative	10,012	27.2	6
Tim Hill, Liberal Democrat	5,790	15.7	4.6

Andrew Roth says: "deft, formerly hard left organiser and behind-the-scenes operator on behalf of the Campaign Group"

Recent parliamentary career: Court of Referees (1999–); junior minister, DETR (1998–99); on committees of various European organisations
Background: author; editor; development officer, NACRO; researcher for MPs, including Barbara Castle and Dennis Skinner; seaman; honorary citizen of Cyprus
Born: July 31 1949 in Bishop Auckland
Education: St. Joseph Roman Catholic School, Bishop Auckland
Higher education: Durham University; Oxford, Ruskin
Constituency: bleak ex-mining town north of Nottingham

Mercer, Patrick
Conservative MP for Newark since 2001

Majority: 4,073 (9.0%)
Turnout: 63.5%

	Votes	Share %	Change %
Patrick Mercer, Conservative	20,983	46.5	7.1
Fiona Jones, Labour	16,910	37.5	−7.7
David Harding-Price, Liberal Democrat	5,970	13.2	1.7
Donald Haxby, Independent	822	1.8	n/a
Ian Thomson, Socialist Alliance	462	1	n/a

Maiden speech: "What brought me into politics was the men with whom I served in the Foresters [Nottinghamshire regiment] and their families"

Recent parliamentary career: entered parliament 2001, taking seat from Labour; defence committee (2001–)
Background: BBC defence correspondent; radio journalist with Radio 4's *Today* programme; second lieutenant, the Sherwood Foresters (1974–99); lecturer; awarded medals for service in Ulster and Serbia
Born: June 26 1956 in Newark
Education: King's School, Chester
Higher education: Oxford University
Constituency: historic town east of Nottingham, Conservatives regained (2001) after disputed election (1997)

Merron, Gillian
Labour MP for Lincoln since 1997

Majority: 8,420 (22.7%)
Turnout: 56%

	Votes	Share %	Change %
Gillian Merron, Labour	20,003	53.9	−1
Christine Talbot, Conservative	11,583	31.2	0.2
Lisa Gabriel, Liberal Democrat	4,703	12.7	1.9
Roger Doughty, UK Independence party	836	2.3	n/a

Andrew Roth says: "former centre-left mainstreamer, turned Blairite loyalist"

Recent parliamentary career: PPS to John Reid (2001–); PPS to Baroness Symons (1999–2001); PPS to Doug Henderson (1998–99)
Background: senior regional official, NUPE and Unison (1987–97); local government officer
Born: April 12 1959 in London

Education: Wanstead High School
Higher education: Lancaster University
Constituency: hard-to-reach cathedral city in eastern England

Michael, Rt Hon Alun
Labour MP for Cardiff South and Penarth since 1987

Majority: 12,287 (34.4%)
Turnout: 57.6%

	Votes	Share %	Change %
Alun Michael, Labour	20,094	56.2	2.8
Maureen Kelly-Owen, Conservative	7,807	21.8	1.1
Rodney Berman, Liberal Democrat	4,572	12.8	3.5
Lila Haines, Plaid Cymru	1,983	5.6	2.4
Justin Callan, UK Independence party	501	1.4	n/a
Dave Bartlett, Socialist Alliance	427	1.2	n/a
Anne Savoury, ProLife Alliance	367	1	n/a

Andrew Roth says: "quietly persuasive: 'has an extraordinarily lucid style of debate; he shouts at nobody'"

Recent parliamentary career: minister of state, DEFRA (2001–); first minister, Welsh Assembly (1999); secretary of state, Welsh Office (1998–99); resigned to lead Labour in Welsh Assembly; junior minister, HO (1997–99)
Background: journalist, youth and community worker; national vice president of YHA; Welsh-speaking; was briefly first minister in Welsh Assembly (resigned 2000)
Born: August 22 1943 in north Wales
Education: Colwyn Bay Grammar School
Higher education: Keele University
Constituency: docklands Cardiff around redeveloping bay; Bute, Splott and Grangetown

Milburn, Rt Hon Alan
Labour MP for Darlington since 1992

Majority: 9,529 (23.4%)
Turnout: 63.4%

	Votes	Share %	Change %
Alan Milburn, Labour	22,479	55.2	–6.4
Tony Richmond, Conservative	12,950	31.8	3.5
Robert Adamson, Liberal Democrat	4,358	10.7	3.5
Alan Docherty, Socialist Alliance	469	1.2	n/a
Craig Platt, Independent	269	0.7	n/a
Amanda Rose, Socialist Labour Party	229	0.6	n/a

Andrew Roth says: "highly intelligent, impressive former left-wing poacher turned revisionist gamekeeper"

Recent parliamentary career: secretary of state, DoH (1999–); chief secretary to the Treasury (1998–99); minister of state, DoH (1997–98)
Background: trade unionist (MSF); business development officer for Tyneside council
Born: January 27 1958 in Birmingham
Education: John Marley School, Newcastle; Stokesely Comprehensive School
Higher education: Newcastle University; Lancaster University
Constituency: railway and engineering town in County Durham

Miliband, David
Labour MP for South Shields since 2001

Majority: 14,090 (46.3%)
Turnout: 49.3%

	Votes	Share %	Change %
David Miliband, Labour	19,230	63.2	–8.2
Joanna Gardner, Conservative	5,140	16.9	2.3
Marshall Grainger, Liberal Democrat	5,127	16.8	8
Alan Hardy, UK Independence party	689	2.3	n/a
Roger Nettleship, Independent	262	0.9	n/a

Maiden speech: "In South Shields, icy North Sea winds lead people to say 'cold hands, but warm heart'. Today, we need a government with helping hands and a warm heart."

Background: head, Downing Street Policy Unit (1997–2001); head of policy in Tony Blair's office in opposition; co-author of 1997 and 2001 Labour manifestos; research fellow, IPPR; speechwriter, Neil Kinnock (1992)
Born: July 15 1965
Education: Haverstock Comprehensive School
Higher education: Oxford, Corpus Christi; MIT
Constituency: one-time shipbuilding town at the mouth of the River Tyne

Miller, Andrew
Labour MP for Ellesmere Port and Neston since 1992

Majority: 10,861 (26.2%)
Turnout: 60.9%

	Votes	Share %	Change %
Andrew Miller, Labour	22,964	55.3	–4.3
Gareth Williams, Conservative	12,103	29.1	0
Stuart Kelly, Liberal Democrat	4,828	11.6	2.7
Henry Crocker, UK Independence party	824	2	n/a
Geoff Nicholls, Green party	809	2	n/a

Andrew Roth says: "an able, indefatigable and computer-literate organiser"

Recent parliamentary career: information committee (1997–2001)
Background: technician; geological analyst; regional officer, MSF union
Born: March 23 1949 in Middlesex
Education: Hayling Island County Secondary School
Higher education: London School of Economics; Highbury Technical College
Constituency: tucked between the Rivers Dee and Mersey at end of the Wirral; dominated by oil refinery and Vauxhall factory

Mitchell, Andrew
Conservative MP for Sutton Coldfield since 2001; Gedling (1987–97)

Majority: 10,104 (23.2%)
Turnout: 60.5%

	Votes	Share %	Change %
Andrew Mitchell, Conservative	21,909	50.4	–1.8
Robert Pocock, Labour	11,805	27.2	3.4
Martin Turner, Liberal Democrat	8,268	19	–0.3
Mike Nattrass, UK Independence party	1,186	2.7	n/a
Ian Robinson, Independent	284	0.7	n/a

Andrew Roth says: "smooth, bright, assiduous climber with all the right connections for a Tory MP"

Recent parliamentary career: re-entered parliament 2001; work and pensions committee (2001–); president, One Nation group of Conservative MPs (1989–92)
Background: merchant banker; army officer
Born: March 23 1956
Education: Rugby School
Constituency: middle class Birmingham suburb east of Birmingham

Mitchell, Austin
Labour MP for Great Grimsby since 1983; Grimsby (1977–83)

Majority: 11,484 (34.8%)
Turnout: 52.3%

	Votes	Share %	Change %
Austin Mitchell, Labour	19,118	57.9	–1.9
James Cousins, Conservative	7,634	23.1	1
Andrew de Freitas, Liberal Democrat	6,265	19	0.9

Andrew Roth says: "brilliant, witty but erratic small-screen Yorkshire Don Quixote and incurable iconoclast"

Recent parliamentary career: agriculture committee (1997–2001)
Background: editor, House magazine; journalist with Yorkshire Television, BBC, Sky TV; politics and history lecturer, New Zealand
Born: September 19 1934 in Baildon, Yorkshire
Education: Bingley Grammar School
Higher education: Manchester University; Oxford, Nuffield
Constituency: isolated north-east seat between Humber and North Sea

Moffatt, Laura
Labour MP for Crawley since 1997

Majority: 6,770 (17.1%)
Turnout: 55.2%

	Votes	Share %	Change %
Laura Moffatt, Labour	19,488	49.3	–5.7
Henry Smith, Conservative	12,718	32.2	0.4
Linda Seekings, Liberal Democrat	5,009	12.7	4.5
Brian Galloway, UK Independence party	1,137	2.9	n/a
Ms Claire Staniford, Official Monster Raving Loony party	388	1	n/a
Arshad Khan, Justice party	271	0.7	0.2
Karl Stewart, Socialist Labour party	260	0.7	n/a
Ms Muriel Hirsch, Socialist Alliance	251	0.6	n/a

Andrew Roth says: "loyal London-born left-wing nurse graduated from local government"

Recent parliamentary career: PPS to Lord Irvine (2001–); defence committee (1997–2001)
Background: general nurse, Crawley hospital; Crawley councillor and mayor
Born: April 9 1954 in London
Education: Hazelwick Comprehensive School, Crawley
Higher education: Crawley Technical College
Constituency: new town between London and Brighton

Moonie, Dr Lewis
Labour MP for Kirkcaldy since 1987

Majority: 8,963 (31.8%)
Turnout: 54.6%

	Votes	Share %	Change %
Lewis Moonie, Labour	15,227	54.1	0.5
Shirley-Anne Somerville, Scottish National party	6,264	22.3	–0.6
Scott Campbell, Conservative	3,013	10.7	–3
Andrew Weston, Liberal Democrat	2,849	10.1	1.4
Dougie Kinnear, Scottish Socialist party	804	2.9	n/a

Andrew Roth says: "potential promise and connections have been belied by his seeming laid-back dilettantism"

Recent parliamentary career: junior minister, MoD (2000–); Treasury committee (1998–2000)
Background: GP, clinical pharmacologist; medical adviser in Netherlands; award-winning bridge player; linguist
Born: February 25 1947 in Dundee
Education: Grove Academy, Dundee
Higher education: Edinburgh University; St Andrews University
Constituency: Forth coastline plus industrial towns

Moore, Michael
Liberal Democrat MP for Tweeddale, Ettrick and Lauderdale since 1997

Majority: 5,157 (15.6%)
Turnout: 63.9%

	Votes	Share %	Change %
Michael Moore, Liberal Democrat	14,035	42.3	11.1
Keith Geddes, Labour	8,878	26.7	–0.7
Andrew Brocklehurst, Conservative	5,118	15.4	–6.7
Richard Thomson, Scottish National party	4,108	12.4	–4.7
Norman Lockhart, Scottish Socialist party	695	2.1	n/a
John Hein, Liberal	383	1.2	0.2

Andrew Roth says: "rising star of the Scottish Lib Dems"

Recent parliamentary career: Lib Dem spokesperson, Scotland (2001–); Lib Dem spokesperson, Transport (1999–2001)
Background: helped arrange Scottish coalition with Labour (1999); chartered accountant; researcher to Archie Kirkwood MP (who was in turn researcher to David Steel, Michael Moore's predecessor)
Born: June 3 1965 in Dundonald
Education: Strathallan School; Jedburgh Grammar School
Higher education: Edinburgh University
Constituency: big, rolling Borders country south of Edinburgh, main towns are Galashiels, Selkirk, and Peebles

Moran, Margaret
Labour MP for Luton South since 1997

Majority: 10,133 (25.8%)
Turnout: 57%

	Votes	Share %	Change %
Margaret Moran, Labour	21,719	55.2	0.4
Gordon Henderson, Conservative	11,586	29.4	–2
Rabi Martins, Liberal Democrat	4,292	10.9	1.3
Marc Scheimann, Green party	798	2	1.3
Charles Lawman, UK Independence party	578	1.5	n/a
Joe Hearne, Socialist Alliance	271	0.7	n/a
Robert Bolton, Workers' Revolutionary party	107	0.3	n/a

Andrew Roth says: "highly rated dynamo from local government with a reputation for toughness"

Recent parliamentary career: PPS to Baroness Morgan (2001–); information committee (2001–); PPS to Mo Mowlam (1998–2001); PPS to Gavin Strang (1997–98)
Background: National President, NALGO housing association branch; director, housing association; Lewisham councillor and leader
Born: April 24 1955 in London
Education: St Ursula's Convent School, Greenwich
Higher education: Birmingham University; Hackney College; St Mary's College of Education
Constituency: town north of London, dominated by airport and closing Vauxhall car plant

Morgan, Julie
Labour MP for Cardiff North since 1997

Majority: 6,165 (14.3%)
Turnout: 69%

	Votes	Share %	Change %
Julie Morgan, Labour	19,845	45.9	−4.5
Alastair Watson, Conservative	13,680	31.6	−2.1
John Dixon, Liberal Democrat	6,631	15.3	4.4
Sion Jobbins, Plaid Cymru	2,471	5.7	3.2
Don Hulston, UK Independence party	613	1.4	n/a

Andrew Roth says: "politically very correct former social worker and stalwart of the South Wales Labour establishment"

Recent parliamentary career: modernisation of the House of Commons committee (2001–); administration committee (2001–); Welsh affairs committee (1997–)
Background: social worker; South Glamorgan councillor; member of Welsh refugee council, race equality council; married to Rhodri Morgan, Labour leader in Welsh Assembly
Born: November 2 1944 in Cardiff
Education: Howell's School
Higher education: London University; Manchester University; Cardiff University
Constituency: middle class Cardiff suburb

Morley, Elliot
Labour MP for Scunthorpe since 1997; Glanford and Scunthorpe (1987–97)
Majority: 10,372 (30.9%)
Turnout: 56.3%

	Votes	Share %	Change %
Elliot Morley, Labour	20,096	59.8	−0.6
Bernard Theobald, Conservative	9,724	28.9	2.6
Bob Tress, Liberal Democrat	3,156	9.4	1
Mike Cliff, UK Independence party	347	1	n/a
David Patterson, Independent	302	0.9	n/a

Andrew Roth says: "straight-talking left-wing teacher"

Recent parliamentary career: junior minister, DEFRA (2001–); junior minister, MAFF (1997–2001)
Background: secondary school and special needs teacher; Hull councillor; interest in environment and wildlife
Born: July 6 1952 in Liverpool
Education: St Margaret's High School, Liverpool
Higher education: Hull College of Education; Lincolnshire; Humberside University
Constituency: industrial seat on north-east coast with steel and food industries

Morris, Estelle
Labour MP for Birmingham Yardley since 1992

Majority: 2,578 (8.6%)
Turnout: 57.2%

	Votes	Share %	Change %
Estelle Morris, Labour	14,085	46.9	−0.1
John Hemming, Liberal Democrat	11,507	38.3	5.3
Barrie Roberts, Conservative	3,941	13.1	−4.7
Alan Ware, UK Independence party	329	1.1	n/a
Colin Wren, Socialist Labour Party	151	0.5	n/a

Andrew Roth says: "widely admired or tolerated and only rarely criticised"

Recent parliamentary career: secretary of state, DFES (2001–); minister of state, DFEE (1998–2001)

Background: teacher and head of sixth form studies (1974–92); Warwick councillor; political career has focused on education
Born: June 17 1952 in Manchester
Education: Whalley Range High School, Manchester
Higher education: Warwick University; Coventry College of Education
Constituency: south-east Birmingham seat next to Solihull that has become rare Lib Dem–Labour marginal

Moss, Malcolm
Conservative MP for North East Cambridgeshire since 1987

Majority: 6,373 (13.2%)
Turnout: 60.2%

	Votes	Share %	Change %
Malcolm Moss, Conservative	23,132	48.1	5.1
Dil Owen, Labour	16,759	34.9	1.1
Richard Renaut, Liberal Democrat	6,733	14	−2.4
John Stevens, UK Independence party	1,189	2.5	n/a
Tony Hoey, ProLife Alliance	238	0.5	n/a

Andrew Roth says: "does his homework thoroughly without shouting or grabbing media lapels"

Recent parliamentary career: opposition spokesperson, DTLGR (2001–); opposition spokesperson, agriculture (1999–2001); Northern Ireland (1997–99)
Background: geography and economics teacher; insurance consultant; company director; Fenland District councillor
Born: March 6 1943 in Manchester
Education: Audenshaw Grammar School
Higher education: Cambridge, St John's
Constituency: flat Cambridgeshire fenland around Ely (but not containing it)

Mountford, Kali
Labour MP for Colne Valley since 1997

Majority: 4,639 (9.9%)
Turnout: 63.3%

	Votes	Share %	Change %
Kali Mountford, Labour	18,967	40.4	−0.9
Philip Davies, Conservative	14,328	30.5	−2.2
Gordon Beever, Liberal Democrat	11,694	24.9	2.3
Richard Plunkett, Green party	1,081	2.3	n/a
Arthur Quarmby, UK Independence party	917	2	n/a

Andrew Roth says: "articulate and very northern-shrewd"

Recent parliamentary career: Treasury committee (2001–); social security committee (1998–99); admitted leaking select committee report to Gordon Brown's PPS (1999)
Background: civil servant in DFEE (1975–96); trade unionist (CPSA); Sheffield councillor
Born: January 12 1954 in Crewe
Education: Crewe Grammar for Girls
Higher education: Manchester Metropolitan University
Constituency: historic three-way marginal in West Yorkshire with Hovis country looks

Mudie, George
Labour MP for Leeds East since 1992

Majority: 12,643 (43.6%)
Turnout: 51.5%

	Votes	Share %	Change %
George Mudie, Labour	18,290	63	–4.5
Barry Anderson, Conservative	5,647	19.4	0.7
Brian Jennings, Liberal Democrat	3,923	13.5	3.2
Raymond Northgreaves, UK Independence party	634	2.2	n/a
Mark King, Socialist Labour party	419	1.4	n/a
Peter Socrates, Independent	142	0.5	n/a

Andrew Roth says: "worries mainly about local innercity dereliction and its impact on the Leeds poor"

Recent parliamentary career: Treasury committee (2001–); junior minister, DFEE (1998–99); government whip (1997–98)
Background: leader of Leeds City Council; trade union official; engineer; seaman
Born: February 6 1945 in Dundee
Education: local state schools; Lawside Academy, Dundee
Higher education: Newbattle Abbey College, Midlothian
Constituency: big council estates on eastern edge of Leeds

Mullin, Chris
Labour MP for Sunderland South since 1987

Majority: 13,667 (43.8%)
Turnout: 48.3%

	Votes	Share %	Change %
Chris Mullin, Labour	19,921	63.9	–4.2
Jim Boyd, Conservative	6,254	20.1	1.2
Mark Greenfield, Liberal Democrat	3,675	11.8	0.3
Joe Dobbie, British National party	576	1.9	n/a
Joseph Moore, UK Independence party	470	1.5	n/a
Ms Rosalyn Warner, Official Monster Raving Loony party	291	0.9	n/a

Andrew Roth says: "built his reputation by pressing the establishment's nose into miscarriages of justice"

Recent parliamentary career: chair, home affairs committee , returning to position where he established reputation as analytical liberal critic of Home Office (2001–); junior minister, DFID (2001), left at his own request; junior minister, DETR (1999–2001); chair, home affairs committee (1997–99)
Background: author; journalist, BBC World Service, especially in Asia; previously a noted left-wing campaigner and author of *How to Select and Re-select your MP*; successfully campaigned for release of wrongly convicted Birmingham Six
Born: December 12 1947 in Chelmsford
Education: St Joseph's College, Ipswich
Higher education: Hull University
Constituency: working-class town on coast south of Newcastle, now has Nissan plant but few shipbuilding jobs

Munn, Meg
Labour MP for Sheffield Heeley since 2001

Majority: 11,704 (34.3%)
Turnout: 54.4%

	Votes	Share %	Change %
Meg Munn, Labour	19,452	57	–3.7
David Willis, Liberal Democrat	7,748	22.7	1.4
Carolyn Abbott, Conservative	4,864	14.3	–1.3
Rob Unwin, Green party	774	2.3	n/a
Brian Fischer, Socialist Labour party	667	2	n/a
David Dunn, UK Independence party	634	1.9	n/a

Maiden speech: "The benefits of the EU appear to me to be threefold – stability, security and economic prosperity"

Recent parliamentary career: entered parliament 2001; education and skills committee (2001–); procedure committee (2001–)
Background: social worker and union official (Unison, Nalgo, GMB); assistant director, children's services, York; Nottingham City councillor; trilingual
Born: August 24 1959 in Sheffield
Education: Rowlinson Comprehensive School, Sheffield
Higher education: York University; Nottingham University
Constituency: south Sheffield seat dominated by valleys and tower blocks

Murphy, Denis
Labour MP for Wansbeck since 1997

Majority: 13,101 (35.0%)
Turnout: 59.4%

	Votes	Share %	Change %
Denis Murphy, Labour	21,617	57.8	–7.7
Alan Thompson, Liberal Democrat	8,516	22.8	6.9
Rachel Lake, Conservative	4,774	12.8	–1.1
Michael Kirkup, Independent	1,076	2.9	n/a
Nic Best, Green party	954	2.6	0.5
Gavin Attwell, UK Independence party	482	1.3	n/a

Andrew Roth says: "part of Labour's dwindling band of proletarian MPs"

Recent parliamentary career: deregulation committee (1998–)
Background: mines electrician (1969–94); Wansbeck councillor and leader
Born: November 2 1948 in Ashington
Education: St Cuthbert's Grammar School, Newcastle upon Tyne
Higher education: Northumberland College
Constituency: Northumberland seat centred on Morpeth

Murphy, Jim
Labour MP for Eastwood since 1997

Majority: 9,141 (18.9%)
Turnout: 70.7%

	Votes	Share %	Change %
Jim Murphy, Labour	23,036	47.6	7.9
Raymond Robertson, Conservative	13,895	28.7	–4.8
Allan Steele, Liberal Democrat	6,239	12.9	1.2
Stewart Maxwell, Scottish National party	4,137	8.6	–4.5
Peter Murray, Scottish Socialist party	814	1.7	n/a
Dr Manar Tayan, Independent	247	0.5	n/a

Andrew Roth says: "eager-beaver clumsy super-loyalist"

Recent parliamentary career: PPS to Helen Liddell (2001–); public accounts committee (1999–2001)
Background: director, Endsleigh Insurance; president, NUS (1994–96)
Born: August 23 1967 in Glasgow
Education: Bellarmine Secondary School, Glasgow; Milnerton High School, Cape Town
Higher education: Strathclyde University, Glasgow
Constituency: stockbroker belt south of Glasgow, once safest Conservative seat in Scotland

Murphy, Rt Hon Paul
Labour MP for Torfaen since 1987

Majority: 16,280 (46.2%)
Turnout: 57.7%

	Votes	Share %	Change %
Paul Murphy, Labour	21,883	62.1	–7
Jason Evans, Conservative	5,603	15.9	3.6
Alan Masters, Liberal Democrat	3,936	11.2	–0.9
Stephen Smith, Plaid Cymru	2,720	7.7	5.3
Brenda Vipass, UK Independence party	657	1.9	n/a
Steve Bell, Socialist Alliance	443	1.3	n/a

Andrew Roth says: "unobtrusive, highly respected Welsh negotiator of Northern Ireland peace talks"

Recent parliamentary career: secretary of state, WO (1999–); minister of state, NIO (1997–99)
Background: consultant, National Association of Teachers; lecturer on government and history; Torfaen councillor
Born: November 25 1948 in Usk, Gwent
Education: West Monmouth School, Pontypool
Higher education: Oxford, Oriel
Constituency: covers Pontypool and Cwmbran new town at east of Welsh valleys

Murrison, Andrew
Conservative MP for Westbury since 2001

Majority: 5,294 (10.5%)
Turnout: 66.7%

	Votes	Share %	Change %
Andrew Murrison, Conservative	21,299	42.1	1.5
David Vigar, Liberal Democrat	16,005	31.6	1.7
Sarah Cardy, Labour	10,847	21.4	0.3
Charles Booth-Jones, UK Independence party	1,261	2.5	n/a
Bob Gledhill, Green party	1,216	2.4	n/a

Maiden speech: "the threat that the proposed Euro force might pose to one of the most successful postwar organisations, NATO, and to our symbiotic relationship with the United States has surely not been adequately explored"

Recent parliamentary career: entered parliament 2001
Background: consultant occupational physician; GP; surgeon in Royal Navy (1984–2000); examiner; school governor; prison visitor
Born: April 24 1961
Education: Harwich High School, Dartmouth
Higher education: Bristol University; Cambridge, Hughes Hall
Constituency: rural seat between Bath and Salisbury including Bradford on Avon, Westbury, and chalk White Horse

N

Naysmith, Dr Doug
Labour MP for Bristol North West since 1997

Majority: 11,087 (23.7%)
Turnout: 60.8%

	Votes	Share %	Change %
Doug Naysmith, Labour	24,436	52.3	2.4
Charles Hansard, Conservative	13,349	28.6	–0.7
Peter Tyzack, Liberal Democrat	7,387	15.8	2.7
Diane Carr, UK Independence party	1,149	2.5	n/a
Vince Horrigan, Socialist Labour party	371	0.8	–0.1

Andrew Roth says: "active in seriously questioning those coming before his committees"

Recent parliamentary career: health committee (2001–); deregulation committee (1998–); social security committee (1999–2001)
Background: immunologist researcher and lecturer at several universities; Bristol councillor
Born: April 1 1941 in Midlothian
Education: Musselburgh Burgh School; George Heriot's School, Edinburgh
Higher education: Edinburgh University; Yale University
Constituency: northern edge of Bristol bordering Northavon, with Filton BAe and Rolls-Royce factory

Norman, Archie
Conservative MP for Tunbridge Wells since 1997

Majority: 9,730 (24.2%)
Turnout: 62.3%

	Votes	Share %	Change %
Archie Norman, Conservative	19,643	48.9	3.7
Keith Brown, Liberal Democrat	9,913	24.7	–5
Ian Carvell, Labour	9,332	23.2	2.8
Victor Webb, UK Independence party	1,313	3.3	n/a

Andrew Roth says: "slow learning Commons novice: 'a businessman in politics, not a politician in business'"

Recent parliamentary career: shadow secretary of state, DETR (2000–01); opposition spokesperson, Europe (1999–2000); party chief executive (1998–99); ally of former leader William Hague
Background: multi-millionaire chairman and chief executive, Asda Group (1991–96); finance director and company director, including Railtrack (1994–2000); vice chairman, Conservative party (1997–98)
Born: May 1 1954 in London
Education: Charterhouse School
Higher education: Minnesota University; Harvard Business School; Cambridge, Emmanuel
Constituency: traditional town in Kent that has long been safe Conservative territory

Norris, Dan
Labour MP for Wansdyke since 1997

Majority: 5,113 (10.4%)
Turnout: 69.4%

	Votes	Share %	Change %
Dan Norris, Labour	22,706	46.3	2.2
Chris Watt, Conservative	17,593	35.9	0.6
Gail Coleshill, Liberal Democrat	7,135	14.6	–2.2
Francis Hayden, Green party	958	2	n/a
Peter Sandell, UK Independence party	655	1.3	n/a

Andrew Roth says: "considered by Millbank to be a West Country specialist at Lib Dem bashing"

Recent parliamentary career: assistant whip (2001–)
Background: researcher; author; child protection officer; Bristol councillor
Born: January 28 1960 in London
Education: Chipping Sodbury Comprehensive School
Higher education: Sussex University; Reading University
Constituency: south of Bristol, small towns including Radstock and Midsomer Norton

O

Oaten, Mark
Liberal Democrat MP for Winchester since 1997

Majority: 9,634 (16.3%)
Turnout: 72.3%

	Votes	Share %	Change %
Mark Oaten, Liberal Democrat	32,282	54.6	−13.4
Andrew Hayes, Conservative	22,648	38.3	9.9
Stephen Wyeth, Labour	3,498	5.9	4.2
Joan Martin, UK Independence party	664	1.1	n/a
Ms Henrietta Rouse, Wessex regionalist	66	0.1	n/a

Andrew Roth says: "young former lobbyist...local issues constituency man"

Recent parliamentary career: Lib Dem spokesperson, CO (2001–); public administration committee (1999–2001); PPS to Charles Kennedy (1999–2001); fought byelection after his 1997 win by two votes was overturned in the courts
Background: company director; lobbyist for Shandwick Public Affairs; Watford councillor; member of SDP
Born: March 8 1964 in Watford
Education: Queen's Secondary Modern School, Watford
Higher education: Hatfield Polytechnic; Hertfordshire College of Further Education
Constituency: upmarket southern cathedral town with lowest Labour vote in Britain

O'Brien, Mike
Labour MP for North Warwickshire since 1992

Majority: 9,639 (21.7%)
Turnout: 60.2%

	Votes	Share %	Change %
Mike O'Brien, Labour	24,023	54.1	−4.3
Geoff Parsons, Conservative	14,384	32.4	1.2
William Powell, Liberal Democrat	5,052	11.4	4
John Flynn, UK Independence party	950	2.1	n/a

Andrew Roth says: "highly intelligent, straight-talking junior minister; previously thought a 'thoughtful prober'"

Recent parliamentary career: junior minister, HO (1997–2001)
Background: solicitor (1987–92); law lecturer; parliamentary adviser to Police Federation
Born: June 19 1954 in Worcester
Education: Blessed Edward Oldcorne Roman Catholic School, Worcester
Higher education: North Staffordshire Polytechnic
Constituency: mixed urban seat that curls around the east of Birmingham

O'Brien, Stephen
Conservative MP for Eddisbury since 1999

Majority: 4,568 (10.3%)
Turnout: 64.2%

	Votes	Share %	Change %
Stephen O'Brien, Conservative	20,556	46.3	1.5
Bill Eyres, Labour	15,988	36	−4.2
Paul Roberts, Liberal Democrat	6,975	15.7	1.9
David Carson, UK Independence party	868	2	n/a

Andrew Roth says: "is sure he lives in 'the real world', battling against a red-tape jungle of government regulations"

Recent parliamentary career: opposition whip (2001–); environment, food, and rural affairs committee (2001–); education and employment committee (1999–2001); education subcommittee (1999–2001); PPS to Rt Hon Michael Ancram (1999–2001);
Background: city solicitor, Freshfields; businessman and company director; member of Law Society; once a member of SDP (1981–88)
Born: April 1 1957 in Mtwara, Tanzania
Education: Loretto School, Kenya; Handbridge School; Heronwater School
Higher education: College of Law, Chester; Cambridge, Emmanuel
Constituency: prosperous rural Cheshire between Crewe and Chester, running to Welsh border

O'Brien, William
Labour MP for Normanton since 1983

Majority: 9,937 (29.1%)
Turnout: 52.2%

	Votes	Share %	Change %
William O'Brien, Labour	19,152	56.1	–4.5
Graham Smith, Conservative	9,215	27	3.4
Stephen Pearson, Liberal Democrat	4,990	14.6	2.2
Mick Appleyard, Socialist Labour party	798	2.3	n/a

Andrew Roth says: "ageing moderate with the practical low-profile approach of an experienced local councillor"

Recent parliamentary career: transport, local government, and the regions committee (2001–); environment, transport and regional affairs committee (1997–2001)
Background: coal miner for nearly 40 years; West Riding councillor
Born: January 25 1929 in Castleford
Education: St Joseph's School, Castleford
Higher education: Leeds University
Constituency: mixed towns around Wakefield of which Normanton is the largest

O'Hara, Edward
Labour MP for Knowsley South since 1990

Majority: 21,316 (58.3%)
Turnout: 51.8%

	Votes	Share %	Change %
Edward O'Hara, Labour	26,071	71.3	–5.8
David Smithson, Liberal Democrat	4,755	13	4.7
Paul Jemetta, Conservative	4,250	11.6	–1
Alan Fogg, Socialist Labour Party	1,068	2.9	n/a
Ms Mona McNee, Independent	446	1.2	n/a

Andrew Roth says: "solid, cerebral, Liverpool Irish Protestant Hellenophile"

Recent parliamentary career: on several European organisations; won 1990 byelection
Background: lecturer in higher education; Knowsley councillor; speaks Modern Greek and Latin
Born: October 1 1937 in Bootle
Education: Liverpool Collegiate School

Higher education: Oxford, Magdalen
Constituency: innercity Merseyside seat containing Ford's Jaguar factory

Olner, Bill
Labour MP for Nuneaton since 1992

Majority: 7,535 (17.4%)
Turnout: 60.1%

	Votes	Share %	Change %
Bill Olner, Labour	22,577	52.1	–4.1
Mark Lancaster, Conservative	15,042	34.7	3.8
Tony Ferguson, Liberal Democrat	4,820	11.1	2.3
Brian James, UK Independence party	873	2	n/a

Andrew Roth says: "a Commons doughnutter and rare working class type"

Recent parliamentary career: environment, food, and rural affairs committee (2001–); environment subcommittee (1997–); standing orders committee (2000–); environment, transport and regional affairs committee (1997–2001); transport subcommittee (1997–2001);
Background: machinist in Rolls-Royce plant; Nuneaton councillor
Born: May 9 1942 in Atherstone, Warwickshire
Education: Atherstone Secondary Modern School
Higher education: North Warwickshire Technical College
Constituency: mixed West Midlands seat on edge of Coventry

O'Neill, Martin
Labour MP for Ochil since 1997; Clackmannan (1983–97); East Stirlingshire and Clackmannan (1979–83)

Majority: 5,349 (15.1%)
Turnout: 61.3%

	Votes	Share %	Change %
Martin O'Neill, Labour	16,004	45.3	0.3
Keith Brown, Scottish National party	10,655	30.2	–4.2
Alasdair Campbell, Conservative	4,235	12	–2.6
Paul Edie, Liberal Democrat	3,253	9.2	4
Pauline Thompson, Scottish Socialist party	751	2.1	n/a
Flash Gordon Approaching, Official Monster Raving Loony party	405	1.2	n/a

Andrew Roth says: "shrewd, pragmatic, cautious defence, then energy, specialist"

Recent parliamentary career: chair, trade and industry committee (1995–)
Background: insurance clerk
Born: January 6 1945 in Edinburgh
Education: Trinity Academy, Edinburgh
Higher education: Heriot Watt University, Edinburgh; Moray House Teacher Training College, Edinburgh
Constituency: low hills between Rivers Forth and Tay, mostly small towns

Öpik, Lembit
Liberal Democrat MP for Montgomeryshire since 1997

Majority: 6,234 (21.5%)
Turnout: 65.5%

	Votes	Share %	Change %
Lembit Öpik, Liberal Democrat	14,319	49.4	3.5
David Jones, Conservative	8,085	27.9	1.8
Paul Davies, Labour	3,443	11.9	−7.2
David Senior, Plaid Cymru	1,969	6.8	1.8
David William Rowlands, UK Independence party	786	2.7	n/a
Ruth Davies, ProLife Alliance	210	0.7	n/a
Reg Taylor, Independent	171	0.6	n/a

Andrew Roth says: "an exotic, soft spoken, political gypsy"

Recent parliamentary career: leader, Welsh Lib Dems (2001–); Lib Dem spokesperson, Wales, Northern Ireland and youth affairs (2001); Lib Dem spokesperson, Northern Ireland and youth (1997–2001); agriculture committee (1999–2001); campaigned in parliament on asteroid-impact risk
Background: human resources training manager; brand manager, Procter and Gamble; Newcastle upon Tyne councillor; president of Shropshire Astronomical Society
Born: March 2 1965 in Bangor, County Down
Education: Royal Belfast Academical Institution
Higher education: Bristol University
Constituency: very rural mid Wales, small towns and few people

Organ, Diana
Labour MP for Forest of Dean since 1997

Majority: 2,049 (4.6%)
Turnout: 67.3%

	Votes	Share %	Change %
Diana Organ, Labour	19,350	43.4	−4.8
Mark Harper, Conservative	17,301	38.8	3.2
David Gayler, Liberal Democrat	5,762	12.9	0.6
Simon Pickering, Green party	1,254	2.8	n/a
Alan Prout, UK Independence party	661	1.5	n/a
Gerald Morgan, Independent	279	0.6	n/a

Andrew Roth says: "'fiery campaigner' and 'strong on women's issues'"

Recent parliamentary career: environment, food and rural affairs committee (2001–); culture, media and sport committee (1999–2001)
Background: special needs and English teacher; researcher for Labour group, Oxfordshire County Council
Born: February 21 1952 in West Bromwich
Education: Edgbaston Church of England School for Girls
Higher education: Bath University; Bristol Polytechnic; Oxford, St Hugh's
Constituency: west Gloucestershire between Rivers Wye and Severn

Osborne, George
Conservative MP for Tatton since 2001

Majority: 8,611 (20.8%)
Turnout: 63.6%

	Votes	Share %	Change %
George Osborne, Conservative	19,860	48.1	10.6
Steve Conquest, Labour	11,249	27.3	n/a
Mike Ash, Liberal Democrat	7,685	18.6	n/a
Mark Sheppard, UK Independence party	769	1.9	n/a
Peter Sharratt, Ind Sh	734	1.8	n/a
Mrs Viviane Allinson, Tatton	505	1.2	n/a
John Batchelor, Ind Batch	322	0.8	n/a
Jonathan Boyd Hunt, Ind Hunt	154	0.4	n/a

Maiden speech: "The lessons that I learn from my family's past are these: one must not impose political systems on peoples who are unwilling to accept them… and one cannot afford to stop listening"

Recent parliamentary career: entered parliament 2001, taking seat from retiring Independent MP Martin Bell; public accounts committee (2001–)
Background: William Hague's political secretary and speechwriter (1997–2001); secretary to the shadow Cabinet; special adviser, MAFF (1995–97); writer for Telegraph group
Born: May 23 1971 in London
Education: Davidson College, North Carolina; St Paul's School, London
Higher education: Magdalen College, Oxford
Constituency: upmarket Cheshire seat that ousted Neil Hamilton in 1997

Osborne, Sandra
Labour MP for Ayr since 1997

Majority: 2,545 (6.6%)
Turnout: 69.3%

	Votes	Share %	Change %
Sandra Osborne, Labour	16,801	43.6	–4.8
Phil Gallie, Conservative	14,256	37	3.2
Jim Mather, Scottish National party	4,621	12	–0.6
Stuart Ritchie, Liberal Democrat	2,089	5.4	0.7
James Stewart, Scottish Socialist party	692	1.8	n/a
Joseph Smith, UK Independence party	101	0.3	n/a

Andrew Roth says: "Blairite moderniser and homeruler"

Recent parliamentary career: PPS to George Foulkes (2001–); PPS to Brian Wilson (1999–2001)
Background: community worker; South Ayrshire councillor; member of Women's Aid
Born: February 23 1956 in Paisley
Education: Camphill Senior Secondary School, Paisley
Higher education: Strathclyde University, Glasgow; Jordanhill College of Education, Glasgow; Anniesland College, Glasgow
Constituency: west coast town south of Glasgow, includes Troon and Prestwick

Ottaway, Richard
Conservative MP for Croydon South since 1992; Nottingham North (1983–87)

Majority: 8,697 (19.3%)
Turnout: 61.4%

	Votes	Share %	Change %
Richard Ottaway, Conservative	22,169	49.2	1.9
Gerry Ryan, Labour	13,472	29.9	4.6
Anne Gallop, Liberal Democrat	8,226	18.3	–2.8
Kathleen Turner, UK Independence party	998	2.2	n/a
Mark Samuel, People's Choice	195	0.4	0.2

Andrew Roth says: "independent-minded, Euro-pragmatic, family planning advocate, has mellowed on capital punishment"

Recent parliamentary career: opposition spokesperson, Treasury (2000–01); PPS to Michael Heseltine (1992–97)
Background: Royal Navy Officer; solicitor; author of papers on international law, debt, fraud; petroleum expert
Born: May 24 1945 in Sonning, Berkshire
Education: Blackwell Secondary Modern School, Somerset
Higher education: Bristol University; Royal Naval College, Dartmouth
Constituency: outer London suburbs of Coulsdon, Sanderstead, Purley and Selsdon

Owen, Albert
Labour MP for Ynys Mon since 2001

Majority: 800 (2.3%)
Turnout: 64%

	Votes	Share %	Change %
Albert Owen, Labour	11,906	35	1.8
Eilian Williams, Plaid Cymru	11,106	32.7	−6.8
Albie Fox, Conservative	7,653	22.5	1
Nick Bennett, Liberal Democrat	2,772	8.2	4.4
Francis Wykes, UK Independence party	359	1.1	n/a
Ms Nona Donald, Independent	222	0.7	n/a

Maiden speech: "Ynys Mon is affectionately known as 'Mon Mam Cymru – the mother of Wales'. History attributes the name to the extensive cornfields that supplied the Welsh nation during many invasions"

Recent parliamentary career: entered parliament 2001, taking seat from Plaid Cymru; accommodation and works committee (2001–); Welsh affairs committee (2001–)
Background: centre manager, Isle of Anglesey Council; welfare rights and employment adviser, Citizens' Advice Bureau; merchant seaman; Unison official
Born: August 10 1959 in Anglesy
Education: Ysgol Uwchradd Holyhead Comprehensive School
Higher education: Coleg Harlech; York University
Constituency: really Anglesey, partly Welsh-speaking, island, ferryport

P

Page, Richard
Conservative MP for South West Hertfordshire since 1979; Workington (1976–79)

Majority: 8,181 (17.3%)
Turnout: 64.4%

	Votes	Share %	Change %
Richard Page, Conservative	20,933	44.3	−1.7
Graham Dale, Labour	12,752	27	−0.9
Ed Featherstone, Liberal Democrat	12,431	26.3	4
Colin Dale-Mills, UK Independence party	847	1.8	n/a
Julia Goffin, ProLife Alliance	306	0.7	n/a

Andrew Roth says: "boasts of doing the reverse of anything backed by Dennis Skinner"

Recent parliamentary career: opposition spokesperson, trade and industry (2000–01); public accounts committee (1997–)
Background: director, family-owned Page Holdings; mechanical engineer; apprentice, Vauxhall Motors; Banstead councillor
Born: February 22 1941 in Tredegar, South Wales
Education: Hurstpierpoint College
Higher education: Luton Technical College
Constituency: prosperous towns from Rickmansworth to Tring

Paice, James
Conservative MP for South East Cambridgeshire since 1987

Majority: 8,990 (17.3%)
Turnout: 63.5%

	Votes	Share %	Change %
James Paice, Conservative	22,927	44.2	1.3
Sal Brinton, Liberal Democrat	13,937	26.9	1.8
Andrew Inchley, Labour	13,714	26.4	−0.1
Neil Scarr, UK Independence party	1,308	2.5	n/a

Andrew Roth says: "sensible, sensitive and knowledgeable low-profile pro-European"

Recent parliamentary career: opposition spokesperson, HO (2001–); opposition spokesperson, agriculture (1997–2001)
Background: farm manager; director of farming companies; Suffolk councillor; former pro-European who now opposes single currency
Born: April 24 1949 in Felixstowe, Suffolk
Education: Framlingham College, Suffolk
Higher education: Writtle College of Agriculture, Essex
Constituency: centred on Cambridgeshire cathedral city of Ely

Paisley, Rev Ian
Democratic Unionist party MP for North Antrim since 1970

Majority: 14,224 (28.9%)
Turnout: 66.1%

	Votes	Share %	Change %
Ian Paisley, Democratic Unionist party	24,539	49.9	3.4
Lexie Scott, Ulster Unionist party	10,315	21	−2.6
Sean Farren, Social Democratic and Labour party	8,283	16.8	0.9
John Kelly, Sinn Fein	4,822	9.8	3.5
Jane Dunlop, Alliance party of Northern Ireland	1,258	2.6	−3.6

Andrew Roth says: "tiring but still sulphur and brimstone hardline voice of paranoid loyalists"

Recent parliamentary career: founder and leader, DUP (1971–)
Background: MEP (1979–), member of NIA (1973–74, 1982 1998–); resigned seat 1985 to fight byelection in protest at Anglo-Irish Agreement, re-elected 1986; minister of Presbyterian Church; founded *Protestant Telegraph*; member of Stormont Assembly (1970–72); author of several books on religion and Northern Ireland
Born: April 6 1926 in Armagh
Education: Ballymena Model School; Ballymena Technical High School
Higher education: Reformed Presbyterian Theological College; South Wales Bible College
Constituency: Moyle, Ballymoney and Ballymena, scenic, a quarter Catholic

Palmer, Dr Nick
Labour MP for Broxtowe since 1997

Majority: 5,873 (11.9%)
Turnout: 66.5%

	Votes	Share %	Change %
Nick Palmer, Labour	23,836	48.6	1.6
Pauline Latham, Conservative	17,963	36.7	−0.7
David Watts, Liberal Democrat	7,205	14.7	2.8

Andrew Roth says: "quietly effective, has sought to apply total quality management techniques from business"

Recent parliamentary career: Treasury committee (2001–); Northern Ireland affairs committee (1999–); European scrutiny committee (1998–2001); administration committee (1998–)
Background: computing manager for various medical companies; PhD in mathematics; speaks six languages; one-time member of Swiss Social Democrats
Born: February 5 1950 in London
Education: international schools, Vienna and Copenhagen

Higher education: Birkbeck College, London University; Copenhagen University
Constituency: residential suburb to west of Nottingham

Paterson, Owen
Conservative MP for North Shropshire since 1997

Majority: 6,241 (13.5%)
Turnout: 63.1%

	Votes	Share %	Change %
Owen Paterson, Conservative	22,631	48.7	8.5
Michael Ion, Labour	16,390	35.2	−0.8
Ben Jephcott, Liberal Democrat	5,945	12.8	−7.6
David Trevanion, UK Independence party	1,165	2.5	n/a
Russell Maxfield, Independent	389	0.8	n/a

Andrew Roth says: "beneath a charming veneer, is a pugnacious performer in the Commons and division lobby"

Recent parliamentary career: PPS to party leader (2001–); opposition whip (2000–01); Welsh affairs committee (1997–2001); agriculture committee (2000–2001)
Background: leather tanner; managing director, British Leather Company
Born: June 24 1956 in Whitchurch, Shropshire
Education: Radley College
Higher education: National Leathersellers' College; Cambridge, Corpus Christi
Constituency: Welsh borders and flat farmland around Oswestry

Pearson, Ian
Labour MP for Dudley South since 1997; Dudley West (1994–97)

Majority: 6,817 (18.7%)
Turnout: 55.4%

	Votes	Share %	Change %
Ian Pearson, Labour	18,109	49.8	−6.8
Jason Sugarman, Conservative	11,292	31.1	1.7
Lorely Burt, Liberal Democrat	5,421	14.9	4
John Westwood, UK Independence party	859	2.4	n/a
Angela Thompson, Socialist Alliance	663	1.8	n/a

Andrew Roth says: "Euro-minded Blairite consultant on regeneration playing a low-profile political role"

Recent parliamentary career: assistant whip (2001–); employment subcommittee (1999–); education and employment committee (1999–2001); PPS to Geoffrey Robinson (1997–98)
Background: locally-born economic development consultant; Dudley councillor; won 1994 byelection from Conservatives
Born: April 5 1959 in Wall Heath
Education: Brierley Hill Grammar School
Higher education: Warwick University; Oxford, Balliol
Constituency: urban Black Country seat with high unemployment

Perham, Linda
Labour MP for Ilford North since 1997

Majority: 2,115 (5.2%)
Turnout: 58.4%

	Votes	Share %	Change %
Linda Perham, Labour	18,428	45.8	−1.6
Vivian Bendall, Conservative	16,313	40.6	−0.2
Gavin Stollar, Liberal Democrat	4,717	11.7	1.4
Martin Levin, UK Independence party	776	1.9	n/a

Andrew Roth says: "Blair-loyal former councillor and mayor who wants NHS improvements above all"

Recent parliamentary career: trade and industry committee (1998–); accommodation and works committee (1997–2001)
Background: librarian; information officer, GLC; Redbridge councillor and mayor
Born: June 29 1947 in London
Education: Mary Datchelor Girls' School, Camberwell
Higher education: Leicester University; Ealing Technical College
Constituency: centred on Hainault on London-Essex border

Picking, Anne
Labour MP for East Lothian since 2001

Majority: 10,830 (29.4%)
Turnout: 62.5%

	Votes	Share %	Change %
Anne Picking, Labour	17,407	47.2	−5.5
Hamish Mair, Conservative	6,577	17.8	−2.1
Judy Hayman, Liberal Democrat	6,506	17.7	7.2
Hilary Brown, Scottish National party	5,381	14.6	−1.1
Derrick White, Scottish Socialist party	624	1.7	n/a
Jake Herriot, Socialist Labour Party	376	1	n/a

Maiden speech: "I was born Anne Moffat of the famous dynasty of Moffats who are steeped in the history of the Scottish miners' trade union movement and who hailed from Fife and East Lothian"

Recent parliamentary career: entered parliament 2001; accommodation and works committee (2001–); modernisation of the House of Commons committee (2001–)
Background: nurse; Unison representative; Ashford borough councillor; on Labour NEC (1990–2000)
Born: March 30 1958
Education: Woodmill High School
Constituency: coastal seat that runs south of Edinburgh towards Dunbar

Pickles, Eric
Conservative MP for Brentwood and Ongar since 1992

Majority: 2,821 (6.4%)
Turnout: 67.3%

	Votes	Share %	Change %
Eric Pickles, Conservative	16,558	38	−7.4
Martin Bell, Independent	13,737	31.6	n/a
David Kendall, Liberal Democrat	6,772	15.6	−10.7
Diana Johnson, Labour	5,505	12.6	−9.5
Ken Gulleford, UK Independence party	611	1.4	n/a
Peter Pryke, Independent	239	0.6	n/a
David Bishop, Elvis	68	0.2	n/a
Tony Appleton, Independent	52	0.1	n/a

Andrew Roth says: "shrewd and pleasant radical right-wing former Yorkshire Thatcherite"

Recent parliamentary career: opposition spokesperson, social security (1998–); brought in private member's bill on food labels (2001); defeated Martin Bell, who challenged him at 2001 election
Background: controversial leader of Bradford Council (1987–88); on several Conservative local government organisations; parliamentary adviser
Born: April 20 1952 in West Yorkshire

Education: Greenhead Grammar School, Keighley
Higher education: Leeds Polytechnic
Constituency: Essex towns in green belt north-east of London

Pickthall, Colin
Labour MP for West Lancashire since 1992

Majority: 9,643 (22.5%)
Turnout: 59%

	Votes	Share %	Change %
Colin Pickthall, Labour	23,404	54.5	−5.8
Jeremy Myers, Conservative	13,761	32	2.9
John Thornton, Liberal Democrat	4,966	11.6	4.4
David Hill, Independent	523	1.2	n/a
David Braid, Independent	317	0.7	n/a

Andrew Roth says: "highly intelligent, fair-minded northern leftist"

Recent parliamentary career: PPS to Jack Straw (1999–); PPS to Alun Michael (1997–98)
Background: head of European studies (1983–92); English teacher and lecturer (1967–83); Lancashire councillor; member of CND
Born: September 13 1944 in Dalton-in-Furness
Education: Ulverston Grammar School
Higher education: University of Wales; Lancaster University
Constituency: struggling Skelmersdale new town

Pike, Peter
Labour MP for Burnley since 1983

Majority: 10,498 (28.4%)
Turnout: 55.6%

	Votes	Share %	Change %
Peter Pike, Labour	18,195	49.3	−8.6
Robert Frost, Conservative	7,697	20.9	0.7
Paul Wright, Liberal Democrat	5,975	16.2	−1.2
Steve Smith, British National party	4,151	11.3	n/a
Richard Buttrey, UK Independence party	866	2.4	n/a

Andrew Roth says: "hardworking, well-informed, respected local sensible leftist"

Recent parliamentary career: modernisation of the House of Commons committee (1997–); chair, deregulation committee (1997–)
Background: Labour party organiser; clerk at Twinings Tea and Midland Bank; Merton and Burnley councillor; Royal Marines
Born: June 26 1937 in Ware, Hertfordshire
Education: Hinchley Wood County Secondary
Higher education: Kingston Technical College
Constituency: mixed seat including Burnley and some surrounding villages

Plaskitt, James
Labour MP for Warwick and Leamington since 1997

Majority: 5,953 (11.1%)
Turnout: 65.8%

	Votes	Share %	Change %
James Plaskitt, Labour	26,108	48.8	4.3
David Bannerman, Conservative	20,155	37.7	−1.2
Linda Forbes, Liberal Democrat	5,964	11.1	−0.8
Alison Kime, Socialist Alliance	664	1.2	n/a
Greville Warwick, UK Independence party	648	1.2	n/a

Andrew Roth says: "relatively unobtrusive business consultant and Blair loyalist"

Recent parliamentary career: Treasury committee (1999–); Treasury subcommittee (1999–); joint committee on consolidation of bills (1997–)
Background: business analyst; lecturer in business and economics at several universities; member of Liberty, Charter 88
Born: June 23 1954 in Grimsby
Education: Pilgrim School, Bedford
Higher education: Oxford, University College; Brunel University
Constituency: twin West Midlands towns mixing industry and residential areas

Pollard, Kerry
Labour MP for St Albans since 1997

Majority: 4,466 (10.3%)
Turnout: 66.3%

	Votes	Share %	Change %
Kerry Pollard, Labour	19,889	45.5	3.5
Charles Elphicke, Conservative	15,423	35.2	2
Nick Rijke, Liberal Democrat	7,847	17.9	–3.1
Christopher Sherwin, UK Independence party	602	1.4	n/a

Andrew Roth says: "among most rebellion-prone MPs…his profile is much higher in St Albans than in Westminster"

Recent parliamentary career: education and skills committee (2001–)
Background: housing association director; development engineer, British Gas; Hertfordshire councillor
Born: April 27 1944 in Pinner, Middlesex
Education: Thornleigh Grammar School, Bolton
Constituency: cathedral city turned London commuter town

Pond, Chris
Labour MP for Gravesham since 1997

Majority: 4,862 (11.1%)
Turnout: 62.7%

	Votes	Share %	Change %
Chris Pond, Labour	21,773	49.9	0.2
Jacques Arnold, Conservative	16,911	38.8	0
Bruce Parmenter, Liberal Democrat	4,031	9.2	1.4
William Jenner, UK Independence party	924	2.1	n/a

Andrew Roth says: "leading expert on low pay, formerly a youngish Fabian redistributionist but after selection became a fervent Blairite"

Recent parliamentary career: PPS to Dawn Primarolo (1999–)
Background: economics lecturer at Surrey and Kent Universities; chair, Low Pay Unit; author of several books on poverty; runs the London Marathon
Born: September 25 1952 in London
Education: Minchenden School, Southgate
Higher education: Sussex University
Constituency: North Kent town of Gravesham and surrounding villages

Pope, Greg
Labour MP for Hyndburn since 1992

Majority: 8,219 (21.5%)
Turnout: 57.6%

	Votes	Share %	Change %
Greg Pope, Labour	20,900	54.7	−0.9
Peter Britcliffe, Conservative	12,681	33.2	1.3
Bill Greene, Liberal Democrat	3,680	9.6	1
John Tomlin, UK Independence party	982	2.6	n/a

Andrew Roth says: "his earliest declared ambition was to turn Eton into a miners' convalescent home"

Recent parliamentary career: foreign affairs committee (2001–); government whip (1997–2001)
Background: paperworker; local government officer for Blackburn Council; Hyndburn councillor
Born: August 29 1960 in Blackburn
Education: St Mary's College, Blackburn
Higher education: Hull University
Constituency: centred on Accrington, between Blackburn and Burnley

Portillo, Rt Hon Michael
Conservative MP for Kensington and Chelsea since 1999; Enfield Southgate (1984–97)

Majority: 8,771 (31.3%)
Turnout: 45.2%

	Votes	Share %	Change %
Michael Portillo, Conservative	15,270	54.5	−1.9
Simon Stanley, Labour	6,499	23.2	1.2
Kishwer Falkner, Liberal Democrat	4,416	15.8	6.4
Julia Stephenson, Green party	1,158	4.1	1.8
Damian Hockney, UK Independence party	416	1.5	n/a
Josephine Quintavalle, ProLife Alliance	179	0.6	n/a
Ginger Crab, Wrestling	100	0.4	n/a

Michael Portillo: after defeat in leadership contest, July 2001 "everyone will be constantly looking for splits, saying I was still planning to be leader. I would just get in the way"

Recent parliamentary career: challenged for party leadership (2001) and on his defeat announced he would leave politics; shadow chancellor of the exchequer (2000–01); returned to parliament in byelection (1999); secretary of state, MoD (1995–97) chief secretary to the Treasury (1992–94)
Background: consultant to oil industry firm Kerr McGee (1981–83, 1997–); TV presenter; admitted he had been bisexual (1999); Conservative Research Department (1976–78); multilingual
Born: May 26 1953 in Bushey, Hertfordshire
Education: Harrow County Grammar
Higher education: Cambridge, Peterhouse
Constituency: the most blue-chip seat in Britain, contains Harrod's, the King's Road and many millionaires

Pound, Stephen
Labour MP for Ealing North since 1997

Majority: 11,837 (26.4%)
Turnout: 58%

	Votes	Share %	Change %
Stephen Pound, Labour	25,022	55.7	2
Charles Walker, Conservative	13,185	29.3	−7.9
Francesco Fruzza, Liberal Democrat	5,043	11.2	4.2
Astra Seibe, Green party	1,039	2.3	n/a
Daniel Moss, UK Independence party	668	1.5	n/a

Andrew Roth says: "Austin Mitchell's only rival as Labour's best stand up comedian"

Recent parliamentary career: Northern Ireland affairs committee (1999–); broadcasting committee (1997–2001)
Background: housing association worker; Ealing councillor; bus conductor; seaman
Born: July 3 1948 in Hammersmith
Education: Hertford Grammar School
Higher education: London School of Economics
Constituency: covers A40 road as it comes into London, many Polish residents

Powell, Sir Raymond
Labour MP for Ogmore since 1979

Majority: 14,574 (48.1%)
Turnout: 58.2%

	Votes	Share %	Change %
Ray Powell, Labour	18,833	62.1	–11.9
Ms Angela Pulman, Plaid Cymru	4,259	14	7
Ian Lewis, Liberal Democrat	3,878	12.8	3.6
Richard Hill, Conservative	3,383	11.2	1.4

Andrew Roth says: "excluded, formerly powerful whip and fixer prised out by Blair"

Recent parliamentary career: chair, accommodation and works committee (1997–2001)
Background: fireman; shop assistant; senior administration officer; Welsh Water Authority
Born: June 19 1928 in Treorchy, Rhondda
Education: Pentre Grammar School, Rhondda Valley
Higher education: London School of Economics; National Council Labour Colleges
Constituency: former mining valleys west of Cardiff

Prentice, Bridget
Labour MP for Lewisham East since 1992

Majority: 8,959 (29.9%)
Turnout: 51.5%

	Votes	Share %	Change %
Bridget Prentice, Labour	16,116	53.7	–4.6
David McInnes, Conservative	7,157	23.8	–2.1
David Buxton, Liberal Democrat	4,937	16.4	5.2
Barry Roberts, British National party	1,005	3.4	n/a
Jean Kysow, Socialist Alliance	464	1.5	n/a
Maurice Link, UK Independence party	361	1.2	n/a

Andrew Roth says: "former Tribune Group chairman pragmatically moving rightward"

Recent parliamentary career: home affairs committee (2001–); PPS to Lord Irvine of Lairg (1999–); PPS to Brian Wilson (1998–99); government whip (1997–98)
Background: English and history teacher; head of careers; Hammersmith and Fulham councillor; formerly married to Gordon Prentice MP
Born: December 28 1952 in Glasgow
Education: Our Lady and St Francis School, Glasgow
Higher education: London University; Glasgow University; South Bank University
Constituency: inner London including middle class Blackheath and big estates

Prentice, Gordon
Labour MP for Pendle since 1992

Majority: 4,275 (10.7%)
Turnout: 63.2%

	Votes	Share %	Change %
Gordon Prentice, Labour	17,729	44.6	–8.7
Rasjid Skinner, Conservative	13,454	33.9	3.6
David Whipp, Liberal Democrat	5,479	13.8	2.2
Chris Jackson, British National party	1,976	5	n/a
Graham Cannon, UK Independence party	1,094	2.8	n/a

Andrew Roth says: "sardonic left critic of New Labour, 'splendidly off message'"

Recent parliamentary career: public administration committee (2001–); modernisation of the House of Commons (1999–); PPS to Dr Gavin Strang (1997–97), resigned over benefit cuts
Background: leader of Hammersmith and Fulham Council; Labour party local government officer; formerly married to Bridget Prentice MP
Born: January 28 1951 in Edinburgh
Education: George Heriot's School, Edinburgh
Higher education: Glasgow University
Constituency: small Lancashire towns including Nelson and Colne, dominated by manufacturing

Prescott, Rt Hon John
Labour MP for Kingston upon Hull East since 1970

Majority: 15,325 (49.7%)
Turnout: 46.5%

	Votes	Share %	Change %
John Prescott, Labour	19,938	64.6	–6.7
Jo Swinson, Liberal Democrat	4,613	14.9	5.1
Sandip Verma, Conservative	4,276	13.9	0.2
Jeanette Jenkinson, UK Independence party	1,218	3.9	n/a
Linda Muir, Socialist Labour Party	830	2.7	n/a

Andrew Roth says: "a heavyweight politician with a thin skin and long toes, anyone who steps on his toes or pricks his skin can expect an explosion"

Recent parliamentary career: deputy prime minister and first secretary of state, based in CO (2001–); deputy prime minister and secretary of state, DETR (1997–2001); deputy leader of Labour party (1994–)
Background: Labour transport spokesperson as far back as 1972; famously punched a protester during 2001 election; steward, merchant navy; trade union official, National Union of Seamen;
Born: May 31 1938 in Prestatyn
Education: Grange Secondary Modern
Higher education: Hull University; Oxford, Ruskin
Constituency: dense residential area in east Hull, many council tenants

Price, Adam
Plaid Cymru MP for Carmarthen East and Dinefwr since 2001

Majority: 2,590 (6.8%)
Turnout: 70.4%

	Votes	Share %	Change %
Adam Price, Plaid Cymru	16,130	42.4	7.8
Alan Williams, Labour	13,540	35.6	–7.3
David Thomas, Conservative	4,912	12.9	0.9
Doiran Evans, Liberal Democrat	2,815	7.4	–0.1
Mike Squires, UK Independence party	656	1.7	n/a

Maiden speech: "As the youngest of three working-class children to go to university I am passionately committed to ensuring that the same opportunities are afforded to today's generation of young people"

Recent parliamentary career: entered parliament 2001, taking seat from Labour; Welsh affairs committee (2001–)
Background: director, economic development consultancy; campaigner for EU objective funding for west Wales; author of books on Welsh development
Born: September 23 1968 in Carmarthen
Education: Dyffryn Aman
Higher education: Cardiff University; Saarland University, Saarbrucken, Germany
Constituency: big, Welsh-speaking, rural seat in south-west Wales; also contains part of Camarthen

Primarolo, Dawn
Labour MP for Bristol South since 1987

Majority: 14,181 (34.6%)
Turnout: 56.5%

	Votes	Share %	Change %
Dawn Primarolo, Labour	23,299	56.9	–3
Richard Eddy, Conservative	9,118	22.3	1.1
James Main, Liberal Democrat	6,078	14.8	1.4
Glenn Vowles, Green party	1,233	3	1.6
Brian Drummond, Socialist Alliance	496	1.2	n/a
Chris Prasad, UK Independence party	496	1.2	n/a
Giles Shorter, Socialist Labour Party	250	0.6	n/a

Andrew Roth says: "changed from 'Red Dawn' to 'Rosy Pink'"

Recent parliamentary career: paymaster general, Treasury (1999–); financial secretary to the Treasury (1997–99)
Background: book-keeper; legal secretary, and advice worker; Avon councillor; member of Labour's Campaign Group
Born: May 2 1954 in London
Education: Thomas Bennett Comprehensive School, Crawley
Higher education: Bristol University; Bristol Polytechnic
Constituency: least prosperous Bristol seat, contains big estates

Prisk, Mark
Conservative MP for Hertford and Stortford since 2001

Majority: 5,603 (11.9%)
Turnout: 62.8%

	Votes	Share %	Change %
Mark Prisk, Conservative	21,074	44.7	0.7
Simon Speller, Labour	15,471	32.8	1.4
Mione Goldspink, Liberal Democrat	9,388	19.9	2.2
Stuart Rising, UK Independence party	1,243	2.6	n/a

Maiden speech: "I passionately believe that we must strengthen the house's committees... and ensure that the career of a parliamentarian is as respected as that of a minister"

Recent parliamentary career: entered parliament 2001; Welsh affairs committee (2001–)
Background: chartered surveyor; ran own PR firm, the Mark Prisk Connection (1991–96); joint national coordinator, Conservative Countryside Campaign; national vice chairman, Federation of Conservative Students; chairman, Youth for Peace Through Nato (1983–85)
Born: June 12 1962
Education: Truro School, Cornwall
Higher education: Reading University
Constituency: twin towns north of London, mix of commuters and local business

Prosser, Gwyn
Labour MP for Dover since 1997

Majority: 5,199 (11.6%)
Turnout: 65.1%

	Votes	Share %	Change %
Gwyn Prosser, Labour	21,943	48.8	−5.7
Paul Watkins, Conservative	16,744	37.2	4.4
Anthony Hook, Liberal Democrat	5,131	11.4	3.5
Lee Speakman, UK Independence party	1,142	2.5	n/a

Andrew Roth says: "thoroughly local loyalist; preoccupied with economic regeneration"

Recent parliamentary career: information committee (2000–); home affairs committee (2001–)
Background: chartered marine engineer, working on Sealink Ferries; Dover councillor
Born: April 27 1943 in Swansea
Education: Dunvant Secondary
Higher education: Swansea Technical College
Constituency: port town with famous white cliffs, hit by Channel Tunnel

Pugh, Dr John
Liberal Democrat MP for Southport since 2001

Majority: 3,007 (7.3%)
Turnout: 58.1%

	Votes	Share %	Change %
John Pugh, Liberal Democrat	18,011	43.8	−4.3
Laurence Jones, Conservative	15,004	36.5	0.6
Paul Brant, Labour	6,816	16.6	4.5
David Green, Liberal	767	1.9	1.1
Gerry Kelley, UK Independence party	555	1.4	n/a

Maiden speech: "the time is now overdue to state the ancient but unhappily no longer orthodox view that public services are best delivered by those whose personal destiny lies with rendering public benefits, not private profits"

Recent parliamentary career: entered parliament 2001; transport, local government, and the regions committee (2001–)
Background: head of philosophy and teacher for 30 years; PhD in logic; leader, Sefton Borough Council
Born: June 28 1948
Education: Prescott and Maidstone Grammar Schools
Higher education: Durham University
Constituency: faded seaside resort north of Liverpool

Purchase, Ken
Labour MP for Wolverhampton North East since 1992

Majority: 9,965 (31.7%)
Turnout: 52.1%

	Votes	Share %	Change %
Ken Purchase, Labour	18,984	60.3	1
Maria Miller, Conservative	9,019	28.6	0.7
Steven Bourne, Liberal Democrat	2,494	7.9	2.6
Thomas McCartney, UK Independence party	997	3.2	n/a

Andrew Roth says: "low-profiled but bulky…proud of his industrial working class origins"

Recent parliamentary career: PPS to Robin Cook (1997–)
Background: tools machinist; business development adviser; Wolverhampton councillor for 20 years
Born: January 8 1939 in Wolverhampton

Education: Springfield Secondary Modern
Higher education: Wolverhampton Polytechnic
Constituency: traditional industrial West Midlands seat

Purnell, James
Labour MP for Stalybridge and Hyde since 2001

Majority: 8,859 (27.7%)
Turnout: 48.4%

	Votes	Share %	Change %
James Purnell, Labour	17,781	55.5	−3.4
Andrew Reid, Conservative	8,922	27.8	3.3
Brendon Jones, Liberal Democrat	4,327	13.5	1.5
Frank Bennett, UK Independence party	1,016	3.2	n/

Maiden speech: "The people of my constituency have shown that the best way to respond to change is not to suffer it, nor to resist it, but to welcome it and be in its vanguard so that we can shape it to our ends"

Recent parliamentary career: entered parliament 2001; work and pensions committee (2001–)
Background: Downing Street Policy Unit; IPPR;researcher, Tony Blair (1989–92); head of corporate planning, BBC; Islington councillor
Born: March 2 1970
Education: Oxford, Balliol
Constituency: working-class residential seat on western edge of Manchester

Q

Quin, Rt Hon Joyce
Labour MP for Gateshead East and Washington West since 1997; Gateshead East (1987–97)

Majority: 17,904 (53.2%)
Turnout: 52.5%

	Votes	Share %	Change %
Joyce Quin, Labour	22,903	68.1	−4
Ron Beadle, Liberal Democrat	4,999	14.9	4.2
Elizabeth Campbell, Conservative	4,970	14.8	0.6
Martin Rouse, UK Independence party	743	2.2	n/a

Andrew Roth says: "hard-working, self-effacing, Tyneside-raised moderate"

Recent parliamentary career: intelligence and security committee (2001–); minister of state, MAFF (1999–2001), left office at own request; minister of state, FCO (1998–99); minister of state, HO (1997–98)
Background: MEP (1979–89); French and politics lecturer, Durham and Bath Universities;
Born: November 26 1944 in Tynemouth
Education: Whitley Bay Grammar School
Higher education: London School of Economics; Newcastle University
Constituency: at the heart of Tyneside, includes half of Washington New Town

Quinn, Lawrie
Labour MP for Scarborough and Whitby since 1997

Majority: 3,585 (7.5%)
Turnout: 63.2%

	Votes	Share %	Change %
Lawrie Quinn, Labour	22,426	47.2	1.6
John Sykes, Conservative	18,841	39.7	3.5
Tom Pearce, Liberal Democrat	3,977	8.4	-5.7
Jonathan Dixon, Green party	1,049	2.2	n/a
John Jacob, UK Independence party	970	2	n/a
Theresa Murray, ProLife Alliance	260	0.6	n/a

Andrew Roth says: "over-eager low-profile loyalist capable of fumbling even planted questions"

Recent parliamentary career: PPS to Douglas Alexander (2001–)
Background: chartered civil engineer for British Rail and then Railtrack; North Yorkshire councillor; rail enthusiast
Born: December 25 1956 in Carlisle
Education: Harraby School, Carlisle
Higher education: Hatfield Polytechnic
Constituency: North Yorkshire moors, Scarborough seaside resort and Whitby fishing port, relies on agriculture and tourism

R

Rammell, Bill
Labour MP for Harlow since 1997

Majority: 5,228 (13.0%)
Turnout: 59.8%

	Votes	Share %	Change %
Bill Rammell, Labour	19,169	47.8	-6.3
Robert Halfon, Conservative	13,941	34.8	2.7
Lorna Spenceley, Liberal Democrat	5,381	13.4	3.9
Tony Bennett, UK Independence party	1,223	3.1	n/a
John Hobbs, Socialist Alliance	401	1	n/a

Andrew Roth says: "soft-left graduate of the student union movement"

Recent parliamentary career: PPS to Tessa Jowell (2001–); European scrutiny committee (2000–2001)
Background: head of youth services, Basildon Council; regional officer, NUJ; university business manager; Harlow councillor
Born: October 10 1959 in London
Education: Burnt Mill Comprehensive School, Harlow
Higher education: Cardiff University
Constituency: West Essex new town on Hertfordshire border; once rural, now commuter belt

Randall, John
Conservative MP for Uxbridge since 1997

Majority: 2,098 (6.2%)
Turnout: 57.6%

	Votes	Share %	Change %
John Randall, Conservative	15,751	47.1	-4
Dave Salisbury-Jones, Labour	13,653	40.9	1.6
Catherine Royce, Liberal Democrat	3,426	10.3	4.7
Paul Cannons, UK Independence party	588	1.8	n/a

Andrew Roth says: "a quiet pro-Serb environmentally-sensitive local shop owning mainstreamer"

Recent parliamentary career: opposition whip (1999–); deregulation committee (1997–2001); won byelection (1997)
Background: director of family department store in Uxbridge; ornithologist
Born: August 5 1955 in Ealing
Education: Rutland House School, Hillingdon; Merchant Taylors' School, Northwood
Higher education: School of Slavonic and East European Studies, London
Constituency: independent town on west London fringe, end of tube line

Rapson, Syd
Labour MP for Portsmouth North since 1997

Majority: 5,134 (14.0%)
Turnout: 57.4%

	Votes	Share %	Change %
Syd Rapson, Labour	18,676	50.7	3.6
Chris Day, Conservative	13,542	36.7	–0.9
Darren Sanders, Liberal Democrat	3,795	10.3	–0.3
William McCabe, UK Independence party	559	1.5	n/a
Brian Bundy, Independent	294	0.8	n/a

Andrew Roth says: "an unusual New Labour combination: a loyal, self-effacing skilled working-class fitter"

Recent parliamentary career: accommodation and works committee (2001–); defence committee (2001–); sits on several European committees
Background: trade unionist (AEEU); aircraft industrial technician, MoD; Portsmouth councillor, mayor and deputy leader
Born: April 17 1942 in Lake, Isle of Wight
Education: Southsea and Paulsgrove Secondary Modern School; Portsmouth Dockyard College; National Council of Labour Colleges
Constituency: relatively affluent northern part of Britain's premier naval centre, on south coast of England

Raynsford, Nick
Labour MP for Greenwich and Woolwich since 1997; Greenwich (1992–97); Fulham (1986–87)

Majority: 13,433 (41.3%)
Turnout: 52%

	Votes	Share %	Change %
Nick Raynsford, Labour	19,691	60.5	–2.9
Richard Forsdyke, Conservative	6,258	19.2	0.6
Russell Pyne, Liberal Democrat	5,082	15.6	3.1
Stan Gain, UK Independence party	672	2.1	n/a
Kirstie Paton, Socialist Alliance	481	1.5	n/a
Margaret Sharkey, Socialist Labour party	352	1.1	n/a

Andrew Roth says: "skilled, respected but uncharismatic technocrat"

Recent parliamentary career: minister of state, DTLGR (2001–); minister of state, DETR (1999–2001); junior minister, DETR (1997–99); led Greater London Authority Act through parliament and considered running for London mayor
Background: director, London Housing Aid Centre; Hammersmith and Fulham councillor
Born: January 28 1945 in Northampton
Education: Repton School
Higher education: Chelsea School of Art; Cambridge, Sidney Sussex
Constituency: south London borough on the south-east side of the Thames; home to Millennium Dome

Redwood, Rt Hon John
Conservative MP for Wokingham since 1987

Majority: 5,994 (13.7%)
Turnout: 64.1%

	Votes	Share %	Change %
John Redwood, Conservative	20,216	46.1	−4
Royce Longton, Liberal Democrat	14,222	32.4	1
Matthew Syed, Labour	7,633	17.4	0.6
Franklin Carstairs, UK Independence party	897	2.1	n/a
Peter Owen, Official Monster Raving Loony party	880	2	0.2

Andrew Roth says: "sharp minded aggressively dynamic ideologist of the Eurosceptic right"

Recent parliamentary career: shadow secretary of state, DETR (1999–2000); shadow secretary of state, DTI (1997–99)
Background: investment analyst; banker; company director; Oxfordshire councillor; contested leadership of Conservative party (1995 and 1997); author; head, Downing Street Policy Unit (1983–85); fellow of All Soul's, Oxford
Born: June 15 1951 in Dover
Education: Kent College, Canterbury
Higher education: Oxford, Magdalen; Oxford, St Antony's
Constituency: Berkshire town west of London; bordered by Oxfordshire to the north and Hampshire to the south-west

Reed, Andrew
Labour MP for Loughborough since 1997

Majority: 6,378 (14.5%)
Turnout: 63.2%

	Votes	Share %	Change %
Andy Reed, Labour	22,016	49.8	1.2
Neil Lyon, Conservative	15,638	35.3	−2.4
Julie Simons, Liberal Democrat	5,667	12.8	1
John Bigger, UK Independence party	933	2.1	n/a

Andrew Roth says: "over-eager Blair loyalist and stooge questioner"

Recent parliamentary career: PPS to Margaret Beckett (2001–)
Background: trade unionist (NALGO, Unison); parliamentary assistant to Keith Vaz; adviser to Leicestershire Council; Birstall councillor; rugby player
Born: September 17 1964 in Kettering
Education: Stonehill High School; Longsdale Community College, Birstall
Higher education: Leicester Polytechnic
Constituency: East Midlands market town, 20 miles from Leicester, Nottingham and Derby

Reid, Alan
Liberal Democrat MP for Argyll and Bute since 2001

Majority: 1,653 (5.4%)
Turnout: 63%

	Votes	Share %	Change %
Alan Reid, Liberal Democrat	9,245	29.9	−10.3
Hugh Raven, Labour	7,592	24.5	8.8
David Petrie, Conservative	6,436	20.8	1.8
Agnes Samuel, Scottish National party	6,433	20.8	−2.4
Des Divers, Scottish Socialist party	1,251	4	n/a

Maiden speech: "Because of the vast size of my constituency and the sparsity of its population, many rural economic problems that affect other areas are magnified"

Recent parliamentary career: entered parliament 2001; broadcasting committee (2001–)
Background: computer project manager; Renfrewshire councillor; chess player
Born: August 7 1954 in Scotland
Education: Prestwick Academy; Ayr Academy
Higher education: Strathclyde University; Jordanhill College; Bell College
Constituency: vast seat on west coast of Scotland; includes many remote islands

Reid, Rt Hon Dr John
Labour MP for Hamilton North and Bellshill since 1997; Motherwell North (1987–97)

Majority: 13,561 (44.6%)
Turnout: 56.8%

	Votes	Share %	Change %
John Reid, Labour	18,786	61.8	–2.2
Chris Stephens, Scottish National party	5,225	17.2	–1.9
Bill Frain Bell, Conservative	2,649	8.7	–1.7
Keith Legg, Liberal Democrat	2,360	7.8	2.7
Shareen Blackall, Scottish Socialist party	1,189	3.9	n/a
Steve Mayes, Socialist Labour party	195	0.6	n/a

Andrew Roth says: "highly regarded, no-nonsense defence specialist and Scots devolutionist"

Recent parliamentary career: secretary of state, Northern Ireland (2001–); secretary of state, SO (1999–2001); junior minister, DETR (1998–99); junior minister, MoD (1997–98)
Background: member of Labour party NEC (to 2001); research officer, Labour party; adviser to Neil Kinnock; organiser, Trade Unionists for Labour
Born: May 8 1947 in Bellshill
Education: St Patrick's Senior Secondary School
Higher education: Stirling University
Constituency: central Scottish seat ten miles south-east of Glasgow

Rendel, David
Liberal Democrat MP for Newbury since 1993

Majority: 2,415 (4.7%)
Turnout: 67.3%

	Votes	Share %	Change %
David Rendel, Liberal Democrat	24,507	48.2	–4.7
Richard Benyon, Conservative	22,092	43.5	5.7
Steve Billcliffe, Labour	3,523	6.9	1.4
Ms Delphine Gray-Fisk, UK Independence party	685	1.4	n/a

Andrew Roth says: "Old Etonion hostile to the Lib–Lab project; speeches can range from the brilliant to pedestrian"

Recent parliamentary career: Lib Dem spokesperson, education and skills (2001–); procedure committee (2001–); public accounts committee (2001–); ran for party leadership (1999); spokesperson, social security and welfare (1997–99); spokesperson, housing (1997)
Background: financial analyst; manager at Shell International, British Gas, and Esso; Oxford rowing Blue; volunteer teacher overseas; Newbury councillor
Born: April 15 1949
Education: Eton College
Higher education: Oxford, Magdalen; Oxford, St Cross
Constituency: at the crossroads of southern England, booming market town just off M4

Robathan, Andrew
Conservative MP for Blaby since 1992

Majority: 6,209 (13.0%)
Turnout: 64.5%

	Votes	Share %	Change %
Andrew Robathan, Conservative	22,104	46.4	0.6
J David Morgan, Labour	15,895	33.4	−0.4
Geoff Welsh, Liberal Democrat	8,286	17.4	2.5
Edward Scott, British National party	1,357	2.9	1.9

Andrew Roth says: "voluble, right of centre, partisan Eurosceptic"

Recent parliamentary career: international development committee (2001–)
Background: officer, Coldstream Guards; Hammersmith and Fulham councillor
Born: July 17 1951 in Surrey
Education: Merchant Taylors' School, Northwood
Higher education: Oxford, Oriel
Constituency: suburban town on the south bank of the River Soar outside Leicester

Robertson, Angus
Scottish National party MP for Moray since 2001

Majority: 1,744 (5.2%)
Turnout: 57.3%

	Votes	Share %	Change %
Angus Robertson, Scottish National party	10,076	30.3	−11.3
Catriona Munro, Labour	8,332	25.1	5.3
Frank Spencer-Nairn, Conservative	7,677	23.1	−4.5
Linda Gorn, Liberal Democrat	5,224	15.7	6.8
Norma Anderson, Scottish Socialist party	821	2.5	n/a
Bill Jappy, Independent	802	2.4	n/a
Nigel Kenyon, UK Independence party	291	0.9	n/a

Maiden speech: "I can make the happy claim to represent more than 50% of Scotland's distilleries, which is something that I plan to research fully."

Recent parliamentary career: entered parliament 2001
Background: journalist: BBC reporter in Austria and news editor, Austrian Broadcasting Corporation; European policy adviser, SNP group, Scottish parliament
Born: September 28 1969
Education: Broughton High School, Edinburgh
Higher education: Aberdeen University
Constituency: rural north-east Scotland including Elgin

Robertson, Hugh
Conservative MP for Faversham and Mid Kent since 2001

Majority: 4,183 (10.2%)
Turnout: 60.4%

	Votes	Share %	Change %
Hugh Robertson, Conservative	18,739	45.7	1.3
Grahame Birchall, Labour	14,556	35.5	−0.5
Mike Sole, Liberal Democrat	5,529	13.5	1.1
Jim Gascoyne, UK Independence party	828	2	n/a
Penny Kemp, Green party	799	2	n/a
Norman Davidson, R & R Loony	600	1.5	n/a

Maiden speech: "In many ways, the countryside defines my constituency. Not for nothing is it known as the Garden of England."

Recent parliamentary career: entered parliament 2001

Background: army officer, served in Northern Ireland, the Gulf War, Bosnia, and Cyprus; investment banker
Born: October 9 1962 in Canterbury
Education: King's School, Canterbury
Higher education: Royal Military Academy, Sandhurst; Reading University
Constituency: borders Maidstone; carved from mid Kent and Canterbury

Robertson, John
Labour MP for Glasgow Anniesland since 2000

Majority: 11,054 (41.3%)
Turnout: 50.1%

	Votes	Share %	Change %
John Robertson, Labour	15,102	56.5	4.4
Grant Thoms, Scottish National party	4,048	15.2	–5.6
Christopher McGinty, Liberal Democrat	3,244	12.1	4
Stewart Connell, Conservative	2,651	9.9	–0.9
Charlie McCarthy, Scottish Socialist party	1,486	5.6	–1.5
Katherine McGavigan, Socialist Labour party	191	0.7	n/a

Maiden speech: "I was born in the constituency – more years ago than I care to remember – and I live there now. I am proud to be a Glaswegian"

Recent parliamentary career: Scottish affairs committee (2001–); entered parliament in 2000 byelection
Background: British Telecom customer manager; post office engineer; union organiser (NCU, POEU, CWU)
Born: April 17 1952 in Glasgow
Education: Shawlands Academy; Langside College; Stow College
Constituency: outer suburbs to the north-west of Glasgow; once held by Donald Dewar

Robertson, Laurence
Conservative MP for Tewkesbury since 1997

Majority: 8,663 (19.2%)
Turnout: 64.3%

	Votes	Share %	Change %
Laurence Robertson, Conservative	20,830	46.1	0.3
Keir Dhillon, Labour	12,167	26.9	0.7
Stephen Martin, Liberal Democrat	11,863	26.3	–1.7
Charles Vernall, Independent	335	0.7	n/a

Andrew Roth says: "constituency focussed, Redwood-backing, hard-line Eurosceptic and anti-devolutionist"

Recent parliamentary career: opposition whip (2001–); education and skills committee (2001); European scrutiny committee (1999–2001); joint committee on consolidation of bills (1997–2001); social security committee (1999–2001)
Background: industrial management consultant; factory owner; charity fundraiser and public relations consultant
Born: March 29 1958 in Bolton
Education: St James's Church of England Secondary School; Farnworth Grammar School
Higher education: Bolton Institute of Higher Education
Constituency: historic English country town nestled among the Cotswolds and Malvern Hills, in Gloucestershire and on the M5 corridor

Robinson, Geoffrey
Labour MP for Coventry North West since 1976

Majority: 10,874 (25.6%)
Turnout: 55.5%

	Votes	Share %	Change %
Geoffrey Robinson, Labour	21,892	51.5	-5.4
Andrew Fairburn, Conservative	11,018	25.9	-0.4
Geoffrey Sewards, Liberal Democrat	5,832	13.7	3.2
Ms Christine Oddy, Independent	3,159	7.4	n/a
Mark Benson, UK Independence party	650	1.5	n/a
Tim Logan, Socialist Labour party	-1.7		

Andrew Roth says: "controversial millionaire businessman-politico"

Recent parliamentary career: paymaster general (1997–99); faced suspension from Commons after investigation by the parliamentary commissioner for standards into his links with Robert Maxwell (2001)
Background: former chief executive, Jaguar cars, Triumph motorcycles, TransTec; Labour research assistant; noted ally of Gordon Brown after 1997; owner of *New Statesman* (1996–)
Born: May 25 1938 in Sheffield
Education: Emmanuel School, London
Higher education: Yale University; Cambridge, Clare
Constituency: urban West Midlands seat, home to Jaguar car factory

Robinson, Iris
Democratic Unionist party MP for Strangford since 2001

Majority: 1,110 (2.6%)
Turnout: 59.9%

	Votes	Share %	Change %
Iris Robinson, Democratic Unionist party	18,532	42	12.6
David McNarry, Ulster Unionist party	17,422	40.3	-4
Kieran McCarthy, Alliance party of Northern Ireland	2,902	6.7	-6.4
Danny McCarthy, Social and Democratic Labour party	2,646	6.1	-0.6
Liam Johnston, Sinn Fein	930	2.2	0.9
Cedric Wilson, Northern Ireland Unionist party	822	1.9	n/a

Maiden speech: "I am not a polished or professional politician…I can only hope that down to earth loyalty, compassion, honesty and effort can substitute for all else that I lack."

Recent parliamentary career: entered parliament 2001, taking seat from Ulster Unionist MP
Background: Castlereagh councillor and first woman mayor; member of NIA; married to DUP MP Peter Robinson
Born: September 6 1949
Education: Knockbrea Intermediate School
Higher education: Cregagh Technical College
Constituency: the shores of Strangford Lough to Belfast suburbs

Robinson, Peter
Democratic Unionist party MP for Belfast East since 1979

Majority: 7,117 (19.3%)
Turnout: 63%

	Votes	Share %	Change %
Peter Robinson, Democratic Unionist party	15,667	42.5	–0.1
Tim Lemon, Ulster Unionist party	8,550	23.2	–2.1
David Alderdice, Alliance party of Northern Ireland	5,832	15.8	–8
David Ervine, Progressive Unionist Northern Ireland	3,669	10	n/a
Joe O'Donnell, Sinn Fein	1,237	3.4	1.3
Ciara Farren, Social Democratic and Labour party	880	2.4	0.8
Terry Dick, Conservative	800	2.2	–0.2
Joe Bell, Workers' party	123	0.3	–0.3
Rainbow George Weiss, Ind Vote	71	0.2	n/a

Andrew Roth says: "Ian Paisley's lieutenant acolyte, more deft and less stentorian but equally unbending"

Recent parliamentary career: deputy leader, DUP (1980–); Northern Ireland affairs committee (1997–)
Background: minister for regional development, NIA (1999–); estate agent; Castlereagh Borough council; resigned his seat in protest against the Anglo-Irish Agreement in 1985; re-elected 1986; married to DUP MP Iris Robinson
Born: December 29 1948 in Belfast
Education: Annadale Grammar School; Castlereagh College of Further Education
Constituency: most Protestant Belfast seat, includes Harland & Wolff shipyard, Short's aircraft factory, and Stormont Castle

Roche, Barbara
Labour MP for Hornsey and Wood Green since 1992

Majority: 10,614 (24.1%)
Turnout: 58%

	Votes	Share %	Change %
Barbara Roche, Labour	21,967	49.9	–11.8
Lynne Featherstone, Liberal Democrat	11,353	25.8	14.5
Jason Hollands, Conservative	6,921	15.7	–6.2
Jayne Forbes, Green party	2,228	5.1	n/a
Louise Christian, Socialist Alliance	1,106	2.5	n/a
Ella Rule, Socialist Labour Party	294	0.7	–0.4
Erdil Ataman, Reform 2000	194	0.4	n/a

Andrew Roth says: "able, fast-rising, soft-left barrister and self-declared 'supreme pragmatist'"

Recent parliamentary career: minister of state, CO (2001–); minister of state, HO (1999–2001); financial secretary, Treasury (1999–99); junior minister, Treasury (1997–99)
Background: barrister; adviser on crime prevention to Hackney council
Born: April 13 1954 in London
Education: Jewish Free School Comprehensive School, Camden
Higher education: Oxford, Lady Margaret Hall
Constituency: plush north London heights plus diverse suburbs to east

Roe, Mrs Marion
Conservative MP for Broxbourne since 1983

Majority: 8,993 (23.7%)
Turnout: 54.9%

	Votes	Share %	Change %
Marion Roe, Conservative	20,487	54.1	5.2
David Prendergast, Labour	11,494	30.4	–4.3
Julia Davies, Liberal Democrat	4,158	11	–0.3
Martin Harvey, UK Independence party	858	2.3	n/a
John Cope, British National party	848	2.2	0.9

Andrew Roth says: "assiduous, commonsensical, right-wing loyalist, sensitive to constituents without breaking party ranks"

Recent parliamentary career: chair, administration committee (1997–); health committee (2000–2001)
Background: trilingual secretary; Bromley councillor
Born: July 15 1936 in London
Education: Bromley and Croydon High Schools
Higher education: English School of Languages, Switzerland
Constituency: north-east London on River Lea, includes Waltham Cross and Cheshunt

Rooney, Terry
Labour MP for Bradford North since 1990

Majority: 8,969 (25.6%)
Turnout: 52.7%

	Votes	Share %	Change %
Terry Rooney, Labour	17,419	49.7	–6.4
Zahid Iqbal, Conservative	8,450	24.1	–1.5
David Ward, Liberal Democrat	6,924	19.8	5.3
John Brayshaw, British National party	1,613	4.6	n/a
Steven Schofield, Green party	611	1.7	n/a

Andrew Roth says: "loyalism masks a class-conscious leftish fundamentalist who believes in the redistribution of wealth"

Recent parliamentary career: PPS to Michael Meacher (1997–)
Background: commercial insurance broker; welfare rights worker; Bradford councillor; the first Mormon in the Commons
Born: November 11 1950 in Bradford
Education: Buttershaw Comprehensive School
Higher education: Bradford Technical College
Constituency: north of West Yorkshire's second city; large Asian community; troubled by riots

Rosindell, Andrew
Conservative MP for Romford since 2001

Majority: 5,977 (16.7%)
Turnout: 59.6%

	Votes	Share %	Change %
Andrew Rosindell, Conservative	18,931	53	11.4
Eileen Gordon, Labour	12,954	36.3	–6.9
Nigel Meyer, Liberal Democrat	2,869	8	0.1
Stephen Ward, UK Independence party	533	1.5	n/a
Frank McAllister, British National party	414	1.2	0

Maiden speech: "I want to challenge the reports found in the popular press that Spike, my Staffordshire bull terrier, was the real victor of Romford... may I reassure you that Spike has no immediate plans to take his seat on these benches"

Recent parliamentary career: entered parliament 2001, taking seat from Labour; deregulation committee (2001–); down to earth right-winger supported by Norman Tebbit during his election campaign
Background: freelance journalist; parliamentary researcher, Vivian Bendall MP; director, the European Foundation; outspoken Eurosceptic
Born: March 17 1966 in Romford
Education: Marshall's Park Comprehensive School, Romford
Constituency: outer-east London suburbs, almost Essex

Ross, Ernie
Labour MP for Dundee West since 1979

Majority: 6,800 (23.3%)
Turnout: 54.4%

	Votes	Share %	Change %
Ernie Ross, Labour	14,787	50.6	–3.2
Gordon Archer, Scottish National party	7,987	27.3	4.1
Ian Hail, Conservative	2,656	9.1	–4.1
Elizabeth Dick, Liberal Democrat	2,620	9	1.3
Jim McFarlane, Scottish Socialist party	1,192	4.1	n/a

Andrew Roth says: "former hard-left zealot, recently a Blair loyalist"

Recent parliamentary career: standing orders committee (1997–); court of referees committee (1997–); suspended from Commons for ten days for helping to leak a foreign affairs committee report (1999); foreign affairs committee (1997–98)
Background: quality control engineer, Timex (1970–79)
Born: July 27 1942 in Dundee
Education: St John's Junior Secondary School
Constituency: industrial Dundee, includes city centre, university and airport

Roy, Frank
Labour MP for Motherwell and Wishaw since 1997

Majority: 10,956 (36.9%)
Turnout: 56.6%

	Votes	Share %	Change %
Frank Roy, Labour	16,681	56.2	–1.2
Jim McGuigan, Scottish National party	5,725	19.3	–3.2
Mark Nolan, Conservative	3,155	10.6	–0.4
Iain Brown, Liberal Democrat	2,791	9.4	3
Stephen Smellie, Scottish Socialist party	1,260	4.3	n/a
Claire Watt, Socialist Labour party	61	0.2	–2

Andrew Roth says: "politically astute, pro-Blair moderate"

Recent parliamentary career: defence committee (2001–); PPS to Dr John Reid (1999–2001); PPS to Helen Liddell (1998–99)
Background: steelworker; PA to Helen Liddell MP
Born: August 29 1958 in Motherwell
Education: Our Lady's High School, Motherwell; Motherwell College
Higher education: Glasgow Caledonian University
Constituency: once home to Ravenscraig steel plant, now closed; hard-hit working-class seat

Ruane, Chris
Labour MP for Vale of Clwyd since 1997

Majority: 5,761 (17.8%)
Turnout: 63.1%

	Votes	Share %	Change %
Chris Ruane, Labour	16,179	50	–2.7
Brendan Murphy, Conservative	10,418	32.2	2.4
Graham Rees, Liberal Democrat	3,058	9.5	0.7
John Penri Williams, Plaid Cymru	2,300	7.1	1.2
William Campbell, UK Independence party	391	1.2	n/a

Andrew Roth says: "very loyal, former local councillor who concentrates on pursuing local problems"

Recent parliamentary career: Welsh affairs committee (1999–); was present when John Prescott punched a protester during election (2001)
Background: primary school deputy head teacher; NUT organiser; Rhyl town councillor
Born: July 8 1958 in Clwyd
Education: Blessed Edward Jones Comprehensive School
Higher education: Liverpool University; Aberystwyth University
Constituency: North Wales towns around Rhyl and Prestatyn, includes Denbigh

Ruddock, Joan
Labour MP for Lewisham, Deptford since 1987

Majority: 15,293 (52.6%)
Turnout: 46.3%

	Votes	Share %	Change %
Joan Ruddock, Labour	18,915	65	–5.8
Cordelia McCartney, Conservative	3,622	12.4	–2.3
Andrew Wiseman, Liberal Democrat	3,409	11.7	2.8
Darren Johnson, Green party	1,901	6.5	n/a
Ian Page, Socialist Alliance	1,260	4.3	n/a

Andrew Roth says: "able, dynamic, former semi hard-left opponent of nuclear arms and energy"

Recent parliamentary career: modernisation of the House of Commons committee (2001–); junior minister, DSS (1997–98)
Background: director: Shelter, National Campaign for Homeless, Oxford Housing Aid centre; manager, Citizens' Advice Bureau, Reading
Born: December 28 1943 in Pontypool
Education: Pontypool Grammar School for Girls
Higher education: Imperial College, London
Constituency: innercity south London along Thames, includes New Cross

Ruffley, David
Conservative MP for Bury St Edmunds since 1997

Majority: 2,503 (5.0%)
Turnout: 66%

	Votes	Share %	Change %
David Ruffley, Conservative	21,850	43.5	5.2
Mark Ereira, Labour	19,347	38.5	0.8
Richard Williams, Liberal Democrat	6,998	13.9	–4.3
John Howlett, UK Independence party	831	1.7	n/a
Mike Brundle, Independent	651	1.3	n/a
Michael Benwell, Socialist Labour party	580	1.2	n/a

Andrew Roth says: "has settled in as a skilled debater and baiter of Labour's chancellor ... articulate, abrasive, arrogant"

Recent parliamentary career: Treasury committee (1998–); Treasury subcommittee (1999–); reputed to have backed three candidates in different rounds of the 1997 Conservative leadership election
Background: economic consultant to the Conservative party (1996–97); special adviser to Kenneth Clarke, Treasury and HO; vice president, Small Business Bureau; solicitor
Born: April 18 1962 in Bolton
Education: Bolton Boys' School
Higher education: Cambridge, Queens'
Constituency: agricultural Suffolk seat centred on market town of Bury St Edmunds

Russell, Bob
Liberal Democrat MP for Colchester since 1997

Majority: 5,553 (12.7%)
Turnout: 55.4%

	Votes	Share %	Change %
Bob Russell, Liberal Democrat	18,627	42.6	8.2
Kevin Bentley, Conservative	13,074	29.9	−1.5
Christopher Fegan, Labour	10,925	25	−5.6
Roger Lord, UK Independence party	631	1.4	n/a
Leonard Overy-Owen, Grey	479	1.1	n/a

Andrew Roth says: "a rival for Norman Baker as the Liberal Democrats' most mocked MP"

Recent parliamentary career: Lib Dem spokesperson, culture, media, and sport (2001–); home affairs committee (1998–); catering committee (2000–2001); spokesperson, sport (1999–2001); spokesperson, legal affairs (1997–99)
Background: journalist on several local papers in Essex; fastest typist in the Commons; publicity officer for NUJ; stood for Labour party in Colchester (1979) and then joined SDP (1981)
Born: March 31 1946 in Colchester
Education: St Helena School, Colchester
Higher education: North East Essex Technical College; NCTJ
Constituency: growing Essex town on River Colne, mostly urban, seat contains some farms

Russell, Christine
Labour MP for City of Chester since 1997

Majority: 6,894 (15.4%)
Turnout: 63.8%

	Votes	Share %	Change %
Christine Russell, Labour	21,760	48.5	−4.5
David Jones, Conservative	14,866	33.1	−1.1
Eleanor Burnham, Liberal Democrat	6,589	14.7	5.2
Allan Weddell, UK Independence party	899	2	n/a
George Rogers, Independent	763	1.7	n/a

Andrew Roth says: "Chester's first ever Labour MP and first ever woman MP; low-profile and loyal"

Recent parliamentary career: transport, local government, and the regions committee (2001–); environmental audit committee (1999–2001)
Background: chartered librarian; assistant to Labour MEPs; JP; Chester councillor; project coordinator, Mind
Born: March 25 1945
Education: Spalding High School
Higher education: London School of Librarianship; North West London Polytechnic
Constituency: grand medieval city plus partly industrial surrounds towards Ellesmere Port

Ryan, Joan
Labour MP for Enfield North since 1997

Majority: 2,291 (6.0%)
Turnout: 56.3%

	Votes	Share %	Change %
Joan Ryan, Labour	17,888	46.9	−3.8
Nick De Bois, Conservative	15,597	40.9	4.6
Hilary Leighter, Liberal Democrat	3,355	8.8	−0.1
Ramon Johns, British National party	605	1.6	0.4
Brian Hall, UK Independence party	247	0.7	n/a
Michael Akerman, ProLife Alliance	241	0.6	n/a
Richard Course, Independent	210	0.6	n/a

Andrew Roth says: "ultra-loyal backbencher who asks prompted questions and enthusiastically welcomes the answers"

Recent parliamentary career: PPS to Andrew Smith (1999–)
Background: teacher and head of humanities; deputy leader, Barnet council; NUT member
Born: September 8 1955
Education: St Joseph's Secondary School; Notre Dame High School
Higher education: City of Liverpool College; South Bank Polytechnic
Constituency: mixed seat on edge of London, runs into green belt around Enfield Chase

S

Salmond, Alex
Scottish National party MP for Banff and Buchan since 1987

Majority: 10,503 (34.0%)
Turnout: 54.5%

	Votes	Share %	Change %
Alex Salmond, Scottish National party	16,710	54.2	–1.6
Alexander Wallace, Conservative	6,207	20.2	3.6
Edward Harris, Labour	4,363	14.2	2.4
Douglas Herbison, Liberal Democrat	2,769	9	3
Alice Rowan, Scottish Socialist party	447	1.5	n/a
Eric Davidson, UK Independence party	310	1	n/a

Andrew Roth says: "bright, aggressive, leftish Scottish Nationalist who astonished the political world by his sudden retirement from the leadership"

Recent parliamentary career: leader of SNP in Westminster (2001–); leader of SNP until decided to retire (1990–2000)
Background: MSP for Banff and Buchan; economist at Scottish Office and Royal Bank of Scotland (1999–2001)
Born: December 31 1954 in Linlithgow
School: Linlithgow Academy
Higher education: St Andrews University
Constituency: north-east Scottish coast beyond Aberdeen, main towns are Peterhead and Fraserburgh

Salter, Martin
Labour MP for Reading West since 1997

Majority: 8,849 (21.1%)
Turnout: 58.6%

	Votes	Share %	Change %
Martin Salter, Labour	22,300	53.1	8
Stephen Reid, Conservative	13,451	32	–6.9
Polly Martin, Liberal Democrat	5,387	12.8	0.1
David Black, UK Independence party	848	2	n/a

Andrew Roth says: "former union activist and demonstrator for CND, recently a crusader for 'a new politics'"

Recent parliamentary career: modernisation of the House of Commons committee (2001–); set up all-party campaign to fight bank closures; has achieved attention for his bluff backbench-common sense and support for electoral reform
Background: regional development coordinator for housing cooperative; trade union shop steward (TGWV, UCATT); lorry driver; scaffolder; builder's labourer; dustman; Reading councillor

Born: April 19 1954 in Hampton, Middlesex
Education: Hampton Grammar School
Higher education: Sussex University
Constituency: the safer half (for Labour) of a successful, modern town west of London

Sanders, Adrian
Liberal Democrat MP for Torbay since 1997

Majority: 6,708 (14.1%)
Turnout: 65.7%

	Votes	Share %	Change %
Adrian Sanders, Liberal Democrat	24,015	50.5	10.9
Christian Sweeting, Conservative	17,307	36.4	−3.1
John McKay, Labour	4,484	9.4	−5.5
Graham Booth, UK Independence party	1,512	3.2	n/a
Pam Neale, Independent	251	0.5	n/a

Andrew Roth says: "former Ashdown aide, experienced and sensible on local government with an old fashioned and moralistic approach"

Recent parliamentary career: introduced private member's bill on playgrounds (2001); Lib Dem spokesperson, DTLGR (2001–); spokesperson, environment (1999–2001)
Background: worked in insurance industry; seven years working for the Liberal party and later Lib Dems; ran organisation which helps charities access grants from Europe
Born: April 25 1959 in Paignton
Education: Torquay Boys' Grammar School
Constituency: sunny south-west coast resort with many pensioners

Sarwar, Mohammed
Labour MP for Glasgow Govan since 1997

Majority: 6,400 (25.3%)
Turnout: 46.8%

	Votes	Share %	Change %
Mohammed Sarwar, Labour	12,464	49.3	5.2
Karen Neary, Scottish National party	6,064	24	−11.1
Bob Stewart, Liberal Democrat	2,815	11.1	5.2
Mark Menzies, Conservative	2,167	8.6	−0.2
Wullie McGartland, Scottish Socialist party	1,531	6.1	n/a
John Foster, Communist party	174	0.7	n/a
Badar Mirza, Independent	69	0.3	n/a

Andrew Roth says: "Britain's first Muslim MP, bald, trim moustache, the victim of many conspiracies"

Recent parliamentary career: Scottish affairs committee (1999–); suspended by Labour briefly after 1997 election amid concern about election processes, name cleared
Background: director, United Wholesale cash and carry business, which turns over £2m a week; moved to Scotland in mid-1970s
Born: August 18 1952 in Faisalabad, Pakistan
Higher education: University of Faisalabad, Pakistan
Constituency: poor, west of central Glasgow, ex-shipbuilding, perpetual SNP challenge

Savidge, Malcolm
Labour MP for Aberdeen North since 1997

Majority: 4,449 (14.6%)
Turnout: 57.6%

	Votes	Share %	Change %
Malcolm Savidge, Labour	13,157	43.3	–4.6
Alasdair Allan, Scottish National party	8,708	28.7	6.9
Jim Donaldson, Liberal Democrat	4,991	16.4	2.3
Richard Cowling, Conservative	3,047	10	–5
Shona Foreman, Scottish Socialist party	454	1.5	n/a

Andrew Roth says: "knowledgeable pursuer of world peace, his abilities well disguised by his dull delivery"

Recent parliamentary career: environmental audit committee (1997–)
Background: maths teacher in Aberdeen for 24 years; Aberdeen councillor
Born: May 9 1956 in Redhill, Surrey
Education: Wallington County Grammar School for Boys
Higher education: Aberdeen University; Aberdeen College of Education
Constituency: Aberdeen suburbs running into countryside around Dyce

Sawford, Philip
Labour MP for Kettering since 1997

Majority: 665 (1.2%)
Turnout: 67.5%

	Votes	Share %	Change %
Philip Sawford, Labour	24,034	44.7	1.4
Philip Hollobone, Conservative	23,369	43.5	0.6
Roger Aron, Liberal Democrat	5,469	10.2	–0.5
Barry Mahoney, UK Independence party	880	1.6	n/a

Andrew Roth says: "onetime carpenter and steelworker who re-educated himself after redundancy"

Recent parliamentary career: environment, food, and rural affairs committee (2001–); information committee (1997–2001); environmental audit committee (2000–01)
Background: made redundant as a steelworker from Corby steelworks; spent 12 years until his election in 1997 working with the long term unemployed
Born: June 26 1950 in Loddington, Northants
Education: Kettering Grammar School
Higher education: Leicester University; Oxford, Ruskin; Leicester University
Constituency: mixed industrial town in Northamptonshire with good links to London

Sayeed, Jonathan
Conservative MP for Mid Bedfordshire since 1997; Bristol East (1983–92)

Majority: 8,066 (17.3%)
Turnout: 66.1%

	Votes	Share %	Change %
Jonathan Sayeed, Conservative	22,109	47.4	1.4
James Valentine, Labour	14,043	30.1	–2.4
Graham Mabbutt, Liberal Democrat	9,205	19.7	2.9
Christopher Laurence, UK Independence party	1,281	2.8	n/a

Andrew Roth says: "left of centre on racism and social matters but has moved rightward on defence and Europe"

Recent parliamentary career: opposition spokesperson, DEFRA (2001–)broadcasting committee (1997–2001)
Background: businessman; joined Marks & Spencer in 1974; Royal Navy (1964–74)
Born: March 20 1948 in Westminster
Education: Wolverstone Hall; Royal Naval College, Dartmouth; Engineering College, Manadon
Constituency: rural Bedfordshire constituency north of Luton, main towns are Flitwick and Ampthill

Sedgemore, Brian
Labour MP for Hackney South and Shoreditch since 1983; Luton West (1974–79)

Majority: 15,049 (49.6%)
Turnout: 47.4%

	Votes	Share %	Change %
Brian Sedgemore, Labour	19,471	64.2	4.8
Tony Vickers, Liberal Democrat	4,422	14.6	–0.4
Paul White, Conservative	4,180	13.8	0.5
Cecilia Prosper, Socialist Alliance	1,401	4.6	n/a
Saim Kokshal, Reform 2000	471	1.6	n/a
Ivan Beavis, Communist party	259	0.9	0
William Rogers, Workers' Revolutionary party	143	0.5	0.1

Andrew Roth says: "rude about Blair and 'Blair's babes' but much more hostile to Ken Livingstone"

Recent parliamentary career: Treasury committee (1997–2001); Treasury subcommittee (1998–2001)
Background: civil servant; barrister (1966–74) before being asked to leave chambers for conveying legal information to Private Eye, for which he freelanced in the 1970s; TV journalist
Born: March 17 1937 in Exmouth
Education: Heles School, Exeter
Higher education: Oxford, Corpus Christi
Constituency: southern end of innercity London borough with intemperate local politics

Selous, Andrew
Conservative MP for South West Bedfordshire since 2001

Majority: 776 (1.7%)
Turnout: 60.8%

	Votes	Share %	Change %
Andrew Selous, Conservative	18,477	42.1	1.4
Andrew Date, Labour	17,701	40.4	–0.1
Martin Pantling, Liberal Democrat	6,473	14.8	0.5
Tom Wise, UK Independence party	1,203	2.7	n/a

Maiden speech: "My motivation for aspiring to become a member of this house is my Christian faith. It is my wish to see the Conservative party become the party for the poor and disadvantaged."

Recent parliamentary career: elected to parliament 2001; work and pensions committee (2001–)
Background: insurer; Territorial Army soldier for 12 years; director, Christian Voter Initiative
Born: April 27 1962
Education: prefers not to reveal
Higher education: London School of Economics
Constituency: north of London, Whipsnade zoo, Leighton Buzzard and Dunstable

Shaw, Jonathan
Labour MP for Chatham and Aylesford since 1997

Majority: 4,340 (10.9%)
Turnout: 57%

	Votes	Share %	Change %
Jonathan Shaw, Labour	19,180	48.3	5.2
Sean Holden, Conservative	14,840	37.4	0
David Lettington, Liberal Democrat	4,705	11.8	–3.2
Gregory Knopp, UK Independence party	1,010	2.5	n/a

Andrew Roth says: "socially-concerned former social worker"

Recent parliamentary career: education and skills committee (2001–); introduced private member's bill on air guns (2001); environmental audit committee (1997–2001)

Background: social worker, Kent County Council; Unison member; chair of community development committee, Rochester Council
Born: June 3 1966 in Aylesford, Kent
Education: Vintners' Boys' School; Bromley College; West Kent College of Education
Constituency: mixed seat in east Kent, coastal Chatham plus Downs

Sheerman, Barry

Labour MP for Huddersfield since 1983; Huddersfield East (1979–83)

Majority: 10,046 (28.4%)
Turnout: 55%

	Votes	Share %	Change %
Barry Sheerman, Labour	18,840	53.3	–3.2
Paul Baverstock, Conservative	8,794	24.9	4
Neil Bentley, Liberal Democrat	5,300	15	–2.2
John Phillips, Green party	1,254	3.5	n/a
Judith Longman, UK Independence party	613	1.7	n/a
Graham Hellawell, Socialist Alliance	374	1.1	n/a
George Randall, Socialist Labour party	208	0.6	n/a

Andrew Roth says: "Europhile Blairite, ex-lecturer and pleasantly persuasive Christian socialist"

Recent parliamentary career: education and skills committee (2001–); chair, education subcommittee (1999–); chair, education and employment committee (1999–2001); on several international parliamentary organisations
Background: politics lecturer, University of Wales (1966–79); company chairman; once windsurfed from Majorca to France
Born: August 17 1940 in Sunbury-on-Thames
Education: Hampton Grammar School; Kingston Technical College
Higher education: London School of Economics; London University
Constituency: Pennine town east of Leeds with mixed economy

Shephard, Rt Hon Gillian

Conservative MP for South West Norfolk since 1987

Majority: 9,366 (17.7%)
Turnout: 63.1%

	Votes	Share %	Change %
Gillian Shephard, Conservative	27,633	52.2	10.2
Anne Hanson, Labour	18,267	34.5	–3.3
Gordon Dean, Liberal Democrat	5,681	10.7	–3.2
Ian Smith, UK Independence party	1,368	2.6	n/a

Andrew Roth says: "pragmatic centre-right Europhile who rose rapidly under Major and subsided under Hague"

Recent parliamentary career: shadow secretary of state, DETR (1998–99); shadow leader of the House of Commons (1997–98); secretary of state, education (1994–97); secretary of state, agriculture (1993–94); secretary of state, employment (1992–93)
Background: Mental Health Act commissioner; Health Authority chair; worked for Anglia TV; magistrate; French teacher; Norfolk councillor
Born: January 22 1940 in Cromer
Education: North Walsham High School
Higher education: Oxford, St Hilda's
Constituency: small Norfolk towns; very rural, plus military training area

Shepherd, Richard
Conservative MP for Aldridge-Brownhills since 1979

Majority: 3,768 (10.0%)
Turnout: 60.6%

	Votes	Share %	Change %
Richard Shepherd, Conservative	18,974	50.2	3.1
Ian Geary, Labour	15,206	40.2	−1.5
Jim Whorwood, Liberal Democrat	3,251	8.6	−2.6
J Rothery, Socialist Alliance	379	1	n/a

Andrew Roth says: "fastidious and fiercely independent rightish liberty-lover"

Recent parliamentary career: ran for speakership (2000); modernisation of the House of Commons committee (1997–); lost Tory whip for rebellion over Europe (1994–95)
Background: founder and chairman of a London-based grocery business; Lloyd's underwriter; noted parliamentarian and libertarian who supports freedom of information and opposes EU
Born: December 6 1942 in Aberdeen
Education: Isleworth Grammar School
Higher education: London School of Economics; Johns Hopkins University School of Advanced International Studies
Constituency: outer Walsall suburbs and ex-mining Brownhills, all to north-east of Birmingham

Sheridan, James
Labour MP for West Renfrewshire since 2001

Majority: 8,575 (25.6%)
Turnout: 63.3%

	Votes	Share %	Change %
James Sheridan, Labour	15,720	46.9	0.3
Carol Puthucheary, Scottish National party	7,145	21.3	−5.2
David Sharpe, Conservative	5,522	16.5	−2.1
Alex Mackie, Liberal Democrat	4,185	12.5	4.8
Arlene Nunnery, Scottish Socialist party	925	2.8	n/a

Maiden speech: "If we were to accept the Luddite approach to Europe articulated by many in the official opposition, it would be disastrous for our country, our electorate and, more important, our businesses"

Recent parliamentary career: elected to parliament 2001
Background: Renfrewshire councillor; painter; industrial labourer; trade union convenor at Pilkington Optronics, Glasgow, where he worked as a material handler
Born: November 24 1952
Education: St Pius Secondary School
Constituency: rural seat with small towns just west of Glasgow

Shipley, Debra
Labour MP for Stourbridge since 1997

Majority: 3,812 (9.6%)
Turnout: 61.8%

	Votes	Share %	Change %
Debra Shipley, Labour	18,823	47.2	0
Stephen Eyre, Conservative	15,011	37.6	1.8
Chris Bramall, Liberal Democrat	4,833	12.1	−2.2
John Knotts, UK Independence party	763	1.9	n/a
Mick Atherton, Socialist Labour Party	494	1.2	n/a

Andrew Roth says: "one of Labour's most successful frontline women warriors"

Recent parliamentary career: culture, media and sport committee (2001–); her 1999 Protection of Children Act created a blacklist for child abusers
Background: author of 17 books on travel, history, cookery, and architecture; course developer, University of Central England; consultant, Arts Council of Great Britain
Born: June 22 1957 in Shrewsbury
Education: Kidderminster High School
Higher education: London University; Oxford Brookes University
Constituency: self-contained industrial town between Worcestershire and West Midlands

Short, Rt Hon Clare
Labour MP for Birmingham Ladywood since 1983

Majority: 18,143 (57.6%)
Turnout: 44.3%

	Votes	Share %	Change %
Clare Short, Labour	21,694	68.9	–5.2
Benjamin Prentice, Conservative	3,551	11.3	–2
Mahmood Chaudhry, Liberal Democrat	2,586	8.2	0.2
Allah Ditta, PJP	2,112	6.7	n/a
Surinder Virdee, Socialist Labour party	443	1.4	n/a
Mahmood Hussain, Muslim	432	1.4	n/a
Jim Caffery, ProLife Alliance	392	1.2	n/a
Anneliese Nattrass, UK Independence party	283	0.9	n/a

Andrew Roth says: "Tony Blair's hip-shooting stormy petrel...the least conventional of Labour's senior women"

Recent parliamentary career: secretary of state, DFID (1997–)
Background: civil servant at the Home Office; community organiser in Birmingham; Irish roots
Born: February 15 1946 in Birmingham
Education: St Paul's Grammar School, Birmingham
Higher education: Leeds University; Keele University
Constituency: hardpressed innercity Birmingham seat

Simmonds, Mark
Conservative MP for Boston and Skegness since 2001

Majority: 515 (1.3%)
Turnout: 58.4%

	Votes	Share %	Change %
Mark Simmonds, Conservative	17,298	42.9	0.5
Elaine Bird, Labour	16,783	41.6	0.6
Duncan Moffatt, Liberal Democrat	4,994	12.4	–4.2
Cyril Wakefield, UK Independence party	717	1.8	n/a
Martin Harrison, Green party	521	1.3	n/a

Maiden speech: "I am not advocating withdrawal, but arguing forcefully that if Europe is to survive and succeed in the forthcoming years, it must become more democratically accountable"

Recent parliamentary career: elected to parliament 2001; environmental audit committee (2001–)
Background: East Midlands-born chartered surveyor; Wandsworth councillor
Born: April 12 1964
Education: Worksop College, Nottinghamshire
Higher education: Trent University
Constituency: bracing east coast seaside town and surrounding farmland

Simon, Sîon
Labour MP for Birmingham Erdington since 2001

Majority: 9,962 (32.6%)
Turnout: 46.6%

	Votes	Share %	Change %
Sîon Simon, Labour	17,375	56.8	−2
Oliver Lodge, Conservative	7,413	24.2	−3.3
Sandra Johnson, Liberal Democrat	3,602	11.8	1.6
Michael Shore, National Front	681	2.2	n/a
Steve Godward, Socialist Alliance	669	2.2	n/a
Mark Nattrass, UK Independence party	521	1.7	n/a
Judith Sambrook Marshall, Socialist Labour party	343	1.1	n/a

Maiden speech: "I shall not pretend that my constituency is the most conventionally beautiful corner of England. As it happens, I love Spaghetti Junction, which is lucky, because I live almost directly under it. But that is okay – I am a Brummie."

Recent parliamentary career: elected to parliament 2001
Background: journalist on the *Spectator*, *News of the World* and *Daily Telegraph*; very New Labour; MP's researcher
Born: December 23 1968
Education: Handsworth Grammar School
Higher education: Oxford, Magdalen
Constituency: inner-city Birmingham, just to the north of the city centre

Simpson, Alan
Labour MP for Nottingham South since 1992

Majority: 9,989 (27.3%)
Turnout: 50.1%

	Votes	Share %	Change %
Alan Simpson, Labour	19,949	54.5	−0.8
Wendy Manning, Conservative	9,960	27.2	−0.5
Kevin Mulloy, Liberal Democrat	6,064	16.6	3.7
David Bartrop, UK Independence party	632	1.7	n/a

Andrew Roth says: "the Liverpudlian would-be heir to Tony Benn"

Recent parliamentary career: secretary, Socialist Campaign for Labour MPs (1995–)
Background: research officer for the Nottingham Racial Equality Council (1979–92); community development worker and Nottinghamshire County councillor; environmental activist
Born: September 20 1948 in Bootle
Education: Bootle Grammar School
Higher education: Nottingham Trent University
Constituency: mixed suburbs to south of Nottingham plus university

Simpson, Keith
Labour MP for Mid Norfolk since 1997

Majority: 4,562 (8.7%)
Turnout: 70.2%

	Votes	Share %	Change %
Keith Simpson, Conservative	23,519	44.8	5.2
Daniel Zeichner, Labour	18,957	36.1	−1.2
Vivienne Clifford-Jackson, Liberal Democrat	7,621	14.5	−0.5
Stuart Agnew, UK Independence party	1,333	2.5	n/a
Peter Reeve, Green party	1,118	2.1	−0.1

Andrew Roth says: "fun-loving but shrewd, assiduous and hardhitting former Sandhurst lecturer"

Recent parliamentary career: opposition whip (1999–2001); opposition spokesperson, defence (1998–99)
Background: senior lecturer in war studies and international affairs, Royal Military Academy; head, foreign affairs and defence, Conservative Research Department; special adviser to defence ministers; director, Cranfield Securities Studies Institute; author of five books on military history
Born: March 29 1949 in Norwich
Education: Thorpe Grammar School, Norfolk
Higher education: Hull University; King's College, London
Constituency: big rural seat plus Broads; few towns, many villages

Singh, Marsha
Labour MP for Bradford West since 1997

Majority: 4,165 (10.9%)
Turnout: 53.6%

	Votes	Share %	Change %
Marsha Singh, Labour	18,401	48	6.5
Mohammed Riaz, Conservative	14,236	37.1	4.1
John Robinson, Green party	2,672	7	5.1
Rauf Khan, Liberal Democrat	2,437	6.4	–8.4
Imran Hussein, UK Independence party	427	1.1	n/a
Farhan Khokhar, AL	197	0.5	n/a

Andrew Roth says: "leftish Sikh with a background in secular and expansive politics"

Recent parliamentary career: home affairs committee (1997–)
Background: worked for Bradford Council's education directorate and Bradford Community Health Trust (1990–97)
Born: October 11 1954 in India
Education: Belle Vue Grammar School
Higher education: Loughborough University
Constituency: innercity, Asian Bradford; Green beats Liberal Democrat here

Skinner, Dennis
Labour MP for Bolsover since 1970

Majority: 18,777 (49.1%)
Turnout: 56.7%

	Votes	Share %	Change %
Dennis Skinner, Labour	26,249	68.6	–5.4
Simon Massey, Conservative	7,472	19.5	2.8
Marie Bradley, Liberal Democrat	4,550	11.9	2.6

Andrew Roth says: "unyielding, incorruptible, puritanical, abrasively proletarian conscience of the hard left"

Recent parliamentary career: outspoken backbench wit and constructive left-wing critic of New Labour whose energy has faded slightly; hostile to EU
Background: miner, Derbyshire councillor and part-time singer; on Labour NEC (1978–92 and 1994–98)
Born: February 11 1932 in Clay Cross, Derbyshire
Education: Tupton Hall Grammar School
Higher education: Sheffield University; Oxford, Ruskin
Constituency: eastern ex-mining part of Derbyshire, famous for its castle

Smith, Rt Hon Andrew
Labour MP for Oxford East since 1987

Majority: 10,344 (26.0%)
Turnout: 53.5%

	Votes	Share %	Change %
Andrew Smith, Labour	19,681	49.4	–7.4
Steve Goddard, Liberal Democrat	9,337	23.4	8.7
Cheryl Potter, Conservative	7,446	18.7	–3.3
Pritam Singh, Green party	1,501	3.8	1.8
John Lister, Socialist Alliance	708	1.8	n/a
Peter Gardner, UK Independence party	570	1.4	n/a
Fahim Ahmed, Socialist Labour Party	274	0.7	n/a
L Hodge, ProLife Alliance	254	0.6	n/a
Pathmanathan Mylvaganan, Independent	77	0.2	n/a

Andrew Roth says: "long expected to reach the Cabinet, initially held back by lack of charisma"

Recent parliamentary career: chief secretary to the Treasury (1999–); minister of state, DFEE (1997–99); opposition spokesperson, Transport (1996–97)
Background: joined Labour at 22; relations officer, Oxford and Swindon Co-operative Society; sociology lecturer; Oxford councillor
Born: February 1 1951 in Wokingham, Berkshire
Education: Reading Grammar School
Higher education: Oxford, St John's
Constituency: Cowley Mini factory and gentrifying Oxford terraces east of River Cherwell

Smith, Angela
Labour MP for Basildon since 1997

Majority: 7,738 (18.9%)
Turnout: 55.2%

	Votes	Share %	Change %
Angela Smith, Labour	21,551	52.7	–3.1
Dominic Schofield, Conservative	13,813	33.8	3
Jane Smithard, Liberal Democrat	3,691	9	0.3
Frank Mallon, UK Independence party	1,397	3.4	n/a
Dick Duane, Socialist Alliance	423	1	n/a

Andrew Roth says: "critically loyal, centre-left activist and multi-good-cause groupie"

Recent parliamentary career: government whip (2001–); PPS to Paul Boateng (1999–2001)
Background: head of political and public relations, League Against Cruel Sports (1983–95); researcher for Alun Michael MP; Essex county councillor
Born: January 7 1959 in London
Education: Chalvedon Comprehensive School, Basildon
Higher education: Leicester Polytechnic
Constituency: famous as 1992 weather vane; Essex new town with an economy that never quite took off

Smith, Rt Hon Chris
Labour MP for Islington South and Finsbury since 1983

Majority: 7,280 (25.9%)
Turnout: 47.4%

	Votes	Share %	Change %
Chris Smith, Labour	15,217	54	–8.5
Keith Sharp, Liberal Democrat	7,937	28.1	6.8
Nicky Morgan, Conservative	3,860	13.7	0.7
Janine Booth, Socialist Alliance	817	2.9	n/a
Thomas McCarthy, Independent	267	1	0.7
Charles Thomson, Stuck	108	0.4	n/a

Andrew Roth says: "hard-working, highly intelligent, cultivated, not-too-soft left intellectual"

Recent parliamentary career: secretary of state, DCMS (1997–2001); opposition spokesperson, DoH (1996–97)
Background: gained a first and PhD in English at Cambridge; Islington councillor; the first openly gay MP; high-profile victim in 2001 reshuffle
Born: July 24 1951 in Barnet, Hertfordshire
Education: George Watson's College, Edinburgh
Higher education: Harvard University; Cambridge, Pembroke
Constituency: part-grand, part-poor metaphor for new Labour; Lib Dems win council, Labour general elections

Smith, Geraldine
Labour MP for Morecambe and Lunesdale since 1997

Majority: 5,092 (12.3%)
Turnout: 60.7%

	Votes	Share %	Change %
Geraldine Smith, Labour	20,646	49.6	0.7
David Nuttall, Conservative	15,554	37.3	0.6
Chris Cotton, Liberal Democrat	3,817	9.2	–2.2
Gregg Beaman, UK Independence party	935	2.2	n/a
Ms Cherith Adams, Green party	703	1.7	n/a

Andrew Roth says: "her heart thrills to the beauties of her constituency and bleeds for the deprived"

Recent parliamentary career: on European standing committee; substitute delegate, Council of Europe
Background: postal clerk; joined the Labour party in 1979, climbed the party ladder until her election in 1997
Born: August 29 1961 in Belfast
Education: Morecambe High School; Lancaster and Morecambe College
Constituency: declining north-west seaside town just west of Lancaster

Smith, Jacqui
Labour MP for Redditch since 1997

Majority: 2,484 (6.7%)
Turnout: 59.2%

	Votes	Share %	Change %
Jacqui Smith, Labour	16,899	45.6	–4.2
Karen Lumley, Conservative	14,415	38.9	2.8
Michael Ashall, Liberal Democrat	3,808	10.3	–0.7
George Flynn, UK Independence party	1,259	3.4	n/a
Richard Armstrong, Green party	651	1.8	n/a

Andrew Roth says: "partisan superloyalist and experienced activist"

Recent parliamentary career: minister of state, DoH (2001–); junior minister, DFEE (1999–)
Background: economics teacher; Redditch councillor
Born: November 3 1962 in London
Education: Dyson Perrins High School, Malvern
Higher education: Oxford, Hertford; Worcester College of Education
Constituency: Worcestershire new town south-west of Birmingham

Smith, John
Labour MP for Vale of Glamorgan since 1997

Majority: 4,700 (10.4%)
Turnout: 67.4%

	Votes	Share %	Change %
John Smith, Labour	20,524	45.4	−8.5
Susan Inkin, Conservative	15,824	35	0.6
Dewi Smith, Liberal Democrat	5,521	12.2	3
Chris Franks, Plaid Cymru	2,867	6.4	3.8
Niall Warry, UK Independence party	448	1	n/a

Andrew Roth says: "very loyal, soft-left South Wales politician"

Recent parliamentary career: PPS to John Reid (1997–)
Background: working-class Welshman; RAF; joiner; university tutor; trade unionist (MSF, TASS, NATFE, AUT, NUPE, UCATT)
Born: March 17 1951 in Penarth
Education: Penarth Grammar School
Higher education: Cardiff University; Gwent College of Education
Constituency: perpetual marginal west of Cardiff, including Barry and Cardiff airport

Smith, Llewellyn
Labour MP for Blaenau Gwent since 1992

Majority: 19,313 (60.8%)
Turnout: 59.5%

	Votes	Share %	Change %
Llewellyn Smith, Labour	22,855	72	−7.5
Adam Ryaka, Plaid Cymru	3,542	11.2	6
Edward Townsend, Liberal Democrat	2,945	9.3	0.6
Huw Williams, Conservative	2,383	7.5	0.9

Andrew Roth says: "ageing, rebellion-prone Welsh boyo who has long stood on the burning decks from which others feel the heat, he hates nationalism, capitalism and warfare"

Recent parliamentary career: persistent rebel (1997–2001); denounced devolution plans (1997) and campaigned for "no" in referendum
Background: glassworks labourer; author; MEP (1984–94); complained that speaker Boothroyd discriminated against him (1994)
Born: April 16 1944 in Newbridge
Education: Greenfields Secondary Modern School, Newbridge
Higher education: Cardiff University
Constituency: safe Labour Valleys seat including Ebbw Vale and Tredegar, Michael Foot and Nye Bevan were MPs

Smith, Sir Robert
Liberal Democrat MP for West Aberdeenshire and Kincardine since 1997

Majority: 4,821 (12.7%)
Turnout: 62%

	Votes	Share %	Change %
Robert Smith, Liberal Democrat	16,507	43.5	2.4
Tom Kerr, Conservative	11,686	30.8	−4.1
Kevin Hutchens, Labour	4,669	12.3	3.2
John Green, Scottish National party	4,634	12.2	−0.9
Alan Manley, Scottish Socialist party	418	1.1	n/a

Andrew Roth says: "pragmatic landowner who emerged as a strong defender of his local oil industry"

Recent parliamentary career: trade and industry committee (2001–); procedure committee (2001–); acting Lib Dem whip (1999–); spokesperson, Scotland (1999–); Scottish affairs committee (1999–2001); spokesperson, police and prisons (1999–99)

Background: owns and manages family estate near Chapel of Garrioch; Aberdeenshire councillor; formerly in SDP; grandson of Conservative MP
Born: April 15 1958 in London
Education: Merchant Taylors' School, Northwood
Higher education: Aberdeen University
Constituency: Balmoral and rugged Cairngorm hills west of Aberdeen

Smyth, Rev Martin
Ulster Unionist MP for Belfast South since 1982

Majority: 5,399 (14.2%)
Turnout: 63.9%

	Votes	Share %	Change %
Martin Smyth, Ulster Unionist party	17,008	44.8	8.8
Alasdair McDonnell, Social Democratic and Labour party	11,609	30.6	6.3
Prof Monica McWilliams, Northern Ireland Women	2,968	7.8	4.8
Alex Maskey, Sinn Fein	2,894	7.6	2.5
Geraldine Rice, Alliance party of Northern Ireland	2,042	5.4	−7.5
Ms Dawn Purvis, Progressive Unionist party	1,112	2.9	−11.5
Paddy Lynn, Workers' party	204	0.5	−0.2
Rainbow George Weiss, Ind Vote	115	0.3	n/a

Andrew Roth says: "political cleric and soft spoken hardliner in the UUP's old guard"

Recent parliamentary career: Northern Ireland affairs committee (2001–); Ulster Unionist spokesperson, social security (2000–); spokesperson, health and family policy (1997–2001); chief whip (1995–2000);
Background: Presbyterian minister; company director; grand master, Grand Orange Lodge in Ireland (1972–96)
Born: June 15 1931
Education: Methodist College, Belfast
Higher education: Magee University College, Londonderry; Trinity College, Dublin; Presbyterian College, Dublin
Constituency: middle class academic Belfast voters who favour moderate UUP unionism, not DUP

Soames, Hon Nicholas
Conservative MP for Mid Sussex since 1983; Crawley (1983–97)

Majority: 6,898 (15.1%)
Turnout: 64.9%

	Votes	Share %	Change %
Nicholas Soames, Conservative	21,150	46.2	2.7
Lesley Wilkins, Liberal Democrat	14,252	31.1	0.5
Paul Mitchell, Labour	8,693	19	0.4
Petrina Holdsworth, UK Inependence party	1,126	2.5	n/a
Peter Berry, Official Monster Raving Loony party	601	1.3	n/a

Andrew Roth says: "self-satirising, out-of-step Tory"

Recent parliamentary career: supported Michael Portillo for leadership (2001); minister of state, MoD (1994–97)
Background: the grandson of Winston Churchill and a close friend of Prince Charles; former wine correspondent for the *Spectator*; director of pharmaceutical companies
Born: February 12 1948 in London
Education: Eton College; Mons Officer Cadet School
Constituency: Sussex towns of Haywards Heath, Burgess Hill and East Grinstead

Soley, Clive

Labour MP for Ealing, Acton, and Shepherd's Bush since 1997; Hammersmith (1983–97); Hammersmith North (1979–83)

Majority: 10,789 (29.0%)
Turnout: 52.6%

	Votes	Share %	Change %
Clive Soley, Labour	20,144	54.2	–4.2
Justine Greening, Conservative	9,355	25.2	–0.6
Martin Tod, Liberal Democrat	6,171	16.6	5.9
Nick Bush, Socialist Alliance	529	1.4	n/a
George Lawrie, UK Independence party	476	1.3	n/a
Carlos Rule, Socialist Labour Party	301	0.8	–0.5
Rebecca Ng, ProLife Alliance	225	0.6	0

Andrew Roth says: "grew up in a family of politically-minded trade unionists…egg-shaped head, gentle, modest"

Recent parliamentary career: modernisation of the House of Commons committee (1997–); chair, parliamentary Labour party (1997–2001); challenged for post (2000), accused of being too supportive of government when Ken Livingstone stood for mayor
Background: probation officer; member of NEC (1998–); supporter of press regulation
Born: May 7 1939 in Wanstead
Education: Downshall Secondary Modern School, Ilford
Higher education: Strathclyde University; Southampton University; Newbattle Abbey College of Education
Constituency: inner-west London around A40 and BBC headquarters

Southworth, Helen

Labour MP for Warrington South since 1997

Majority: 7,387 (16.3%)
Turnout: 61.2%

	Votes	Share %	Change %
Helen Southworth, Labour	22,409	49.3	–2.8
Caroline Mosley, Conservative	15,022	33	0.5
Roger Barlow, Liberal Democrat	7,419	16.3	3.2
Joan Kelley, UK Independence party	637	1.4	n/a

Andrew Roth says: "loyalist from the local council and caring professions"

Recent parliamentary career: PPS to Paul Boateng (2001–); trade and industry committee (1998–2001)
Background: chief executive, Age Concern; representative on Community Health Council; St Helens councillor
Born: November 13 1956 in Preston
Education: Larkhill Convent School, Preston
Higher education: Lancaster University
Constituency: on the Manchester Ship Canal between Liverpool and Manchester

Spellar, Rt Hon John

Labour MP for Warley since 1997; Warley West (1992–97); Birmingham Northfields (1982–83)

Majority: 11,850 (37.7%)
Turnout: 54.1%

	Votes	Share %	Change %
John Spellar, Labour	19,007	60.5	–3.3
Mark Pritchard, Conservative	7,157	22.8	–1.3
Ron Cockings, Liberal Democrat	3,315	10.6	0.9
Harbhajan Dardi, Socialist Labour party	1,936	6.2	n/a

Andrew Roth says: "a very right-wing loyalist operator-manipulator"

Recent parliamentary career: minister of state, DETLGR (2001–); minister of state, MoD (1999–2001); junior minister, MoD (1997–99)
Background: researcher, several Labour MPs; parliamentary adviser, PQ parliamentary Information Service
Born: August 5 1947 in Bromley
Education: Dulwich College
Higher education: Oxford, St Edmund Hall
Constituency: mixed seat on edge of Birmingham, includes Smethwick

Spelman, Caroline
Conservative MP for Meriden since 1997

Majority: 3,784 (8.5%)
Turnout: 59.9%

	Votes	Share %	Change %
Caroline Spelman, Conservative	21,246	47.7	5.7
Christine Shawcroft, Labour	17,462	39.2	–1.8
Nigel Hicks, Liberal Democrat	4,941	11.1	–1.9
Richard Adams, UK Independence party	910	2	n/a

Andrew Roth says: "internationally-experienced Tory businesswoman, not overly partisan"

Recent parliamentary career: shadow secretary of state, DFID (2001–); opposition spokesperson, health and women's issues (1999–2001); opposition whip (1998–99)
Background: sugarbeet commodities secretary, NFU; research fellow, Centre for European Agricultural Studies; former assistant to MEP; specialises in food and biotechnology issues
Born: May 4 1958 in Bishops Stortford
Education: Herts and Essex Grammar School for Girls
Higher education: Queen Mary College, London
Constituency: commuter suburbs east of Birmingham and Solihull

Spicer, Sir Michael
Conservative MP for West Worcestershire since 1997; South Worcestershire (1974–97)

Majority: 5,374 (12%)
Turnout: 67.1%

	Votes	Share %	Change %
Michael Spicer, Conservative	20,597	46	1
Mike Hadley, Liberal Democrat	15,223	34	–3.2
Waquar Azmi, Labour	6,275	14	–1.7
Ian Morris, UK Independence party	1,574	3.5	n/a
Malcolm Victory, Green party	1,138	2.5	0.5

Andrew Roth says: "swung from extreme dampness in his political infancy to become a Thatcherite free-competition zealot"

Recent parliamentary career: chair, Conservative 1922 committee (2001–); chair, Treasury subcommittee (1999–2001); Treasury committee (1997–2001)
Background: Eurosceptic economist, author, and novelist
Born: January 22 1943 in Bath
Education: Sacré Coeur, Vienna; Gaunt's House Preparatory School; Wellington College
Higher education: Cambridge, Emmanuel
Constituency: rural, pleasant north-western edge of the Cotswolds around Malvern

Spink, Dr Robert
Conservative MP for Castle Point since 2001; Castle Point (1992–97)

Majority: 985 (2.5%)
Turnout: 58.4%

	Votes	Share %	Change %
Robert Spink, Conservative	17,738	44.6	4.5
Christine Butler, Labour	16,753	42.1	–0.3
Billy Boulton, Liberal Democrat	3,116	7.8	–1.4
Ron Hurrell, UK Independence party	1,273	3.2	n/a
Doug Roberts, Independent	663	1.7	n/a
Nik Searle, Truth	220	0.6	n/a

Maiden speech: "Our constitution and traditions are being eroded and our economy is threatened by inappropriate European integration. Worst of all, our very sovereignty is dangerously dissolving into the European melting pot."

Recent parliamentary career: re-entered parliament 2001, taking seat from Labour; education and skills committee (2001–)
Background: convinced right-wing Conservative; electronics engineer; management consultant; director, Bournemouth International Airport; Dorset councillor
Born: August 1 1948
Education: Holycroft Secondary School, Keighley
Higher education: Manchester University
Constituency: Essex surburbia regained by Conservatives in 2001

Spring, Richard
Conservative MP for West Suffolk since 1997; Bury St Edmunds (1992–97)

Majority: 4,295 (10.1%)
Turnout: 59.6%

	Votes	Share %	Change %
Richard Spring, Conservative	20,201	47.6	6.7
Michael Jeffreys, Labour	15,906	37.5	0.4
Robin Martlew, Liberal Democrat	5,017	11.8	–2.2
Will Burrows, UK Independence party	1,321	3.1	n/a

Andrew Roth says: "can be a stooge questioner but, at his best, is sensitively intelligent"

Recent parliamentary career: opposition spokesperson, FO (2001); opposition spokesperson, FCO (2000–01); opposition spokesperson, DCMS (1998–2000)
Background: vice president of Merrill-Lynch; company director
Born: September 24 1946 in Cape Town
Education: Rondebosch School, Cape Town
Higher education: Cape Town University; Cambridge, Magdalene
Constituency: rural Suffolk including Newmarket and Haverhill

Squire, Rachel
Labour MP for Dunfermline West since 1992

Majority: 10,980 (35.5%)
Turnout: 57.1%

	Votes	Share %	Change %
Rachel Squire, Labour	16,370	52.9	–0.2
Brian Goodall, Scottish National party	5,390	17.4	–1.8
Russell McPhate, Liberal Democrat	4,832	15.6	2
James Mackie, Conservative	3,166	10.2	–2.4
Kate Stewart, Scottish Socialist party	746	2.4	n/a
Alastair Harper, UK Independence party	471	1.5	n/a

Andrew Roth says: "gungho cheerleader of the defence services, very active in the Labour women's network"

Recent parliamentary career: introduced private member's bill on patents (2001); defence committee (2001–); PPS to Estelle Morris (1998–2001); PPS to Stephen Byers (1997–98)
Background: English-born; Labour supporter since the age of seven; education officer in Scotland; trade union officer (NUPE, then Unison)
Born: July 13 1954 in Carshalton
Education: Godolphin and Latimer Girls' School
Higher education: Birmingham and Durham Universities
Constituency: mixed Central Belt Scottish town, including Rosyth docks

Stanley, Rt Hon Sir John
Conservative MP for Tonbridge and Malling since 1974

Majority: 8,250 (19.5%)
Turnout: 64.4%

	Votes	Share %	Change %
John Stanley, Conservative	20,956	49.4	1.4
Victoria Hayman, Labour	12,706	29.9	2.7
Merilyn Canet, Liberal Democrat	7,605	17.9	−1.3
Doug Hall, UK Independence party	1,169	2.8	n/a

Andrew Roth says: "very much his own man: bucked Thatcher over poll tax, praised Blair over Kosovo"

Recent parliamentary career: foreign affairs committee (1997–)
Background: traditionalist long-serving Tory; knighted in 1988; PPS to Margaret Thatcher (1976–79); held various ministerial positions in 1980s
Born: January 19 1942 in London
Education: Repton School
Higher education: Oxford, Lincoln
Constituency: Garden of England Kent seat hit by the Channel Tunnel

Starkey, Dr Phyllis
Labour MP for Milton Keynes South West since 1997

Majority: 6,978 (15.3%)
Turnout: 59.2%

	Votes	Share %	Change %
Phyllis Starkey, Labour	22,484	49.5	−4.3
Iain Stewart, Conservative	15,506	34.2	0.7
Nazar Mohammad, Liberal Democrat	4,828	10.6	−1.3
Alan Francis, Green party	957	2.1	n/a
Clive Davies, UK Independence party	848	1.9	n/a
Patrick Denning, LCA	500	1.1	n/a
Dave Bradbury, Socialist Alliance	261	0.6	n/a

Andrew Roth says: "among the most dynamic and cerebral of Labour's loyalist women MPs"

Recent parliamentary career: foreign affairs committee (1999–)
Background: science policy administrator, Biotechnology and Biological Sciences Research Council; research scientist, Cambridge and Oxford; research fellow in obstetrics, Oxford University
Born: January 4 1947 in Ipswich
Education: Perse School for Girls
Higher education: Cambridge, Clare; Oxford, Lady Margaret Hall
Constituency: southern part of Buckinghamshire new town; includes Bletchley of Enigma fame

Steen, Anthony
Conservative MP for Totnes since 1997; South Hams (1983–97); Liverpool Wavertree (1974–83)

Majority: 3,597 (7.3%)
Turnout: 67.9%

	Votes	Share %	Change %
Anthony Steen, Conservative	21,914	44.5	8
Rachel Oliver, Liberal Democrat	18,317	37.2	2.3
Thomas Wildy, Labour	6,005	12.2	–4.2
Craig Mackinlay, UK Independence party	3,010	6.1	n/a

Andrew Roth says: "socially-concerned, obsessive, unpredictable partisan soloist and admitted plotter"

Recent parliamentary career: public administration committee (2001–); European scrutiny committee (1998–); deregulation committee (1997–)
Background: barrister; law lecturer; Lloyds underwriter since 1972; adviser to Canadian government and various regional airlines
Born: July 22 1939 in London
Education: Westminster School
Higher education: Gray's Inn; University College, London
Constituency: south Devon coast including Dartmouth, Totnes and most of Dartmoor

Steinberg, Gerry
Labour MP for City of Durham since 1987

Majority: 13,441 (32.4%)
Turnout: 59.6%

	Votes	Share %	Change %
Gerry Steinberg, Labour	23,254	56.1	–7.2
Carol Woods, Liberal Democrat	9,813	23.7	8.4
Nick Cartmell, Conservative	7,167	17.3	–0.2
Chris Williamson, UK Independence party	1,252	3	n/a

Andrew Roth says: "popular, militantly compassionate soft-left former head teacher who speaks for the teaching profession"

Recent parliamentary career: public accounts committee (1998–); catering committee (1998–2001)
Background: head teacher; trade union member (TGWU, NUT); Durham councillor
Born: April 20 1945 in Durham
Education: Whinney Hill Secondary Modern School; Durham Johnstone Grammar School
Higher education: Sheffield Technical College; Newcastle Polytechnic
Constituency: beautiful, historic north-east city with Labour tradition

Stevenson, George
Labour MP for Stoke-on-Trent South since 1992

Majority: 10,489 (29.2%)
Turnout: 51.5%

	Votes	Share %	Change %
George Stevenson, Labour	19,366	53.8	–8.2
Philip Bastiman, Conservative	8,877	24.6	2.2
Christopher Coleman, Liberal Democrat	4,724	13.1	2.9
Adrian Knapper, Independent	1,703	4.7	n/a
Steven Batkin, British National party	1,358	3.8	2.6

Andrew Roth says: "shrewd, articulate, now mildly rebellious old Labour type"

Recent parliamentary career: transport, local government, and the regions committee (2001–); environment, transport and regional affairs committee (1997–2001)

Background: MEP (1984–94); bus driver; miner; pottery worker; union shop steward; pro-European; pro-farming
Born: August 30 1938 in Maltby, Yorkshire
Education: Queensbury Road Secondary Modern School, Stoke
Constituency: suburban, skilled manual Potteries seat

Stewart, David
Labour MP for Inverness East, Nairn and Lochaber since 1997

Majority: 4,716 (11.2%)
Turnout: 63.2%

	Votes	Share %	Change %
David Stewart, Labour	15,605	36.8	2.9
Angus MacNeil, Scottish National party	10,889	25.6	–3.4
Patsy Kenton, Liberal Democrat	9,420	22.2	4.7
Richard Jenkins, Conservative	5,653	13.3	–4.2
Steve Arnott, Scottish Socialist party	894	2.1	n/a

Andrew Roth says: "interested in the problems of the Highlands, especially his precarious seat"

Recent parliamentary career: work and pensions committee (2001–); Scottish affairs committee (1997–99)
Background: social worker and team manager (1981–97); community care lecturer; Spice Girls fan
Born: May 5 1956 in Inverness
Education: Inverness High School; Paisley College
Higher education: Stirling University; Open University Business School
Constituency: big, beautiful tourist Scotland with mixed political heritage

Stewart, Ian
Labour MP for Eccles since 1997

Majority: 14,528 (43.8%)
Turnout: 48.3%

	Votes	Share %	Change %
Ian Stewart, Labour	21,395	64.5	–2.2
Peter Caillard, Conservative	6,867	20.7	2
Bob Boyd, Liberal Democrat	4,920	14.8	4.1

Andrew Roth says: "union fixer and dedicated north-western regionalist, a rebel on social questions"

Recent parliamentary career: PPS to Brian Wilson (2001–); deregulation committee (1997–); information committee (1998–2001)
Background: regional officer, TGWU; chemical plant officer; electrician; IT enthusiast
Born: August 28 1950 in Blantyre, Scotland
Education: Calder Street Secondary School, Blantyre; Alfred Turner Secondary Modern School, Irlam
Higher education: Manchester Metropolitan University; Stretford Technical College
Constituency: west of Manchester beyond Salford; very industrial

Stinchcombe, Paul
Labour MP for Wellingborough since 1997

Majority: 2,355 (4.6%)
Turnout: 65.9%

	Votes	Share %	Change %
Paul Stinchcombe, Labour	23,867	46.8	2.6
Peter Bone, Conservative	21,512	42.2	–1.6
Peter Gaskell, Liberal Democrat	4,763	9.3	–0.1
Anthony Ellwood, UK Independence party	864	1.7	n/a

Andrew Roth says: "highly idealistic young Christian socialist internationalist and committed environmentalist"

Recent parliamentary career: environment, food, and rural affairs committee (2001–); home affairs committee (1998–2001)
Background: barrister; Camden councillor; radical, idealist; pro-Kenya and sympathetic to immigrants
Born: April 25 1962 in Haslemere
Education: High Wycombe Royal Grammar School
Higher education: Inns of Court School of Law, London; Harvard; Cambridge, Trinity
Constituency: Northamptonshire town on main rail line north of Bedford, mixed economy, Tories expected to win (2001)

Stoate, Dr Howard
Labour MP for Dartford since 1997

Majority: 3,306 (7.4%)
Turnout: 61.9%

	Votes	Share %	Change %
Howard Stoate, Labour	21,466	48	–0.6
Bob Dunn, Conservative	18,160	40.6	0.3
Graham Morgan, Liberal Democrat	3,781	8.5	–0.9
Mark Croucher, UK Independence party	989	2.2	n/a
Keith Davenport, Fancy Dress party	344	0.8	0.2

Andrew Roth says: "equally loyal to the NHS and Labour"

Recent parliamentary career: PPS to John Denham (2001–); health committee (1997–2001)
Background: practising GP who has treated fellow MPs; hospital doctor and tutor; medical journalist; Dartford councillor; ran London Marathon (2000)
Born: April 14 1954 in Weymouth
Education: Kingston Grammar School
Higher education: King's College, London
Constituency: industrial Thames-side seat on M25 river crossing

Strang, Rt Hon Dr Gavin
Labour MP for Edinburgh East and Musselburgh since 1997; Edinburgh East (1970–97)

Majority: 12,168 (35.3%)
Turnout: 58.2%

	Votes	Share %	Change %
Gavin Strang, Labour	18,124	52.6	–1
Rob Munn, Scottish National party	5,956	17.3	–1.8
Gary Peacock, Liberal Democrat	4,981	14.5	3.8
Peter Finnie, Conservative	3,906	11.3	–4.1
Derek Durkin, Scottish Socialist party	1,487	4.3	n/a

Andrew Roth says: "an old Labour left fundamentalist'

Recent parliamentary career: intelligence and security committee (2001–); cabinet minister, DETR (1997–98)
Background: joined Labour at 18 years old; scientist with the Agricultural Research Council in Edinburgh; long-standing Labour minister and spokesperson dropped from Cabinet soon after 1997
Born: July 10 1943 in Dundee
Education: Morrison's Academy, Crieff
Higher education: Edinburgh University; Cambridge, Churchill
Constituency: commuter seat outside Edinburgh

Straw, Rt Hon Jack
Labour MP for Blackburn since 1979

Majority: 9,249 (22.9%)
Turnout: 55.8%

	Votes	Share %	Change %
Jack Straw, Labour	21,808	53.9	-1.1
John Cotton, Conservative	12,559	31	6.4
Imtiaz Patel, Liberal Democrat	3,264	8.1	-2.4
Dorothy Baxter, UK Independence party	1,185	2.9	n/a
Paul Morris, Independent	577	1.4	n/a
Terry Cullen, Socialist Labour party	559	1.4	0.1
Frederick Nichol, Socialist	532	1.3	n/a

Andrew Roth says: "hard-headed and privately ambitious politician on the soft-left fringe of the Blair-Brown modernising project"

Recent parliamentary career: secretary of state, FCO (2001–); home secretary (1997–2001); shadow home secretary (1994–97); spokesman environment (1992–94); spokesman, education (1987–92)
Background: barrister; parliamentary adviser; former columnist, *The Times* and *Independent*; TV researcher; special adviser, Peter Shore; adviser, Barbara Castle
Born: August 3 1946 in Buckhurst Hill, Essex
Education: Brentwood School
Higher education: Leeds University; Inns of Court School of Law, London
Constituency: declining industrial town north of Manchester

Streeter, Gary
Conservative MP for South West Devon since 1997; Plymouth Sutton (1992–97)

Majority: 7,144 (15.2%)
Turnout: 66.1%

	Votes	Share %	Change %
Gary Streeter, Conservative	21,970	46.8	3.9
Christopher Mavin, Labour	14,826	31.6	2.7
Phil Hutty, Liberal Democrat	8,616	18.4	-5.4
Roger Bullock, UK Independence party	1,492	3.2	n/a

Andrew Roth says: "split personality who sometimes seems a partisan right-wing Tory and sometimes still in the SDP"

Recent parliamentary career: shadow secretary of state for International Development (1998–2001); vice-chairman, Conservative party (2001–)
Background: farming; solicitor with expertise in the area of trade union legislation; company director; former SDP Plymouth councillor
Born: October 2 1955 in Hayling Island, Hampshire
Education: Tiverton Grammar School
Higher education: King's College, London
Constituency: Southern Devon, part Plymouth surrounds, part rural and coast

Stringer, Graham
Labour MP for Manchester Blackley since 1997

Majority: 14,464 (54.5%)
Turnout: 44.9%

	Votes	Share %	Change %
Graham Stringer, Labour	18,285	68.9	-1.1
Lance Stanbury, Conservative	3,821	14.4	-0.9
Gary Riding, Liberal Democrat	3,015	11.4	0.4
Ken Barr, Socialist Labour Party	485	1.8	n/a
Karen Reissmann, Socialist Alliance	461	1.7	n/a
Aziz Bhatti, Anti-Corruption	456	1.7	n/a

Andrew Roth says: "swung from being a hard-left headbanger to an Armani-suited world-travelling airport manager"

Recent parliamentary career: government whip (2001–); junior minister, CO (1999–2001)
Background: high-profile former Manchester Council leader; chairman of expanding local airport who pushed through building of second runway
Born: February 17 1950 in Manchester
Education: Moston Brook High School
Higher education: Sheffield University
Constituency: much of central Manchester, including Strangeways Prison and brewery

Stuart, Gisela
Labour MP for Birmingham Edgbaston since 1997

Majority: 4,698 (12.5%)
Turnout: 56%

	Votes	Share %	Change %
Gisela Stuart, Labour	18,517	49.1	0.5
Nigel Hastilow, Conservative	13,819	36.6	–2
Nicola Davies, Liberal Democrat	4,528	12	2.3
Collis Gretton, Pro European Conservative	454	1.2	n/a
Sam Brackenbury, Socialist Labour party	431	1.1	n/a

Andrew Roth says: "a Bavarian success story, a law lecturer who promised to crusade on pensions; believes in constitution reform"

Recent parliamentary career: foreign affairs committee (2001–); junior minister, DoH (1999–2001); PPS to Paul Boateng (1998–99)
Background: German-born law lecturer; came to England at 19 to study business
Born: November 26 1955 in Velden, Germany
Education: Realschule Vilsbiburg
Higher education: London University; Manchester Polytechnic
Constituency: leafy middle class Birmingham bellwether; Labour gain in 1997, its retention in 2001 spelt end for William Hague

Stunell, Andrew
Liberal Democrat MP for Hazel Grove since 1997

Majority: 8,435 (21.9%)
Turnout: 59.1%

	Votes	Share %	Change %
Andrew Stunell, Liberal Democrat	20,020	52	–2.5
Nadine Bargery, Conservative	11,585	30.1	–0.4
Martin Miller, Labour	6,230	16.2	4.3
Gerald Price, UK Independence party	643	1.7	n/a

Andrew Roth says: "highly intelligent practical reformer, a force for national as well as local government reform"

Recent parliamentary career: Lib Dem acting chief whip (2001–); committee of selection (2001–); modernisation of the House of Commons committee (1997–); spokesperson, energy (1997–2001); spokesperson, environment and transport (1997–99)
Background: vice chairman and assistant. Association of Liberal Democratic Councillors (1985–96); architectural assistant; Cheshire councillor; Baptist lay preacher
Born: November 24 1942 in Sutton, Surrey
Education: Surbiton Grammar School
Higher education: Manchester University; Liverpool Polytechnic
Constituency: middle class Manchester commuter town at the top end of the Peak District

Sutcliffe, Gerry
Labour MP for Bradford South since 1994

Majority: 9,662 (27.5%)
Turnout: 51.3%

	Votes	Share %	Change %
Gerry Sutcliffe, Labour	19,603	55.8	−0.9
Graham Tennyson, Conservative	9,941	28.3	0.3
Alexander Wilson-Fletcher, Liberal Democrat	3,717	10.6	−0.7
Peter North, UK Independence party	783	2.2	n/a
Tony Kelly, Socialist Labour Party	571	1.6	n/a
Ateeq Siddique, Socialist Alliance	302	0.9	n/a
George Riseborough, Def Welfare	220	0.6	n/a

Andrew Roth says: "Bradford trade unionist who sees himself as a 'wheeler-dealer schemer'"

Recent parliamentary career: committee of selection (2001–); government whip (1999–); PPS to Stephen Byers (1998–99); PPS to Harriet Harman (1997–98)
Background: print union official; trade unionist (GPMU); Bradford Labour Council Leader
Born: May 13 1953 in Salford
Education: Cardinal Hinsley Grammar School, Bradford
Higher education: Bradford and Ilkley Community College
Constituency: tough innercity seat with few middle class pockets, Tong and Buttershaw

Swayne, Desmond
Conservative MP for New Forest West since 1997

Majority: 13,191 (29.9%)
Turnout: 65%

	Votes	Share %	Change %
Desmond Swayne, Conservative	24,575	55.7	5.1
Mike Bignell, Liberal Democrat	11,384	25.8	−2
Crada Onuegbu, Labour	6,481	14.7	0.4
Michael Clark, UK Independence party	1,647	3.7	n/a

Andrew Roth says: "hyper-assiduous debater with his own semi-comic style concealing a deeply partisan seriousness"

Recent parliamentary career: opposition spokesperson, MOD (2001–); opposition spokesperson, health (2000–01); Scottish affairs (1997–2001); social security committee (1999–2001)
Background: economics teacher; Territorial Army officer and prison visitor; manager of risk management systems at the Royal Bank of Scotland
Born: August 20 1956 in Berne
Education: Bedford School
Higher education: St Andrews University
Constituency: Bournemouth's eastern borders plus coast and forest

Swire, Hugo
Conservative MP for East Devon since 2001

Majority: 8,195 (17.1%)
Turnout: 68.1%

	Votes	Share %	Change %
Hugo Swire, Conservative	22,681	47.4	4
Tim Dumper, Liberal Democrat	14,486	30.3	1.2
Phil Star, Labour	7,974	16.7	−1
David Wilson, UK Independence party	2,696	5.6	n/a

Maiden speech: "In today's world, agriculture and tourism are interlinked. People come to our part of the world and marvel at our landscape."

Recent parliamentary career: elected to parliament 2001
Background: head of development at the National Gallery; director of Sotheby's; army service
Born: November 30 1959
Education: Eton College
Higher education: St Andrews University; Royal Military Academy, Sandhurst
Constituency: many pensioners, includes Budleigh Salterton and Sidmouth

Syms, Robert
Conservative MP for Poole since 1997

Majority: 7,166 (18.2%)
Turnout: 60.7%

	Votes	Share %	Change %
Robert Syms, Conservative	17,710	45.1	3
David Watt, Labour	10,544	26.9	5.3
Nick Westbrook, Liberal Democrat	10,011	25.5	−5.3
John Bass, UK Independence party	968	2.5	n/a

Andrew Roth says: "thoughtful, orthodox right-wing Eurosceptic loyalist"

Recent parliamentary career: Conservative party vice-chairman (2001–); opposition spokesperson, Transport (1999–2001); PPS to Michael Ancram (1999–2000)
Background: managing director, building and plant hire group; Wiltshire councillor; holds a road haulage manager's certificate
Born: August 15 1956 in Chippenham
Education: Colston's School, Bristol
Constituency: growing Dorset town along the coast from Bournemouth

T

Tami, Mark
Labour MP for Alyn and Deeside since 2001

Majority: 9,222 (26.0%)
Turnout: 58.6%

	Votes	Share %	Change %
Mark Tami, Labour	18,525	52.3	−9.6
Mark Isherwood, Conservative	9,303	26.3	3.5
Derek Burnham, Liberal Democrat	4,585	12.9	3.2
Richard Coombs, Plaid Cymru	1,182	3.3	1.5
Klaus Armstrong-Braun, Green party	881	2.5	n/a
William Crawford, UK Independence party	481	1.4	n/a
Max Cooksey, Independent	253	0.7	n/a
Glyn Davies, Communist party	211	0.6	n/a

Maiden speech: "while my constituency is doing well there are still areas of social deprivation and great need"

Recent parliamentary career: elected to parliament 2001; Northern Ireland affairs (2001–)
Background: national head of policy, AEEU; member, Labour National Policy committee (1997–)
Born: October 3 1962
Education: Enfield Grammar School
Higher education: Swansea University
Constituency: north-east Wales by the English border. Gladstone lived here; Shotton steelworks; Toyota and BAe factory

Tapsell, Sir Peter
Conservative MP for Louth and Horncastle since 1997; Lindsey East (1983–97); Horncastle (1966–83); Nottingham West (1959–64)

Majority: 7,554 (17.0%)
Turnout: 62.1%

	Votes	Share %	Change %
Peter Tapsell, Conservative	21,543	48.5	5.1
David Bolland, Labour	13,989	31.5	1.9
Fiona Martin, Liberal Democrat	8,928	20.1	–4.3

Andrew Roth says: "wealthy, world-travelling, Macmillanite one nation type; somewhat of a doommonger"

Recent parliamentary career: able Conservative MP never given office but who would have liked to have been chancellor; considered running for speaker (2000)
Background: banker; corporate adviser; financial adviser to former Sultan of Brunei; army service and life member of the 6th Squadron RAF; over 40 years as a Conservative MP; the only pro-spending Eurosceptic;
Born: February 1 1930 in Sussex
Education: Tonbridge School
Higher education: Oxford, Merton
Constituency: farming villages and seaside towns, includes Mablethorpe and inland Lincolnshire

Taylor, Rt Hon Ann
Labour MP for Dewsbury since 1987; Bolton West (1974–83)

Majority: 7,449 (20.3%)
Turnout: 58.8%

	Votes	Share %	Change %
Ann Taylor, Labour	18,524	50.5	1.1
Robert Robert Cole, Conservative	11,075	30.2	0.1
Ian Cuthbertson, Liberal Democrat	4,382	12	1.7
Russell Smith, British National party	1,632	4.5	–0.7
Brenda Smithson, Green party	560	1.5	n/a
David Pearce, UK Independence party	478	1.3	n/a

Andrew Roth says: "sharp-minded, hard-hitting, talented, a 'traditionalist of the old right'"

Recent parliamentary career: chair, intelligence and security committee (2001–); government chief whip (1998–2001); leader of House of Commons (1997–98)
Background: Open University tutor; monitoring officer, Housing Corporation
Born: July 2 1947 in Motherwell
Education: Bolton School
Higher education: Sheffield and Bradford Universities
Constituency: industrial West Yorkshire town that has lost its textile industry

Taylor, Dari
Labour MP for Stockton South since 1997

Majority: 9,086 (20.6%)
Turnout: 62.2%

	Votes	Share %	Change %
Dari Taylor, Labour	23,414	53	–2.2
Tim Devlin, Conservative	14,328	32.4	–0.6
Suzanne Fletcher, Liberal Democrat	6,012	13.6	4.5
Lawrie Coombes, Socialist Alliance	455	1	n/a

Andrew Roth says: "energetic left of centre Fabian and ex-CND feminist"

Recent parliamentary career: vice chair, Labour women's group (1999–); defence committee (1997–99)
Background: regional education officer; GMB; college lecturer; Sunderland City councillor

Born: December 13 1944 in Rhondda
Education: Ynyshir Girls School, Rhondda
Higher education: Nottingham and Durham Universities; Burnley Municipal College
Constituency: middle class Teesside seat south of Middlesbrough

Taylor, David
Labour MP for North West Leicestershire since 1997

Majority: 8,157 (18.2%)
Turnout: 65.8%

	Votes	Share %	Change %
David Taylor, Labour	23,431	52.1	–4.3
Nick Weston, Conservative	15,274	33.9	2.9
Charlie Fraser-Fleming, Liberal Democrat	4,651	10.3	1.7
William Nattrass, UK Independence party	1,021	2.3	n/a
Robert Nettleton, Independent	632	1.4	n/a

Andrew Roth says: "a highly intelligent, critical Christian socialist, deeply-rooted locally"

Recent parliamentary career: environment, food, and rural affairs committee (2001-);
modernisation of the House of Commons committee (1999–2001)
Background: accountant; computer manager; Leicestershire councillor
Born: August 22 1946 in Ashby de la Zouch
Education: Ashby Grammar School
Higher education: Open University; Coventry Polytechnic; Leicester Polytechnic
Constituency: ex-mining (Coalville); covers historic Ashby de la Zouch and East Midlands Airport

Taylor, Ian
Conservative MP for Esher and Walton since 1997; Esher (1987–97)

Majority: 11,538 (25.4%)
Turnout: 61.9%

	Votes	Share %	Change %
Ian Taylor, Conservative	22,296	49	–0.8
Joe McGowan, Labour	10,758	23.6	0.8
Mark Marsh, Liberal Democrat	10,241	22.5	2.1
Bernard Collignon, UK Independence party	2,236	4.9	n/a

Andrew Roth says: "self-retired Europhile, better regarded by Labour ministers than Tory Eurosceptics"

Recent parliamentary career: had to fight for reselection (2001); opposition spokesperson,
Northern Ireland (1997–97); left frontbench at own request over policy towards single currency
Background: merchant banker; stockbroker; corporate finance and management adviser; company
director; vice chair, European Movement; interested in science
Born: April 18 1945 in Coventry
Education: Whitley Abbey School
Higher education: London School of Economics; Keele University
Constituency: Home Counties stockbroker belt on Thames west of London, includes Thames Ditton

Taylor, John Mark
Conservative MP for Solihull since 1983

Majority: 9,407 (19.4%)
Turnout: 62.6%

	Votes	Share %	Change %
John Mark Taylor, Conservative	21,935	45.4	0.8
Jo Byron, Liberal Democrat	12,528	26	0.7
Brendan O'Brien, Labour	12,373	25.6	1.3
Andy Moore, UK Independence party	1,061	2.2	n/a
J Caffery, ProLife Alliance	374	0.8	–0.3

Andrew Roth says: "no-nonsense, affable rightish loyalist pragmatist"

Recent parliamentary career: opposition spokesperson, Northern Ireland (1999–2001); opposition whip (1997–99)
Background: company director; solicitor; Solihull councillor; MEP (1979–84)
Born: August 19 1941 in Hampton-in-Arden
Education: Bromsgrove School
Higher education: College of Law, London
Constituency: safe, leafy Conservative suburb west of Birmingham

Taylor, Matthew
Liberal Democrat MP for Truro and St Austell since 1997; Truro (1987–97)

Majority: 8,065 (16.0%)
Turnout: 63.5%

	Votes	Share %	Change %
Matthew Taylor, Liberal Democrat	24,296	48.3	–0.2
Tim Bonner, Conservative	16,231	32.3	5.9
David Phillips, Labour	6,889	13.7	–1.6
James Wonnacott, UK Independence party	1,664	3.3	n/a
Conan Jenkin, Mebyon Kernow	1,137	2.3	1.5
John Lee, Independent	78	0.2	n/a

Andrew Roth says: "bright, preening, young hyperactive word-gusher; part of the Kennedy leadership team"

Recent parliamentary career: Lib Dem shadow chancellor (1999–); spokesperson, environment and transport (1997–99)
Background: elected at 24 he was the youngest MP in 1987 and 1992 parliaments; research assistant to David Penhaligon MP, replaced him in parliament after David Penhaligon's death
Born: January 30 1963 in London
Education: Treliske School, Truro
Higher education: Oxford, Lady Margaret Hall; Oxford, University College
Constituency: mainly urban Cornish seat with china clay pits

Taylor, Dr Richard
Kidderminster Hospital and Health Concern MP for Wyre Forest since 2001
Majority: 17,630 (36.0%)
Turnout: 68%

	Votes	Share %	Change %
Richard Taylor, KHHC	28,487	58.1	n/a
David Lock, Labour	10,857	22.1	–26.7
Mark Simpson, Conservative	9,350	19.1	–17
James Millington, UK Independence party	368	0.8	n/a

Maiden speech: "I became an MP because of an all-consuming passion, born out of an intense anger about the arrogant, dismissive and unfair treatment that my friends at home have had to suffer"

Recent parliamentary career: independent backbencher who entered parliament 2001, taking seat from Labour MP and minister; health committee (2001–)
Background: retired consultant physician who ran in the 2001 election as an independent opposing changes at Kidderminster General Hospital
Born: July 7 1934
Education: The Leys School, Cambridge
Higher education: Cambridge, Clare; Westminster Medical School
Constituency: West Midlands seat containing Kidderminster, Bewdley, and rural woodland

Taylor, Sir Teddy
Conservative MP for Rochford and Southend East since 1997; Southend East (1980–97); Glasgow Cathcart (1964–79)

Majority: 7,034 (18.8%)
Turnout: 53.5%

	Votes	Share %	Change %
Teddy Taylor, Conservative	20,058	53.6	4.9
Chris Dandridge, Labour	13,024	34.8	−4.9
Stephen Newton, Liberal Democrat	2,780	7.4	−2
Adrian Hedges, Green party	990	2.6	n/a
Brian Lynch, Liberal	600	1.6	−0.6

Andrew Roth says: "engagingly articulate, fervent, indefatigable, exiled Scots Thatcherite right-wing crusader"

Recent parliamentary career: secretary, European Reform Goup (1980–); Treasury committee (1997–2001)
Background: outspoken Eurosceptic and rebel against John Major who missed promotion to the Cabinet when he lost his seat in 1979; journalist, *Glasgow Herald*; branch manager, Glasgow and West Scotland NUJ; Clyde Shipbuilders' Association official; author; lost Conservative whip for rebellion over Europe (1994–95)
Born: April 18 1937 in Glasgow
Education: the High School of Glasgow
Higher education: Glasgow University
Constituency: seaside Essex town and commuters around Shoeburyness

Thomas, Gareth
Labour MP for Clwyd West since 1997

Majority: 1,115 (3.2%)
Turnout: 64.1%

	Votes	Share %	Change %
Gareth Thomas, Labour	13,426	38.8	1.7
Jimmy James, Conservative	12,311	35.6	3.1
Elfred Williams, Plaid Cymru	4,453	12.9	−0.6
Bobbie Feeley, Liberal Democrat	3,934	11.4	−1.4
Matthew Guest, UK Independence party	476	1.4	n/a

Andrew Roth says: "thoughtful moderate reformer, Welsh devolutionary in the Fabians and Amnesty"

Recent parliamentary career: PPS to Paul Murphy (2001–); social security committee (1999–2001)
Background: barrister; insurer, loss adjuster; Flintshire councillor; Welsh-speaking
Born: September 25 1954 in Bangor, Gwynedd
Education: Rock Ferry High, Birkenhead
Higher education: University of Wales, Aberystwyth
Constituency: North Wales coast near Colwyn Bay

Thomas, Gareth Richard
Labour MP for Harrow West since 1997

Majority: 6,156 (13.2%)
Turnout: 63.5%

	Votes	Share %	Change %
Gareth Thomas, Labour	23,142	49.6	8.1
Danny Finkelstein, Conservative	16,986	36.4	−2.8
Christopher Noyce, Liberal Democrat	5,995	12.9	−2.6
Peter Kefford, UK Independence party	525	1.1	n/a

Andrew Roth says: "assiduous, quick-thinking loyalist"

Recent parliamentary career: introduced private member's bill on provident societies (2001); PPS to Charles Clarke (1999–)
Background: secondary school teacher and Harrow councillor; chair, Co-operative party
Born: July 15 1967 in London
Education: Hatch End High School; Lowlands College
Higher education: University of Wales, Aberystwyth; King's College, London
Constituency: a smart suburban seat in north-west London

Thomas, Simon

Plaid Cymru MP for Ceredigion since 2000

Majority: 3,944 (11.4%)
Turnout: 61.7%

	Votes	Share %	Change %
Simon Thomas, Plaid Cymru	13,241	38.3	–4.5
Mark Williams, Liberal Democrat	9,297	26.9	3.9
Paul Davies, Conservative	6,730	19.5	3
David Grace, Labour	5,338	15.4	1

Andrew Roth says: "Welsh nationalist and earnest apparatchik"

Recent parliamentary career: catering committee (2001–); environmental audit committee (2001–); introduced private member's bill on Welsh housing (2001); elected byelection (2000)
Background: assistant curator, National Library of Wales; policy and research officer; rural development officer; from a Labour supporting family
Born: December 28 1964 in Aberdare
Education: Aberdare Boys' School
Higher education: University of Wales, Aberystwyth
Constituency: once Liberal Welsh-speaking rural central-west Wales including Aberystwyth

Thurso, Viscount John

Liberal Democrat MP for Caithness, Sutherland, and Easter Ross since 2001

Majority: 2,744 (11.1%)
Turnout: 60.3%

	Votes	Share %	Change %
John Thurso, Liberal Democrat	9,041	36.4	0.8
Michael Meighan, Labour	6,297	25.3	–2.5
John MacAdam, Scottish National party	5,273	21.2	–1.8
Robert Rowantree, Conservative	3,513	14.1	3.3
Karn Marbon, Scottish Socialist party	544	2.2	n/a
Gordon Campbell, Independent	199	0.8	n/a

Maiden speech: "the House of Lords Act 1999…permitted me to shake off the shackles of the peerage and return to being a normal human being"

Recent parliamentary career: elected to parliament 2001; culture, media and sport committee (2001–)
Background: former member of the House of Lords, the first hereditary peer to join the Commons; joined Savoy Group 1971; hotel manager; estate owner
Born: October 9 1953
Education: Eton College
Constituency: huge, remote, beyond Highlands; includes Dounreay nuclear plant

Timms, Stephen
Labour MP for East Ham since 1997; Newham North East (1994–97)

Majority: 21,032 (56.4%)
Turnout: 52.3%

	Votes	Share %	Change %
Stephen Timms, Labour	27,241	73.1	8.5
Peter Campbell, Conservative	6,209	16.7	0.6
Bridget Fox, Liberal Democrat	2,600	7	0.5
Rod Finlayson, Socialist Labour party	783	2.1	–4.7
Ms Johinda Pandhal, UK Indepence party	444	1.2	n/a

Andrew Roth says: "churchy idealist"

Recent parliamentary career: minister of state, DFES (2001–); financial secretary, Treasury (1999–2001); minister of state, DSS (1999–99)
Background: mathematical analyst working in computing and telecommunications; Newham councillor
Born: July 29 1955 in Oldham
Education: Farnborough Grammar School
Higher education: Cambridge, Emmanuel
Constituency: outer east London plus some dockland development

Tipping, Paddy
Labour MP for Sherwood since 1992

Majority: 9,373 (20.5%)
Turnout: 60.7%

	Votes	Share %	Change %
Paddy Tipping, Labour	24,900	54.3	–4.2
Brandon Lewis, Conservative	15,527	33.8	5
Peter Harris, Liberal Democrat	5,473	11.9	3.3

Matthew Parris, *The Times* says: "he's so unimportant that Labour's style police have not even bothered to remove his beard"

Recent parliamentary career: junior minister, Privy Council Office (1999–2001); PPS to Jack Straw (1997–99)
Background: project leader, CE Children's Society; social worker; Nottinghamshire County councillor
Born: October 24 1949 in Halifax
Education: Hipperholme Grammar School
Higher education: Nottingham University
Constituency: diverse seat with rural Tory villages and modern mining industry

Todd, Mark
Labour MP for South Derbyshire since 1997

Majority: 7,851 (15.1%)
Turnout: 64.1%

	Votes	Share %	Change %
Mark Todd, Labour	26,338	50.7	–3.8
James Hakewill, Conservative	18,487	35.6	4.3
Russell Eagling, Liberal Democrat	5,233	10.1	1.1
John Blunt, UK Independence party	1,074	2.1	n/a
Paul Liversuch, Socialist Labour party	564	1.1	n/a
James Taylor, Independent	249	0.5	n/a

Andrew Roth says: "reasonable, respected, and centre-left grandson of a Tory MP"

Recent parliamentary career: environment, food, and rural affairs committee (2001–); agriculture committee (1997–2001)
Background: Cambridge City Council leader; director of information technology company; publisher, Longman Group (1977–92)
Born: December 29 1954 in Dorchester
Education: Sherborne School
Higher education: Cambridge, Emmanuel
Constituency: semi-rural seat, south of Derby; Edwina Currie was MP

Tonge, Dr Jenny
Liberal Democrat MP for Richmond Park since 1997

Majority: 4,964 (10.1%)
Turnout: 67.6%

	Votes	Share %	Change %
Jenny Tonge, Liberal Democrat	23,444	47.7	3
Tom Harris, Conservative	18,480	37.6	–1.9
Barry Langford, Labour	5,541	11.3	–1.3
James Page, Green party	1,223	2.5	n/a
Peter St John Howe, UK Independence party	348	0.7	n/a
Raymond Perrin, Independent	115	0.2	n/a

Andrew Roth says: "on the Liberal Democrats' social democratic wing, infinitely closer to Clare Short than to the Tories"

Recent parliamentary career: Lib Dem spokesperson, international development (1999–); spokesperson, foreign affairs, defence and Europe (1997–99)
Background: NHS clinical medical officer; community health manager
Born: February 19 1941 in Walsall
Education: Dudley Girls' High School
Higher education: University College Hospital, London
Constituency: green, spacious west London residential area

Touhig, Don
Labour MP for Islwyn since 1995

Majority: 15,309 (48.4%)
Turnout: 61.9%

	Votes	Share %	Change %
Don Touhig, Labour	19,505	61.6	–12.6
Kevin Etheridge, Liberal Democrat	4,196	13.2	4.8
Leigh Thomas, Plaid Cymru	3,767	11.9	5.7
Philip Howells, Conservative	2,543	8	0.1
Paul Taylor, Independent	1,263	4	n/a
Mary Millington, Socialist Labour party	417	1.3	n/a

Andrew Roth says: "loyal footsoldier in Blair's model army"

Recent parliamentary career: junior minister, Wales Office (2001–); government whip (1999–2001); PPS to Gordon Brown (1997–99)
Background: newspaper editor; printing company executive; Gwent County councillor
Born: December 5 1947 in Abersychan, Gwent
Education: St Francis School, Abersychan
Higher education: East Monmouthshire College, Pontypool
Constituency: valley towns with recovering economy, Neil Kinnock was MP

Tredinnick, David
Conservative MP for Bosworth since 1987

Majority: 2,280 (5.0%)
Turnout: 64.4%

	Votes	Share %	Change %
David Tredinnick, Conservative	20,030	44.4	3.8
Andrew Furlong, Labour	17,750	39.4	0.7
Jon Ellis, Liberal Democrat	7,326	16.2	−1.6

Andrew Roth says: "indicates that extensive education does not necessarily hone judgement"

Recent parliamentary career: chair, joint committee on statutory instruments (1997–); resigned as a PPS over cash for questions (1994)
Background: marketing manager, QI Europe Ltd; Malden Mitcham Properties; armed forces
Born: January 19 1950 in Worthing
Education: Eton College
Higher education: Cape Town University; Oxford, St John's
Constituency: big Leicestershire seat centred on Hinckley and Bosworth

Trend, Michael
Conservative MP for Windsor since 1997; Windsor and Maidenhead (1992–97)

Majority: 8,889 (21.1%)
Turnout: 60.9%

	Votes	Share %	Change %
Michael Trend, Conservative	19,900	47.3	−0.9
Nick Pinfield, Liberal Democrat	11,011	26.2	−2.5
Mark Muller, Labour	10,137	24.1	5.8
John Fagan, UK Independence party	1,062	2.5	n/a

Andrew Roth says: "highly intelligent mainstreamer and perceptive journalist who cannot 'let himself go' as a politician"

Recent parliamentary career: public administration committee (2001–); opposition spokesperson, social security (1999–); opposition spokesperson, foreign affairs (1998–99)
Background: journalist, *Daily Telegraph* (chief leader writer 1990–92); political aide to Norman Tebbit; author
Born: April 19 1952 in Greenwich
Education: Westminster School
Higher education: Oxford, Oriel
Constituency: upmarket town west of London, including Sunningdale and Ascot

Trickett, Jon
Labour MP for Hemsworth since 1996

Majority: 15,636 (44.4%)
Turnout: 51.8%

	Votes	Share %	Change %
Jon Trickett, Labour	23,036	65.4	−5.2
Elizabeth Truss, Conservative	7,400	21	3.2
Ed Waller, Liberal Democrat	3,990	11.3	2.4
Paul Turek, Socialist Labour Party	801	2.3	n/a
Marie Middleton, UK Independence party			n/a

Andrew Roth says: "quiet, thoughtful left-of-centre local loyalist"

Recent parliamentary career: public accounts committee (2001–); PPS to Peter Mandelson (1997–98); elected byelection (1996)

Background: builder; plumber; Leeds City councillor
Born: July 2 1950 in Leeds
Education: Roundhay High School
Higher education: Leeds University; Hull University
Constituency: bleak South Yorkshire ex-mining towns once famous as the place where Labour votes were said to be weighed, not counted

Trimble, Rt Hon David
Ulster Unionist MP for Upper Bann since 1990

Majority: 2,058 (4.0%)
Turnout: 70.3%

	Votes	Share %	Change %
David Trimble, Ulster Unionist party	17,095	33.5	−10.1
David Simpson, Democratic Unionist party	15,037	29.5	18
Dr Dara O'Hagan, Sinn Fein	10,770	21.1	9
Dolores Kelly, Social Democratic and Labour Party	7,607	14.9	−9.3
Tom French, Workers' party	527	1	−0.2

Andrew Roth says: "a class performer on the slack high wire of Ulster Unionist politics"

Recent parliamentary career: first minister, Northern Ireland Executive (1998–2001) resigning over IRA decommissioning; leader of the Ulster Unionist party (1995–)
Background: senior law lecturer, Queen's University, Belfast; member, NIA; once a hardline Unionist in Vanguard Unionist party, now moderate; supporter of peace process, to dismay of many in his party; awarded Nobel Peace Prize (1998); opera fan
Born: October 15 1944 in Belfast
Education: Bangor Grammar School
Higher education: Queen's University, Belfast
Constituency: rural Ulster plus Portadown and Craigavon new town

Truswell, Paul
Labour MP for Pudsey since 1997

Majority: 5,626 (12.5%)
Turnout: 63.3%

	Votes	Share %	Change %
Paul Truswell, Labour	21,717	48.1	0
John Procter, Conservative	16,091	35.6	−0.7
Stephen Boddy, Liberal Democrat	6,423	14.2	0.2
David Sewards, UK Independence party	944	2.1	n/a

Andrew Roth says: "health, environment and freedom of information crusader"

Recent parliamentary career: introduced private member's bill to prosecute off licence staff for underage sales (1999); environmental audit committee (1997–99)
Background: local government officer; local journalist
Born: November 17 1955 in Sheffield
Education: Firth Park Comprehensive School
Higher education: Leeds University
Constituency: residential area between Leeds and Bradford

Turner, Andrew
Conservative MP for the Isle of Wight since 2001

Majority: 2,826 (4.5%)
Turnout: 59.7%

	Votes	Share %	Change %
Andrew Turner, Conservative	25,223	39.7	5.7
Peter Brand, Liberal Democrat	22,397	35.3	−7.5
Deborah Gardiner, Labour	9,676	15.2	2.1
David Lott, UK Independence party	2,106	3.3	1.9
David Holmes, Independent	1,423	2.2	1.1
Paul Scivier, Green party	1,279	2	1.3
Philip Murray, Isle of Wight party	1,164	1.8	n/a
James Spensley, Independent	214	0.3	n/a

Maiden speech: "I am not the sort of Conservative who is known for wearing his compassion on his sleeve, but I am passionate about education, health and housing"

Recent parliamentary career: elected to parliament 2001, taking seat from Lib Dem; education and skills committee (2001–)
Background: teacher; education consultant and adviser to DHSS ministers; founded Grant Maintained Schools Foundation
Born: October 24 1953
Education: Rugby School
Higher education: Birmingham University
Constituency: island containing Britain's biggest electorate; Lib Dems won in the 1970s and 1997; Tory gain 2001

Turner, Dennis
Labour MP for Wolverhampton South East since 1987

Majority: 12,464 (45.6%)
Turnout: 50.6%

	Votes	Share %	Change %
Dennis Turner, Labour	18,409	67.4	3.7
Adrian Pepper, Conservative	5,945	21.8	1.6
Peter Wild, Liberal Democrat	2,389	8.8	−0.7
James Barry, National Front	554	2	n/a

Andrew Roth says: "Clare Short's Black Country left-wing working class aide"

Recent parliamentary career: introduced private member's bill on energy conservation (2001); PPS to Clare Short (1997–); chair, catering committee (1997–); runs House of Commons bars and restaurants
Background: Wolverhampton steelworker
Born: August 26 1942 in Bilston, Staffordshire
Education: Stonefield Secondary School; Bilston College of Education
Constituency: Black Country industrial seat based around Bilston

Turner, Dr Desmond
Labour MP for Brighton Kemptown since 1997

Majority: 4,922 (12.5%)
Turnout: 58%

	Votes	Share %	Change %
Desmond Turner, Labour	18,745	47.8	1.2
Geoffrey Theobald, Conservative	13,823	35.3	−3.6
Janet Marshall, Liberal Democrat	4,064	10.4	0.7
Hugh Miller, Green party	1,290	3.3	n/a
James Chamberlain-Webber, UK Independence party	543	1.4	n/a
John McLeod, Socialist Labour Party	364	0.9	0.2
Dave Dobbs, Free	227	0.6	n/a
Elaine Cook, ProLife Alliance	147	0.4	n/a

Andrew Roth says: "interlaces rebellions over disability cuts and air traffic control privatisation with sycophantic questions to Blair"

Recent parliamentary career: science and technology committee (1997–2001)
Background: biochemist lecturer who founded a brewery; Brighton and Hove councillor
Born: July 17 1939 in Southampton
Education: Luton Grammar School
Higher education: Imperial College, London; University College, London
Constituency: mixed Brighton seat, includes some big council estates but also an ageing Tory vote

Turner, Neil
Labour MP for Wigan since 1999

Majority: 13,743 (40.9%)
Turnout: 52.5%

	Votes	Share %	Change %
Neil Turner, Labour	20,739	61.7	2.1
Mark Page, Conservative	6,996	20.8	2.8
Trevor Beswick, Liberal Democrat	4,970	14.8	1.5
David Lowe, Socialist Alliance	886	2.6	n/a

Andrew Roth says: "on-message municipal safe pair of hands"

Recent parliamentary career: PPS to Ian McCartney (2001–); public administration committee (2000–2001); elected in byelection (1999)
Background: quantity surveyor; company director; Wigan councillor
Born: September 16 1945 in Carlisle
Education: Carlisle Grammar School
Constituency: proud, industrial north-west town

Twigg, Derek
Labour MP for Halton since 1997

Majority: 17,428 (50.6%)
Turnout: 54.1%

	Votes	Share %	Change %
Derek Twigg, Labour	23,841	69.2	−1.7
Chris Davenport, Conservative	6,413	18.6	0.9
Peter Walker, Liberal Democrat	4,216	12.2	4.9

Andrew Roth says: "super-loyal on-message backbencher"

Recent parliamentary career: PPS to Stephen Byers (2001–); PPS to Helen Liddell (1999–2001); public accounts committee (1998–99)
Background: civil servant, DFEE (1975–96); political adviser to the PST trade union
Born: July 9 1959 in Widnes
Education: Bankfield High School, Widnes; Halton College of Education, Widnes
Constituency: includes Runcorn and Widnes; big chemical plants

Twigg, Stephen
Labour MP for Enfield Southgate since 1997

Majority: 5,546 (13.2%)
Turnout: 63.1%

	Votes	Share %	Change %
Stephen Twigg, Labour	21,727	51.8	7.6
John Flack, Conservative	16,181	38.6	−2.5
Wayne Hoban, Liberal Democrat	2,935	7	−3.7
Ms Elaine Graham-Leigh, Green party	662	1.6	n/a
Roy Freshwater, UK Independence party	298	0.7	n/a
Andrew Malakouna, Independent	105	0.3	n/a

Andrew Roth says: "young, openly gay Portillo-terminator; very talented Blairite Fabian wunderkind"

Recent parliamentary career: parliamentary secretary to leader of the House of Commons (2001–); employment subcommittee (1999–2001); education and employment committee (1999–2001)
Background: general secretary, Fabian Society; parliamentary officer: Amnesty, NCVO, International UK; research assistant, Margaret Hodge MP; political consultant, Rowland Sallingbury Casey; president, NUS; Islington councillor
Born: December 25 1966 in Enfield
Education: Southgate Comprehensive School
Higher education: Oxford, Balliol
Constituency: north London suburbia at western edge of Enfield around Winchmore Hill and Oakwood

Tyler, Paul
Liberal Democrat MP for North Cornwall since 1992; Bodmin (February–October 1974)

Majority: 9,832 (18.2%)
Turnout: 63.8%

	Votes	Share %	Change %
Paul Tyler, Liberal Democrat	28,082	52	–1.2
John Weller, Conservative	18,250	33.8	4.3
Mike Goodman, Labour	5,257	9.7	0.3
Stephen Protz, UK Independence party	2,394	4.4	n/a

Andrew Roth says: "shrewd middle-aged veteran of nine general elections"

Recent parliamentary career: Lib Dem shadow leader of the House (2001–); modernisation of the House of Commons committee (2001–); chief whip and shadow leader of the House (1997–2001); spokesperson, food (1997–99)
Background: founded own PR firm, Western Approaches; consultant and lobbyist, Good Relations; publisher
Born: October 29 1941 in Newton Abbot, Devon
Education: Sherborne School
Higher education: Oxford, Exeter
Constituency: isolated north Cornish Atlantic coast

Tynan, Bill
Labour MP for Hamilton South since 1999

Majority: 10,775 (40.3%)
Turnout: 57.3%

	Votes	Share %	Change %
Bill Tynan, Labour	15,965	59.7	22.9
John Wilson, Scottish National party	5,190	19.4	–14.6
John Oswald, Liberal Democrat	2,381	8.9	n/a
Neil Richardson, Conservative	1,876	7	–0.2
Gena Mitchell, Scottish Socialist party	1,187	4.4	–5.1
Janice Murdoch, UK Independence party	151	0.6	n/a

Andrew Roth says: "safe, loyal pair of hands interested in employment law, social security, equal opportunities and social inclusion"

Recent parliamentary career: Northern Ireland affairs (2001–); European scrutiny committee (2001–); scottish affairs committee (1999–2001); elected in byelection (1999)
Background: press toolmaker; fulltime trade unionist (AEU)
Born: August 18 1940 in Glasgow
Education: St Mungo's Academy, Glasgow
Higher education: Stow College
Constituency: town on the M74, south of Glasgow

Tyrie, Andrew
Conservative MP for Chichester since 1997

Majority: 11,355 (22.9%)
Turnout: 63.7%

	Votes	Share %	Change %
Andrew Tyrie, Conservative	23,320	47.1	0.7
Lynne Ravenscroft, Liberal Democrat	11,965	24.2	–4.8
Celia Barlow, Labour	10,627	21.5	4.3
Douglas Denny, UK Independence party	2,308	4.7	n/a
Gavin Graham, Green party	1,292	2.6	n/a

Andrew Roth says: "came out of the special advisers' back rooms into the light of the parliamentary day"

Recent parliamentary career: Kenneth Clarke's campaign manager (2001); Treasury committee (2001–); joint committee on consolidation of bills (1997–); public administration committee (1997–2001)
Background: senior economist; Treasury special adviser; assisted John Major; campaigner for parliamentary (but not electoral) reform
Born: January 15 1957 in Rochford
Education: Felstead School, Essex
Higher education: Smithsonian Institute; College of Europe; Oxford, Trinity; Cambridge, Wolfson
Constituency: smart, safe Southern Conservative seat, mainly rural

V

Vaz, Keith
Labour MP for Leicester East since 1987

Majority: 13,442 (33.1%)
Turnout: 62.1%

	Votes	Share %	Change %
Keith Vaz, Labour	23,402	57.6	–7.9
John Mugglestone, Conservative	9,960	24.5	0.5
Harpinder Athwal, Liberal Democrat	4,989	12.3	5.3
Dave Roberts, Socialist Labour Party	837	2.1	1.1
Clive Potter, British National party	772	1.9	n/a
Shirley Bennett, Independent	701	1.7	n/a

Andrew Roth says: "a man of fickle flexibility, a preening weathervane interested mainly in admirers"

Recent parliamentary career: minister of state, FCO (1999–2001); minister of state, LCD (1999–99); PPS to law officers (1997–99)
Background: barrister and solicitor; Leicester councillor; controversially involved in Hinduja passports affair (2001); comes from Goanese Catholic family
Born: November 26 1956 in Aden
Education: Latymer Upper School
Higher education: College of Law, London; Cambridge, Gonville and Caius
Constituency: innercity Leicester, strongly Asian

Viggers, Peter
Conservative MP for Gosport since 1974

Majority: 2,621 (6.5%)
Turnout: 57.2%

	Votes	Share %	Change %
Peter Viggers, Conservative	17,364	43.6	0
Richard Williams, Labour	14,743	37.1	6.4
Roger Roberts, Liberal Democrat	6,011	15.1	−4.5
John Bowles, UK Independence party	1,162	2.9	n/a
Kevin Chetwynd, Socialist Labour party	509	1.3	n/a

Andrew Roth says: "fading but intelligent company solicitor who has behind the scenes influence"

Recent parliamentary career: defence committee (2000–2001)
Background: company director; career in the RAF, Lloyds and the City; main interest in defence
Born: March 13 1938 in Gosport
Education: Portsmouth Grammar School
Higher education: College of Law, London; Cambridge, Trinity Hall
Constituency: seaside, working-class town; still Conservative thanks to Royal Navy base

Vis, Dr Rudi
Labour MP for Finchley and Golders Green since 1997

Majority: 3,716 (8.5%)
Turnout: 57.3%

	Votes	Share %	Change %
Rudi Vis, Labour	20,205	46.3	0.2
John Marshall, Conservative	16,489	37.8	−1.9
Sarah Teather, Liberal Democrat	5,266	12.1	0.8
Miranda Dunn, Green party	1,385	3.2	n/a
John de Roeck, UK Independence party	330	0.8	n/a

Andrew Roth says: "Europhile who was surprised at winning his 'hopeless' seat"

Recent parliamentary career: active in Council of Europe (1997–) and Western EU (1997–); less active in Commons
Background: Dutch-born; economics lecturer for 26 years; Barnet councillor; was in the Dutch Army; pro-Euro
Born: April 4 1941 in Alkmaar, Netherlands
Education: High School, Alkmaar, Netherlands
Higher education: London School of Economics; Brunel University; University of Maryland, USA
Constituency: inner-north London suburbs on the Northern Line; once Mrs Thatcher's seat

W

Walley, Joan
Labour MP for Stoke-on-Trent North since 1987

Majority: 11,784 (39.1%)
Turnout: 51.9%

	Votes	Share %	Change %
Joan Walley, Labour	17,460	58	−7.1
Benjamin Browning, Conservative	5,676	18.9	−1.3
Henry Jebb, Liberal Democrat	3,580	11.9	1.2
Lee Wanger, Independent	3,399	11.3	n/a

Andrew Roth says: "worthy, diffuse green feminist and gentle crusader for good causes"

Recent parliamentary career: environmental audit committee (1997–); former opposition frontbencher; close to Neil Kinnock
Background: social work researcher and local government officer; Lambeth councillor; Campaign Group member

Born: January 23 1949 in Congleton, Cheshire
Education: Biddulph Grammar School
Higher education: University College, Swansea ; Hull University
Constituency: archetypal Potteries towns including Burslem and much of Stoke

Walter, Robert
Conservative MP for North Dorset since 1997

Majority: 3,797 (8.0%)
Turnout: 66.3%

	Votes	Share %	Change %
Robert Walter, Conservative	22,314	46.7	2.4
Emily Gasson, Liberal Democrat	18,517	38.7	−0.4
Mark Wareham, Labour	5,334	11.2	1
Peter Jenkins, UK Independence party	1,019	2.1	n/a
Joseph Duthie, Low Excise	391	0.8	n/a
Mrs Cora Bone, Independent	246	0.5	n/a

Andrew Roth says: "international banker and sheep farmer in the parliamentary mainstream of pro-European Tories"

Recent parliamentary career: opposition spokesperson, Wales (1999–2001); unopposed bills panel (1997–); backed Kenneth Clarke for leader (1997 and 2001)
Background: farmer; international banker
Born: May 30 1948 in Swansea
Education: Lord Weymouth School
Higher education: Aston University, Birmingham
Constituency: rolling north Dorset farmland and elegant Shaftesbury

Ward, Claire
Labour MP for Watford since 1997

Majority: 5,555 (12.0%)
Turnout: 61.2%

	Votes	Share %	Change %
Claire Ward, Labour	20,992	45.3	0
Michael McManus, Conservative	15,437	33.3	−1.5
Duncan Hames, Liberal Democrat	8,088	17.4	0.6
Denise Kingsley, Green party	900	1.9	n/a
Edmund Stewart-Mole, UK Independence party	535	1.2	n/a
Jon Berry, Socialist Alliance	420	0.9	n/a

Andrew Roth says: "cautious young politico…and assiduous wide-ranging activist"

Recent parliamentary career: PPS to John Hutton (2001–); culture, media and sport committee (1997–2001); joint secretary, all-party Film Group
Background: solicitor; mayor of Borehamwood
Born: May 9 1972 in North Shields
Education: Loretto School, St Albans
Higher education: College of Law, London; Brunel University; Hertfordshire University
Constituency: town on north-west edge of London with much light industry

Wareing, Robert
Labour MP for Liverpool West Derby since 1983

Majority: 15,853 (51.3%)
Turnout: 45.5%

	Votes	Share %	Change %
Robert Wareing, Labour	20,454	66.2	−5
Steve Radford, Liberal	4,601	14.9	5.3
Patrick Moloney, Liberal Democrat	3,366	10.9	1.9
Bill Clare, Conservative	2,486	8	−0.7

Andrew Roth says: "warm-hearted, wordy survivor of local Labour factionalism in Liverpool"

Recent parliamentary career: secretary, British-Russian Parliamentary Group (1997–); treasurer, British-Azerbaijan Parliamentary Group (1997–)
Background: pro-Serb; suspended by parliamentary Labour party (1997) after failing to disclose directorship of a company which has provided consultancy services for a blacklisted company with Serb links; rebelled against Labour (1997) over benefit cuts; narrowly reselected (2000); further education lecturer
Born: August 20 1930 in Liverpool
Education: Alsop High School, Liverpool
Higher education: London University; Bolton College of Education
Constituency: outer Liverpool suburbs and council estates; Liberals (not Lib Dems) come second here

Waterson, Nigel
Conservative MP for Eastbourne since 1992

Majority: 2,154 (4.8%)
Turnout: 60.7%

	Votes	Share %	Change %
Nigel Waterson, Conservative	19,738	44.1	2
Chris Berry, Liberal Democrat	17,584	39.3	1
Gillian Roles, Labour	5,967	13.3	0.8
Roy Maryon, UK Independence party	907	2	n/a
Ms Theresa Williamson, Liberal	574	1.3	−0.1

Andrew Roth says: "mainstream immigration and asylum-preoccupied marine lawyer"

Recent parliamentary career: opposition spokesperson, DTI (2001–); opposition spokesperson, environment (1999–2001); opposition whip (1997–99); PPS to Michael Heseltine (1996–97)
Background: solicitor and barrister
Born: October 12 1950 in Bradford
Education: Leeds Grammar School
Higher education: Oxford, Queen's
Constituency: southern seaside town; many pensioners

Watkinson, Angela
Conservative MP for Upminster since 2001

Majority: 1,241 (3.6%)
Turnout: 59.6%

	Votes	Share %	Change %
Angela Watkinson, Conservative	15,410	45.5	6
Keith Darvill, Labour	14,169	41.9	−4.3
Peter Truesdale, Liberal Democrat	3,183	9.4	−0.1
Terry Murray, UK Independence party	1,089	3.2	n/a

Maiden speech: "having spent 12 years working in a special needs school, I know that it is impossible to generalise about special needs pupils"

Recent parliamentary career: elected to parliament 2001, taking seat from Labour; home affairs committee (2001–)
Background: banker; school governor; worked at special school for physically handicapped children

Born: November 18 1941
Education: Wanstead County High School
Higher education: Anglia University
Constituency: Essex-London border town at the end of the District line, with some farms

Watson, Tom
Labour MP for West Bromwich East since 2001

Majority: 9,763 (29.9%)
Turnout: 53.4%

	Votes	Share %	Change %
Tom Watson, Labour	18,250	55.9	–1.3
David MacFarlane, Conservative	8,487	26	1.6
Ian Garrett, Liberal Democrat	4,507	13.8	–1.1
Steven Grey, UK Independence party	835	2.6	n/a
Sheera Johal, Socialist Labour Party	585	1.8	n/a

Maiden speech: "One of the most frightening experiences of the election campaign was drawing the bingo numbers at the Friar Park millennium centre in Wednesbury"

Recent parliamentary career: elected to parliament 2001; home affairs committee (2001–)
Background: trade union official: political organiser for AEEU; member of Labour party since 16; anti-electoral reform
Born: January 8 1967
Education: King Charles I school, Kidderminster
Constituency: urban West Midlands seat

Watts, David
Labour MP for St Helens North since 1997

Majority: 15,901 (42.3%)
Turnout: 53.3%

	Votes	Share %	Change %
David Watts, Labour	22,977	61.1	–3.8
Simon Pearce, Conservative	7,076	18.8	1.5
John Beirne, Liberal Democrat	6,609	17.6	4.9
Steve Watham, Socialist Labour party	939	2.5	0.8

Andrew Roth says: "self described as 'middle of the road Labour'"

Recent parliamentary career: PPS to John Spellar (2001–); finance and services committee (1997–2001)
Background: research assistant to the seat's former MP John Evans; St Helen's councillor and leader
Born: August 26 1951
Education: Seel Road Secondary Modern School
Constituency: Merseyside industrial town, includes Newton-le-Willows

Webb, Professor Steve
Liberal Democrat MP for Northavon since 1997

Majority: 9,877 (17.7%)
Turnout: 70.7%

	Votes	Share %	Change %
Steve Webb, Liberal Democrat	29,217	52.4	10
Carrie Ruxton, Conservative	19,340	34.7	–4.3
Robert Hall, Labour	6,450	11.6	–4
Carmen Carver, UK Independence party	751	1.4	n/a

Andrew Roth says: "social security specialist and economist with Christian beliefs"

Recent parliamentary career: Lib Dem spokesperson, work and pensions (2001–); spokesperson, social security and welfare (1997–2001)
Background: Professor of Social Policy, Bath University; professional economist; programme director, Institute of Fiscal Studies; noted Commons expert on social security
Born: July 18 1965 in Birmingham
Education: Dartmouth High School, Birmingham
Higher education: Oxford, Hertford
Constituency: commuter land north of Bristol, M4 and the Severn Bridge

Weir, Michael
Scottish National party MP for Angus since 2001

Majority: 3,611 (10.3%)
Turnout: 59.3%

	Votes	Share %	Change %
Michael Weir, Scottish National party	12,347	35.3	–13
Marcus Booth, Conservative	8,736	25	0.4
Ian McFatridge, Labour	8,183	23.4	7.8
Peter Nield, Liberal Democrat	5,015	14.3	4.9
Bruce Wallace, Scottish Socialist party	732	2.1	n/a

Maiden speech: "Angus includes my home town of Arbroath, where the first declaration of Scottish independence was signed in 1320 and where we look forward to hosting the signing of the next"

Recent parliamentary career: elected to parliament 2001; Scottish affairs committee (2001–)
Background: solicitor; local councillor
Born: March 24 1957
Education: Arbroath High School
Higher education: Aberdeen University
Constituency: Montrose and Arbroath; rural but not remote Scotland

White, Brian
Labour MP for Milton Keynes North East since 1997

Majority: 1,829 (3.9%)
Turnout: 62.4%

	Votes	Share %	Change %
Brian White, Labour	19,761	42	2.6
Marion Rix, Conservative	17,932	38.1	–0.9
David Yeoward, Liberal Democrat	8,375	17.8	0.4
Michael Phillips, UK Independence party	1,026	2.2	n/a

Andrew Roth says: "cadaverous, pragmatic realist"

Recent parliamentary career: deregulation committee (2001–); joint committee on statutory instruments (2001–); public administration committee (1999–); backs electoral reform and freedom of information
Background: developer and designer of computer systems; Milton Keynes councillor for ten years
Born: May 5 1957 in Isleworth
Education: Methodist College, Belfast
Constituency: upmarket part of new town plus villages and Newport Pagnell on the M1

Whitehead, Dr Alan
Labour MP for Southampton Test since 1997

Majority: 11,207 (27.0%)
Turnout: 56.3%

	Votes	Share %	Change %
Alan Whitehead, Labour	21,824	52.5	−1.6
Richard Gueterbock, Conservative	10,617	25.5	−2.6
John Shaw, Liberal Democrat	7,522	18.1	4.4
Garry Rankin-Moore, UK Independence party	792	1.9	n/a
Mark Abel, Socialist Alliance	442	1.1	n/a
Paramjit Bahia, Socialist Labour party	378	0.9	n/a

Andrew Roth says: "moved from being a semi-hard left-winger twenty years ago to a soft-leftist now"

Recent parliamentary career: junior minister, DTLGR (2001–); PPS to Baroness Blackstone (1999–2001)
Background: professor of Public Policy, Southampton Institute; Southampton councillor and leader; member of Labour National Policy Forum (1999–)
Born: September 15 1950 in Isleworth
Education: Isleworth Grammar School
Higher education: Southampton University
Constituency: western part of Southampton including Ford Transit factory and suburbs

Whittingdale, John
Conservative MP for Maldon and Chelmsford East since 1997; South Colchester and Maldon (1992–97)

Majority: 8,462 (19.2%)
Turnout: 63.7%

	Votes	Share %	Change %
John Whittingdale, Conservative	21,719	49.3	0.6
Russell Kennedy, Labour	13,257	30.1	1.4
Jane Jackson, Liberal Democrat	7,002	15.9	−3.5
Geoffrey Harris, UK Independence party	1,135	2.6	n/a
Walter Schwartz, Green party	987	2.2	0.8

Andrew Roth says: "former political secretary to Margaret Thatcher who lost favour with John Major for his Maastricht rebellions"

Recent parliamentary career: shadow secretary of state, DTI (2001–); trade and industry committee (2001); PPS to William Hague (1999–2001); opposition spokesperson, Treasury (1998–99); opposition whip (1997–98)
Background: special adviser, DTI; banker; political secretary to Margaret Thatcher; part of Conservative Research Department before the 1979 election
Born: October 16 1959 in Sherborne, Dorset
Education: Winchester College; Sandroyd School, Wiltshire
Higher education: University College, London
Constituency: North Sea coast, centred on Maldon and Burnham-on-Crouch

Wicks, Malcolm
Labour MP for Croydon North since 1997; Croydon North West (1992–97)
Majority: 16,858 (40.2%)
Turnout: 54.7%

	Votes	Share %	Change %
Malcolm Wicks, Labour	26,610	63.5	1.3
Simon Allison, Conservative	9,752	23.3	−3.9
Sandra Lawman, Liberal Democrat	4,375	10.5	2.8
Alan Smith, UK Independence party	606	1.5	n/a
Don Madgwick, Socialist Alliance	539	1.3	n/a

Andrew Roth says: "soft-left academic family policy specialist, a prolific author on social problems"

Recent parliamentary career: junior minister, DWP (2001–); junior minister, DFEE (1999–2001);

Background: sociologist; lecturer in social administration; founded Family Policy Studies Centre; company director
Born: July 1 1947 in Hatfield, Hertfordshire
Education: Elizabeth College, Guernsey
Higher education: London School of Economics; North West London Polytechnic
Constituency: suburban sprawl on northern edge of booming Croydon

Widdecombe, Rt Hon Ann
Conservative MP for Maidstone and The Weald since 1997; Maidstone (1987–97)

Majority: 10,318 (22.6%)
Turnout: 61.6%

	Votes	Share %	Change %
Ann Widdecombe, Conservative	22,621	49.6	5.5
Mark Davis, Labour	12,303	27	0.8
Allison Wainman, Liberal Democrat	9,064	19.9	–2.5
John Botting, UK Independence party	978	2.2	n/a
Neil Hunt, Independent	611	1.3	n/a

Andrew Roth says: "sharp minded, forthright, hard right veteran"

Recent parliamentary career: shadow home secretary (1999–2001); spoke out against Michael Portillo's bid for leadership (2001) while admitting she did not have the support of enough MPs to stand herself; shadow health secretary (1998–99); minister of state, HO (1995–1997)
Background: Unilever marketing department; senior administrator, University of London; Runnymede councillor
Born: October 31 1947 in Bath
Education: Royal Naval School, Singapore; La Sainte Union Convent, Bath
Higher education: Oxford, Lady Margaret Hall; Birmingham University
Constituency: safe urban-rural seat in prosperous part of Kent

Wiggin, Bill
Conservative MP for Leominster since 2001

Majority: 10,367 (22.2%)
Turnout: 68%

	Votes	Share %	Change %
Bill Wiggin, Conservative	22,879	49	3.7
Celia Downie, Liberal Democrat	12,512	26.8	–1
Stephen Hart, Labour	7,872	16.9	–0.6
Pippa Bennett, Green party	1,690	3.6	n/a
Christopher Kinglsey, UK Independence party	1,590	3.4	n/a
John Haycock, Independent	186	0.4	n/a

Maiden speech: "The seat of Leominster has a history of unusual members… one shot himself, one was hanged and another was imprisoned in the Tower during the South Sea bubble crisis"

Recent parliamentary career: elected to parliament 2001; transport, local government, and the regions committee (2001–); Welsh affairs committee (2001–)
Background: foreign exchange banker; officer in Territorial Army; father was MP for Weston-super-Mare
Born: June 4 1966
Education: Eton College
Higher education: University College, North Wales
Constituency: Marches border seat that runs from Wales into Worcestershire and from Shropshire to the Wye Valley

Wilkinson, John
Conservative MP for Ruislip Northwood since 1979; Bradford West (1970–74)

Majority: 7,537 (20.3%)
Turnout: 61.1%

	Votes	Share %	Change %
John Wilkinson, Conservative	18,115	48.8	−1.4
Gillian Travers, Labour	10,578	28.5	−4.4
Mike Cox, Liberal Democrat	7,177	19.3	3.1
Graham Lee, Green party	724	2	n/a
Ian Edwards, British National party	547	1.5	n/a

Andrew Roth says: "changeable defence intellectual and one-time Europhile turned Eurosceptic"

Recent parliamentary career: delegate to Council of Europe; active in many parliamentary groups
Background: company director; author; consultant; correspondence tutor, Open University; pilot; RAF flying instructor; lost whip (1994–95) for rebellion over Europe
Born: September 23 1940 in Slough
Education: Eton College
Higher education: RAF College, Cranwell; Cambridge, Churchill
Constituency: greenbelt suburban seat on north-west edge of London

Willetts, David
Conservative MP for Havant since 1992

Majority: 4,207 (10.4%)
Turnout: 57.6%

	Votes	Share %	Change %
David Willetts, Conservative	17,769	43.9	4.2
Peter Guthrie, Labour	13,562	33.5	1.5
Helen Cole, Liberal Democrat	7,508	18.6	−3.8
Kevin Jacks, Green party	793	2	n/a
Tim Cuell, UK Independence party	561	1.4	n/a
Roy Stanley, Independent	244	0.6	n/a

Andrew Roth says: "a top-class, coolly-creative radical right-wing philosopher of modern Conservatism"

Recent parliamentary career: shadow secretary of state, DWP (2001–); shadow secretary of state for social security [now work and pensions] (1999–2001); shadow education and employment secretary (1998–99); paymaster general (1996), resigned after misleading the Commons standards and privileges committee
Background: civil servant; company director; consultant director of Conservative Research Department (1987–92); author of several books on Conservatism
Born: March 9 1956 in Birmingham
Education: King Edward VI School, Birmingham
Higher education: Oxford, Christ Church
Constituency: mainly urban south coast seat, not posh; home of the Royal Navy

Williams, Rt Hon Alan
Labour MP for Swansea West since 1964

Majority: 9,550 (29.7%)
Turnout: 56.2%

	Votes	Share %	Change %
Alan Williams, Labour	15,644	48.7	−7.5
Margaret Harper, Conservative	6,094	19	−1.5
Mike Day, Liberal Democrat	5,313	16.6	2.1
Ian Titherington, Plaid Cymru	3,404	10.6	4
Richard Lewis, UK Independence party	653	2	n/a
Martyn Shrewsbury, Green party	626	2	n/a
Alec Thraves, Socialist Alliance	366	1.1	n/a

Andrew Roth says: "a still-assiduous former frontbencher and former Wilson-Callaghan minister...long-memoried and long-winded"

Recent parliamentary career: standards and privileges committee (1997–); public accounts committee (1997–)
Background: economist; economics lecturer; broadcaster and journalist; company director
Born: October 14 1930 in Caerphilly
Education: Cardiff High School
Higher education: Oxford, University College; Cardiff Technical College
Constituency: middle class Swansea around university and redeveloped docks

Williams, Betty
Labour MP for Conwy since 1997

Majority: 6,219 (18.1%)
Turnout: 62.8%

	Votes	Share %	Change %
Betty Williams, Labour	14,366	41.8	6.8
David Logan, Conservative	8,147	23.7	−0.6
Vicky MacDonald, Liberal Democrat	5,800	16.9	−14.3
Ann Owen, Plaid Cymru	5,665	16.5	9.7
Alan Barham, UK Independence party	388	1.1	n/a

Andrew Roth says: "late-emerging rebel who believes that socialism, not nationalism, is the answer to Welsh problems"

Recent parliamentary career: Welsh affairs committee (1997–); rebelled agaisnt government on four major occasions (1997–2001)
Background: journalist; councillor, and mayor of Arfon
Born: July 31 1944 in Bangor, Gwynedd
Education: Ysgol Dyffryn Nantlle, Penygroes
Higher education: Normal College, Bangor
Constituency: seaside town and castle on road to Holyhead

Williams, Hywel
Plaid Cymru MP for Caernarfon since 2001

Majority: 3,511 (12.1%)
Turnout: 61.4%

	Votes	Share %	Change %
Hywel Williams, Plaid Cymru	12,894	44.4	−6.6
Martin Eaglestone, Labour	9,383	32.3	2.8
Bronwen Naish, Conservative	4,403	15.2	2.9
Mel ab Owain, Liberal Democrat	1,823	6.3	1.4
Ifor Lloyd, UK Independence party	550	1.9	n/a

Maiden speech: "my constituency is an area of astonishing natural beauty; but, as the saying goes, 'you can't eat the scenery'"

Recent parliamentary career: elected to parliament 2001
Background: social worker; researcher in social work policy, University of Wales; adviser to House of Commons Welsh affairs committee
Born: May 14 1953 in Pwllheli
Education: Ysgol Glan y Mor, Pwllheli
Higher education: University of Wales, Bangor; University of Wales, Cardiff
Constituency: most Welsh-speaking seat; castles and Snowdonia; Lloyd George was once MP

Williams, Roger
Liberal Democrat MP for Brecon and Radnorshire since 2001

Majority: 751 (2.0%)
Turnout: 71.8%

	Votes	Share %	Change %
Roger Williams, Liberal Democrat	13,824	36.9	–3.9
Peter Gooderham, Conservative	13,073	34.9	5.9
Huw Irranca-Davis, Labour	8,024	21.4	–5.2
David Diprose, Plaid Cymru	1,301	3.5	2
Ian Mitchell, Independent	762	2	n/a
Elizabeth Phillips, UK Independence party	452	1.2	n/a
Robert Nicholson, Independent	80	0.2	n/a

Maiden speech: "The good people of Brecon and Radnorshire rarely elect members with a large majority: we come on probation. My majority, which is in the hundreds, is the second largest in that constituency in the past 20 years"

Recent parliamentary career: elected to parliament 2001; Welsh affairs committee (2001–)
Background: degree in agriculture; sheep farmer; Brecon councillor for 20 years
Born: January 22 1948
Education: Llanfilo County Primary School, Powys; Christ's College, Brecon
Higher education: Cambridge, Selwyn College
Constituency: beautiful Welsh seat containing Brecon Beacons National Park

Willis, Phil
Liberal Democrat MP for Harrogate and Knaresborough since 1997

Majority: 8,845 (21.0%)
Turnout: 64.7%

	Votes	Share %	Change %
Phil Willis, Liberal Democrat	23,445	55.6	4.1
Andrew Jones, Conservative	14,600	34.6	–3.9
Alastair MacDonald, Labour	3,101	7.4	–1.3
Bill Brown, UK Independence party	761	1.8	n/a
John Cornforth, ProLife Alliance	272	0.6	n/a

Andrew Roth says: "Lamont terminator…from the social democratic wing of his party"

Recent parliamentary career: Lib Dem spokesperson, education and skills (2001–): senior spokesperson, education and employment (1999–2001), spokesperson, education (1997–99)
Background: head-teacher (1978–97); Harrogate Council leader
Born: November 30 1941 in Burnley
Education: Burnley Grammar School
Higher education: Birmingham University; Carnegie College, Leeds
Constituency: elegant and affluent twin Yorkshire towns

Wills, Michael
Labour MP for North Swindon since 1997

Majority: 8,105 (19.2%)
Turnout: 61.1%

	Votes	Share %	Change %
Michael Wills, Labour	22,371	52.9	3.1
Nick Martin, Conservative	14,266	33.7	–0.2
David Nation, Liberal Democrat	4,891	11.6	–1.3
Brian Lloyd, UK Independence party	800	1.9	n/a

Andrew Roth says: "one of Peter Mandelson's and Gordon Brown's very bright but surprisingly quiet friends"

Recent parliamentary career: junior minister, LCD (2001–); junior minister, DFEE (1999–2001); junior minister, DTI (1999–99)

Background: TV producer, LWT; director of TV production company; FO civil servant
Born: May 20 1952
Education: Haberdashers' Aske's School, Elstree
Higher education: Cambridge, Clare
Constituency: boom town in western England on M4, includes Honda factory

Wilshire, David
Conservative MP for Spelthorne since 1987

Majority: 3,262 (7.8%)
Turnout: 60.8%

	Votes	Share %	Change %
David Wilshire, Conservative	18,851	45.1	0.2
Andrew Shaw, Labour	15,589	37.3	−0.9
Martin Rimmer, Liberal Democrat	6,156	14.7	1.6
Richard Squire, UK Independence party	1,198	2.9	n/a

Andrew Roth says: "leading defender of rate-capping and fat-paring in local government"

Recent parliamentary career: opposition whip (2001–); delegate to Council of Europe; foreign affairs committee (1997–2001)
Background: codirector of Brunel University's political management programme; company director; political consultant; established sports gear business; grammar school teacher; Wansdyke councillor and leader
Born: September 16 1943 in Bristol
Education: Kingswood School, Bath
Higher education: Cambridge, Fitzwilliam
Constituency: Surrey seat across the Thames from Heathrow, includes Staines and Shepperton

Wilson, Brian
Labour MP for Cunninghame North since 1987

Majority: 8,398 (24.9%)
Turnout: 61.5%

	Votes	Share %	Change %
Brian Wilson, Labour	15,571	46.1	−4.2
Campbell Martin, Scottish National party	7,173	21.2	2.8
Dorothy Luckhurst, Conservative	6,666	19.7	−3.8
Ross Chmiel, Liberal Democrat	3,060	9.1	3.6
Sean Scott, Scottish Socialist party	964	2.9	n/a
Louise McDaid, Socialist Labour party	382	1.1	−0.1

Andrew Roth says: "hard-hitting, bright, combative, maverick, radical journalist with a searing flamethrower of a tongue"

Recent parliamentary career: minister of state, DTI (2001–), responsible for energy and attracting attention for his support for nuclear power; minister of state, FCO (2001–2001); minister of state, SO (1999–2001)
Background: writer and journalist who founded radical West Highland Free Press
Born: December 13 1948 in Dunoon
Education: Dunoon Grammar School
Higher education: University College, Cardiff; Dundee University
Constituency: ex-mining southern Scotland plus the Isle of Arran; partly rural

Winnick, David
Labour MP for Walsall North since 1979; Croydon South (1964–70)

Majority: 9,391 (29.0%)
Turnout: 48.9%

	Votes	Share %	Change %
David Winnick, Labour	18,779	58.1	1.5
Melvin Pitt, Conservative	9,388	29.1	1.6
Michael Heap, Liberal Democrat	2,923	9.1	−0.3
Jenny Mayo, UK Independence party	812	2.5	n/a
David Church, Socialist Alliance	410	1.3	n/a

Andrew Roth says: "a member of Labour's rebellious awkward squad"

Recent parliamentary career: home affairs committee (1997–)
Background: advertising manager, *Tribune*; clerk in the engineering industry; trade unionist (APEX)
Born: June 26 1933 in Brighton
Education: various state schools
Higher education: London School of Economics
Constituency: outer edge of the West Midlands, self-contained town north of Birmingham

Winterton, Ann
Conservative MP for Congleton since 1983

Majority: 7,134 (15.8%)
Turnout: 62.7%

	Votes	Share %	Change %
Ann Winterton, Conservative	20,872	46.3	5.1
John Flanagan, Labour	13,738	30.5	3
David Lloyd-Griffiths, Liberal Democrat	9,719	21.6	−8.1
Bill Young, UK Independence party	754	1.7	n/a

Andrew Roth says: "a dulcet voice and restrained manner conceals a steely right-wing backbone and an independent mind"

Recent parliamentary career: opposition spokesperson, DEFRA (2001–); opposition spokesperson, CO with responsibility for drugs (1999–2001)
Background: company director; comes from a staunch Conservative-supporting family; married to Nicholas Winterton MP
Born: March 6 1941 in Sutton Coldfield
Education: Erdington Grammar School for Girls
Constituency: prosperous Cheshire middle class seat south-east of Manchester

Winterton, Nicholas
Conservative MP for Macclesfield since 1971

Majority: 7,200 (15.8%)
Turnout: 62.3%

	Votes	Share %	Change %
Nicholas Winterton, Conservative	22,284	48.9	−0.7
Stephen Carter, Labour	15,084	33.1	−0.5
Mike Flynn, Liberal Democrat	8,217	18	1.3

Andrew Roth says: "blonde John Wayne who presides over Westminster Hall"

Recent parliamentary career: deputy speaker, Westminster Hall (1999–); chair, procedure committee (1997–); modernisation of the House of Commons committee (1997–); married to Ann Winterton MP; noted Conservative Eurosceptic
Background: sales manager; director of several companies
Born: March 31 1938
Education: Rugby School
Constituency: prosperous town at the foot of Cheshire's Peak hills

Winterton, Rosie
Labour MP for Doncaster Central since 1997

Majority: 11,999 (35.4%)
Turnout: 52.1%

	Votes	Share %	Change %
Rosie Winterton, Labour	20,034	59.1	–3
Gary Meggitt, Conservative	8,035	23.7	2.7
Michael Southcombe, Liberal Democrat	4,390	13	3.6
David Gordon, UK Independence party	926	2.7	n/a
Janet Terry, Socialist Alliance	517	1.5	n/a

Andrew Roth says: "enthusiastic cheerleader for the Blair government"

Recent parliamentary career: junior minister, LCD (2001–)
Background: managing director of public affairs firm; assistant to John Prescott MP; parliamentary officer for Southwark Council and Royal College of Nursing
Born: August 10 1958 in Leicester
Education: Doncaster Grammar School
Higher education: Hull University
Constituency: developing ex-mining town on A1 south of Leeds

Wishart, Peter
Scottish National party MP for North Tayside since 2001

Majority: 3,283 (8.5%)
Turnout: 62.5%

	Votes	Share %	Change %
Peter Wishart, Scottish National party	15,441	40.1	–4.7
Murdo Fraser, Conservative	12,158	31.6	–4.1
Thomas Docherty, Labour	5,715	14.8	3.5
Julia Robertson, Liberal Democrat	4,363	11.3	3.1
Rosie Adams, Scottish Socialist party	620	1.6	n/a
Ms Tina MacDonald, Independent	220	0.6	n/a

Maiden speech: "I am reliably informed that I am the first member who has ever appeared on *Top of the Pops* in his own right, so you can imagine the onerous responsibility that that places on my shoulders"

Recent parliamentary career: elected to parliament 2001
Background: trained community worker; concerned about problem of drugs in Scottish society; member of the successful Scottish rock group Runrig for 15 years
Born: March 9 1962
Education: Queen Anne High School, Dunfermline
Higher education: Moray House College of Education, Edinburgh
Constituency: scenic tourist Scotland between Perth and Dundee

Wood, Mike
Labour MP for Batley and Spen since 1997

Majority: 5,064 (13.2%)
Turnout: 60.5%

	Votes	Share %	Change %
Mike Wood, Labour	19,224	49.9	0.5
Elizabeth Peacock, Conservative	14,160	36.7	0.3
Kath Pinnock, Liberal Democrat	3,989	10.4	1.6
Clive Lord, Green party	595	1.5	n/a
Allen Burton, UK Independence party	574	1.5	n/a

Andrew Roth says: "a quietly but persistently rebellious old Labour off-message left-winger"

Recent parliamentary career: interested in further education; transport and the environment; claims to have introduced free second-class postal envelopes to Commons
Background: social worker; probation officer; Kirklees District councillor; director, housing charity
Born: March 3 1946 in Crewe
Education: Nantwich and Acton Grammar School, Nantwich
Higher education: Salisbury and Wells Theological College; Leeds University; Leeds Metropolitan University
Constituency: West Yorkshire seat around Dewesbury

Woodward, Shaun

Labour MP for St Helen's South since 2001; Labour MP for Witney (2000); Conservative MP for Witney (1997–2000)

Majority: 8,985 (26.6%)
Turnout: 51.9%

	Votes	Share %	Change %
Shaun Woodward, Labour	16,799	49.7	–18.9
Brian Spencer, Liberal Democrat	7,814	23.1	9.7
Lee Rotherham, Conservative	4,675	13.8	–1.2
Neil Thompson, Socialist Alliance	2,325	6.9	n/a
Michael Perry, Socialist Labour Party	1,504	4.5	n/a
Robert Barker, UK Independence party	336	1	n/a
Michael Murphy, Independent	271	0.8	n/a
David Braid, Ind Braid	80	0.2	n/a

Andrew Roth says: "socially-mobile with a safe seat, costly homes and a Sainsbury millionairess wife"

Recent parliamentary career: selected for safe Labour seat, St Helen's South, immediately ahead of 2001 election, to local protests; joint committee on human rights (2001–); broadcasting committee (2000–2001); opposition spokesperson, London (1999–99)
Background: defected to Labour party (December 1999) in protest at Conservative policy on Section 28; Conservative party director of communications; television producer; *Newsnight* reporter;
Born: October 26 1958 in Bristol
Education: Bristol Grammar School
Higher education: Harvard; Cambridge, Jesus
Constituency: north-west town dominated by glass industry

Woolas, Philip

Labour MP for Oldham East and Saddleworth since 1997

Majority: 2,726 (6.0%)
Turnout: 61%

	Votes	Share %	Change %
Philip Woolas, Labour	17,537	38.6	–3.1
Howard Sykes, Liberal Democrat	14,811	32.6	–2.8
Craig Heeley, Conservative	7,304	16.1	–3.6
Mike Treacy, British National party	5,091	11.2	n/a
Barbara Little, UK Independence party	677	1.5	n/a

Andrew Roth says: "infinitely flexible and ambitious low profile young politician"

Recent parliamentary career: government whip (2001–); PPS to Lord MacDonald of Tradeston
Background: television producer, *Newsnight* and *Channel 4 News*; director of communications, GMB; ex NUS president; came second to Lib Dems in 1995 byelection
Born: December 11 1959 in Scunthorpe
Education: Nelson Grammar School
Higher education: Manchester University; Nelson and Colne College
Constituency: mix of Oldham terraces and Pennine Hills; BNP vote notable

Worthington, Tony
Labour MP for Clydebank and Milngavie since 1987

Majority: 10,724 (33.0%)
Turnout: 61.9%

	Votes	Share %	Change %
Tony Worthington, Labour	17,249	53.1	−2.1
Jim Yuill, Scottish National party	6,525	20.1	−1
Rod Ackland, Liberal Democrat	3,909	12	1.5
Catherine Pickering, Conservative	3,514	10.8	−1.7
Dawn Brennan, Scottish Socialist party	1,294	4	n/a

Andrew Roth says: "able, thoughtful, international aid and human rights idealist"

Recent parliamentary career: international development committee (1999–); junior minister, NIO (1997–98)
Background: lecturer at HM Borstal and FE college; Clydebank councillor; one of few English-born Labour MPs to be elected in Scotland; interest in African development
Born: October 11 1941 in Lemsford, Hertfordshire
Education: City School, Lincoln
Higher education: London School of Economics; York, Durham, and Glasgow Universities
Constituency: diverse seat, part industrial decline and part middle class Glasgow suburbs

Wray, James
Labour MP for Glasgow Baillieston since 1987; Glasgow Provan (1987–97)

Majority: 9,839 (42.3%)
Turnout: 47.2%

	Votes	Share %	Change %
Jimmy Wray, Labour	14,200	61.1	−4.6
Lachlan McNeill, Scottish National party	4,361	18.8	−0.3
David Comrie, Conservative	1,580	6.8	−0.9
Jim McVicar, Scottish Socialist party	1,569	6.8	n/a
Charles Dundas, Liberal Democrat	1,551	6.7	2.9

Andrew Roth says: "an old school Gorbals-born working class professional politician of Irish origins"

Recent parliamentary career: UK delegation to Council of Europe, Western Europe Union
Background: lorry driver; Strathclyde councillor and housing campaigner; jewellery salesman; boxer; unemployed for seven years; opposed repeal of Section 28
Born: April 28 1938 in Glasgow
Education: St Bonaventure's, Gorbals
Constituency: outer Glasgow seat troubled by huge council estates such as Easterhouse

Wright, Anthony
Labour MP for Great Yarmouth since 1997

Majority: 4,564 (11.3%)
Turnout: 58.4%

	Votes	Share %	Change %
Anthony Wright, Labour	20,344	50.4	−3
Charles Reynolds, Conservative	15,780	39.1	3.5
Maurice Leeke, Liberal Democrat	3,392	8.4	−2.6
Bertie Poole, UK Independence party	850	2.1	n/a

Andrew Roth says: "low-profile, loyal, GMB-backed former local council leader"

Recent parliamentary career: public administration committee (1998–)
Background: engineer; Yarmouth Council leader; ran the local Labour party
Born: August 12 1954
Education: Secondary Modern Hospital School
Constituency: port town on Norfolk coast with rural hinterland

Wright, Dr Tony W
Labour MP for Cannock Chase since 1997; Cannock and Burntwood (1992–97)

Majority: 10,704 (26.0%)
Turnout: 55.9%

	Votes	Share %	Change %
Tony Wright, Labour	23,049	56.1	1.3
Gavin Smithers, Conservative	12,345	30.1	2.9
Stewart Reynolds, Liberal Democrat	5,670	13.8	5.1

Andrew Roth says: "leading Labour moderniser and freedom of information campaigner"

Recent parliamentary career: chair, public administration committee (1999–); PPS to Lord Irvine of Lairg (1997–98)
Background: honorary professor of politics and lecturer in political thought, Birmingham University; author; noted intellectual commentator and supporter of constitutional reform
Born: March 11 1948 in Leicester
Education: Kettering Grammar School
Higher education: London School of Economics; Harvard University; Oxford, Balliol
Constituency: south Staffordshire, power stations, small towns of Rugely and Cannock

Wright, David
Labour MP for Telford since 2001

Majority: 8,383 (27.2%)
Turnout: 51.9%

	Votes	Share %	Change %
David Wright, Labour	16,854	54.6	–3.2
Andrew Henderson, Conservative	8,471	27.4	0
Sally Wiggin, Liberal Democrat	3,983	12.9	1.1
Nicola Brookes, UK Independence party	1,098	3.6	n/a
Mike Jeffries, Socialist Alliance	469	1.5	n/a

Maiden speech: "I belong to the first generation of people from the area who would describe themselves as Telfordians"

Recent parliamentary career: elected to parliament 2001; administration committee (2001–); procedure committee (2001–); environmental audit committee (2001–)
Background: local government officer; district councillor; has always lived in Shropshire
Born: December 22 1966 in Shropshire
Education: Wrockwardine Wood Comprehensive School, Telford
Higher education: Wolverhampton Polytechnic
Constituency: Shropshire new town with many social problems

Wyatt, Derek
Labour MP for Sittingbourne and Sheppey since 1997

Majority: 3,509 (9.3%)
Turnout: 57.5%

	Votes	Share %	Change %
Derek Wyatt, Labour	17,340	45.8	5.2
Adrian Lee, Conservative	13,831	36.5	0.1
Elvie Lowe, Liberal Democrat	5,353	14.1	−4.2
Michael Young, R & R Loony	673	1.8	n/a
Robert Oakley, UK Independence party	661	1.8	n/a

Andrew Roth says: "the Commons' most active proponent of the internet"

Recent parliamentary career: culture, media and sport committee (1997–)
Background: England rugby union player; Haringey councillor; worked in the corporate department of BSkyB; ran IT company
Born: December 12 1949 in London
Education: Westcliff County High School; Colchester Royal Grammar School; St Luke's College, Exeter
Higher education: Open University; Oxford, St Catherine's
Constituency: Isle of Sheppy and port of Sheerness plus north Kent coast

Y

Yeo, Tim
Conservative MP for South Suffolk since 1983

Majority: 5,081 (11.2%)
Turnout: 66.2%

	Votes	Share %	Change %
Tim Yeo, Conservative	18,748	41.4	4.1
Marc Young, Labour	13,667	30.2	0.9
Tessa Munt, Liberal Democrat	11,296	24.9	−2.8
Derek Allen, UK Independence party	1,582	3.5	n/a

Andrew Roth says: "an aggressive but flexible politician and an ambitious, socially-conscious reformer"

Recent parliamentary career: shadow secretary of state, DCMS (2001–); opposition spokesperson, MAFF (1998–2001), handling response to foot and mouth; opposition spokesperson, DETR (1997–98); minister of state, environment (1993–94)
Background: company director and city businessman; resigned ministerial job over tabloid reports of his private life (1994)
Born: March 20 1945 in London
Education: Charterhouse School
Higher education: Cambridge, Emmanuel
Constituency: rolling south Suffolk around Sudbury and Lavenham

Young, Rt Hon Sir George
Conservative MP for North West Hampshire since 1997; Ealing Acton (1974–97)

Majority: 12,009 (24.7%)
Turnout: 63.7%

	Votes	Share %	Change %
George Young, Conservative	24,374	50.1	4.9
Mick Mumford, Labour	12,365	25.4	1.8
Alex Bentley, Liberal Democrat	10,329	21.2	−2.9
Stanley Oram, UK Independence party	1,563	3.2	n/a

Andrew Roth says: "very able, socially-conscious liberal-traditional Tory"

Recent parliamentary career: chair, standards and privileges committees (2001–); committee of selection (2001–); defeated in effort to win speakership (2000); shadow leader of the House of Commons (1998–2000); shadow defence secretary (1997–98)
Background: author and writer; economist; enthusiast for parliamentary reform; GLC councillor
Born: July 16 1941 in Oxford
Education: Eton College
Higher education: Surrey University; Oxford, Christ Church
Constituency: rural Hampshire seat around Andover

Younger-Ross, Richard
Liberal Democrat MP for Teignbridge since 2001

Majority: 3,011 (5.1%)
Turnout: 69.3%

	Votes	Share %	Change %
Richard Younger-Ross, Liberal Democrat	26,343	44.4	5.7
Patrick Nicholls, Conservative	23,332	39.3	0.1
Christopher Bain, Labour	7,366	12.4	–5.6
Paul Exmouth, UK Independence party	2,269	3.8	1.3

Maiden speech: "ball clay is one of my constituency's most important exports. At some time, most members will have sat on products made from ball clay"

Recent parliamentary career: elected to parliament 2001, taking seat from Conservative
Background: self-employed architectural consultant; Commons researcher; active Christian
Born: January 29 1953
Education: Walton on Thames Secondary School
Higher education: Oxford Polytechnic; Ewell Technical College
Constituency: 660 square miles of rolling Devon countryside from granite tors on Dartmoor to sandy beaches at Teignmouth and Dawlish

Summary of Voting in Great Britain   2001 General Election

Party	Votes Number	Share %	Change in sh
Labour	10,724,895	42.0	-2.4
Conservative	8,355,200	32.7	+1.2
Liberal Democrat	4,812,833	18.8	+1.6
SNP	464,305	1.8	-0.2
UK Independence	390,575	1.5	+1.2
Plaid Cymru	195,892	0.8	+0.2
Green	166,487	0.7	+0.4
Independent	119,211	0.5	+0.2
Scottish Socialist	72,279	0.3	n/a
Socialist Alliance	60,496	0.2	n/a
Socialist Labour	57,536	0.2	+0.1
BNP	47,129	0.2	+0.1
Speaker	16,053	0.1	0.0
Liberal	10,920	0.0	-0.1
Pro-Life Alliance	9,453	0.0	n/a
Legalise Cannabis	8,677	0.0	0.0
People's Justice	7,443	0.0	n/a
Monster Raving Loony	6,655	0.0	0.0
Mebyon Kernow	3,199	0.0	0.0
Liberated	3,127	0.0	n/a
Scottish	2,728	0.0	n/a
Rock 'n' Roll Loony	2,634	0.0	n/a
National Front	2,484	0.0	0.0
Socialist Alternative	1,454	0.0	n/a
Reform 2000	1,418	0.0	n/a
Isle of Wight	1,164	0.0	n/a
Muslim	1,150	0.0	n/a
Communist	1,003	0.0	0.0

Candidates	MPs elected		Lost deposits	Average share %
	Number	Change from 1997		
640	412	-6	0	43.8
640	166	+1	2	31.0
639	52	+6	2	18.2
72	5	-1	0	20.2
428	0		422	2.1
40	4		5	14.8
145	0		135	2.8
136	1		126	2.1
72	0		62	3.3
98	0		95	1.8
114	0		113	1.4
33	0		28	3.9
1	1		0	66.6
9	0		8	3.2
37	0		37	0.7
13	0		13	1.6
3	0		1	7.3
15	0		15	1.0
3	0		3	2.1
6	0		6	1.2
2	0		1	4.9
7	0		7	0.9
5	0		5	1.5
2	0		2	2.2
5	0		5	0.9
1	0		1	1.8
4	0		4	0.9
6	0		6	0.5

Party	Votes		Change in sh
	Number	Share %	
New Britain	888	0.0	n/a
Free	832	0.0	n/a
Left Alliance	770	0.0	n/a
New Millennium Bean	727	0.0	n/a
Workers Revolutionary	607	0.0	0.0
Tatton Group	505	0.0	n/a
Christian People's Alliance	479	0.0	n/a
Grey	479	0.0	n/a
Others	6,737	0.0	n/a
Total	**25,558,424**	**100**	

	MPs elected			
Candidates	Number	Change from 1997	Lost deposits	Average share %
1	0		1	2.3
3	0		3	0.7
1	0		1	1.9
1	0		1	2.4
6	0		6	0.3
1	0		1	1.2
1	0		1	1.2
1	0		1	1.1
28	0		28	0.0
3,219	641		1,147	

Summary of Voting in Northern Ireland   2001 General Election

Party	Votes Number	Share %	Change in sh
Ulster Unionist	216,839	26.8	-5.9
Democratic Unionist	181,999	22.5	+8.9
Sinn Fein	175,933	21.7	+5.7
SDLP	169,865	21.0	-3.2
Alliance	28,999	3.6	-4.4
UK Unionist	13,509	1.7	0.0
Independent	8,379	1.0	+0.4
Progressive Unionist	4,781	0.6	-0.8
Northern Ireland Women's Coalition	2,968	0.4	n/a
Conservative	2,422	0.3	-0.9
Workers	2,352	0.3	-0.1
Northern Ireland Unionist	1,794	0.2	n/a
Vote for Yourself	418	0.1	n/a
Ulster Third Way	116	0.0	n/a
Total	**810,374**	**100**	

Candidates	MPs elected		Lost deposits	Average share %
	Number	Change from 1997		
17	6	-4	0	29.2
14	5	+3	0	29.2
18	4	+2	4	20.7
18	3		2	20.0
10	0		5	7.1
1	0	-1	0	36.3
3	0		2	5.8
2	0		1	6.4
1	0		0	7.8
3	0		3	2.2
6	0		6	0.9
2	0		2	2.1
4	0		4	0.3
1	0		1	0.3
100	**18**		**30**	

MPs by Constituency

A

Aberavon	Dr Hywel Francis
Aberdeen Central	Frank Doran
Aberdeen North	Malcolm Savidge
Aberdeen South	Miss Anne Begg
Airdrie & Shotts	Rt Hon Helen Liddell
Aldershot	Gerald Howarth
Aldridge-Brownhills	Richard Shepherd
Altrincham & Sale West	Graham Brady
Alyn & Deeside	Mark Tami
Amber Valley	Judy Mallaber
Angus	Michael Weir
Argyll & Bute	Alan Reid
Arundel & South Downs	Howard Flight
Ashfield	Rt Hon Geoff Hoon
Ashford	Damian Green
Ashton-under-Lyne	David Heyes
Aylesbury	David Lidington
Ayr	Sandra Osborne

B

Banbury	Tony Baldry
Banff & Buchan	Alex Salmond
Barking	Margaret Hodge
Barnsley Central	Eric Illsley
Barnsley East & Mexborough	Jeff Ennis
Barnsley West & Penistone	Michael Clapham
Barrow & Furness	Rt Hon John Hutton
Basildon	Angela Smith
Basingstoke	Andrew Hunter
Bassetlaw	John Mann
Bath	Don Foster
Batley & Spen	Mike Wood
Battersea	Martin Linton
Beaconsfield	Dominic Grieve
Beckenham	Mrs Jacqui Lait
Bedford	Patrick Hall
Belfast East	Peter Robinson
Belfast North	Nigel Dodds
Belfast South	The Reverend Martin Smyth
Belfast West	Gerry Adams
Berwick-upon-Tweed	Rt Hon A. J. Beith
Bethnal Green & Bow	Ms Oona King
Beverley & Holderness	James Cran
Bexhill & Battle	Gregory Barker
Bexleyheath & Crayford	Nigel Beard
Billericay	John Baron
Birkenhead	Rt Hon Frank Field
Birmingham, Edgbaston	Ms Gisela Stuart
Birmingham, Erdington	Siôn Simon
Birmingham, Hall Green	Stephen McCabe
Birmingham, Hodge Hill	Rt Hon Terry Davis
Birmingham, Ladywood	Rt Hon Clare Short
Birmingham, Northfield	Richard Burden
Birmingham, Perry Barr	Khalid Mahmood
Birmingham, Selly Oak	Lynne Jones
Birmingham, Sparkbrook & Small Heath	Roger Godsiff

Birmingham, Yardley	Rt Hon Estelle Morris
Bishop Auckland	Rt Hon Derek Foster
Blaby	Andrew Robathan
Blackburn	Rt Hon Jack Straw
Blackpool North & Fleetwood	Mrs Joan Humble
Blackpool South	Gordon Marsden
Blaenau Gwent	Llew Smith
Blaydon	John McWilliam
Blyth Valley	Ronnie Campbell
Bognor Regis & Littlehampton	Nick Gibb
Bolsover	Dennis Skinner
Bolton North East	David Crausby
Bolton South East	Dr Brian Iddon
Bolton West	Ruth Kelly
Bootle	Joe Benton
Boston & Skegness	Mark Simmonds
Bosworth	David Tredinnick
Bournemouth East	David Atkinson
Bournemouth West	John Butterfill
Bracknell	Rt Hon Andrew Mackay
Bradford North	Terry Rooney
Bradford South	Gerry Sutcliffe
Bradford West	Marsha Singh
Braintree	Alan Hurst
Brecon & Radnorshire	Roger Williams
Brent East	Paul Daisley
Brent North	Barry Gardiner
Brent South	Rt Hon Paul Boateng
Brentford & Isleworth	Ann Keen
Brentwood & Ongar	Eric Pickles
Bridgend	Win Griffiths
Bridgwater	Ian Liddell-Grainger
Brigg & Goole	Ian Cawsey
Brighton, Kemptown	Dr Desmond Turner
Brighton, Pavilion	David Lepper
Bristol East	Jean Corston
Bristol North West	Dr Doug Naysmith
Bristol South	Dawn Primarolo
Bristol West	Valerie Davey
Bromley & Chislehurst	Rt Hon Eric Forth
Bromsgrove	Miss Julie Kirkbride
Broxbourne	Mrs Marion Roe
Broxtowe	Dr Nick Palmer
Buckingham	John Bercow
Burnley	Peter Pike
Burton	Mrs Janet Dean
Bury North	David Chaytor
Bury South	Ivan Lewis
Bury St Edmunds	David Ruffley

C

Caernarfon	Hywel Williams
Caerphilly	Wayne David
Caithness, Sutherland, & Easter Ross	John Thurso
Calder Valley	Chris McCafferty
Camberwell & Peckham	Rt Hon Harriet Harman QC

Constituency	Member
Cambridge	Mrs Anne Campbell
Cannock Chase	Tony Wright
Canterbury	Julian Brazier
Cardiff Central	Jon Owen Jones
Cardiff North	Julie Morgan
Cardiff South & Penarth	Rt Hon Alun Michael
Cardiff West	Kevin Brennan
Carlisle	Eric Martlew
Carmarthen East & Dinefwr	Adam Price
Carmarthen West & South Pembrokeshire	Nick Ainger
Carrick, Cumnock, & Doon Valley	George Foulkes
Carshalton & Wallington	Tom Brake
Castle Point	Bob Spink
Central Fife	John MacDougall
Central Suffolk & North Ipswich	Sir Michael Lord
Ceredigion	Simon Thomas
Charnwood	Rt Hon Stephen Dorrell
Chatham & Aylesford	Jonathan R. Shaw
Cheadle	Patsy Calton
Cheltenham	Nigel Jones
Chesham & Amersham	Mrs Cheryl Gillan
Chester, City of	Christine Russell
Chesterfield	Paul Holmes
Chichester	Andrew Tyrie
Chingford & Woodford Green	Iain Duncan Smith
Chipping Barnet	Sir Sydney Chapman
Chorley	Lindsay Hoyle
Christchurch	Christopher Chope
Cities of London & Westminster	Mark Field
Cleethorpes	Shona McIsaac
Clwyd South	Martyn Jones
Clwyd West	Gareth Thomas
Clydebank & Milngavie	Tony Worthington
Clydesdale	Jimmy Hood
Coatbridge & Chryston	Rt Hon Tom Clarke
Colchester	Bob Russell
Colne Valley	Kali Mountford
Cogleton	Mrs Ann Winterton
Conwy	Mrs Betty Williams
Copeland	Rt Hon Dr Jack Cunningham
Corby	Phil Hope
Cotswold	Geoffrey Clifton-Brown
Coventry North East	Bob Ainsworth
Coventry North West	Geoffrey Robinson
Coventry South	Jim Cunningham
Crawley	Laura Moffatt
Crewe & Nantwich	Hon Gwyneth Dunwoody
Crosby	Mrs Claire Curtis-Thomas
Croydon Central	Geraint Davies
Croydon North	Malcolm Wicks
Croydon South	Richard Ottaway
Cumbernauld & Kilsyth	Rosemary McKenna
Cunninghame North	Brian Wilson
Cunninghame South	Brian H. Donohoe
Cynon Valley	Ann Clwyd

D

Constituency	Member
Dagenham	Jon Cruddas
Darlington	Rt Hon Alan Milburn
Dartford	Dr Howard Stoate
Daventry	Tim Boswell
Delyn	David Hanson
Denton & Reddish	Andrew Bennett
Derby North	Bob Laxton
Derby South	Rt Hon Margaret Beckett
Devizes	Rt Hon Michael Ancram QC
Dewsbury	Rt Hon Ann Taylor
Don Valley	Caroline Flint
Doncaster Central	Ms Rosie Winterton
Doncaster North	Kevin Hughes
Dover	Gwyn Prosser
Dudley North	Ross Cranston QC
Dudley South	Ian Pearson
Dulwich & West Norwood	Rt Hon Tessa Jowell
Dumbarton	John McFall
Dumfries	Russell Brown
Dundee East	Iain Luke
Dundee West	Ernie Ross
Dunfermline East	Rt Hon Gordon Brown
Dunfermline West	Rachel Squire
Durham, City of	Gerry Steinberg

E

Constituency	Member
Ealing, Acton & Shepherd's Bush	Clive Soley
Ealing North	Stephen Pound
Ealing Southall	Piara S. Khabra
Easington	John Cummings
East Antrim	Roy Beggs
East Devon	Hugo Swire
East Ham	Stephen Timms
East Hampshire	Michael Mates
East Kilbride	Rt Hon Adam Ingram
East Londonderry	Gregory Campbell
East Lothian	Anne Picking
East Surrey	Peter Ainsworth
East Worthing & Shoreham	Tim Loughton
East Yorkshire	Rt Hon Greg Knight
Eastbourne	Nigel Waterson
Eastleigh	David Chidgey
Eastwood	Jim Murphy
Eccles	Ian Stewart
Eddisbury	Stephen O'Brien
Edinburgh Central	Rt Hon Alistair Darling
Edinburgh East & Musselburgh	Rt Hon Dr Gavin Strang
Edinburgh North & Leith	Mark Lazarowicz
Edinburgh Pentlands	Dr Lynda Clark QC
Edinburgh South	Nigel Griffiths
Edinburgh West	John Barrett
Edmonton	Andrew Love
Ellesmere Port & Neston	Andrew Miller
Elmet	Colin Burgon
Eltham	Clive Efford

Enfield North	Joan Ryan	Halifax	Alice Mahon
Enfield, Southgate	Stephen Twigg	Haltemprice & Howden	Rt Hon David Davis
Epping Forest	Mrs Eleanor Laing	Halton	Derek Twigg
Epsom & Ewell	Chris Grayling	Hamilton North	
Erewash	Mrs Liz Blackman	& Bellshill	Rt Hon Dr John Reid
Erith & Thamesmead	John Austin	Hamilton South	Bill Tynan
Esher & Walton	Ian Taylor	Hammersmith & Fulham	Iain Coleman
Exeter	Ben Bradshaw	Hampstead & Highgate	Glenda Jackson
		Harborough	Edward Garnier QC
		Harlow	Bill Rammell
F		Harrogate &	
Falkirk East	Michael Connarty	Knaresborough	Phil Willis
Falkirk West	Eric Joyce	Harrow East	Tony McNulty
Falmouth & Camborne	Ms Candy Atherton	Harrow West	Gareth R. Thomas
Fareham	Mark Hoban	Hartlepool	Rt Hon Peter
Faversham & Mid Kent	Hugh Robertson	Mandelson	
Feltham & Heston	Alan Keen	Harwich	Ivan Henderson
Fermanagh & South		Hastings & Rye	Michael Jabez Foster
Tyrone	Michelle Gildernew	Havant	David Willetts
Finchley & Golders		Hayes & Harlington	John McDonnell
Green	Dr Rudi Vis	Hazel Grove	Andrew Stunell
Folkestone & Hythe	Rt Hon Michael	Hemel Hempstead	Tony McWalter
	Howard	Hemsworth	Jon Trickett
Forest of Dean	Diana Organ	Hendon	Andrew Dismore
Foyle	John Hume	Henley	Boris Johnson
Fylde	Rt Hon Michael Jack	Hereford	Paul Keetch
		Hortford & Stortford	Mark Prisk
G		Hertsmere	James Clappison
Gainsborough	Edward Leigh	Hexham	Peter Atkinson
Galloway & Upper		Heywood & Middleton	Jim Dobbin
Nithsdale	Peter Duncan	High Peak	Tom Levitt
Gateshead East &		Hitchin & Harpenden	Rt Hon Peter Lilley
Washington West	Rt Hon Joyce Quin	Holborn & St Pancras	Rt Hon Frank
Gedling	Vernon Coaker		Dobson
Gillingham	Paul Clark	Hornchurch	John Cryer
Glasgow Anniesland	John Robertson	Hornsey & Wood Green	Mrs Barbara Roche
Glasgow Baillieston	James Wray	Horsham	Rt Hon Francis
Glasgow Cathcart	Tom Harris		Maude
Glasgow Govan	Mohammad Sarwar	Houghton & Washington	
Glasgow Kelvin	George Galloway	East	Fraser Kemp
Glasgow Maryhill	Ann McKechin	Hove	Ivor Caplin
Glasgow Pollok	Ian Davidson	Huddersfield	Barry Sheerman
Glasgow Rutherglen	Thomas McAvoy	Huntingdon	Jonathan Djanogly
Glasgow Shettleston	David Marshall	Hyndburn	Greg Pope
Glasgow Springburn	Rt Hon Michael J.		
	Martin	**I**	
Gloucester	Parmjit Dhanda	Ilford North	Linda Perham
Gordon	Malcolm Bruce	Ilford South	Mike Gapes
Gosport	Peter Viggers	Inverness East,	
Gower	Martin Caton	Nairn, & Lochaber	David Stewart
Grantham & Stamford	Quentin Davies	Ipswich	Jamie Cann
Gravesham	Chris Pond	Isle of Wight	Andrew Turner
Great Grimsby	Austin Mitchell	Islington North	Jeremy Corbyn
Great Yarmouth	Anthony D. Wright	Islington South &	
Greenock & Inverclyde	David Cairns	Finsbury	Rt Hon Chris Smith
Greenwich & Woolwich	Rt Hon Nick	Islwyn	Don Touhig
	Raynsford		
Guildford	Sue Doughty	**J**	
		Jarrow	Stephen Hepburn
H			
Hackney North &		**K**	
Stoke Newington	Ms Diane Abbott	Keighley	Mrs Ann Cryer
Hackney South &		Kensington & Chelsea	Rt Hon Michael
Shoreditch	Brian Sedgemore		Portillo
Halesowen & Rowley		Kettering	Phil Sawford
Regis	Sylvia Heal		

Kilmarnock & Loudoun — Desmond Browne
Kingston & Surbiton — Edward Davey
Kingston upon Hull East — Rt Hon John Prescott
Kingston upon Hull North — Kevin McNamara
Kingston upon Hull West & Hessle — Alan Johnson
Kingswood — Roger Berry
Kirkcaldy — Dr Lewis Moonie
Knowsley North & Sefton East — George Howarth
Knowsley South — Edward O'Hara

L

Lagan Valley — Jeffrey M. Donaldson
Lancaster & Wyre — Hilton Dawson
Leeds Central — Hilary Benn
Leeds East — George Mudie
Leeds North East — Fabian Hamilton
Leeds North West — Harold Best
Leeds West — John Battle
Leicester East — Keith Vaz
Leicester South — Jim Marshall
Leicester West — Rt Hon Patricia Hewitt
Leigh — Andy Burnham
Leominster — Bill Wiggin
Lewes — Norman Baker
Lewisham, Deptford — Joan Ruddock
Lewisham East — Bridget Prentice
Lewisham West — Jim Dowd
Leyton & Wanstead — Harry Cohen
Lichfield — Michael Fabricant
Lincoln — Gillian Merron
Linlithgow — Tam Dalyell
Liverpool, Garston — Maria Eagle
Liverpool, Riverside — Mrs Louise Ellman
Liverpool, Walton — Peter Kilfoyle
Liverpool, Wavertree — Jane Kennedy
Liverpool, West Derby — Robert N. Wareing
Livingston — Rt Hon Robin Cook
Llanelli — Rt Hon Denzil Davies
Loughborough — Andy Reed
Louth & Horncastle — Sir Peter Tapsell
Ludlow — Matthew Green
Luton North — Kelvin Hopkins
Luton South — Margaret Moran

M

Macclesfield — Nicholas Winterton
Maidenhead — Mrs Theresa May
Maidstone & The Weald — Rt Hon Ann Widdecombe
Makerfield — Rt Hon Ian McCartney
Maldon & East Chelmsford — John Whittingdale
Manchester, Blackley — Graham Stringer
Manchester Central — Tony Lloyd
Manchester, Gorton — Rt Hon Gerald Kaufman
Manchester, Withington — Rt Hon Keith Bradley
Mansfield — Alan Meale
Medway — Robert Marshall-Andrews QC
Meirionnydd Nant Conwy — Elfyn Llwyd

Meriden — Mrs Caroline Spelman
Merthyr Tydfil & Rhymney — Dai Havard
Mid Bedfordshire — Jonathan Sayeed
Mid Dorset & North Poole — Annette Brooke
Mid Norfolk — Keith Simpson
Mid Sussex — Hon Nicholas Soames
Mid Ulster — Martin McGuinness
Mid Worcestershire — Peter Luff
Middlesbrough — Stuart Bell
Middlesbrough South & East Cleveland — Dr Ashok Kumar
Midlothian — David Hamilton
Milton Keynes South West — Dr Phyllis Starkey
Mitcham & Morden — Siobhain McDonagh
Mole Valley — Sir Paul Beresford
Monmouth — Huw Edwards
Montgomeryshire — Lembit Öpik
Moray — Angus Robertson
Morecambe & Lunesdale — Geraldine Smith
Morley & Rothwell — Colin Challen
Motherwell & Wishaw — Frank Roy

N

Neath — Rt Hon Peter Hain
New Forest East — Dr Julian Lewis
New Forest West — Desmond Swayne
Newark — Patrick Mercer
Newbury — David Rendel
Newcastle-under-Lyme — Paul Farrelly
Newcastle upon Tyne Central — Jim Cousins
Newcastle upon Tyne East & Wallsend — Rt Hon Nicholas Brown
Newcastle upon Tyne North — Doug Henderson
Newport East — Rt Hon Alan Howarth
Newport West — Paul Flynn
Newry & Armagh — Seamus Mallon
Normanton — Bill O'Brien
North Antrim — The Reverend Ian Paisley
North Cornwall — Paul Tyler
North Devon — Nick Harvey
North Dorset — Robert Walter
North Down — Lady Sylvia Hermon
North Durham — Kevan Jones
North East Bedfordshire — Alistair Burt
North East Cambridgeshire — Malcolm Moss
North East Derbyshire — Harry Barnes
North East Fife — Rt Hon Menzies Campbell QC
North East Hampshire — Rt Hon James Arbuthnot
North East Hertfordshire — Oliver Heald
North East Milton Keynes — Brian White
North Essex — Hon Bernard Jenkin
North Norfolk — Norman Lamb
North Shropshire — Owen Paterson
North Southwark & Bermondsey — Simon Hughes

North Swindon — Michael Wills
North Tayside — Pete Wishart
North Thanet — Roger Gale
North Tyneside — Rt Hon Stephen Byers
North Warwickshire — Mike O'Brien
North West Cambridgeshire — Rt Hon Sir Brian Mawhinney
North West Durham — Rt Hon Hilary Armstrong
North West Hampshire — Rt Hon Sir George Young Bt
North West Leicestershire — David Taylor
North West Norfolk — Henry Bellingham
North Wiltshire — James Gray
Northampton North — Ms Sally Keeble
Northampton South — Tony Clarke
Northavon — Steve Webb
Norwich North — Dr Ian Gibson
Norwich South — Rt Hon Charles Clarke
Nottingham East — John Heppell
Nottingham North — Graham Allen
Nottingham South — Alan Simpson
Nuneaton — Bill Olner

O
Ochil — Martin O'Neill
Ogmore — Sir Raymond Powell
Old Bexley & Sidcup — Derek Conway
Oldham East & Saddleworth — Phil Woolas
Oldham West & Royton — Rt Hon Michael Meacher
Orkney & Shetland — Alistair Carmichael
Orpington — John Horam
Oxford East — Rt Hon Andrew Smith
Oxford West & Abingdon — Dr Evan Harris

P
Paisley North — Irene Adams
Paisley South — Douglas Alexander
Pendle — Gordon Prentice
Penrith & The Border — Rt Hon David Maclean
Perth — Annabelle Ewing
Peterborough — Mrs Helen Clark (formerly Brinton)
Plymouth, Devonport — David Jamieson
Plymouth, Sutton — Linda Gilroy
Pontefract & Castleford — Yvette Cooper
Pontypridd — Dr Kim Howells
Poole — Robert Syms
Poplar & Canning Town — Jim Fitzpatrick
Portsmouth North — Syd Rapson
Portsmouth South — Mike Hancock
Preseli Pembrokeshire — Mrs Jackie Lawrence
Preston — Mark Hendrick
Pudsey — Paul Truswell
Putney — Tony Colman

R
Rayleigh — Mark Francois
Reading East — Jane Griffiths
Reading West — Martin Salter

Redcar — Vera Baird
Redditch — Jacqui Smith
Regent's Park & Kensington North — Ms Karen Buck
Reigate — Crispin Blunt
Rhondda — Chris Bryant
Ribble Valley — Nigel Evans
Richmond (Yorks) — Rt Hon William Hague
Richmond Park — Dr Jenny Tonge
Rochdale — Mrs Lorna Fitzsimons
Rochford & Southend East — Sir Teddy Taylor
Romford — Andrew Rosindell
Romsey — Sandra Gidley
Ross, Skye, & Inverness West — Rt Hon Charles Kennedy
Rossendale & Darwen — Janet Anderson
Rother Valley — Kevin Barron
Rotherham — Denis MacShane
Roxburgh & Berwickshire — Archie Kirkwood
Rugby & Kenilworth — Andy King
Ruislip – Northwood — John Wilkinson
Runnymede & Weybridge — Philip Hammond
Rushcliffe — Rt Hon Kenneth Clarke QC
Rutland & Melton — Alan Duncan
Ryedale — John Greenway

S
Saffron Walden — Rt Hon Sir Alan Haselhurst
Salford — Ms Hazel Blears
Salisbury — Robert Key
Scarborough & Whitby — Lawrie Quinn
Scunthorpe — Elliot Morley
Sedgefield — Rt Hon Tony Blair
Selby — John Grogan
Sevenoaks — Michael Fallon
Sheffield Attercliffe — Clive Betts
Sheffield Brightside — Rt Hon David Blunkett
Sheffield Central — Rt Hon Richard Caborn
Sheffield, Hallam — Richard Allan
Sheffield Heeley — Ms Meg Munn
Sheffield, Hillsborough — Helen Jackson
Sherwood — Paddy Tipping
Shipley — Christopher Leslie
Shrewsbury & Atcham — Paul Marsden
Sittingbourne & Sheppey — Derek Wyatt
Skipton & Ripon — Rt Hon David Curry
Sleaford & North Hykeham — Rt Hon Douglas Hogg QC
Slough — Fiona Mactaggart
Solihull — John Taylor
Somerton & Frome — David Heath
South Antrim — David Burnside
South Cambridgeshire — Andrew Lansley
South Derbyshire — Mark Todd
South Dorset — Jim Knight
South Down — Eddie McGrady
South East Cambridgeshire — James Paice

South East Cornwall	Colin Breed
South Holland & The Deepings	John Hayes
South Norfolk	Richard Bacon
South Ribble	David Borrow
South Shields	David Miliband
South Staffordshire	Sir Patrick Cormack
South Suffolk	Tim Yeo
South Swindon	Julia Drown
South Thanet	Dr Stephen Ladyman
South West Bedfordshire	Andrew Selous
South West Devon	Gary Streeter
South West Hertfordshire	Richard Page
South West Norfolk	Rt Hon Gillian Shephard
South West Surrey	Rt Hon Virginia Bottomley
Southampton, Itchen	Rt Hon John Denham
Southampton, Test	Dr Alan Whitehead
Southend West	David Amess
Southport	Dr John Pugh
Spelthorne	David Wilshire
St Albans	Kerry Pollard
St Helens North	Dave Watts
St Helens South	Shaun Woodward
St Ives	Andrew George
Stafford	David Kidney
Staffordshire Moorlands	Charlotte Atkins
Stalybridge & Hyde	James Purnell
Stevenage	Barbara Follett
Stirling	Mrs Anne McGuire
Stockport	Ann Coffey
Stockton North	Frank Cook
Stockton South	Ms Dari Taylor
Stoke-on-Trent Central	Mark Fisher
Stoke-on-Trent North	Joan Walley
Stoke-on-Trent South	George Stevenson
Stone	William Cash
Stourbridge	Ms Debra Shipley
Strangford	Mrs Iris Robinson
Stratford-on-Avon	John Maples
Strathkelvin & Bearsden	John Lyons
Streatham	Keith Hill
Stretford & Urmston	Beverley Hughes
Stroud	David Drew
Suffolk Coastal	Rt Hon John Gummer
Sunderland North	Bill Etherington
Sunderland South	Chris Mullin
Surrey Heath	Nick Hawkins
Sutton & Cheam	Paul Burstow
Sutton Coldfield	Andrew Mitchell
Swansea East	Rt Hon Donald Anderson
Swansea West	Rt Hon Alan Williams
T	
Tamworth	Brian Jenkins
Tatton	George Osborne
Taunton	Adrian Flook
Teignbridge	Richard Younger-Ross
Telford	David Wright
Tewkesbury	Laurence Robertson
Thurrock	Andrew Mackinlay
Tiverton & Honiton	Mrs Angela Browning
Tonbridge & Malling	Rt Hon Sir John Stanley
Tooting	Tom Cox
Torbay	Adrian Sanders
Torfaen	Rt Hon Paul Murphy
Torridge & West Devon	John Burnett
Totnes	Anthony Steen
Tottenham	David Lammy
Truro & St Austell	Matthew Taylor
Tunbridge Wells	Archie Norman
Tweeddale, Ettrick & Lauderdale	Michael Moore
Twickenham	Dr Vincent Cable
Tyne Bridge	David Clelland
Tynemouth	Alan Campbell
U	
Upminster	Angela Watkinson
Upper Bann	Rt Hon David Trimble
Uxbridge	John Randall
V	
Vale of Clwyd	Chris Ruane
Vale of Glamorgan	John Smith
Vale of York	Anne McIntosh
Vauxhall	Kate Hoey
W	
Wakefield	David Hinchliffe
Wallasey	Angela Eagle
Walsall North	David Winnick
Walsall South	Rt Hon Bruce George
Walthamstow	Neil Gerrard
Wansbeck	Denis Murphy
Wansdyke	Dan Norris
Wantage	Robert Jackson
Warley	Rt Hon John Spellar
Warrington North	Helen Jones
Warrington South	Helen Southworth
Warwick & Leamington	James Plaskitt
Watford	Ms Claire Ward
Waveney	Bob Blizzard
Wealden	Charles Hendry
Weaver Vale	Mike Hall
Wellingborough	Paul Stinchcombe
Wells	Rt Hon David Heathcoat-Amory
Welwyn Hatfield	Miss Melanie Johnson
Wentworth	John Healey
West Aberdeenshire & Kincardine	Sir Robert Smith
West Bromwich East	Tom Watson
West Bromwich West	Adrian Bailey
West Chelmsford	Simon Burns
West Derbyshire	Patrick McLoughlin
West Dorset	Oliver Letwin

West Ham	Tony Banks	Wolverhampton North	
West Lancashire	Colin Pickthall	East	Ken Purchase
West Renfrewshire	Jim Sheridan	Wolverhampton South	
West Suffolk	Richard Spring	East	Dennis Turner
West Tyrone	Pat Doherty	Wolverhampton South	
West Worcestershire	Sir Michael	West	Rob Marris
	Spicer	Woodspring	Dr Liam Fox
Westbury	Dr Andrew	Worcester	Michael Foster
	Murrison	Workington	Tony
Western Isles	Calum		Cunningham
	MacDonald	Worsley	Terry Lewis
Westmorland & Lonsdale	Tim Collins	Worthing West	Peter Bottomley
Weston-Super-Mare	Brian Cotter	Wrekin, The	Peter Bradley
Wigan	Neil Turner	Wrexham	Ian Lucas
Wimbledon	Roger Casale	Wycombe	Paul Goodman
Winchester	Mark Oaten	Wyre Forest	Dr Richard Taylor
Windsor	Michael Trend	Wythenshawe & Sale	
Wirral South	Ben Chapman	East	Paul Goggins
Wirral West	Stephen Hesford		
Witney	David Cameron	**Y**	
Woking	Humfrey Malins	Yeovil	David Laws
Wokingham	Rt Hon John	Ynys Mon	Albert Owen
	Redwood	York, City of	Hugh Bayley

The House of Lords

What is the Point of the House of Lords?

Julian Glover

No other parliament in the world has a chamber anything like the House of Lords. Even in its post-1999 semi-reformed state, it includes 26 bishops and archbishops, 27 earls, 17 viscounts, two dukes and a marquess among its active members. Everyone, apart from ministers, who takes part in its debates is a volunteer, unpaid apart from an expenses allowance. Most remain members until they die. Only 16% are women. None have been elected, apart from 90 hereditary peers voted in by their fellows.

Swathed in ermine and silk and with an average age of 67, Britain's peers look like nothing more than a dusty adornment to a dated constitution. The fact that, after two Labour landslides, the chamber still contains more Conservative than Labour members seems to confirm its oddity. So does its status as the pinnacle of Britain's legal system.

Yet there is a fresher side to the institution, even before the government's much promised further reform. It contains more ethnic-minority members than the Commons and – unlike that supposedly more democratic chamber – offers room to voices from the political margins. The only Green parliamentarian at Westminster sits in the Lords, and so does the only independent Eurosceptic conservative.

The Chamber is one of the most active legislative assemblies in the world, sitting (in some years) for longer than its Commons neighbour and for almost three times as many days a year as the European parliament. At £30m a year it costs less than the Scottish parliament. It is Britain's main parliamentary bulwark against the European Union and its committees produce thoughtful and respected reports on issues such as illegal drug use.

But what is it really for?

The traditional answer is to point to four roles: as a place to revise legislation; as a check on government, scrutinising its actions; as a source of independent expertise; and, in its judicial capacity, to serve as a final court of appeal.

The House of Lords spends about 60% of its time legislating and – without a party majority – its members have bite. Governments have been defeated on average 23 times a session since 1970, and the frequency is increasing. In 1998–99, the last year of the unreformed house, 31% of Lords divisions led to a government defeat. The new Lords has proved just as uncomfortable for Tony Blair, defeating the government 36 times in the 1999–2000 session.

In July 2000 the chamber threw out the government's legislation repealing

Section 28 of the Local Government Act, which restricts the teaching of homosexuality in schools. Two months later peers rejected (for the second time) government plans to restrict the right to jury trials. And in March 2001 they defeated government proposals to ban or restrict hunting with dogs.

Each of these issues was at the forefront of political debate and all of them brought the upper house directly into conflict with the views of the elected lower chamber.

Who sits in the Lords?

The number of peers with the right to sit in the Lords varies: the number rises when new peers are created and falls when members retire or die.

Until 1999, when the first stage of Lords reform came into effect, there were more than 1,000 members – although many did not attend sessions. By excluding most hereditary peers, reform brought this number to just over 700.

Of these some 560 are life peers; another 28 are law lords, also serving for life; 92 are hereditary peers reappointed for life; and 26 are bishops or archbishops serving either for life or for a term.

Further reform is likely to leave the overall number of peers at around 700. A limited number of directly elected peers may join the chamber – probably 87 – and the number of Church of England peers is likely to fall from 26 to 10.

Committees

Committees are at the heart of the Lords' scrutiny work. Although ministers make statements, are questioned, and take part in debates on the floor of the House, just as they do in the Commons, these activities are often less influential than the Lords' committee work.

Three committees count in particular. The first, the European Union committee, with its various sub-committees – set up in 1974 – publishes regular reports on EU documents, proposals, and policies. Most reports are debated on the floor of the House. Nothing on this scale happens in the Commons or in most other EU parliaments.

The second committee, the select committee on delegated powers and deregulation – perhaps the dullest title for a body in Westminster – attempts to plug another gap in parliamentary scrutiny.

Much government policy is enforced by so-called secondary legislation. This consists of extra-parliamentary orders, issued by ministers but with the same legal force as Acts of Parliament. (For more on secondary legislation, see page 353.

Only the House of Lords, through the delegated powers committee, makes any major effort to keep an eye on this remarkable breach of the established constitutional order. The task is gargantuan – 3,000 pieces of secondary legislation are issued a year.

Finally a third committee, the House of Lords committee on science and technology, brings together the chamber's expertise to address long-term issues ignored in the cut and thrust of Commons politics, such as climate change, drugs policy, and the conservation of fish stocks. These reports shake off the Lords' stuffy image to put it at the front edge of social change.

Judicial role

Meanwhile the House of Lords' judicial role functions independently of the rest of the chamber's work. The Lords hears appeals from the Court of Appeal in England and Wales and Northern Ireland in both civil and criminal matters and from the Court of Session in Scotland in civil matters.

Various conditions govern which cases can come to the Lords, the broad principle being that cases can be heard if the issues involved are of general, rather than individual, importance and questions of law, rather than questions of fact, are at issue.

Only specially appointed peers qualified to take part in legal decisions, known as law lords, are involved in the Lords' judicial role. They sit in committee, rather than on the floor of the House and, if reformers get their way, may at some point form an independent supreme court.

Reform

None of the House of Lords' functions will be much affected by the completion of the government's reform plans (the first stage of reform, completed in 2000, saw the removal of all hereditary peers other than a limited number of office-holders and 90 peers elected by their fellows). The government has resisted calls for radical change to remove the Lords' judicial role, elect all its members or rename the chamber the Senate.

Current plans for reform concentrate on the chamber's composition, not its role, removing the remaining hereditary peers and convicted criminals and introducing at least some directly elected members.

These plans were drawn up by the Royal Commission on the Reform of the House of Lords, under the chairmanship of Lord Wakeham, in 2000. In the Queen's speech in June 2001, the government promised to "introduce legislation to implement the second phase of House of Lords reform" but no deadline was set. In July 2001 the leader of the House of Commons, Robin Cook, indicated that reform might be introduced within two years.

The government says it intends to consult on draft legislation before introducing a formal bill. It may also try to achieve cross-party consensus on the issue.

If it does take place, change is likely to lead to a chamber whose membership more closely resembles that of the House of Commons.

In that case, the chamber's set-piece revolts against government legislation are likely to become less frequent, although there is evidence that the first stage of Lords reform increased peers' willingness to rebel by adding to their sense of legitimacy.

The result may be an institution that is more democratic but less likely to make the headlines, one that depends, more than ever, on the work of its committees and its lawyers for its claim to effectiveness.

Composition of the House of Lords

Party	Life peers	Hereditary:elected by party holders	Hereditary: elected office holders	Hereditary: appointed royal office
Conservative	173	40	9	1
Labour	189	2	2	
Liberal Democrats	56	3	2	
Cross-bench	141	29	2	1
Archbishops and Bishops				
Other	31			
TOTAL	**590**	**74**	**15**	**2**

Source: House of Lords. Information correct as at August 1, 2001.

Members of the House of Lords

Full Title	Name	Gender	Created/took
Aberdare, Lord	Morys George Lyndhurst Bruce	M	1999
Ackner, Lord	Desmond James Conrad Ackner	M	1986
Acton, Lord	Richard Gerald Lyon-Dalberg-Acton	M	2000
Addington, Lord	Dominic Bryce Hubbard	M	1999
Ahmed, Lord	Nazir Ahmed	M	1998
Alderdice, Lord	John Thomas Alderdice	M	1996
Alexander of Weedon, Lord	Robert Scott Alexander	M	1988
Allen of Abbeydale, Lord	Philip Allen	M	1976
Allenby of Megiddo, Viscount	Michael Jaffray Hynman Allenby	M	1999
Alli, Lord	Waheed Alli	M	1998
Alton of Liverpool, Lord	David Patrick Paul Alton	M	1997
Amos, Baroness	Valerie Ann Amos	F	1997
Ampthill, Lord	Geoffrey Denis Erskine Russell	M	1999
Andrews, Baroness	Elizabeth Kay Andrews	F	2000
Anelay of St Johns, Baroness	Joyce Anne Anelay	F	1996
Archer of Sandwell, Lord	Peter Kingsley Archer	M	1992
Archer of Weston-Super-Mare, Lord	Jeffrey Howard Archer	M	1992
Armstrong of Ilminster, Lord	Robert Temple Armstrong	M	1988
Arran, Earl of	Arthur Desmond Colquhoun Gore	M	1999

Bishops	Total
	223
	195
	61
	173
26	26
	26
26	**709**

Status	Party	Details
Elected hereditary peer	Conservative	Former businessman
Life peer	Cross bench	Barrister and retired law lord
Hereditary peer given life peerage	Labour	Barrister, senior law officer and writer
Elected hereditary peer	Liberal Democrat	Liberal Democrat spokesman
Life peer	Labour	Businessman
Life peer	Liberal Democrat	Speaker, Northern Ireland assembly
Life peer	Conservative	Barrister and non-executive director
Life peer	Cross bench	Former under-secretary of state
Elected hereditary peer	Cross bench	Former company director
Life peer	Labour	Media companies director
Life peer	Cross bench	University professor
Life peer	Labour	Parliamentary secretary, Foreign and Commonwealth Office 2001–
Elected hereditary peer	Cross bench	Former businessman
Life peer	Labour	Former policy adviser to Neil Kinnock
Life peer	Conservative	Conservative spokeswoman
Life peer	Labour	Barrister
Life peer	Other	Former Conservative party chairman
Life peer	Cross bench	Former head of the home civil service. Company director
Elected hereditary peer	Conservative	Non-executive director

Full Title	Name	Gender	Created/took s
Ashcroft, Lord	Michael Ashcroft	M	2000
Ashdown, Lord	Jeremy John Dunham	M	2001
Ashley of Stoke, Lord	Jack Ashley	M	1992
Ashton of Upholland, Baroness	Catherine Margaret Ashton	F	1999
Astor, Viscount	William Waldorf Astor	M	1999
Astor of Hever, Lord	John Jacob Astor	M	1999
Attenborough, Lord	Richard Samuel Attenborough	M	1993
Attlee, Earl of	John Richard Attlee	M	1999
Avebury, Lord	Eric Reginald Lubbock	M	1999
Bach, Lord	William Stephen Goulden Bach	M	1998
Bagri, Lord	Raj Kumar Bagri	M	1997
Baker of Dorking, Lord	Kenneth Wilfred Baker	M	1997
Baldwin of Bewdley, Earl of	Edward Alfred Alexander Baldwin	M	1999
Barber, Lord	Anthony Perrinott Lysberg Barber	M	1974
Barber of Tewkesbury, Lord	Derek Coates Barber	M	1992
Barker, Baroness	Elizabeth Jean Barker	F	1999
Barnett, Lord	Joel Barnett	M	1983
Bassam of Brighton, Lord	(John) Steven Bassam	M	1997
Bath and Wells, Bishop of	James Lawton Thompson	M	1997
Bauer, Lord	Peter Thomas Bauer	M	1983
Beaumont of Whitley, Lord	Timothy Wentworth Beaumont	M	1967
Bell, Lord	Timothy John Leigh Bell	M	1998
Belstead, Lord	John Julian Ganzoni	M	1999
Berkeley, Lord	Anthony Fitzhardinge Gueterbock	M	1999
Bernstein of Craigweil, Lord	Alex Bernstein	M	2000
Biffen, Lord	John Biffen	M	1997
Billingham, Baroness	Angela Theodora Billingham	F	2000
Bingham of Cornhill, Lord	Thomas Henry Bingham	M	1996
Birmingham, Bishop of	Mark Santer	M	1994
Birt, Lord	John Birt	M	2000
Lord Black	Conrad Black	M	2001
Blackburn, Bishop of	Alan Chesters	M	1995
Blackstone, Baroness	Tessa Ann Vosper Blackstone	F	1987
Blackwell, Lord	Norman Roy Blackwell	M	1997
Blake, Lord	Robert Norman William Blake	M	1971
Blaker, Lord	Peter Allan Renshaw Blaker	M	1994
Blatch, Baroness	Emily May Blatch	F	1987
Blease, Lord	William John Blease	M	1978
Bledisloe, Viscount	Christopher Hiley Ludlow Bathurst	M	1999
Blood, Baroness	May Blood	F	1999
Blyth of Rowington, Lord	James Blyth	M	1995
Boardman, Lord	Thomas Gray Boardman	M	1980

Parliamentary Processes

Parliament under New Labour

Jonathan Freedland

Never mind the Tories – the clear loser of the 1997 election was parliament. Until then, the institution had clung to the reassuring conviction that it was the heart and lungs of British democracy, the great arena where all the action happened.

After all, the 90s had not been bad for Westminster. John Major's wafer-thin majority turned every vote into a battle for survival, producing night after night of edge-of-the-seat drama. First came the rebellion over the Maastricht Treaty, as Conservative MPs plotted against their own government. Later, the nation saw the PM's unspoken pact with the Ulster Unionists, a tiny party who nevertheless held the crucial handful of seats that stood between the prime minister and defeat. In between, there was the Tory leadership contest, as the prime minister did battle with one of his own cabinet colleagues, John Redwood. It was all action, all the time, and it all happened in parliament. Small wonder that these were the TV years of Francis Urquhart and his *House of Cards*: Urquhart-style plotting in the tearoom and backbiting in the lobby was happening in reality every night of the week.

That all changed when Labour came to town. It was not that the party had some unique, ideological animus against Westminster (though that thought did cross the mind of some of Labour's enemies). The explanation was more basic than that. Labour began to bypass and eclipse parliament for the same reason that would have motivated any government: because it could.

Unlike John Major, Tony Blair arrived armed with a huge majority (of 179 seats). That meant he could sustain an enormous revolt of his backbench MPs and still breeze through any vote on any bill. Overnight the Commons became a rubber stamp. The illusion of the 1990s was suddenly shattered as MPs were confronted with the harsh truth: Westminster matters when majorities are tiny. The rest of the time, they are a talking shop/hot-air factory/poodle of the executive – choose your cliché.

That things had changed became clear from the very beginning. Within days of arriving in Downing Street, Tony Blair announced he would no longer come before the Commons twice a week to face Prime Minister's Questions. Instead the ritual Tuesday and Thursday sessions would be rolled up into a single bout at 3pm on Wednesdays. Labour's defence was that MPs would still have the same amount of time to grill the PM – 30 minutes – but parliamentary veterans felt they had been cheated. Now any event that broke on a Wednesday night or Thursday would escape the instant scrutiny of old.

The Commons felt it had been downgraded and there was soon more evidence to confirm these fears, with the lead being set at the very top. Blair notched up the worst attendance record of any prime minister since 1945 – participating in just 5% of Commons votes. Many of his senior colleagues sent similar messages, coming to the house to deliver set-piece statements or open debates and then hurrying off to more urgent business elsewhere.

Parliament felt slighted by New Labour, and the insults kept coming. Like an abandoned spouse, MPs soon realised that, when anything interesting happened, they were always the last to know: ministers would either leak news to the papers or make announcements on BBC Radio 4's *Today* programme – now the true debating chamber of British democracy. More than once, the then speaker, Betty Boothroyd, had to admonish ministers for their disregard of parliament, reminding them that it had the right to know government decisions first.

But MPs must have known they were swimming against a rising tide. Under Labour, the energy was shifting away from the Palace of Westminster. Often the most influential players in the government weren't in the House of Commons at all. They were either unelected special advisers – like press secretary Alistair Campbell at Number Ten or the "deputy chancellor", Ed Balls, at Number Eleven – or they were unelected peers, inserted into government via the back door of the House of Lords. Thus the PM's former college chum and fellow barrister, Charles Falconer, became a peer and minister for the Millennium Dome (among other things). David Simon from BP, David Sainsbury, Gus McDonald from Scottish Television – all were ennobled and handed key ministries.

One Blairite friend, music-business tycoon Michael Levy, was draped in ermine and dispatched as the PM's personal envoy to the Middle East. Restless MPs began to wonder whether they'd made the right career decision: if the Commons was no longer the recruiting ground for future ministers, what was the point of being there at all? Labour backbenchers – and there were so many of them – suddenly doubted they would ever get the chance of office, fearing they were doomed to serve as glorified social workers, toiling away for their constituents and watching million-aire industrialists leapfrog over them to take the best government jobs.

Impotence and irrelevance seemed to be the new watchwords: impotence, because no matter how much the Commons rebelled, the government still got its way. Now that the razor-thin majority of the Major era had given way to the Blairite bulldozer, 45 or 50 MPs could revolt, and still make not a dent on the government programme. Labour left-wingers saw tuition fees or the cut in lone parents' benefits go through, and there was nothing that they could do about it.

Perhaps the hardest moment of realisation came when it dawned on MPs that they couldn't even influence themselves, let alone the government. The 1997 result had prompted expectations of a new wave of reforms to the way parliament did its business. The arrival of 101 women on the Labour side alone led many to assume that great changes were afoot, that now the Commons would modernise its ancient working practices – introduce decent, family-friendly hours and ditch some of the public-school traditions and yah-boo adversarial style of debate that had long discredited the place.

A modernisation committee was soon established, but its work produced only minor tweaks at the margins. The chief whip, Ann Taylor, and the leader of the House, Margaret Beckett, proved to be stubborn conservatives, too attached to the Commons and all its encrusted ways. The symbolic moment came when Julia Drown, a new mother in the Mother of Parliaments, wanted to breast-feed her baby in the chamber. Madam Speaker Boothroyd said no: rules were rules. Another new Labour MP, Tess Kingham, was so frustrated by the medieval ways of the house that she stood down at the 2001 election, declaring life at Westminster to be "stuck in the Dark Ages".

Soon the media, and then the public, got the message. The newspapers had already stopped reporting Commons debates, except as joke fodder for the sketch-writers; then the BBC dropped "Yesterday in Parliament" from the *Today* programme (eventually reinstated on long wave). Most damning of all, viewers who glimpsed the House at times other than PMQs could see the proof for themselves: row upon row of empty green benches. MPs seemed to have abandoned the place, so why should anyone else pay any attention? The clearest verdict came on June 7, 2001, when Britons showed such disregard for parliament that only 59% of them bothered to vote for a person to represent them in it.

In the blame game that followed, the chief targets were either ministers, accused of control-freakery and disrespect for a great British institution, or the MPs, themselves, lambasted as craven, robotic servants of their pagers, marching like zombies through the division lobbies at the behest of their masters, the whips. The truth may be less hard on the individuals, and much harder on the system.

For the weakness of parliament has less to do with the moral fibre of the people who sit in it than with the nature of the institution itself. For Britain asks the impossible of the Commons, demanding that it be two things at once: simultaneously the home of the executive and the legislature.

In most democracies, those two functions are kept strictly separate: think of the president (executive) and Congress (legislature) in the United States. But the Commons houses both the executive, in the form of the prime minister and his Cabinet, and the lawmakers charged with keeping an eye on him. Ours is not a system of separated powers, but one where they are fused together.

The result affects the behaviour of MPs, no matter how well intentioned. For the chief function of MPs of the governing party is to maintain the executive in power, by granting the PM his Commons majority. According to Roy Jenkins, the Commons is little more than an "electoral college" which meets every day to reinstall the prime minister as exactly that. No wonder MPs vote predictably on party lines: our system forces them to do so.

In other words, the sheer logic of a parliamentary system prevents parliament doing its job properly: any government has, by definition, a majority in the very chamber that is meant to restrain it. If votes always go the government's way, that is not because MPs are mindless zombies: it's the nature of our system. The only time that a rule is broken is when a governing party is reduced to a tiny, unreliable majority and has to fight for every vote. That's what happened in the Major years, feeding the illusion that parliament could act independently of government. But in normal times, when the majorities are fat, the Commons sleeps.

This penny finally dropped after the 2001 election. Labour MPs realised the way the system works and how it was stacked against them. They had once, for example, believed they could hold the government to account through Commons select committees. But weeks after the election, the executive showed it could bring even these supposedly independent watchdogs to heel, by announcing the removal of two inquisitive MPs from the chairs of two key committees. Gwyneth Dunwoody and Donald Anderson had asked tough questions on transport and foreign affairs respectively, and so the government sacked them.

For many Labour MPs this proved an insult too far. It was too blatant a demonstration of the executive's might over the legislature, too crude a shattering of the illusion of separated powers. One hundred and eighteen of them defied the government line and voted for the return of Dunwoody and Anderson. The mouse had roared.

Such rebellions were not expected to happen often in Labour's second term; under our system, the government cannot be repeatedly defeated or else it stops being the government. But the Commons had flexed what was left of its muscles. More importantly, MPs, especially those who now realised they would never get a sniff of the ministerial leather in the chauffeured car, gave up on a job in government and began to concentrate their energies on the duties of a legislature: to scrutinise the executive.

In 2001, MPs started looking at new ways to pursue that end. They became interested in reform of the House of Lords, the second chamber, which, unlike the Commons, is sufficiently distant from the exccutive to be a viable scrutiniser. Having long feared granting the Upper House too much power, lest it rival the Commons, MPs began to see the Lords as an invaluable check, and sought to make it democratic.

And they looked to a new champion. Demoted from the Foreign Office, Robin Cook arrived as the new leader of the House with a long record of interest in constitutional reform. His ministerial aide was Stephen Twigg, the young MP who had been a firm advocate of electoral reform for the Commons. Between them, these two looked like people who would do more than merely maintain the rules of the Westminster gentlemen's club. Surely Cook in particular would want to leave a legacy of reform? By the summer of 2001 a growing band of MPs had become tired of impotence and irrelevance – interrupted only by brief spells of intrigue during the rare moments of paper-thin majorities – and had come to hope for something better. Whether they will succeed looks set to be one of the crucial battles of the early 21st century.

Jonathan Freedland is policy editor of the Guardian.

Parliament First

Paul Flynn MP

The Mother of Parliaments has been battered but not destroyed. As a backbench Labour MP, I have watched Conservative and Labour governments alike cut into her power. Now MPs are beginning to bite back.

In July 2001, the new parliament crackled into life when Labour MPs voted against the government's attempt to remove two long-serving select committee chairmen from their posts. I hope that the vote signals the rebirth of democracy in the parliamentary Labour party.

My colleagues and I feel liberated. Many did not expect to be re-elected in 2001. Back in the House, we are no longer prepared to be subservient. We have been joined by Conservatives, aware that their party may not return to power for a generation, and by former Labour ministers culled in the government's repeated reshuffles. All are bewildered, resentful and seeking new outlets for their energies.

The House of Commons will provide that outlet. Reform of the House is much needed but even before it is in place (and the new leader of the House, Robin Cook, is an enthusiastic reformer), there is much that MPs can do.

Cases of injustice, corruption and stupidity arrive daily on MPs' desks. If they are capable of being resolved by parliament and can engage public opinion, they transform the member into a dragon slayer. Independent-minded MPs, though stripped of power by the whips, can nonetheless change the way the country is run.

Opposition MPs need to change the way they work just as much as Government backbenchers do. At present they are trapped in a bleak task, instructed by their whips that their only role is obstruction and delay. Their weapon is streams of words, meaningless verbal ectoplasm that fills the time spaces and clogs the legislative machine.

Parliament's great powers of inquiry, innovation and innovative lawmaking are often deployed as crude, blunt instruments. There is great talent and experience among members, especially in the fields of law, industry, trade unions and the arts.

The number of distinguished scientists on the green benches is unprecedented but scientific thinking in the legislative process is embryonic. As a scientist, I find that disrespect for scientific thought and objective reasoning is institutionalised.

Yet, by speaking out in the Commons against what I believe to be the perversity of Britain's drugs laws, I, along with my fellow campaigners, have been rewarded by a shift in public and political opinion. Frustrated by the fact that many MPs do not know how to exploit their rights, I wrote a book for new members, *Commons Knowledge: How to Be a Backbencher*. It celebrated the sumptuous campaigning powers that all elected Members have.

After the 2001 general election, I helped found a new all-party group, Parliament First, dedicated to reclaiming parliament's rights. Our aim is to persuade our colleagues to put tribal loyalties and personal ambitions on hold to fight the cause of reform.

Backbenchers are not failed frontbenchers – or never-will-be frontbenchers. They have had a splendid history that is now being rediscovered. Chris Mullin, a Labour MP who stood down as a minister in 2001, has promoted himself from the straitjacket of the front bench to the freedom of the back bench. Karen Buck, offered a job by Tony Blair in the Whip's Office, spurned promotion to serve her constituents more ably from her higher perch on the back benches.

Backbenchers need to restore their powers in two areas in particular. Select committees have been regularly mugged by the executive, and genuine legislation from the back benches is almost extinct.

Winners of the private member's bill lottery that takes place every session are offered hand-me-down government bills. These are the only ones with a chance of reaching the statute book. A team of legislative assassins, tutored by government whips, kill off all other original private bills. Both parties have shamelessly stolen backbenchers' legislative time to expand their own agenda.

Likewise, select committees usually underachieve. The position of chairman is agreed through horse-trading by the whips and independent-minded backbenchers are excluded from membership.

At best, select committees can be blissful oases of intelligence and calm, remote from the inter-party fracas. In 1992, members of the Transport Committee defied the whips and made a Tory railway buff, Robert Adley, their chairman. He produced a remarkably prophetic report on rail privatisation. Had the government listened to the unanimous voice of their own MPs, the transport chaos that followed would have been avoided.

More recently two most momentous reports challenged government policy: Gwynneth Dunwoody chaired the Transport Committee's forensic filleting of the proposed privatisation of air-traffic control and Donald Anderson's Foreign-Affairs Committee produced a report that demolished the government's approach to the Star Wars project.

But these are the exceptions. Most select committees avoid controversial subjects. Vacuous reports are churned out on anodyne subjects where consensus is easily achieved.

In many cases, too, MPs' interrogation of witnesses is amateurish and poorly prepared. Former ministers often recall how select committees failed to ask the right questions when they appeared before them. Ministers, civil servants and other well-prepared witnesses frequently bamboozle committee members. Often MPs with specialist knowledge, excluded from the committee, fume from the public gallery while their ill-informed colleagues are duped.

It is essential, therefore, that select committees should be able to enrol additional MPs in the ranks for specialist questioning.

And there is much else that can be done. Parliamentarians have minuscule influence in initiating and influencing government policy. Backbenchers' speeches in the chamber, in Westminster Hall and in committees do nothing but ventilate pent-up feelings of frustration.

The only worthwhile reform has been the introduction of prelegislative hearings that have reshaped new laws. In the 2001 parliament, Robin Cook plans to extend prelegislative work. He is a natural reformer with a gleam in his eye when he talks of modernisation that was absent from his recent predecessors.

The revolt of July 2001 was a triumph for the Parliament First group but the work continues. A fusion of the progressive zeal of a gifted Commons Leader and the frustration of disregarded backbench talent is unique.

Reforms have been delayed for a century. I hope they will be achieved by this holy alliance.

Paul Flynn is the Labour MP for Newport West.

Westminster Whips

Nicholas Watt

Gyles Brandreth, the daytime television host who enjoyed a brief interlude as the Conservative MP for Chester in the 1990s, gave a colourful taste in his diaries of how new members are cut down to size when they first arrive at Westminster.

Within days of his election, Brandreth was told by party managers that every MP must vote – almost on pain of death – when a "three-line whip" is in force. "You will be here to vote – unless you can produce a doctor's certificate showing you are dead," the shaking MP was told by a senior Tory whip.

Such blunt messages, which are delivered to new MPs in all parties, provide a telling reminder of where the real power lies at Westminster. Any newly elected members with grandiose ideas of emulating Tony Benn, the former Labour minister who became a respected voice of dissent in his last years in parliament, are soon brought to book by their party's whips who control discipline and dispense patronage.

Whips, who are named after "whippers-in", who kept hunting hounds in line, are the prime minister's central instrument for ensuring that the government's business makes it onto the statute book and life is made uncomfortable for disloyal backbenchers. The government's 15 whips – from the chief whip down to lowly assistant whips – work as a close-knit group monitoring the Commons chamber and myriad committees to check for signs of dissent and to ensure that the government's business sails through both chambers. Their work is mirrored by 11 Tory whips and two Liberal Democrat whips.

The main focus of the government whips' week is a lengthy meeting which kicks off at 9.30am every Wednesday in Downing Street to discuss forthcoming Commons business. Whips should feel free to speak their mind – no notes are taken – to warn of difficulties ahead, either from troublesome backbenchers or from foolish government plans.

The meeting produces "The Whip", a two-page document outlining the government's parliamentary business on a weekly basis, which is shown on page 338. This is released to Labour MPs in two stages – a white provisional version, which is released ten days before the week in question, and a pink final version, which is released four days ahead.

In the Labour "Whip" shown, MPs are told that Commons business will begin at 2.30pm on Monday July 2, 2001, with questions to Home Office ministers. The column on the right tells Labour MPs that, if they want to question the culture secretary in two weeks' time, they must table their questions that day.

Attendance was voluntary for backbenchers on July 2 until 6.30pm when the three thick lines under the homelessness bill indicated that a three-line whip was in place for the main second reading debate on the bill. Only the frail, or MPs with genuine excuses, such as the need to be with a newborn child, will have been allowed the night off.

The note at the bottom of the page, which tells MPs that they must not miss deferred voting, signals one of the reforms introduced to the Commons after the 1997 election. Votes on less important matters, such as orders, are now deferred after late-night debates to allow MPs to go home earlier.

Three-line whips were in place every night until Thursday July 5, when MPs faced the least harsh one-line whip for two votes. These votes appeared at the time to be trivial, but subsequently gave the first taste of a post-election rebellion by Labour MPs.

On July 5, Labour MPs were asked to turn up to vote as they liked on the SSRB (the Senior Salaries Review Body) report on their pay and on a motion to set up select committees. On the first vote Labour MPs staged a mini rebellion, when they defied government advice and voted for an increase in their pensions.

The second vote – to set up the select committees that monitor government departments – passed without a hitch. But, six days later, the issue blew up in the government's face, when Hilary Armstrong, the chief whip, summarily sacked two independent-minded Labour committee chairmen. Within days, Ms Armstrong was forced to reinstate Gwyneth Dunwoody and Donald Anderson, demonstrating the limits of the whips' powers if they misjudge the mood on their benches.

Tory MPs savoured the government's embarrassment, muttering that Tony Blair made an error by appointing Ms Armstrong as his chief whip. Although she is a considerable figure in the Labour party, Ms Armstrong has never served in the Whips' Office, depriving her of the instinctive feel for the atmosphere of the Commons that whips never lose.

Conservatives also believe that the prime minister is wrong to appoint whips on his own. When the Tories were in office, any whip was allowed to blackball a proposed new entrant to "the Office", ensuring that a camaraderie and a degree of continuity was established. Such niceties, which ensured that John Major's government limped through to the end of its term in the face of extraordinary odds, appear not to bother Mr Blair, who has even deprived his chief whip of her official office at 12 Downing Street.

The rebellion over the select committees may signal a gradual decline in the power of the whips, after the government agreed to give MPs a say in the appointment of future chairmen. Opposition calls for a less centralised system ring hollow, however. In 1976, when the Tories were last in opposition, Lord Hailsham complained that MPs were so weak that the government had become an "elective dictatorship".

Within three years, Lord Hailsham was an enthusiastic member of Margaret Thatcher's Cabinet, which maintained a vicelike grip over its MPs.

Nicholas Watt is a *Guardian* political correspondent.

The Whip showing a three-line whip

PARLIAMENTARY LABOUR PARTY

MONDAY 2ND JULY 2001.

The House will meet at 2.30 pm.

1. Home Office Questions.

Tabling for Culture, Media and Sport, Church Commissioners and Public Accounts Commission.

2. HOMELESSNESS BILL:
    (Rt Hon Stephen Byers and Sally Keeble)

SECOND READING.

YOUR ATTENDANCE FROM 6.30PM IS ESSENTIAL.
===

TUESDAY 3RD JULY 2001.

The House will meet at 2.30 pm.

1. Transport, Local Government and Regions Questions.

Tabling for Scotland, Advocate General, Lord Chancellor's Dept. , President of the Council and House of Commons Commission.

2. EUROPEAN COMMUNITIES (FINANCE) BILL:
    (Rt Hon Andrew Smith and Ruth Kelly)

SECOND READING.

YOUR ATTENDANCE AT 9.00PM FOR 10.00PM IS ESSENTIAL.
===

WEDNESDAY 4TH JULY 2001.

The House will meet at 2.30 pm.

1. International Development and Prime Minister's Questions.

Tabling for Northern Ireland and Prime Minister.

2. EUROPEAN COMMUNITIES (AMENDMENT) BILL:
    (Rt Hon Jack Straw and Peter Hain)

SECOND READING.

YOUR ATTENDANCE AT 9.00PM F0R 10.00PM IS ESSENTIAL.
===

****

DEFERRED VOTING
YOUR ATTENDANCE TO HAND IN YOUR VOTE PAPER
BETWEEN 3.30PM AND 5.00PM IS ESSENTIAL.

****

THURSDAY 5TH JULY 2001   The House will meet at 11.30am

1. Education and Skills and   Tabling for Treasury.
    Solicitor General Questions.

2. MOTIONS RELATING TO THE SSRB REPORT AND RELATED ISSUES.
    (Rt Hon Robin Cook and Stephen Twigg)

    YOUR ATTENDANCE IS REQUESTED.

3. MOTION TO AMEND THE STANDING ORDERS RELATING TO SELECT COMMITTEES.
    (Rt Hon Robin Cook and Stephen Twigg)

    YOUR CONTINUED ATTENDANCE IS REQUESTED.

FRIDAY 6TH JULY 2001.   The House will not be sitting.

HILARY ARMSTRONG

Summer Adjournment.
Subject to the progress of business it is proposed that the House rise at the end of business on
Friday 20th July for the Summer Recess and return on Monday 15th October 2001

Life in the Chamber

Julian Glover

The chamber of the House of Commons

Parliament has a problem. Its reputation is built upon work in the chamber of the House of Commons and public attention depends upon it. Yet MPs mostly spend their time elsewhere. The result is an uncertain institution with an empty core.

Research in the 1997 parliament found that there are often fewer than 50 MPs in the chamber and sometimes fewer than ten. Only for 30 minutes a week, during Prime Minister's Questions, can the chamber be guaranteed to be full – and even then a Hansard Society survey found that MPs are sceptical about the point of turning up. Only 8% of MPs regard Prime Minister's Questions as effective, according to the research.

Yet the same report found that 84% of MPs believe that the work of select committees – which takes place away from the chamber – makes a difference.

Reporting in 2001, a Hansard Society commission concluded that the chamber is "in decline ... simply one option among many for the active politician and in many respects the least appealing".

Role of the chamber

Does the chamber of the House of Commons matter in a modern parliament more and more dependent on committee work and on media-savvy MPs building a reputation in their constituencies?

The answer is yes. The chamber remains the pinnacle of parliament. It is the best parliamentary forum for party politics, for holding ministers to account and for raising issues. Even in decline, it can be thrilling at moments of political tension and engaging at the quietest of times.

It tests and examines, makes and destroys, in a way no other political institution can manage. Its green benches are a symbol of British democracy and the arguments thrown in stark, partisan form across the floor of the House are the ones judged in a general election.

Ultimately, it is the balance of forces in the chamber that decides who governs the nation. The last two prime ministers fell, at least in part, because they lost the confidence of their Commons colleagues.

The problem facing the chamber is confusion, not about its role but about how it can best be fulfilled. Much time on the floor of the House is wasted; what goes on is second-rate.

"The chamber should be the plenary session of the House of Commons," reported the Hansard Society commission. "In order to perform this function, it should meet less often and meet for a purpose."

Activity in the chamber

Whatever the faults of the modern chamber, inactivity is not one of them. Since 1960, the number of sitting hours per session has remained constant; indeed it has grown with the addition, in 1999, of a secondary chamber in Westminster Hall. This was added to allow an airing to issues that do not find time in the main chamber but its success has been mixed at best.

The House of Commons year is broken by several recesses. In a non-general-election year, the pattern is as follows:

November: The Queen's speech and state opening of parliament
Late December to early January: Christmas recess
February: Half-term recess (since 1999)
Spring: Easter recess
May: Second spring recess
Late July to mid-October: Summer recess
Autumn: Spillover debates for one to two weeks before end of session.

When the house is not sitting it is adjourned. At the end of each parliamentary session, ahead of the Queen's speech, it is prorogued. Ahead of general elections, the house is first prorogued and then dissolved. The normal sitting hours of the main chamber are currently:

Mondays, Tuesdays, Wednesdays
2.30pm to 10.30pm

Thursdays
11.30am to 7.30pm

Fridays
9.30am to 3pm (apart from ten Fridays each session)

In addition, activity takes place in Westminster Hall (in fact, in a specially converted room off the main hall) on:

Tuesdays
10am to 1pm

Wednesdays
9.30am to 2pm

Thursdays
2.30pm for up to 3 hours

Late-night sittings – beyond 10.30pm – have become less common since 1997; until then parliamentary business continued past 11pm most nights. Some MPs would like the Commons to begin work earlier in order to end evening sittings altogether.

The parliamentary day

The House of Commons begins its work each day when the speaker leads a procession through Central Lobby, carrying the mace, the symbol of parliamentary authority. Once the speaker is in the chamber, the Commons chaplain reads prayers and the public galleries are then opened.

By tradition, business is taken in a set order, although not all aspects of the Commons business take place every day.

Immediately after prayers, the speaker makes any necessary formal announcements. These are followed by private business (on private legislation) and then by questions.

Oral questions

Although parliamentary questions take up no more than an hour each parliamentary day, they receive the bulk of media coverage and are by far the best-attended event in the Commons chamber. That does not make them the most fruitful event, however: MPs complain that questions encourage theatrical point-scoring, not dull but effective scrutiny.

Questions are taken on Mondays, Tuesdays, Wednesdays and Thursdays between 2.35pm and 3.30pm.

On Wednesdays the prime minister (or the deputy prime minister if the prime minister is away from London) takes questions from 3pm. On other days and before 3pm on Wednesday, departmental ministers take questions: a rota establishes which department has priority for answering questions, with questions to each department taking place about every two weeks. At most departmental question times, questions are answered by several ministers, although the Cabinet minister will take the lead.

On average, the prime minister answers questions for about two hours a month and major departments for about one hour each.

MPs who want to ask a question must notify the Commons Table Office no more than ten sitting days in advance. Applications are shuffled to decide the order in which they will be asked; only those near the top of the order paper stand a chance.

The speaker calls out questions in the order in which they appear in the day's order paper. By tradition, most MPs submit a bland question and then follow up in the chamber with a surprise "supplementary". Ministers – and particularly the prime minister – are equipped by their civil servants and special advisers with a comprehensive brief to prepare them for these.

The speaker may call several MPs to ask supplementary questions before turning to the next question on the order paper. This gives the speaker substantial power in shaping Question Time.

Questions and supplementaries must relate to issues under the control of the department being questioned – the prime minister can answer on any issue. Questions should either seek information or press for action; they cannot express an opinion.

At Prime Minister's Questions, the leader of the opposition is allowed up to five supplementary questions and the leader of the second largest opposition party can ask two. All other MPs are allowed one.

Written questions

MPs do not always get the chance to ask oral questions in the House but they can submit written questions to ministers. Some have found this a useful way of putting ministers on the spot away from the partisan debating style of oral questions.

In an average session, between 35,000 and 40,000 written questions are submitted; departments can refuse to answer questions that cost more than £550 to answer.

In the 1997 parliament, the Liberal Democrat MP, Norman Baker, became a particular exponent of written questions, authoring one which led to the second resignation of the Northern Ireland minister, Peter Mandelson, in January 2001.

Likewise, ministers sometimes use written questions as a way of making public news that would be politically embarrassing if it came out in a public forum.

Private-notice questions

Private-notice questions are a special form of oral question that allows MPs to raise urgent issues. MPs who wish to raise them must notify the speaker before 12 noon; the speaker then decides whether they can be raised in the chamber.

Every Thursday a PNQ is asked so that the leader of the House can list business scheduled for the week ahead.

Other business

Following questions, the Commons turns to other business before starting the main work of the day. This may include the first reading of bills and applications for emergency debates.

Debates

Once the heart of parliamentary life, reported in depth in the press and responsible for the making and breaking of political careers, debates now linger on in a skeletal form. They dominate the parliamentary day as the "main business" of the house but they are of dubious value.

Debates fall into two categories. Some relate to legislation passing through the House (a process explained on pages 349–53). Others take place on important issues of the day, without any immediate aim of making new laws.

These general debates themselves take two forms: substantive motions and adjournment motions.

Substantive motions

Substantive motions are put forward by an individual MP and propose a particular point of view, which the House considers. An MP from an opposing party will propose an amendment to this and the House then votes on the motion and the amendment.

The government initiates regular debates on substantive motions, including two annual debates on the budget and the Queen's speech.

Most substantive debates take place on the 20 days in each parliamentary session set aside for the opposition. On these days the main opposition parties choose a topic to put to the house (17 opposition days are awarded to the official opposition and three to the second-largest opposition party).

On January 24, 2001, for instance, the Conservative health spokesman, Dr Liam Fox, initiated a debate on the government's health policy:

"That this House notes with concern the failures of Her Majesty's government's public health policy, particularly relating to immunisation and communicable diseases; and calls on the government to consider urgent measures to reduce the risks to public safety and to take urgent action to allay public concerns."

The secretary of state for health, Alan Milburn, proposed an amendment praising the government's record and attacking the situation inherited from the Conservative party.

The debate began at 7.30pm and ran until just before 10.30pm. The government's amendment was carried by a majority of 182.

This predictable result encouraged a formulaic debate that engaged neither MPs nor the public.

No-confidence motions

At moments of high political tension, the opposition may move a debate proposing that the House has "no confidence" in the government. (The government may also announce that a debate carries the status of a confidence motion, as John Major did several times in the 1992 parliament.) If the motion is passed, the government resigns and a general election takes place. The last time this took place was March 28, 1979.

Private members' motions

On ten Fridays and four half-days each session, private members introduce their own motions for debate. The members are decided by ballot and may choose the topic. Most such debates are not taken to a vote and are often used to raise issues of constituency, not national interest.

Adjournment debates

Adjournment debates take several forms. The most common take place each day at the end of parliamentary business when a government whip moves an adjournment motion ("that this House do now adjourn") and a backbencher speaks for around quarter of an hour on a topic of his or her choice (the topic must be announced in advance and involve an issue over which the government has responsibility). A minister with responsibility for the subject replies, also for 15 minutes.

Since these debates take place late at night and usually cover specific constituency issues, they are poorly attended. However, they do allow MPs to put on the record matters that might otherwise be missed, and they often help an MP boost his or her constituency profile.

A second form of adjournment debate takes place before each recess. The parliamentary day is given over to debates initiated by backbenchers ("Whingeing Gits Day", as Tony Banks MP describes it).

On July 20, 2001, debates took place on matters such as the London Underground, mobile phones, the Health Service, safety on London's railways, animal welfare, London hospitals, school building and the planning system, among other issues.

Adjournment debates also take place three times a session on a bill regulating government expenditure, the consolidated fund bill.

Finally, adjournment motions may also be proposed by the government. This allows debate on controversial issues or ones on which the government lacks a policy, without the government running the risk of defeat on a motion that actually mentions the policy.

Standing order No 24

This rule allows MPs to apply to the speaker for time for an emergency adjournment debate on an issue of national importance. MPs applying for this form of adjournment debate are allowed three minutes to put their case for a longer debate to take place next time.

Although the speaker rarely allows an application for an emergency adjournment debate, MPs sometimes use the three-minute application speech to put an issue before the House.

Divisions

At the end of all debates, whether on legislation or motions, the House divides (parliamentary language for voting). Traditionally, there is a "ten o'clock vote" at the end of main business each day.

Recently, a change to parliamentary standing orders allows some votes to be held over to the next day, so called "deferred voting". If this happens, the vote is listed on the order paper and MPs may vote at any time between 3.30pm and 5pm.

Normally, divisions are taken first in the chamber, with supporters crying "aye" and opponents "no".

The speaker may decide that one side has won, and calls out, "The ayes [or the nos] have it." If MPs continue to cry out, the speaker calls out, "Clear the lobby," and voting begins. Division bells ring across Westminster, summoning MPs, who vote in person by passing through either the "aye" or the "no" lobby.

After eight minutes, the doors of the lobby are locked and MPs are counted leaving the lobby by tellers (MPs who do not take part in the vote). There are two tellers for each lobby.

The result is handed to the speaker, who then reads it out in the House.

Early-day motions

Early-day motions are used by MPs to signify their interest in an issue and to attract support for it from other members. In theory, they are applications for a debate "on an early day" but in practice the debate never takes place.

The main benefit is that the EDM is printed on the Commons order paper together with the name of the MP who sponsored it and (initially) others who have signed. Some EDMs are signed by more than 200 MPs; most by no more than one or two.

Many EDMs cover cross-party issues, such as arms control. Since 1997, the number of lightweight EDMs raising constituency issues has grown; indeed, in the 1997 parliament, more EDMs were put down praising local football teams than on any other issue.

Points of order

MPs may make points of order at any time, but do not normally do so during Questions. In theory, MPs must use a point of order to draw the speaker's attention to a breach of the standing orders of the house. In practice, MPs often make points of order to interrupt other speakers or to raise a political issue.

The official report

The proceedings of parliament are published in the official report, known as Hansard. Separate publications cover the House of Commons and the Lords. Hansard consists of a verbatim record of what is said in the chamber, available on the web at: www.publications.parliament.uk/pa/cm/cmpubns.htm

Julian Glover is editor of *Guardian Unlimited Politics*.

Activity in parliament – leading MPs (1997–2001)

Member	Recorded activity	Member	Recorded activity
The Speaker	3,616	Key, Robert	1,204
Baker, Norman	3,549	Chope, Christopher	1,203
Bercow, John	3,207	Swayne, Desmond	1,184
Hancock, Mike	2,073	Mackinlay, Andrew	1,182
Prentice, Gordon	2,040	Redwood, John	1,172
Taylor, Matthew	1,880	Bruce, Malcolm	1,167
Burstow, Paul	1,788	Wigley, Dafydd	1,162
McNamara, Kevin	1,785	Boswell, Tim	1,149
Dalyell, Tam	1,725	Evans, Nigel	1,134
Mitchell, Austin	1,640	Cohen, Harry	1,108
Flynn, Paul	1,606	Jenkin, Bernard	1,102
Maclean, David	1,575	Smith, Llew	1,100
Cox, Tom	1,565	Dismore, Andrew	1,093
Tonge, Jenny	1,544	Yeo, Tim	1,089
Hughes, Simon	1,469	Brady, Graham	1,079
Corbyn, Jeremy	1,456	Chaytor, David	1,073
Gillan, Cheryl	1,388	Campbell Savours, Dale	1,062
Cable, Vincent	1,348	Forth, Eric	1,041
McIntosh, Anne	1,335	Drew, David	1,040
Hoyle, Lindsay	1,314	Field, Frank	1,024
Vaz, Keith	1,309	Dunwoody, Gwyneth	1,000
Webb, Steve	1,270	Marsden, Paul	986
Clappison, James	1,266	Cunningham, Jim	982
Lidington, David	1,264	Foster, Don	974
Robertson, Laurence	1,217		

Data relates to the 1997–2001 parliament. Activity includes oral, written, and private notice questions; divisions; EDMs; standing committee contributions; Hansard references; parliamentary papers and legislation.

Source: parlianet.com

Prime Minister's Questions – most-asked topics (1997–)

Subject Terms	Counts	Subject Terms	Counts	Subject Terms	Counts
Finance	202	Pensioners	46	Redundancy	29
NHS	103	Schools	42	Industry	29
Taxation	80	Refugees	42	Poverty	28
Education	80	Disease control	41	Iraq	28
Economic and		Unemployment	39	Crime	28
monetary union	80	Compensation	38	Railways	27
Northern Ireland	71	Children	37	Manufacturing industries	27
Reform	70	Referendums	35	Labour party	27
Foot and mouth disease	57	Minimum wage	35	Fees and charges	27
Public expenditure	54	Euro	33	Devolution	26
Waiting lists	53	Rural areas	32	Asylum seekers	26
Police	53	Elections	32	Weapons	25
Northern Ireland		Serbia	31	Wales	25
Government	53	Policy	31	USA	25
Kosovo	53	Health services	31	Private sector	25
Scotland	52	Social security benefits	30	Housing	25
Armed conflict	52	Manpower	30		
Ministers	47	Closures	30		

Source: parlianet.com

Early-day motions – most common topics (1997–)

Subject	References	Subject	References
Football	128	Females	26
Human rights	97	Licensing	26
Children	64	Abuse	25
Finance	52	Disclosure of information	25
Armed conflict	48	Festivals and special occasions	25
Closures	42	Health services	25
Medical treatments	42	Pay	25
USA	40	Reform	25
Members	39	Disabled	24
Death	38	Homicide	24
Fees and charges	38	Housing	24
Environment protection	37	Nature conservation	24
Wales	37	Nuclear weapons	24
Compensation	35	Cyprus	23
Safety	33	Elderly	23
Northern Ireland	32	India	23
Television	32	Health hazards	22
Elections	31	NHS	22
Banks	30	Regulation	22
Rugby	30	Research	22
Scotland	30	Animal welfare	21
Sports competitors	30	Hunting	21
Peace negotiations	29	Police	21
Schools	29	Prisoners	21
Anniversaries	28	Cricket	21
Drugs	28		

Source: parlianet.com

Written questions – most active MPs (1997–)

Member	Written questions	Member	Written questions
Baker, Norman	3319	Tonge, Jenny	1365
Taylor, Matthew	1973	Flynn, Paul	1327
Hancock, Mike	1914	Lidington, David	1317
Bercow, John	1891	Gillan, Cheryl	1254
McNamara, Kevin	1781	Vaz, Keith	1212
Prentice, Gordon	1764	Cable, Vincent	1190
Maclean, David	1741	Bruce, Malcolm	1141
Burstow, Paul	1640	Hoyle, Lindsay	1139
Cox, Tom	1602	Webb, Steve	1133
Mitchell, Austin	1497	Dalyell, Tam	1129

Source: parlianet.com

Legislation

Julian Glover

Parliament's right to make the law is central to its existence. Though the details change, the process – proposal, debate, amendment, and enactment – has been settled for more than 500 years.

But critics, including the respected Hansard Society, point out that, for all the ritual, parliament is failing in its job of producing good legislation. Certainly the current process soaks up lots of MPs' time, for mixed reward.

Bills

All legislation begins as a bill – a draft law, not yet in force. There are two types: private bills and public bills.

Private bills are pieces of legislation put forward for the benefit of an individual person, company, or government authority.

Public bills, which make up the bulk of legislation, have wider scope. Most are put forward by the government as part of its legislative programme, the bulk of which is announced at the start of the parliamentary session in the Queen's speech.

These government bills are allocated time for debate and the government Whips' Office does its best to ensure they become law. This usually works; in 1995–96, all 43 government bills were passed, even though the government of the day lacked a secure majority.

Private member's legislation

A handful of public bills are also introduced by individual MPs (confusingly, these bills are known as private members' bills). At the start of each parliamentary session, 20 MPs win parliamentary time for a piece of legislation of their choice, although only the top few MPs have any chance of their bill becoming law. Such members' legislation takes precedence over public on 13 Fridays in each parliamentary session.

Another version of a private member's bill, known as a ten-minute rule bill, is only technically a form of legislation. The intention is to allow MPs a short debate on a topical issue rather than bring in a law (although some ten-minute rule bills do reach the statute book).

Passage through parliament

Bills need to be passed by both Houses in parliament and receive royal assent to become law, but all bills (apart from some financial measures) can begin their passage in either House.

The rules governing the passage of legislation are broadly the same in both Houses but the details below refer to procedure in the House of Commons.

Full details on which bills are proceeding through parliament, as well as information on other major developments, can be found in the Weekly Information Bulletin on the web at: www.parliament.the-stationery-office.co.uk/pa/cm/cmwib. htm

First reading

The first reading is a technical stage, used to introduce a bill. There is no debate or decision. Following the first reading, the bill is printed, and also put on the web at: www.parliament.the-stationery-office.co.uk/pa/pabills.htm/

Second reading

The second reading is the first test of the legislation and normally takes place within a fortnight of the first reading. Government bills are proposed by a senior minister and generally opposed by the equivalent opposition spokesperson.

The debate ends with a speech by another government minister. In theory, this winding-up speech responds to points made in the debate. Some MPs complain that these speeches are getting shorter and less relevant and that second reading debates are now badly attended.

At the second reading, the House debates the principle behind the bill, rather than the detail. Although government bills are almost never defeated at this point – the exception, in April 1986, was the government's plan to liberalise rules on Sunday trading – the second reading of a bill is often a major parliamentary moment. Many MPs also use second readings as a chance to make speeches that might get news coverage in their constituencies.

Any bill that involves a significant charge on central government funds or sets taxes theoretically requires the passing of a money resolution or a ways-and-means resolution immediately after the second reading (though this stage has been optional since 1995).

Some non-controversial bills receive their second readings in committee, rather than on the floor of the House.

Committee stage

The committee stage is the first significant test of the bill and can run for several weeks. In theory, it involves clause-by-clause consideration and amendment of the measure – normally by 16 to 20 MPs serving on a standing committee. In practice, it is a flawed process in need of reform, more of which below.

Some contentious or significant bills are considered, not in the usual standing committees, but by the House of Commons as a whole, sitting in committee, such as the 1993 Maastricht Treaty legislation. Most bills in the Lords are also considered by a similar committee of the whole house.

In a busy parliamentary session, there can be up to 20 standing committees, each dealing with up to two bills at a time.

The aim is to allow MPs to bring individual expertise to bear on legislation in a less confrontational atmosphere than on the floor of the House.

The reality is that standing committees are dominated by party whips and most amendments are brought in by government departments to correct errors in hastily drafted bills, rather than by MPs trying to improve the legislation. As the writer Ferdinand Mount puts it:

"Only a somewhat shamefaced conspiracy between the two front benches and the parliamentary lobby prevents the scandalous spectacle of committee proceedings being more fully brought home to us: ministers wearily reading out their briefs, the opposition spokesman trotting out the same old amendments purely for the purposes of party rhetoric and without any serious hope of improving the bill, the government backbencher – pressed men present merely to make up the government's majority – reading the newspapers or answering their letters; it requires only a few top hats, brocade waistcoats and cigars to complete a tableau of almost Regency sloth."

Many MPs would like to reform the committee stage to allow them to spend time investigating issues before considering the bill – talking to outside experts, for instance. A procedure to allow this was introduced in 1980 and has been tried on a limited amount of legislation since 1997.

If a bill is amended in committee – and most are – it is reprinted before being returned to the House.

Report stage

At the report stage, MPs consider the bill as amended by committee. All MPs can speak and vote on the bill at this stage and changes can be made.

Third reading

This is the final stage and often takes place immediately after the report. The aim is to allow the House to consider a bill as a whole, after amendment. No major changes can be made to the legislation at this point and the third reading is often very brief.

The House of Lords

If a bill has begun its progress in the Commons, it is now sent to the House of Lords. Likewise, bills that originate in the Lords are sent on to the Commons.

The procedure in the Lords is similar. Minor differences are that bills are considered by the whole House, rather than in standing committee; there is no guillotine to curtail debate; amendments can be made at the third reading as well as at the committee and report stages.

The House of Lords rarely prevents a bill passed by the Commons from becoming law but often amends it. Sometimes this amendment can have the effect of defeating it.

Both Houses need to agree a common text of a bill before it can receive royal assent. If the Lords does not amend a bill after it has gone through the Commons, the Commons is told and the bill is considered passed.

If changes are made, the Commons debates the changes and either agrees with them, agrees but adds further changes, or rejects them. This process can be very brief.

If the Commons rejects the Lords' amendments, the Lords considers the matter once more. If the two Houses of Parliament fail to agree, the will of the Commons prevails after a year's delay, if the government chooses to use the 1949 Parliament Act to enforce it.

Royal assent

When a bill has been passed by both Houses, it is sent for royal assent. This is a formality – assent has not been denied since 1707.

Sessions

Traditionally, public bills had to complete all their parliamentary stages in one session. If the session ended with the bill only partly considered, the process had to begin again from the start.

This rule has now been eased to allow some legislation to continue from one session to another. The first bill to receive this treatment was the complex and controversial financial services and markets bill.

Timetabling

Traditionally, parliament considered legislation stage by stage, with no clear timetable in mind. This changed in the late 19th century, when governments began to curtail debate to speed legislation.

Initially, this was done by passing a so-called guillotine motion, which allocates a certain amount of time to debate a bill before it moves on to the next stage. Guillotine motions were not normally passed until a bill had completed its second reading, and until slow progress in committee had made it necessary.

In December 2000, a new, more formalised system of allocating time was introduced on an experimental basis. This has been continued in the new parliament. Under the system, a programme motion is introduced at the start of a bill's second reading, curtailing debate at 10.30pm and timetabling the bill's progress through committee.

Draft legislation

Many MPs complain that bills arrive at the House of Commons in poor shape and that parliamentary time is wasted making corrections that should have been made earlier (a particular bugbear at the committee stage). As a result, pressure has grown for some bills to be issued in draft form for consideration by select committee before being formally introduced.

This was tried in 1999 with the freedom of information bill, which was studied by the Public Administration Select Committee. The committees made a series of criticisms of the legislation but they were mostly ignored in the final drafting. The bill sent to Parliament was little different from that seen by committee.

Nonetheless, the 2001 Queen's speech contained proposals for several draft bills, including one further reforming the House of Lords.

Secondary legislation

Acts of Parliament are passed using the process described above. Although it has faults, it does at least allow for some scrutiny. But much of what government does avoids any thorough examination at all, beyond some oversight by the House of Lords. This is because it is passed in the form of delegated or secondary legislation, issued directly by ministers.

These orders and instruments are as much the law of the land as an Act of Parliament. About 3,000 are issued each year.

Parliamentary authority over them is preserved nominally by ensuring that secondary legislation can only be issued by a body answerable to Westminster.

Parliament does have the right to affirm or annul certain secondary legislation and a House of Lords committee checks some secondary legislation.

However secondary legislation can be used to amend or abolish some parliamentary Acts – a sweeping and rather undemocratic power known in Whitehall as Henry VIII clauses.

One Act, passed in 1994, allows ministers to amend or repeal any Act of Parliament if "the minister is of the opinion that this can be done without removing any necessary protection".

Committees

Julian Glover

Does parliament's future lie in the committee corridor? Action in the chamber of the House of Commons gets the glory but Westminster's most effective work is done by committees. And, if reformers get their way, their power will grow.

Nothing illustrates this more than the row that blew up in July 2001, when Labour whips removed two respected committee chairmen and replaced them with members more sympathetic to the government. In a Commons motion to approve the change, 124 Labour MPs defied the government and voted to restore the sacked chairmen, Labour MPs Gwyneth Dunwoody and Donald Anderson. This "peasants' revolt", the first Commons defeat for Tony Blair, set down an intriguing marker for parliamentary independence in Labour's second term.

Supporters of select committees look with envy towards the work of the US Congress, an institution based on the British parliament, but that now carries out much of its business away from the floor of the House. As a result, say British reformers, Congress does a better job of holding the president to account than the Commons ever does with the prime minister.

Could the model work on this side of the Atlantic? Even the existing departmental select committees have occasionally punched above their weight to make themselves heard. Suitably beefed up, they could point the way to a revival of parliamentary power.

But committee critics argue that they lack the excitement and prestige that has given parliament its historic strength, and say that increased committee work will lead to the bureaucratisation of parliament.

Select committees

The backbone of Westminster's committee system is the House of Commons' network of departmental select committees. This was set up by Mrs Thatcher in 1979, immediately after her first general election success, building upon a long tradition of parliamentary work away from the floor of the House. Although some issue-based select committees were created in the mid-1960s, only after 1979 did Commons committees shadow every government department.

The aim was to improve the Commons' scrutiny of government without threatening the government's power to pass legislation. Because the timetable of the chamber of the Commons is entirely under the control of the party whips, reformers saw select committees as an escape route, leading the way to less confrontational politics.

The select committee system's impact has been mixed: intermittently reports have hit the headlines and changed government policy, sometimes they have had an impact behind the scenes, but more often their work has been ignored by the press and undermined by the executive.

Neither have all committees performed as well as the best. A report in 2000 by the Liaison Committee (which runs select committees) pointed out that "their success has not been consistent and success not unalloyed. In each of the five parliaments since 1979, different committees have shone; some have found it difficult to surmount the difficulties they have encountered."

Departmental committees are intended to operate on a cross-party basis and it is to their credit that, for much of the time, they do, but the pressures against this are great. Governments prefer committees not to reach conclusions that may hinder their re-election; oppositions, naturally, want the opposite. Self-interest among committee members, informal channels run by whips, and simple rule-bending can all taint what should be impartial reports.

How are members chosen?

Select committee places – between 11 and 17 on each committee – are filled after a general election by backbench MPs of all parties in proportion to each party's parliamentary representation.

Some MPs have places on more than one committee. Ministers and frontbench spokesmen from the main opposition do not serve on departmental committees, although they do on some others.

Each select committee is chaired by a senior MP, chosen at the start of each parliament. Chairmen can serve for more than one parliament.

Members are currently chosen by the committee of selection, a secretive body of nine MPs, including five whips, although, following the debacle after the 2001 election, this committee is likely to be re-formed. By convention, MPs on this committee do not challenge party nominations. Most nominations are agreed without discussion and meetings often last no more than five minutes.

This system means that select committees, nominally free of party control, are actually far from independent. Troublesome MPs may find themselves without committee places, or serving on a committee that does not cover their main interest.

Changes by the party whips take place all the time. The composition of the social security select committee changed by 66% in one year in the 1997 parliament, greatly lessening its chances of coming to grips with the complex department it shadows.

Many MPs see reform of the committee of selection to give power to backbenchers, not whips, as a priority.

How do select committees work?

Individual committees have developed their own culture and practices, but all of them work along the same lines. Committees do not try to scrutinise everything all the time, but choose specific topics to investigate.

In spring 2001, for instance, the defence committee investigated Gulf veterans' illnesses and depleted uranium, while the culture committee reported on public libraries.

Topics are chosen informally by the chairmen of the committees, which is a strength in that committees sometimes investigate important issues off the news agenda, and a weakness in that chairmen keen not to trouble the government can usually avoid doing so. This independence also means that committees often spurn undramatic issues, such as finance and administration, for more glamorous policy issues.

In the 1997 parliament, the culture committee did not investigate the Millennium Dome, just as, a decade earlier, the poll tax was passed and then abandoned without parliamentary scrutiny.

In 2001, a Hansard Society commission also pointed out the poor links between select committees and the 500 statutory bodies that are supposed to report to parliament.

Neither do all committees work at the same rate. Between 1997 and 1999, the committee on the Environment, Transport and Regions produced 33 reports; the Scottish affairs committee had an output of just four.

Investigation often begins with private briefings and specialist advice. The committee then starts a process of information gathering, through written and oral evidence that might take several months.

Normally ministers and government officials will give evidence, as well as witnesses from outside government. Most witnesses speak in public and television cameras film the more high-profile proceedings.

When the investigation is complete, this evidence is published, together with (in most cases) a written report. These will usually make recommendations about government policy.

The government is expected to produce a response within two months. Reports may be debated in the Commons or in Westminster Hall but, of the 396 departmental committee reports issued between May 1997 and November 2000, only 29 were debated in the main chamber and just 13 in Westminster Hall.

The fact that many relevant and well-thought-out committee reports are forgotten almost as soon as they are produced, with no structure for putting their recommendations into effect, is a big weakness of the system. There are few firm examples of committee reports influencing government policy. Neither is there any formal system for ensuring investigations and reports get good media coverage: this is left to the skills, or lack of them, of individual committee chairmen.

Committee powers

Select committees have the power to send for people, papers, and records but, with the exception of the Commons standards and privileges committee, they cannot order MPs to appear or force the government to produce documents. (This means that, when the Freedom of Information Act comes into force, members of the public will have stronger powers in this respect than parliamentary committees.)

In addition, select committees have limited powers to scrutinise legislation in draft form. In the 1997 parliament, this happened three times.

It is customary for ministers and civil servants to attend committees when asked, although Tony Blair has rejected an invitation to attend the public administration select committee. By convention, committees do not have the power to ask ministers about civil service advice.

Resources

Select committees are supported by a limited full-time staff – typically three or four clerks for each committee. Some parliamentarians would like to increase the resources available to select committees, arguing that MPs cannot be expected to shadow giant government departments without adequate back-up.

The danger of this is that it would lead to bureaucrats, rather than MPs, doing much of the committees' job.

In 2001, a Hansard Society commission recommended that select committees should be strengthened by integrating them more fully into the work of parliament. The report called for all backbench MPs to serve on committees and suggested an increase in the £7.7m annual budget to pay for more staff and a salary for select committee chairmen.

The aim of this salary is to create an alternative career structure in the Commons for able MPs who do not want to become ministers. But critics point out that paying committee chairs will make party whips more, not less, likely to use the jobs as rewards for loyal behaviour.

Structure

There are currently 14 departmental select committees, as well as other committees able to range across the work of government.

Until 2001, only three select committees had the power to appoint one sub-committee each: now every committee can do this, as well as set up shared committees to carry out investigations that cross departmental boundaries.

In the 1997 parliament, several select committees shadowing large departments worked almost entirely through sub-committees and it is expected that this will continue.

There are also a limited number of joint committees bringing together MPs and peers. These are run under House of Lords regulations.

As of September 2001, the Commons committee structure was as follows:

Departmental committees
* Culture, media and sport committee
* Defence committee
* Education and skills committee
* Environment, food and rural affairs committee
* Foreign affairs committee

- Health committee
- Home affairs committee
- International development committee
- Scottish affairs committee
- Trade and industry committee
- Transport, local government and the regions committee
- Treasury committee
- Welsh affairs committee
- Work and pensions committee

There is no select committee for the Lord Chancellor's Department. This is overseen by the home affairs committee.

All the departmental committees have home pages at: www.parliament. uk/commons/selcom/cmsel.htm

Guardian Unlimited Politics' Ask Aristotle database also carries details on MPs' committee memberships at: www.guardian.co.uk/politics/aristotle

Non-departmental select committees

- Environmental audit
- Information
- Public administration
- Science and technology
- Intelligence and security

Of these, the public administration committee is the most high-profile. It looks at the way government is run – interrogating, for example, the prime minister's press secretary, Alastair Campbell.

Joint committee

- Joint committee on Human Rights

Made up of four members of the House of Commons and members of the House of Lords.

Committee of public accounts

The most powerful committee in Westminster and one of the oldest is the public accounts committee. Previously chaired by the defeated Conservative leadership candidate, David Davis, since 1997, it is the only Commons committee backed by a substantial staff, the National Audit Office.

The PAC was set up in 1861 by William Gladstone to examine the way money voted by parliament is spent but its role has grown since 1983, when the NAO began work. It is now one of the most effective and impressive bodies in parliament.

The committee now produces around 50 reports a year. Some are on specific government projects, others wider-ranging, such as studies of the impact of privatisation and public–private partnerships.

For more on the work of the PAC and the National Audit Office see: www.nao.gov.uk/about/history.htm

Domestic committees

Several committees have been set up to run the Commons:

- Broadcasting
  Regulates radio and television in the Commons.
- Liaison
  Manages select committees.
- Catering
  Runs the House of Commons bars and restaurants.
- Procedure
  Considers changes to the way business is conducted in the Commons.
- Standards and privileges
  Regulates the behaviour of MPs.
- Selection
  Chooses members of select committees.
- Standing orders
  Concerned with private bills.
- Modernisation of the House of Commons
  Aims to strengthen the Commons.

Of these, the most influential are the liaison, the standards and privileges, and the modernisation committees.

The liaison committee is made up of the chairmen of select committees. Although once described by one MP as "a rather seedy travel club", it became increasingly important in the 1997 parliament as a voice for select committee independence.

The standards and privileges committee oversees the work of the parliamentary commissioner for standards (currently Elizabeth Filkin). It considers possible breaches of parliamentary conduct by MPs.

The modernisation committee, established after the 1997 general election, has brought in several changes – above all Westminster Hall – but has so far failed to live up to initial expectations.

Scrutiny committees

Several committees scrutinise proposed legislation.

- Deregulation and regulatory reform
  Examines draft orders under the Deregulation and Contracting Out Act 1994.

- European legislation
  Examines EU documents and legislation (for more on this see pages 286–7).
- Statutory instruments
  Examines delegated legislation (for more on this see pages 286–7).
- Consolidation
  Draws together previous Acts of Parliament.

Devolution

Julian Glover

On July 1 1999, the Scottish parliament and the Welsh assembly began work. On the same day, the UK parliament handed over authority across a wide range of issues, a constitutional about-turn confirmed by the establishment of the Northern Ireland assembly on December 1, 1999.

The impact of these devolved bodies has been twofold. First, the UK parliament has ceased to pass some legislation affecting issues now within the remit of the devolved assemblies. Second, parliament's scrutiny role has been reigned back.

But the balance of authority between Westminster and the devolved assemblies is different in each case. The Scottish parliament, as the only new parliament, is empowered to pass primary legislation and vary income tax by up to 3p either way.

The Welsh and Northern Irish assemblies can only pass secondary legislation under the authority of the UK parliament and cannot raise their own revenue. (For more on secondary legislation see page 353)

This means that the UK parliament continues to be the principal lawmaker for Wales and Northern Ireland, but not for Scotland. However, in practice much new legislation concerning Wales and Northern Ireland is skeletal, simply granting the devolved assembly the power to pass its own secondary legislation.

Reserved powers

Devolution left the UK parliament's powers intact in a limited number of areas concerning Scotland. Broadly, they are:

- The constitution of the UK (including the Crown, the UK parliament, the honours system and the civil service)
- UK foreign policy (including dealings with the EU)
- UK defence policy (including counter-terrorism)
- Protection of national borders (including fishing limits, immigration policy and drugs control)
- Economic policy (including currency)
- Common markets for UK goods and services
- Employment legislation
- Social security administration
- Transport safety
- Some other issues, including abortion policy

Devolution did not remove the UK parliament's authority over other areas; in fact, the legislation setting up the Scottish parliament and executive asserts Westminster's authority "to make laws for Scotland". But, in practice, this right would not be used without the consent of the Scottish parliament.

Similarly, the government would oppose a private member's bill that tried to legislate over Scotland outside the reserved powers.

Wales and Northern Ireland

Legislation introducing the Welsh assembly and Northern Irish assembly differed from that which brought in the Scottish parliament in that it did not grant legislative or tax-raising powers and specified which powers would be devolved, rather than which would not be.

Impact on Westminster

The most immediate effect of devolution on the UK parliament was the curtailment of MPs' right to question UK ministers on devolved issues. Although the posts of Scottish secretary, Welsh secretary, and Northern Irish secretary have been retained – for now, at least – these ministers can only answer questions on reserved issues.

Similarly, the previous system of select and standing committees that dealt with Scottish, Welsh, and Northern Irish issues before devolution has been replaced by three select committees.

Prior to devolution, Wales, Scotland, and Northern Ireland were all over-represented at Westminster in terms of their population (the largest seat in Britain, the Isle of Wight, contains four times as many voters as the smallest Scottish seat).

Devolution will leave the number of Welsh and Northern Irish MPs unaffected but the number of Scottish MPs will fall at the next boundary review.

Parliament and the European Union

Julian Glover

Until the UK joined the EC in 1973, parliament was indisputably sovereign. Since then it has been joined by an alternative and superior source of legislation and government, although it retains the ultimate right to recover full sovereignty by repealing the Act of Parliament that makes Britain a member of the EU.

Parliament's day-to-day involvement with the EU takes two forms. The first is scrutiny of the British government's actions in the Council of Ministers (the EU organisation made up of government representatives). The second is involvement in EU legislation, which makes up an increasingly large part of British law.

In both roles, parliament has much to learn from some of the Scandinavian parliaments, which have adapted well to EU membership. A 2001 survey of MPs by the Hansard Society found that fewer than one in ten think that parliament's scrutiny of the Council of Ministers is effective.

Legislation

EU legislation takes two forms: regulations and directives. The former must be put in place by member states without alteration. The latter give guidance to member states, who then decide how to implement them. Because both forms of EU legislation are directly applicable in member states, bypassing national parliaments, parliament cannot scrutinise EU legislation in the way it passes UK bills.

Instead, parliament uses its expertise and status to influence legislation in two ways. First, the UK parliament can intervene before EU legislation is passed, by trying to shape the government's arguments in the EU's Council of Ministers.

Secondly, parliament can affect the way EU legislation is implemented in Britain once it has been passed in Brussels. Some EU legislation is put into effect by introducing a parliamentary bill, which is then passed in the normal way. More often, ministers make use of delegated legislation, which in itself does not need parliamentary approval to become law.

Underpinning parliament's scrutiny role over EU legislation are two principles: first, that the text of any legislation proposed by the Council of Ministers is deposited with the Commons within two days of its being submitted to the Council of Ministers; and secondly, that the UK government is obliged to delay a decision in the Council of Ministers until parliament has put its view.

There are two big loopholes in this: first, that legislation proposed by the European Commission (rather than the Council of Ministers) is not deposited at Westminster and, secondly, that many directives are implemented by qualified majority voting, which means that they must become law even if the British government or parliament opposes them. Parliament's delaying power is redundant in such cases.

A more fundamental difficulty facing parliament is the quantity and complexity of legislation coming out of the EU. More than 1,000 EU documents are deposited at Westminster every year. Very few items are debated, although all are nominally examined by the parliamentary committees responsible.

House of Commons

In the Commons, this work is done initially by the select committee on European legislation and subsequently by one of three European standing committees. These standing committees debate the more significant pieces of legislation for no more than two-and-a-half hours, in the presence of a minister.

House of Lords

The Lords plays a more significant role than the House of Commons through the work of its European Union committee and its various sub-committees. In total, about 70 peers play a part.

The Lords sub-committees are:

* Economic and Financial Affairs, Trade and External Relations (A)
* Energy, Industry and Transport (B)
* Common Foreign and Security Policy (C)
* Environment, Agriculture, Public Health and Consumer Protection (D)
* Law and Institutions (E)
* Social Affairs, Education and Home Affairs (F)

The sub-committees operate in the same way as other select committees of the House of Lords and the House of Commons. They take written and oral evidence from government departments, EU institutions and other interested bodies and individuals. Reports setting out conclusions and recommendations are agreed.

More than half the reports published are subsequently debated in the House. The government has undertaken to reply to all reports, whether debated or not, within two months of publication.

One strength of this system is that the Lords committee considers not just immediate legislation but the wider impact of the EU's work. Recent reports include ones on issues such as genetically modified organisms in food and airline competition.

Reports from the House of Lords European Union committee can be found at: www.parliament.the-stationery-office.co.uk/pa/ld/ldeucom.htm

Who Else Works in Parliament?

Ian Valvona

A flick through the pages of the national press gives the impression that the only people who work in parliament are the people who legislate but, alongside the MPs and peers, there are around 1,400 permanent parliamentary staff members and 8,000–12,000 other Palace of Westminster pass-holders.

The number of permanent staff members has increased since the early 1990s and the number of pass-holders fluctuates depending on civil servants, media staff and building contractors who come and go. Like a busy airport, parliament is a self-contained city where the people providing the most important function are in a distinct minority. So who else works there?

Parliamentary support staff

MP's support staff, including researchers and secretaries, are not civil servants, although they are indirectly paid for by the taxpayer, or occasionally by MPs themselves. Generally, their salaries come out of an MP's office allowance (currently £52,720 a year), which has to cover the MP's London and constituency expenses. Many MPs claim that, in order to pay a competitive salary, they have to dip into their own pockets. Nearly 600 new members of staff are appointed to work for MPs each year and some members are keen to halt this huge turnover by paying more competitive salaries.

As a result, on July 5, 2001, MPs voted not only for a pay rise but also in favour of a report from the Senior Salaries Review Board (the body that sets pay for MPs, ministers and senior civil servants), which recommended that each MP receive between £60,000 and £70,000 per year for staff pay, as well as extra staff for MPs with particularly large case workloads.

Commons-funded researchers are not supposed to undertake party research or campaigning for their MP but this rule is often broken. Last year the Northern Ireland secretary, John Reid, was the subject of an inquiry by Elizabeth Filkin, the commissioner of standards, into claims that he used his Westminster allowance to pay political researchers in Scotland, including his son Kevin.

Employing a relative isn't necessarily an illegitimate use of an MP's allowance. Leo Beckett is the parliamentary assistant and husband of Margaret Beckett, and she is just one of many MPs who employ their partners. For some politicians, it is the only way they keep in contact with their families.

Contracted working hours for parliamentary support staff vary, but are usually around 35 hours per week. Many more hours will be worked in the evenings and at weekends, especially when preparing for conferences or during elections. Salaries vary between £12,000 and £25,000, depending on experience, although the average is £12,000, while many full-time professional staff are paid just £9,000. Predictably, MPs rely heavily on volunteers and unpaid students.

More information on this can be found at: www.working4anmp.co.uk

The House of Commons service

The House of Commons service looks after matters of housekeeping, provision of information, procedure, accounting, reporting debates and food. Unlike an MP's support staff, employees on the parliamentary estate keep their jobs despite elections or changes of government and will deal with everything from answering the telephones and dealing with complaints to maintaining the computers and ordering stationery.

In charge of the House of Commons service is the clerk of the House. In recent years, as well as the traditional role of giving advice on House procedure, he has assumed the duties of chief executive of the service and its staff of 1,400. This means that the six departments of the Commons: the clerk's own, the serjeant's, the library, the official report, the Finance and Administration Department and the Refreshment Department answer to William McKay, the present clerk.

Security

Anyone who has visited parliament and waited to be cheerily waved through the X-ray machines by a police officer will know that security staff are well represented. The parliamentary police, fire officers, and security officers are known as The Palace of Westminster Division and they enforce the regulations of Parliament at the Palace of Westminster and the various outbuildings used to accommodate both MPs and their 700 or so constituency staff.

The Metropolitan Police are in charge of policing the Palace of Westminster, as well as recruiting the security staff, who are paid a starting wage of £10,911, plus an extra £1,622 London and shift allowance. While this may compare favourably with other security-guard employees, the Home Office reported recruitment difficulties in 2000.

Other staff

The provision of food and drink is a major operation undertaken by the 300-strong Refreshment Department. More than one million meals are served each year at the Palace, about 4,500 each day during a parliamentary session, in seven dining rooms, seven bars, six cafeterias and three sets of banqueting rooms.

Requiring an effort on a similar scale to catering is the job of keeping the Palace of Westminster clean. Spare a thought for the army of Commons workers who do the unglamorous job of cleaning 1,200 rooms, 100 staircases and more than two miles of passageways. Except of course the office of Jane Griffiths, the MP for Reading East, who insists on keeping her pet rats at Westminster, ensuring the cleaners stay away and her office, presumably, stays dirty.

Ian Valvona is a freelance writer.

Glossary of Parliamentary Terms

Adjournment debate – usually a half-hour debate introduced by a backbencher at the end of business for the day. The subjects raised are often local or personal issues. There is also a series of short adjournment debates on Wednesday mornings.

Allocation of time motion (guillotine) – a means by which time for one or more stages of a bill is restricted, and the question is put on outstanding business, even though members may still wish to speak on that business (see **Programme order**).

Ballot (for private members' bills) – drawn on the second Thursday that the House sits in each session. The 20 successful members put their bills down for discussion on particular days (Fridays).

Closure – the question "that the question be now put", i.e. that, although there are still members speaking or wishing to speak, the debate should be ended and the House proceed immediately to a decision. The speaker has discretion as to whether to accept the closure and, if opposed, it requires not just a majority but also at least 100 members voting in favour; otherwise, the original debate is resumed. If the closure is agreed to, the question is then put immediately on the matter previously under debate.

Committee of the whole House – when the entire House sits as a committee in the chamber. It is presided over by the chairman of ways and means or one of his deputies (sitting at the clerk's table), and the mace is placed under the table instead of upon it. The committee stages of bills of constitutional importance, urgent bills and parts of the finance bill are usually taken in committee of the whole House instead of in standing committee.

Consolidated fund bill – a bill to authorise issue of sums to maintain government service. In the Commons, the second and third readings are taken without debate.

Consolidation bill – a bill that seeks to draw together several previous enactments on a subject. In the Commons, the second and third readings are taken without debate.

Deferred divisions – for certain types of business, after 10pm (or 7pm on a Thursday), any division is deferred until the following Wednesday at 3.30pm. In such cases, the questions to be decided are listed on a ballot paper in the vote bundle and members may vote in the "no" lobby at any time from 3.30pm to 5pm (with extra time, if such voting is interrupted by ordinary divisions). The result is then announced in the House.

Delegated legislation – legislation made by ministers under powers granted to them in Acts of Parliament, usually by means of a statutory instrument.

Deregulation order – an order to amend or repeal a provision in primary legislation that is considered to impose a burden on business or others.

Dissolution – parliament is dissolved by a royal proclamation issued when a general election is to be called or when five years has expired (the maximum life of a parliament is five years).

Early-day motion – a colloquial term for notices of motions given by a member for debate "on an early day" but for which no date has been fixed. Few are actually debated.

Generally, EDMs are a way by which members can put on record their opinion on a subject and canvass support for it from fellow members.

General synod measure – a measure passed by the General Synod of the Church of England under the Church of England Assembly (Powers) Act 1919. These measures, once considered by the ecclesiastical committee, and a report having been made by it are considered by both Houses and, if approved, sent for the royal assent. These are noted at the end of the public bill list.

Hansard – a full report of what was said in the House of Commons (including written questions and their answers) is published in the official report. Hansard is normally published daily when the House is sitting. It is also published weekly, and in bound volumes.

Hybrid bill – a public bill which, though general in its application, affects the private interests of particular individuals or organisations differently from those of the population at large.

Official report – see **Hansard**.

Opposition days – 20 days are allotted in each session for proceedings on opposition business, of which 17 are at the disposal of the leader of the opposition, and three are at the disposal of the leader of the second-largest opposition party.

Oral questions – questions must be tabled by a member in person or by another member acting on his or her behalf. A member may table only one oral question on behalf of another for each minister each day.

Parliament Acts 1911, 1949 – restrict the powers of the Lords to amend money bills or delay other bills agreed by the Commons.

Parliamentary agent – promotes private bills on behalf of organisations or acts for petitioners opposing a private bill. Agents must be registered with the private bill office.

Parliamentary counsel – are responsible for drafting government bills and amendments to bills, and advising government departments on all aspects of parliamentary procedure.

Points of order – a method whereby members bring supposed breaches of the House's rules of order to the speaker's attention. Members may seek to raise them at any time, but the speaker has discretion as to when to hear them, and will not normally do so during Question Time.

Presentation bill – motion for leave to bring in a bill made under standing order No 57. Member presents the bill for first reading; there is no debate.

Private bill – a bill promoted by a body or an individual to give powers additional to, or in conflict with, the general law, and to which a separate procedure applies.

Private member's bill – a public bill promoted by a member or peer who is not a member of the government.

Private notice question – a question judged to be of urgent importance on submission to the speaker, answered at the end of oral questions, usually at 3.30pm.

Programme orders – a motion restricting time for one or more stages of a bill.

Prorogation – event that marks the end of a parliamentary session.

Royal assent – the monarch's assent to make the bill an Act of Parliament.

Select committees (departmental) – appointed for the duration of a parliament to examine the expenditure, administration and policy of the main government departments and amendments to bills.

SO (standing order) No 24 application – a means whereby a member may attempt to initiate an emergency debate, by interrupting business to discuss a specific and important matter that should have urgent consideration. If the speaker is satisfied that the matter is proper to be so discussed, a motion is put to the House. If the House gives leave, the business is discussed, usually on the following day.

Standing committee – constituted to consider public bills in detail, clause by clause. Membership is determined by the selection committee, and is established for each bill.

Standing order – an order made by the House (Commons or Lords) for the regulation of its proceedings.

Swearing of members – at the start of a new parliament or after a byelection, members take the oath holding the New Testament (or in the case of a Jew or Muslim, the Old Testament or Koran) and say the words of the oath (which are on a card held by a clerk). Members may also take the oath in the Scottish manner – take an alternative form of oath or make a solemn affirmation instead of an oath.

Ten-minute rule bill – colloquial term for standing order No 23, under which backbenchers have an opportunity on Tuesdays and Wednesdays to introduce a bill and speak in its favour for about ten minutes. Time is also available for a short opposing speech.

Vote bundle – includes the order paper, giving the agenda for the current day's sitting, lists of parliamentary proceedings, notices of meetings of standing and select committees, amendments tabled to public bills, a summary of the proceedings of standing committees that sat the previous day.

Votes and proceedings – the record of the proceedings of the House of Commons on the previous day.

Westminster Hall – sittings in "Westminster Hall" (actually in the room up the staircase in the north-west corner of Westminster Hall) constitute sittings of the House (effectively a parallel chamber), and any member may take part. Debates are held on Tuesday, Wednesday and Thursday.

Writ – form of written command in the name of the monarch.

Further reading

History

Twentieth Century British Political Facts 1900-2000
David Butler and Gareth Butler (Macmillan, 2000)
A vital guide to Westminster and electoral politics.

The Houses of Parliament
eds. Jacqueline Riding and Christine Riding (Merrell Publishers, 2000)
Describes the art and architecture of the Palace of Westminster.

Great Parliamentary Scandals: Four Centuries of Calumny, Smear and Innuendo
Matthew Parris (Robson Books, 1997)
The seamier side of Westminster life in all its glory.

The Pimlico Companion to Parliament
Christopher Silvester (Pimlico, 1998)
A magnificent literary anthology.

Parliamentary procedure

Griffith and Ryle on Parliament
Robert Blackburn and Andrew Kennon (Sweet & Maxwell, 2001)
Updated, excellent guide to parliamentary procedure.

Politico's Guide to Parliament
Susan Child (Politico's Publishing, 1999)
Written by an insider, this is a useful guide to the workings of parliament.

Erskine May's Treatise on the Law, Privileges, Proceedings and the Usage of Parliament (Butterworths, 1997)
The parliamentary bible, a complete but overwhelming record of the operations of both Houses.

The BBC Guide to Parliament
David Davis MP (Penguin, 1997)
A short but entertaining and clear explanation of life in parliament.

How to be a Backbencher
Paul Flynn MP (Seren, 1997)
Parliament as it is lived by many MPs. A fun read.

Parliamentary reform

The Challenge for Parliament
(Hansard Society, 2001)
The report of the commission on parliamentary scrutiny, this is a road map to reform.

Mr Blair's Poodle
Andrew Tyrie MP (Centre for Policy Studies, 2000)
A short but clear call for a more effective House of Commons.

Parliament Under Blair
Peter Riddell (Politico's Publishing, 2000)
The best modern analysis of the battle between parliament and government.

Does Parliament Matter?
Philip Norton (Macmillan, 1998)
Explores the link between parliament and the citizen.

A more extensive reading list can be found at: www.parliament.uk/commons/lib/fs10.pdf

Contact details

Contact details for most MPs can be found on Ask Aristotle, the Guardian Unlimited Politics' database. This offers biographical and political data, phone, fax and postal addresses, as well as email addresses for some MPs.

Ask Aristotle can be found at:
www.guardian.co.uk/politics/aristotle

In addition, another website, Fax Your MP, allows constituents to contact their MPs free of charge. This site can be found at:
www.faxyourmp.com

To contact an MP write to:

[MP's name]
The House of Commons
London SW1A 0AA
Tel: 020 7219 3000

Parliament

General questions about the working of the House of Commons should be addressed to:

House of Commons Information Office
House of Commons
London SW1A 2TT
Tel: 020 7219 4272
Fax: 020 7219 5839

Information about the planned work of the Commons can be heard on the recorded business statement line: 020 7219 5532

For information on the House of Lords, contact:

House of Lords Information Office
House of Lords
London SW1A 0PW
Tel: 020 7219 3107
Fax: 020 7219 0620

For information for schools, teachers, and students, contact:

Parliamentary Education Unit
House of Commons
London SW1A 2TT
Tel: 020 7219 2105
Fax: 020 7219 0818
email: edunit@parliament.uk

For information on select committees, contact:

Committee Office
Tel: 020 7219 3267/4300 (general enquiries)
Tel: 020 7219 2033 (recorded message providing information on forthcoming meetings, subjects under discussion)

To complain about an MP, contact:

Elizabeth Filkin
Parliamentary Commissioner for Standards
House of Commons
London SW1A 0AA
Tel: 020 7219 0320
Fax: 020 7219 0490
email: filkine@parliament.uk

'indispensable'

Andrew Rawnsley

Parliamentary Profiles

Andrew Roth and Byron Criddle

£50 post free; due October 2001
4 volumes £150 post free; due seriatim

34 Somali Road, London SW2 3RL
Tel: 0207 222 5884/5889 (Fax)
Roth@rothprofiles.demon.co.uk

PARLIAMENTARY PROFILES